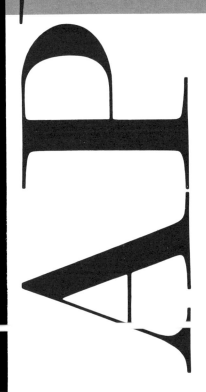

Department of Education and Science
Welsh Office
Department of Education for Northern Ireland

Assessment of Performance Unit

# Science at Age 11

## A Review of APU Survey Findings 1980-84

Terry Russell (Editor)
Paul Black
Wynne Harlen
Sandra Johnson
David Palacio

London
Her Majesty's Stationery Office

0041475100

© Crown Copyright 1988
First published 1988

ISBN 0 11 270617 7

# Contents and authorship

Editor: Terry Russell

iv

# Tables and figures

# Figures

# Preface

This report presents a review of the findings of five national surveys on the performance of 11 year old children in science. The surveys were conducted for the Assessment of Performance Unit by research teams at King's College, University of London, and at the University of Leeds. The report gives an overview of the initial series of five annual surveys of this age, carried out between 1980 and 1984. Surveys will in future take place at five-yearly intervals. Companion reports are also available for ages 13 and 15, together with a technical report, 'National assessment: the APU science approach', which considers issues of interpretation raised by the monitoring programme.

This report describes in detail the approach to the surveys and the findings. It is intended primarily for administrators, education advisers and researchers but it will also be of interest to those teachers who found the previous reports of value. Further copies of this and the other review reports may be purchased from HMSO or through booksellers. A full list of APU publications and details of their availability can be obtained from: APU, Room 5/98, Department of Education and Science,

Elizabeth House, York Road, London, SE1 7PH (telephone: 01-934 9323).

Details of short reports for science teachers drawing on the findings of the APU surveys are available from the above address.

Reports now available in the series:

| | |
|---|---|
| Number 1 | Science at Age 11 |
| Number 2 | Science Assessment Framework Ages 13 and 15 |
| Number 3 | Science at Age 13 |
| Number 4 | Science Assessment Framework Age 11 |
| Number 5 | Science at Age 15 |
| Number 6 | Practical Testing at Ages 11, 13 and 15 |
| Number 7 | Electricity at Age 15 |
| Number 8 | Planning Scientific Investigations at Age 11 |
| Number 9 | Assessing Investigations at Ages 13 and 15 |
| Number 10 | Metals at Age 15 |
| Number 11 | The Language of Science |

# The research teams

The teams are based at two centres: the Centre for Educational Studies, King's College London, University of London*, and the Centre for Studies in Science and Mathematics Education, University of Leeds. The work of monitoring at three ages (11, 13 and 15) in science is divided between these centres so that the responsibility for monitoring at the lower age groups rests with King's, and responsibility for monitoring at age 15 and for the data processing and analysis rests with Leeds.

**Team members at King's** (*January 1987*)

| | |
|---|---|
| Director | Paul Black |
| Research and Development (ages 11 and 13) | Patricia Murphy (Deputy Director) Anne Qualter Peter Swatton Robert Taylor |
| Secretary | Julie Jones |

**Team members at Leeds** (*January 1987*)

| | |
|---|---|
| Director | Fred Archenhold |
| Technical Director | Roger Hartley |
| Research and Development (age 15) | Geoff Welford (Project coordinator) James Donnelly |
| Data Analysis | Sandra Johnson (Deputy Director) John Bell |
| Secretary | Jan Akkermans |

**Past team members**

Dennis Child (Director 1982–83); Angela Davey (1982–84); Brenda Denvir (Jan–Aug 1981); Rosalind Driver (1977–82, Deputy Director 1979–82); Reed Gamble (1982–85); Richard Gott (1980–84, Deputy Director 1982–84); Wynne Harlen (1977–1984, Deputy Director (1978–84); Jenny Head (1981–84); Peter Kelly (Director 1977–82); Nasrin Khaligh (1984–85); David Layton (Director 1977–82); Brian Maher (1979–83); Cynthia Millband (1980–81); Tony Orgee (1982–85); David Palacio (1980–85); Terry Russell (1982–86); Beta Schofield (1977–85, Deputy Director 1985); Karen Spencer (1985–86); Ardrie VanderWaal (1979–80); Iain Watson (1984–85); Christopher Worsley (1978–82); Fiona Wylie (1980–82).

**The preparation of this report**

The statistical analyses for this report were carried out by Sandra Johnson, Iain Watson and John Bell.

---

* Formerly Centre for Science and Mathematics Education, Chelsea College.

# Acknowledgements

The work reported in this review has been conducted collaboratively over a number of years. All colleagues past and present, members of the research teams and of the Steering Group, have contributed time and effort which has made this review possible. Special thanks are due to those who have offered constructive comments on early drafts of chapters.

We would like to thank Mrs Barbara Bloomfield and the members of the APU Monitoring Services Unit at the NFER (see Appendix 13) for their work in drawing the sample, contacting schools and administering the survey.

We are grateful to the advisers in the LEAs who enabled us to have the services of teachers for administration of the practical tests, and to the testers themselves (Appendix 14) for their efforts on our behalf. Also to the considerable efforts of markers who contributed valuable feedback bearing on question development.

Special thanks are due to Julie Jones for all her efforts and for using her organisational skills in assembling this review.

Thanks are also due to the Heads, teachers and pupils in the sample schools on whose cooperation, willingly given, the survey depended.

# 1

# Introduction

## 1.1 The compass of this report

This is the fifth major report on the science performance of pupils at age 11 as assessed by the science monitoring team of the Assessment of Performance Unit. The four earlier reports (DES, 1981, 1983a, 1984a and 1985a) have described the results drawn from the annual surveys conducted from 1980 to 1983. The results of the 1984 survey have not been reported separately but are incorporated into this report as a contribution to the retrospective overview. Novel aspects of the 1984 survey as opposed to those which confirm the findings of 1980–83 will be found in the appendices.

This review attempts the formidable task of pulling into focus the experiences gained from discussion, interviews, question trials, monitoring, data analysis and reporting in the five year development phase. The scale and nature of the development work in the assessment of primary science reported here is in many ways unprecedented, so it should come as no surprise that more issues are raised than can be settled. Consequently, although this review will be principally concerned with what has been achieved and learned so far, it will be neither the last chapter in the story, nor the epitaph to the APU science programme. For example, the issue of population changes in performance over time is only touched upon in Chapters 2 and 4, and receives a full treatment in the accompanying technical report (DES, 1988c). This review will look forward also in the sense of considering some of the questions which will be central to the continuing work of the science teams in the research leading up to the next monitoring of pupils at age 11 which is planned to take place in 1989.

While of no greater length than any of the four single survey reports which preceded it, this volume combines information from five surveys. Readers should be aware that this is only possible as a result of compression of and selection from available information. Access to earlier published materials is assumed, particularly for illustrative question examples. Furthermore, the review of survey findings at age 11 is complemented by three other volumes: the parallel review reports for ages 13 and 15 and the separate technical report (DES, 1988c). The technical report discusses the more general issues arising from question banking, domain sampling and generalisability theory, as well as subcategory performance estimates from 1980 to 1984 against a variety of background variables.

While the age 11 review cannot be free-standing for these reasons, it will nonetheless attempt to be independently coherent.

## 1.2 The development of the science assessment programme to date

The Assessment of Performance Unit dates from 1975, when it was set up within the DES, 'to promote the development of methods of assessing and monitoring the achievement of children at school and to seek to identify the incidence of underachievement'. Advice on general questions and balance in the APU's programme is provided by a broadly based Consultative Committee, while a Coordinating Group (from 1976–1981) had oversight of the assessment model adopted by the APU. A Science Steering Group has guided the policy under which the monitoring teams at King's College London, University of London* (for ages 11 and 13) and at the University of Leeds (age 15 and data analysis) have developed and implemented the science assessment strategy. Finally, a Statistics Advisory Group has offered guidance throughout.

The science monitoring teams were appointed in 1977 and produced an agreed outline assessment framework which was published in the Science Progress Report (DES, 1978a). This document made the point, particularly relevant to the education of the age group under consideration, that 'science is to be regarded as a mode of thought and activity which may be encountered in a number of the subjects appearing in the school curriculum'. Science assessment would consequently be justifiable and relevant even where the schools had not exposed pupils to an explicit science programme.

## 1.3 The assessment framework

The foundation upon which all subsequent development work has been built is the framework for the construction, organisation and reporting of the assessment exercise. Wide consultation at the early stages of the enterprise contributed to the generation of a framework which has

---

* Formerly CSME, Chelsea College

proved workable throughout the rigours of five rounds of monitoring at each of the three ages assessed, with relatively minor modifications and refinements. Four prin cipal facets of science performance spanning the entire cognitive-affective spectrum are identified:

Processes
Concepts
Contexts of process and concepts deployment
Attitudes

It was intended that the first two of these would be the main focus of attention in the initial stages of the primary assessment. The range of science processes is represented by the six science activity categories (see Table 1.1 below) which in broad terms are common to all three ages. An agreed list of science concepts appropriate to the primary age group was formulated. This list defines the range of concepts to be used in the subcategory **Applying science concepts** to make sense of new information. Straight definitions or descriptions of concepts by means of recall is not included in the framework.

**Table 1.1** *The assessment framework*

| Category | Subcategories | Form of test |
| --- | --- | --- |
| 1 Use of graphical and symbolic representation | **Reading information from graphs, tables and charts** **Representing information as graphs, tables and charts** | Written |
| 2 Use of apparatus and measuring instruments | **Using measuring instruments** **Estimating physical quantities** | Individual practical |
| 3 Observation | **Making and interpreting observations** | Group practical |
| 4 Interpretation and application | i **Interpreting presented information** Judging the applicability of a given generalisation Distinguishing degrees of inference ii **Applying science concepts to make sense of new information** Generating alternative hypotheses | Written |
| 5 Planning of investigations | **Planning parts of investigations** **Planning entire investigations** Identifying or proposing testable statements | Written |
| 6 Performance of investigations | **Performing entire investigations** | Individual practical |

While the bank of questions has been structured primarily to assess performance in terms of science processes and concepts, it is acknowledged that the *context* in which a question is embedded may also have a significant effect on performance. Different contexts, for example whether a question describes a situation in the home or in the classroom (albeit addressing the same science processes and concepts), may have an important influence on per formance. Pupils' decisions about the skills and knowl edge which are appropriate to deploy in their reading of

the questions' demands and also their feelings of com petence or alienation in relation to the setting described seem to depend on context. A sense of familiarity or of apprehension are each capable of either enhancing or impairing performance. While questions have been broadly labelled by context, by the use of the labels 'Science', 'everyday' or 'other school subject', the assess ment of context effects has not been a *systematic* part of the assessment programme. However, awareness of the subtle effects context may have on the quality of perform ance has grown, and readers are alerted to the fact that reference will be made to these factors throughout this review, particularly in the category chapters. Furthermore, at a level of still greater specificity, reference will be made to question *content* and its effects on performance. Just as conservation of volume becomes a more engaging task when it is lemonade rather than water which children are sharing, there is often evidence suggesting that it is at the level of the particular content presented that children become involved in questions. The dependence of these responses on context and content serve as a reminder of the typically 'concrete' level of operation in the age group. They may also be read as an indicator that the kinds of questions children are being asked, in the absence of widespread exposure to science process skills, may be unfamiliar to many. The research phase of the pro gramme, between 1984 and the next projected national surveys in 1989, will include examination of these issues in its programme.

As the aim of development and trials of the many hun dreds of questions required to provide reliable national estimates of science performance has been gradually achieved, it has been possible to give some attention to the fourth facet of performance, children's attitudes to science. This work, which was included as part of the 1983 and 1984 surveys, is also reported in this review.

A separate publication explaining the rationale for the framework and the component subcategories (DES 1984d) has been circulated to all relevant schools and education bodies. While this framework is in one sense the starting point which enables the assessment exercise to be imple mented, in another sense it is itself a significant output of the science assessment exercise. The minor refinements in the framework have evolved after extensive monitoring experience and exploratory work, and reflect a growing understanding of the range and subtlety of children's science-related behaviours. The assessment instruments, at the category, subcategory or individual question level have all been tempered by exposure to children and subsequent interpretations of this type of feedback.

## 1.4 Assessment in practice

In each of the years 1980–84 inclusive, a representative sample of pupils has been drawn from the 10–11 age group in both independent and state education. Testing has taken place during April and May in England and during June in Wales and Northern Ireland. Approximately 1.5 per cent of the age group (about 12,000 pupils drawn from over 1,000 schools) have participated in each of the annual surveys. The sampling has in all cases been conducted by the APU's Monitoring Services Unit (MSU) at the NFER. This obviates the need for any direct contact between the monitoring team and the pupils and schools, thus guaranteeing anonymity. Since the intention of the surveys was to obtain a national profile of pupils' performance in science at the end of the primary stage of education, the identities of particular pupils, schools or education authorities have played no part. (See Appendix 7 for details of survey sampling.)

Three distinct methods of assessment were used. In Categories 2 and 6, a trained tester conducted individual interviews and recorded information additional to that recorded by the children themselves. Category 3 used group practical assessments administered by a trained tester, with children recording their own responses. The remaining Categories, (1, 4 and 5) were assessed by means of written responses to pencil and paper questions in test booklets sent to schools and administered by school staff in accordance with the accompanying instructions. Distribution and collection of scripts was via the MSU. Trained markers familiar with the age groups applied the variety of quantitative and qualitative marking techniques which have been developed.

More detailed information on the variety of techniques employed can be found in 'The science assessment framework at age 11' (DES, 1984d) and 'Practical testing at ages 11, 13 and 15' (DES, 1985d).

**Table 1.2** *Numbers of questions monitored in each sub-category, 1981–84*

| | 1980 | 1981 | 1982 | 1983 | 1984 |
|---|---|---|---|---|---|
| Reading | 22 *(24) | 18 (45) | 42 (60) | 20 (90) | 42 (139) |
| Representing | 14 (24) | 16 (44) | 42 (59) | 20 (89) | 42 (118) |
| Apparatus and measuring instruments | 5 | 5 | 5 | – | 15 |
| Observation | 40 (49) | 26 (49) | (91) | 40 (128) | 40 (116) |
| Interpreting | 42 (55) | 42 (90) | 42 (110) | 56 (156) | 70 (196) |
| Judging generalisations | – | 2 | – | 8 | – |
| Distinguishing inferences | 3 | 2 | 3 | – | – |
| Applying concepts | 42 (63) | 42 (114) | 42 (162) | 56 (211) | 70 (196) |
| Generating hypotheses | 3 | 2 | 2 | 3 | 1 |
| Planning (parts) | – | 13 (43) | category restructured | 56 (124) | 70 (206) |
| Planning (whole) | – | 4 | 4 | 2 | 2 |
| Investigating | 6 | 6 | 5 | – | 2 |

\* The numbers of questions in the domain from which the survey questions were randomly selected are shown in parentheses.

The major categories which are assessed by large groups of questions **Reading, Representing, Observation, Interpreting, Applying** (concepts) and **Planning** (parts of investigations) are identified as separate domains. Each domain is closely defined by a set of Question types which describe admissible question characteristics. The number of questions used to represent any one domain in a survey has a lower limit determined by the need to minimise measurement errors in any randomly selected sub-sample of questions from which a performance estimate is to be derived. There is, in theory, no upper limit to the universe of questions which comprise a domain.

Although distinct in educational terms, **Reading** and **Representing** were found to have similar performance characteristics and are combined for comparisons against background variables. The development of the practical questions for **Observation** was a time-consuming and expensive exercise, which explains the relatively small number of questions in this category. The remaining domain-sampled areas, **Interpreting, Applying** and **Planning**, are each represented by about 200 questions, giving a total of over 1,000 questions in all on the age 11 question bank. Table 1.2 shows the number of questions exposed in each annual monitoring.

As Table 1.2 reveals, many more pencil and paper questions were used than could be presented to any single pupil; over 300 questions distributed through 22 test booklets were administered during the 1984 survey. This was possible as the result of a survey design which matched the characteristics of the sub-samples responding to each particular test booklet.

Any single pencil and paper test booklet, which is all any one pupil would have responded to, contained about 15 questions demanding an estimated testing time of about 45 minutes. Each question was presented on one page of A4, usually with a line drawing or diagram, and using a large, clear type. A great deal of thought was given to vocabulary and sentence construction so as to minimise language demands. A guiding principle has been to make questions as clear and as attractive as possible.

In addition to the pencil and paper tests, the pupils in some schools also took part in the practical assessment. This amounted to about 5 per cent of the whole sample for Category 3, and about the same proportion for Categories 6 and 2.

## 1.5 The interpretation of results

An important element of the APU science monitoring results consists of the population performance estimates which are derived from aggregated overall mean scores on pools of questions. These pools of questions comprise the 'domains' representing any particular category or sub-category of science activity, and the technical considerations of their use are elaborated in Chapter 4, and in the technical report (DES, 1988c). While the measures obtained by these means are not simply arbitrary (though judgement of, for example, age-appropriateness of questions does play a part), nor are they absolute (DES, 1983c). The two or three tier definition by Category, Subcategory and Question type on the process dimension, the prescribed list of concepts, the permissible contextual setting and an acceptable affective component can be thought of as a series of filters which exclude a great deal which is irrelevant and lead to fairly homogeneous question groups. Satisfactory question/subcategory correlations within each domain are also required. In practice this tends to exclude the extremes of the facility range, but essentially age-appropriateness is judged by question writers with the help of feedback from question trials. External validation of sample questions or whole question domains has also been undertaken, with adjustments being made where necessary. Expert opinion has been welcomed and carefully heeded throughout. The evidence of the similar profiles across domains at all three ages assessed is some evidence in support of the view that the categories have intrinsic qualities which remain discernible not just in terms of face validity, but also in differential levels of performance. It nevertheless remains true that aggregate mean scores could be raised or lowered by a large influx of questions of higher or lower facility than the existing mean. In practice, this would be avoided, but in theory the *actual* mean level is for some purposes not important. Domain-referenced scores are principally of value in that they permit *comparisons* to be made between performances of various groups of pupils distinguished by reference to a variety of background measures. Re-stated, domain-referenced scores are useful devices for comparing the educational outcomes of different sub-groups within the target population. After the assessment framework itself, performance levels can be thought of as the second major output of the science monitoring exercise. The technical report is concerned with performance scores at the domain-referenced level.

As well as domain-referenced estimates of science performance, another major output of the science programme consists of the detailed qualitative descriptions of children's activities and responses. This type of reporting occurred fairly extensively in the first four age 11 survey reports, particularly by reference to individual questions. Whilst they have been assembled to represent some common burden in terms of science activity, the groups of questions which represent any given process can be re-examined in the search for the features which appear to have a particular impact on performance. These various demands might be described in terms of skills which reflect an underlying process substructure. This level of reporting can also be diagnostic in the sense of distinguishing levels and qualities of performance suggesting characteristic difficulties.

Detailed analysis of individual questions or groups of questions sharing a particular attribute, using detailed category marking systems which are beyond the basic domain-sampling requirement, is often of great educational interest. However, it must be borne in mind that within the domain-sampled areas, it has not always been possible to explore systematically some interesting effects, since to include the necessary questions would have introduced a bias into the question pools. Such explorations have been possible to a limited extent by the use of supplementary 'probe' questions, which are specially written to investigate specific issues and are distributed to sub-samples in whatever test package space is available. Consequently, some of the diagnostic information emerging has the incidental and exploratory feel of clues rather than conclusions, despite the large number of questions developed. Some of these effects will be explored more systematically before the next national monitoring of performance.

The remaining source of information which has played an important role in the interpretation of results is the school questionnaire. This document asks participating schools to report on the provision for science activities, (see Appendix 1), as well as more general school characteristics. This information is important both in providing a profile of the state of science in schools, and also as the source of background variable information, permitting some relationships between pupil performance and fairly broad school characteristics to be explored.

## 1.6 The organisation of this report

The next two chapters present a broad backdrop to the more specific science performance measures. Chapter 2 presents the information gathered from participating schools, as described in the above paragraph. Chapter 3 moves from the school end of the spectrum to examine pupils' experience, activities and interests relating to science, their opportunities and interests, rather than actual performance. Chapter 4 moves to a consideration of science performance at the domain-referenced level, and relates performance to background variables. Chapters 5 to 11 inclusive describe the detailed results obtained from the pools of questions representing the various categories of science activity. Chapter 12 attempts to present a coherent overview of the detail presented in the seven preceding chapters. Chapter 13 briefly touches on some of the issues arising from the fact that the assessment exercise is conducted also with pupils aged 13 and 15. Finally, Chapter 14 summarises the results of five years of monitoring and considers the important issues emerging.

# 2

# Science in the survey schools

## 2.1 Introduction

The information presented in this chapter has been gathered by means of questionnaires sent to all participating schools. The questionnaires have been published in full in each of the previous reports and the particular one used in the 1984 survey can be found in Appendix 1.

The information considered in this chapter concerns the schools' organisation, policies and resources for science work (section 2.2), the goals and emphases of this work and the topics encountered by children (section 2.3), and the use of curriculum materials, television programmes and microcomputers (section 2.4).

Where appropriate, data are presented separately for schools in England, Wales and Northern Ireland. Differences in practice and provision among schools of different type and among those with different catchment areas are explored by reference to four school types: Junior-with-Infant, Junior, Middle and Independent. Three catchment areas are defined: inner city, other urban and rural. Performance by reference to school type and catchment area is reported for England only. This is to avoid confusion of school type and catchment area differences with country differences, the pattern of distribution being different in Northern Ireland and Wales.

Whilst the collection of information by questionnaire has obvious limitations, the findings provide a necessary background against which performance data can be considered. Some information has been gathered regularly, using the same form of question, so that any change in practice over the five years of the surveys could be reported. In these cases any clear trends or sharp changes in the figures over the period are noted.

In addition to these regular questions, others have occasionally been included to explore certain aspects of practice. Questions of this kind include enquiries about the use of curriculum materials, field centres, television and radio programmes. This information has not been gathered every year, mainly in the interests of keeping the questionnaire as short as possible. Thus the findings reported for section 2.4 do not span the whole five years as do those in section 2.3 for the most part.

When considering any of the data presented in this chapter, whether specific to one survey or compared across surveys, it is important to bear in mind the fact that survey participation is voluntary on the part of schools. In no survey have all invited schools taken part, and the degree of non-participation has varied from year to year and from country to country. As Chapter 4 shows, the participation rate in England and Wales has been 85–90 per cent of invited schools; in Northern Ireland the corresponding range is 65–75 per cent. It is not known to what extent the organisation and provision of science in the non-participants might differ from that in those schools which have taken part in the surveys. Clearly this is a point to bear in mind when the findings in this chapter are discussed.

Each survey questionnaire asked schools to indicate whether they had been involved in any kind of reorganisation (such as a change of age range or a merger) in the previous three years, which may have affected the school programme. In each year about 10 per cent of schools in the survey answered this question in the affirmative. There were generally proportionally more schools so disrupted in England, with Wales the next and Northern Ireland having the least. In England proportionally more Middle schools than other types of school reported that they had been involved in reorganisation, with the proportion of Junior-with-infant schools undergoing reorganisation being slightly greater than that of Independent and Junior schools.

## 2.2 Incidence and organisation of science in the survey schools

Obtaining information by questionnaire about whether or not science was included in the curriculum of the survey schools was found to be a difficult task. It was felt not appropriate to impose a definition of science work, but to allow schools to use their own understanding of the term. In 1980 and 1981 a question was posed as to the schools' policy for 10/11 year old pupils' work in science, with one of the alternative responses being that science was not included at all. In 1980 only 1 per cent of schools in England and Wales and 5 per cent in Northern Ireland indicated that no science was taught. In 1981 this fell to zero in England and Wales and 2 per cent in Northern Ireland.

From 1982 onwards the question was changed to 'Is science-based work included in the curriculum for 10/11 year olds in the school?' The proportions of the sample answering in the affirmative were 95 per cent in England, 91 per cent in Wales and 80 per cent in Northern Ireland. However, cross-checking with answers to other questions in the questionnaire suggested some misunderstanding and that there was not a real drop in the incidence of science work from the previous years (DES, 1984a, page 12). The evidence from the 1983 and 1984 questionnaires supports the conclusion that about 99 per cent of survey schools in England and Wales and about 90 per cent of those in the Northern Ireland surveys included some science activities in the work of their 10/11 year olds.

*Time spent on science*

Schools were asked to estimate the amount of time spent on science as a percentage of total lesson time. This is not any easy estimate to make, particularly where science is part of an integrated topic, but schools were free to calculate the proportion over whatever period of time they wished. The necessary roughness of the estimates means that only large differences and sustained trends are worthy of note.

Table 2.1 shows that in the 1984 survey, as in previous surveys, the majority of schools spent about 5 per cent of time on science, with a sizeable minority spending 10 per cent or more of the time in this way. A smaller proportion of schools in Northern Ireland than in Wales and England spent 10 per cent or more of time on science.

**Table 2.1** *Proportion of lesson time spent on science activity at age 10/11 in the survey schools in 1984*
(Percentage of schools indicating each time allocation)

|  | No. schools | Less than 5% | About 5% | About 10% | 20% or more |
|---|---|---|---|---|---|
| England | 431 | 8 | 58 | 32 | 2 |
| Wales | 133 | 7 | 61 | 30 | 2 |
| Northern Ireland | 114 | 19 | 62 | 18 | 1 |
| **Within England** | | | | | |
| Junior and infant | 263 | 9 | 56 | 33 | 2 |
| Junior | 78 | 10 | 72 | 18 | – |
| Middle | 54 | 4 | 63 | 31 | 2 |
| Independent | 36 | 6 | 42 | 46 | 6 |
| **Primary schools in England** | | | | | |
| Inner city | 36 | 8 | 72 | 17 | 3 |
| Other urban | 200 | 11 | 61 | 28 | 1 |
| Rural | 100 | 7 | 52 | 38 | 3 |

If we look at the different types of school in England, a pattern which is familiar from earlier reports is found. Proportionally more of the Independent schools compared with the maintained schools indicated that they spent 10 per cent or more of curriculum time on science.

The national picture over the period of the surveys is given in Table 2.2, which shows that in every country there has been an increase in time spent on this area of the curriculum (especially between 1980 and 1981, and between 1983 and 1984).

**Table 2.2** *Proportion of lesson time on science at age 10/11 in the survey schools, 1980–84*
(Percentage of schools indicating each time allocation)

|  | England | | | Wales | | | N. Ireland | | |
|---|---|---|---|---|---|---|---|---|---|
|  | <5% | 5% | >10% | <5% | 5% | >10% | <5% | 5% | >10% |
| 1980 | 19 | 57 | 26 | 19 | 58 | 23 | 42 | 46 | 12 |
| 1981 | 12 | 52 | 35 | 15 | 56 | 32 | 34 | 48 | 17 |
| 1982 | 11 | 62 | 27 | 8 | 54 | 38 | 22 | 54 | 23 |
| 1983 | 12 | 57 | 31 | 12 | 64 | 24 | 33 | 52 | 15 |
| 1984 | 8 | 58 | 34 | 7 | 61 | 32 | 19 | 62 | 19 |

The overall figures for the proportions of schools spending 10 per cent of time on science, which remain small, perhaps deserve some comment in the light of recent recommendations as to the amount of curriculum time that should be allocated to science. In their survey of some 9–13 Middle schools*, HMI noted that the time allocated varied from 6 per cent for the youngest to 10 per cent for the oldest and commented that 'some of the schools need to consider whether more time should be given to science' (DES, 1983d, para. 7.47). Presumably the two-thirds of Middle schools spending 5 per cent or less of time on science would attract similar comment. Since 11 year olds are not different whether in Middle or other types of school, it seems reasonable to suppose that the preferred proportion of time is nearer to 10 per cent than 5 per cent for all 11 year olds. Although no recommendation about the proportion of time for science in primary schools was made in 'Science 5–16: A statement of Policy' (DES, 1985f), the figure of 10 per cent for 11 year olds in secondary schools was recognised as appropriate. It would appear inappropriate for 11 year olds in primary or middle schools to have much less than this. The survey findings therefore suggest that two-thirds of schools in England and Wales and four out of five in Northern Ireland fall short of providing adequate time for science activities.

*Responsibility for science*

Table 2.3 provides the 1984 figures on the survey schools' arrangements for assigning responsibility for science work. The table shows that while almost half of the survey schools in England held special posts for science, fewer than a third of Welsh schools sampled and only a fifth of the survey schools in Northern Ireland had such a post. Indeed, half or more of the schools in Wales and Northern Ireland did not allocate responsibility for science even on a voluntary basis.

Table 2.3 shows that as in previous years the Junior with infant schools were less well provided with special posts than were all other kinds of school, and rural schools were similarly less fortunate than schools in urban areas. A higher proportion of rural schools are Junior-with-infant, whilst all but a few Junior-only schools are inner city or other urban* and so the two categorisations in

---

* '9–13 Middle schools: an illustrative survey', HMSO, 1983.

**Table 2.3** *Responsibility for science in the survey schools in 1984*

(Percentage of schools indicating each arrangement)

| | No. schools | Special post | Voluntarily assigned | Not allocated |
|---|---|---|---|---|
| England | 437 | 48 | 23 | 29 |
| Wales | 138 | 28 | 22 | 50 |
| Northern Ireland | 119 | 20 | 19 | 61 |
| **Within England** | | | | |
| Junior with infant | 268 | 35 | 25 | 40 |
| Junior | 81 | 68 | 17 | 15 |
| Middle | 54 | 83 | 9 | 7 |
| Independent | 34 | 47 | 38 | 15 |
| **Primary schools in England** | | | | |
| Inner city | 41 | 68 | 17 | 15 |
| Other urban | 200 | 57 | 21 | 22 |
| Rural | 100 | 21 | 30 | 49 |

**Table 2.4** *Responsibility for science in the survey schools, 1980–84*

(Percentage of schools indicating each arrangement)

| | England | | | Wales | | | N. Ireland | | |
|---|---|---|---|---|---|---|---|---|---|
| | Spec. post | Volun. assign. | Not alloc. | Spec. post | Volun. assig. | Not alloc. | Spec. post | Volun. assig. | Not alloc. |
| 1980 | 30 | 22 | 48 | 9 | 20 | 71 | 1 | 13 | 87 |
| 1981 | 35 | 23 | 42 | 9 | 20 | 71 | 14 | 11 | 75 |
| 1982 | 37 | 24 | 39 | 23 | 17 | 60 | 15 | 19 | 66 |
| 1983 | 57 | 18 | 25 | 27 | 20 | 53 | 17 | 19 | 64 |
| 1984 | 48 | 23 | 29 | 28 | 22 | 50 | 20 | 19 | 61 |

Table 2.3 are not independent. The small size of many rural Junior-with-infant schools no doubt presents a difficulty in allocating responsibility for all areas of the curriculum among a small number of staff. Some grouping of small schools for the purpose of sharing a post of responsibility, or consultant, for science has been suggested (DES, 1985f).

Since data have been collected in all five surveys about the allocation of responsibility for science in the schools it is possible to look for trends over the period. The findings for the three countries, brought together in Table 2.4, show that there has been a marked increase in the allocation of responsibility in all cases. The number of survey schools having a post of responsibility allocated to science rose over the five years by 60 per cent in England, tripled in Wales and rose from hardly any to 20 per cent of survey schools in Northern Ireland. It appears that the increase in post holders has been most rapid in England since 1982, though the very sharp rise to 1983 and the small decrease in 1984 could be a sampling effect. In Wales the largest increase occurred between 1981 and 1982, while in Northern Ireland the greatest rise in the numbers of special posts occurred between 1980 and 1981. In both these countries there has been a steady increase to 1984.

The proportions of schools assigning responsibility for science on a voluntary basis has remained steady in Wales and England over the entire period, and in Northern Ireland since 1982 at much the same levels.

*Policy for science*

Information has been gathered as to how science was included in the curriculum: as a specified part, as a planned part of broader topics, brought in 'as it arises' or whether there was no general policy on this matter. The last two categories of response have been combined in Table 2.5.

In their survey of primary education in England (DES, 1978a), HMI indicated that very little science was evident in those schools where science was expected to arise as an unplanned part of other work. Despite good intentions, then, it is likely that having this *laissez-faire* policy or no policy at all is an indication *in general* (though there will be exceptions) of little sustained work in science. Table 2.5 shows how the proportion of English schools falling in this category varied with school type and school catchment area in 1984.

The school type results in Table 2.5 show that Middle and Independent schools were more likely to have a positive policy than either Junior or Junior-with-infant schools.

Table 2.6 (p. 8) shows that the position in England and Wales has remained largely stable over the five years, whilst in Northern Ireland there has been a steady increase in the proportion of schools adopting a positive policy towards the position of science in the curriculum.

In Northern Ireland the trend towards adopting a science policy has taken the form of a large increase in the proportion including science as a specified part of the curriculum and a smaller increase in the proportion including science as a planned part of broader topics. In both

**Table 2.5** *Policy for science in the survey schools in England, Wales and Northern Ireland in 1984*

(Percentage of schools including science in the curriculum)

| | Eng | Wales | NI | Within England | | | | | | |
|---|---|---|---|---|---|---|---|---|---|---|
| | | | | J + I | Jun | Mid | Ind | Inner city | Urban | Rural |
| Specified part of curriculum | 47 | 47 | 40 | 38 | 35 | 89 | 91 | 22 | 38 | 38 |
| Planned part of broader topics | 39 | 36 | 26 | 45 | 52 | 9 | – | 65 | 46 | 42 |
| Included 'as it arises'/no policy | 14 | 17 | 35 | 17 | 14 | 2 | 9 | 13 | 8 | 10 |
| Number of schools | 435 | 135 | 166 | 267 | 81 | 53 | 34 | 37 | 207 | 103 |

**Table 2.6** *Policy for science in the survey schools in England, Wales and Northern Ireland, 1980–84*

(Percentage of schools including science in the curriculum)

| | England | | | Wales | | | N. Ireland | | |
|---|---|---|---|---|---|---|---|---|---|
| | Spec. part | Plan. part | No policy | Spec. part | Plan. part | No policy | Spec. part | Plan. part | No policy |
| 1980 | 56 | 31 | 12 | 43 | 35 | 21 | 21 | 19 | 59 |
| 1981 | 52 | 31 | 17 | 46 | 32 | 21 | 27 | 17 | 56 |
| 1982 | 55 | 29 | 16 | 43 | 40 | 17 | 31 | 22 | 48 |
| 1983 | 54 | 37 | 9 | 45 | 42 | 13 | 30 | 37 | 33 |
| 1984 | 47 | 39 | 14 | 47 | 36 | 17 | 40 | 26 | 35 |

these categories, however, the proportions remain lower in Northern Ireland than in Wales and England.

## School documents relating to science policy

Closely related to the school's policy for science is the existence of a written document. What this might ideally be has been the subject of debate and proposals during the five years covered by the surveys, beginning with the publication of the Learning Through Science guidelines (Schools Council, 1980), which have been widely quoted in many LEA documents, and ending with the statement from the DES that 'An essential part of a primary school's policy for science education must therefore be to produce a properly constructed scheme of work' (DES, 1985f).

The 1980 and 1981 school questionnaires asked survey schools' whether their written science document took the form of a scheme of work or broad guidelines. In 1982 the wording was changed in order to gather more specific information, and three alternatives were then provided: specific activities forming a scheme of work, specific topics or areas of study, or broad guidelines. This more precise wording was used also in 1983 and 1984. The detailed figures for 1984 are shown in Table 2.7.

Table 2.7 shows that in 1984 fewer than one in five survey schools in England and just over one in five in Wales had a policy document taking the form of a scheme of work.

**Table 2.7** *The availability of a policy document in the schools in 1984*

(Percentage of schools possessing each kind)

| | Number of schools | Scheme of work | Topics or areas | Broad guide-lines | None |
|---|---|---|---|---|---|
| England | 440 | 17 | 27 | 26 | 31 |
| Wales | 137 | 23 | 25 | 23 | 29 |
| Northern Ireland | 120 | 13 | 25 | 18 | 44 |
| **Within England** | | | | | |
| Junior-with-infant | 270 | 9 | 23 | 30 | 38 |
| Junior | 81 | 18 | 30 | 25 | 27 |
| Middle | 53 | 34 | 41 | 19 | 6 |
| Independent | 36 | 42 | 31 | 6 | 22 |
| **Primary schools in England** | | | | | |
| Inner city | 37 | 8 | 24 | 22 | 43 |
| Other urban | 208 | 12 | 30 | 28 | 30 |
| Rural | 103 | 10 | 15 | 35 | 43 |

In Northern Ireland about one in seven had such a school policy document. Although a high proportion of Middle schools had a written document (Table 2.7), this took the form of a scheme of work in only a third of the survey schools. Consistently, Junior schools were more likely to have a more detailed document than Junior-with-infant schools. This general picture for 1984 confirms that previously reported for 1982 and 1983.

As Table 2.8 shows, there was an increase between 1982 and 1983 in the proportions of Northern Ireland survey schools indicating the availability of a document of some kind for science. The general picture for England and Wales has been rather stable over the period.

**Table 2.8** *The availability of a written document in the schools of England, Wales and Northern Ireland, 1980–84*

(Percentage of schools possessing a document of some kind)

| Survey | England | | Wales | | N. Ireland | |
|---|---|---|---|---|---|---|
| | Doc. | None | Doc. | None | Doc. | None |
| 1980 | 69 | 31 | 77 | 23 | 41 | 59 |
| 1981 | 74 | 26 | 73 | 27 | 47 | 53 |
| 1982 | 78 | 42 | 62 | 38 | 40 | 60 |
| 1983 | 73 | 27 | 71 | 29 | 56 | 44 |
| 1984 | 69 | 31 | 71 | 29 | 56 | 44 |

## Group or class size for science activities

Table 2.9 presents the results into the enquiry about class/group size for science. As in previous years we see that the most common group size overall was 26–30 pupils, and that among schools of different type it continues to be the case that the majority of the Independent schools enjoy very much smaller class/group sizes than do the maintained schools.

Table 2.10 shows that in England there has been a tendency towards a smaller proportion of very large classes (more than 30) for science, but it remains true that in more than half of the survey schools science was undertaken with more than 25 working together. In Wales and

**Table 2.9** *Size of class or group for science activities at age 10/11 in 1984*

(Percentage of schools indicating each size)

| | No. of schools | <12 | 12–21 | 22–25 | 26–30 | 30+ |
|---|---|---|---|---|---|---|
| England | 431 | 13 | 20 | 15 | 32 | 21 |
| Wales | 136 | 21 | 18 | 14 | 33 | 13 |
| Northern Ireland | 114 | 11 | 21 | 22 | 26 | 19 |
| **Within England** | | | | | | |
| Junior with infant | 261 | 17 | 19 | 14 | 28 | 22 |
| Junior | 81 | 6 | 14 | 10 | 41 | 30 |
| Middle | 54 | 6 | 4 | 22 | 54 | 15 |
| Independent | 35 | 6 | 69 | 17 | 9 | – |
| **Primary schools in England** | | | | | | |
| Inner city | 37 | 16 | 14 | 27 | 32 | 11 |
| Other urban | 203 | 8 | 15 | 11 | 32 | 34 |
| Rural | 97 | 26 | 25 | 13 | 27 | 9 |

**Table 2.10** *Size of class or group for science activities at age 10/11, 1980–84*

(Percentage of schools indicating each size)

| | England | | | Wales | | | N. Ireland | | |
|---|---|---|---|---|---|---|---|---|---|
| | <12 | 12–30 | 30+ | <12 | 12–30 | 30+ | <12 | 12–30 | 30+ |
| 1980 | 13 | 60 | 27 | 34 | 52 | 14 | 26 | 64 | 10 |
| 1981 | 14 | 61 | 25 | 26 | 62 | 12 | 17 | 63 | 20 |
| 1982 | 13 | 64 | 23 | 21 | 64 | 15 | 13 | 65 | 22 |
| 1983 | 10 | 70 | 20 | 18 | 72 | 10 | 17 | 64 | 19 |
| 1984 | 13 | 66 | 21 | 21 | 66 | 13 | 11 | 70 | 19 |

Northern Ireland this proportion is slightly less but there has nevertheless been a tendency for very small group or class sizes to become less common in the survey schools.

*Teachers' in-service course experience*

Teachers themselves are schools' most important resource for science. However the initial training of most teachers of 10/11 year olds has not given them an adequate background in science. Previous science reports at this age, for instance, have shown that only a very small percentage of primary school teachers hold a science degree. In-service experience therefore has a vital role in supporting science work in the schools. In each survey information has been sought about teachers' recent experience of in-service courses in science. Changes were made to the wording of the question posed in 1983 and 1984 in order to increase the detail and validity of the responses. The findings for 1984 are shown in Table 2.11.

**Table 2.11** *The in-service science course experience of teachers in the survey schools in 1984 in England, Wales and Northern Ireland*

(Percentage of teachers with indicated experience within previous 3 years)

| Nature of course | England | Wales | Northern Ireland |
|---|---|---|---|
| Leading to a certificate or award | 1 | 3 | 1 |
| Amounting to at least 3 days (excl. above) | 9 | 9 | 7 |
| Number of teachers | 4,220 | 987 | 1,029 |

The immediate message of Table 2.11, which confirms that revealed in 1983, is that only very small proportions of teachers have any in-service experience in science at all, particularly extensive experience leading to a formal award.

## 2.3 Goals, emphases and topics in the pupils' science work

The extent to which information about children's experiences of science activities can go beyond the description of organisation and the kinds of quantitative details given in the previous section, to indicate something of the nature and quality of their work, is strictly limited in questionnaire surveys. This section reports the results of attempts to investigate what kinds of activities pupils in the survey schools were engaged in, but in the interpretation of the findings it has to be kept in mind that the information was supplied by the schools themselves, allowing a variety of criteria to be applied.

*Goals of science work*

In four of the five surveys the questionnaire has asked schools to declare their priorities in relation to a given list of 12 goals of science-based activities. In the 1980, 1981 and 1982 surveys schools were required to select the five goals they considered most important. The goals enquiry was not included in the 1983 survey, but was reintroduced in 1984 when schools were asked to rate each item on a 1–5 scale (1 = least important; 5 = most important). The change in method of responding was found to make no difference to the order of priority.

The results showed a remarkable consistency throughout. The goals are listed in Table 2.12 in descending order of rating overall in the 1984 survey. Table 2.12 shows that in all three countries, the most highly rated goals were those which are often general goals of primary education while the least rated goals were those more specific to science activity. This confirms the pattern previously reported. Of interest also is the tendency for the lower-rated 'experimental science' goals to be given a lower rating by the Northern Ireland schools than by the schools in England and Wales.

**Table 2.12** *Average ratings given to various goals of science activity in 1984*

(1 = least important, 5 = most important)

| Development of: | Eng | Wales | N.I. |
|---|---|---|---|
| Ability to observe carefully | 4.6 | 4.6 | 4.5 |
| Enjoyment of science-based activity | 4.4 | 4.6 | 4.2 |
| Questioning attitude to surroundings | 4.4 | 4.3 | 4.4 |
| Knowledge of natural and physical world | 4.1 | 4.2 | 4.3 |
| Problem-solving skills | 4.1 | 3.7 | 3.8 |
| Ability to find information from reference books | 3.8 | 4.1 | 4.1 |
| Ability to carry out simple experiments | 3.8 | 3.9 | 3.5 |
| Recognition of patterns in observations or data | 3.6 | 3.5 | 3.2 |
| Appreciation of relevance of maths to problems | 3.4 | 3.5 | 2.8 |
| Understanding of basic science concepts | 3.3 | 3.5 | 2.8 |
| Familiarity with correct use of simple equipment | 3.3 | 3.3 | 2.9 |
| Ability to plan experiments | 3.1 | 3.1 | 2.7 |

There were also some differences between types of school which are worthy of mention and which also confirm previous survey findings. Independent and Middle schools gave a higher rating to *ability to carry out experiments carefully and safely* and to *familiarity with the correct use of simple science equipment* than did primary schools. Conversely primary schools rated *ability to find information from reference books* and *appreciation of the* relevance of mathematics to real problems more highly than Middle and Independent schools. This may well reflect the greater tendency in the primary schools for science to be integrated with other subjects and to be seen as serving the learning of basic numeracy and literacy, whilst in Middle and Independent schools science is more frequently taught as a separate subject and more often in a separate room from the rest of the curriculum. Differences between schools in different catchment areas in England were negligible.

There is no indication in the data that there have been any changes in priority over the period of the surveys.

*Activities emphasised in science work*

In each survey questionnaire a list has been given of 18 statements about things which pupils might be encouraged to do in science activities. In the first three age 11 surveys a 'forced choice' type of response was requested, schools being asked to pick out the eight items representing the kinds of activities most emphasised in the science work of their 10/11 year olds. In the fourth survey schools were asked to rate each one using a 1–5 scale (1 = least emphasis) and also to select the eight most emphasised. The results (DES, 1985a, page 11) showed that the two methods of responding gave very similar results for overall order of emphases. In the 1984 survey the response was by rating only. As in the case of the goals, the results for emphases in various activities showed a consistent picture across all the surveys. The results are given, therefore, only for 1984 in Table 2.13, with items arranged in order of priority established by the overall results.

*The general picture is that the most emphasis has been given to making observations, drawing conclusions, making notes during their work, making a satisfactory written record of the work and following instructions carefully.* The last three of these reflect a view of science as a vehicle for encouraging basic reading and writing. In contrast to the high emphasis on producing a written record, the emphasis on children choosing the kind of record to make is much lower. It has been noted in earlier reports (eg DES, 1983a, page 199) that among those activities given least emphasis were many which are more specifically scientific relating to designing experiments, whilst those at the top of the list have a more general application across the curriculum. This mirrors the pattern previously discussed for the goals of science activity.

Differences between catchment areas in England have not been consistent across the three years for which these data have been collected, apart from a slightly lower emphasis in inner city schools than in others on children *designing their own experiments.*

Emphases have varied across types of school in England, however, with consistently more emphasis being given by Independent and Middle schools than primary schools to *making a satisfactory written record, using scientific words correctly, paying careful attention to demonstrations,* and

**Table 2.13** *Average ratings given to various emphases of science activities in 1984*
(1 = least emphasis, 5 = most emphasis)

| Pupils are encouraged to: | England | Wales | N. Ireland |
|---|---|---|---|
| Make careful observations at first hand | 4.4 | 4.2 | 4.9 |
| Draw conclusions from results or make generalisations based on observations | 4.2 | 4.1 | 3.7 |
| Make notes of observations and results during the course of their work | 4.0 | 4.2 | 3.8 |
| Make a satisfactory written record of their work | 3.9 | 4.2 | 3.8 |
| Follow carefully instructions given on a card, in a book or on the blackboard | 3.8 | 4.1 | 4.0 |
| Estimate a measurement before taking it | 3.7 | 3.9 | 3.8 |
| Use scientific words correctly in discussion and in written records | 3.4 | 3.4 | 3.0 |
| Pay careful attention to demonstrations | 3.4 | 4.0 | 3.7 |
| Repeat any measurements or readings to reduce error | 3.2 | 3.5 | 3.3 |
| Identify the variables operating in certain situations | 3.1 | 3.1 | 2.8 |
| Apply scientific knowledge to many different problems or situations | 3.1 | 3.3 | 2.9 |
| Examine their work critically for flaws in exp. method | 3.0 | 3.1 | 2.9 |
| Incorporate controls in experiments | 2.9 | 3.1 | 2.6 |
| Decide on the problems they wish to investigate | 2.8 | 2.8 | 2.7 |
| Choose what kind of record to make of their work | 2.8 | 2.6 | 2.5 |
| Design their own experiments | 2.8 | 2.9 | 2.3 |
| Check results using reference books where possible | 2.6 | 3.1 | 2.9 |
| Read about experiments which it is not possible for them to carry out | 2.2 | 2.3 | 2.2 |
| Number of schools | 417 | 124 | 110 |

*incorporating controls in experiments.* Junior and Junior-with-infant schools gave more emphasis than the other two types to children *deciding the problem they wish to investigate, choosing what kind of record to make of their work, estimating a measurement before taking it* and *designing their own experiments.* Consistently, Middle schools have given more emphasis than other school types to *drawing conclusions or making generalisations.*

These school differences suggest that primary schools' emphases were more in harmony with the process-oriented view of science, as widely advocated in primary science curriculum projects, than Middle and Independent schools which gave greater emphasis to activities more typical of secondary school science. These differences might well be considered in the light of the recent DES statement in which all schools are urged to give greater emphasis to processes and to the application of science to problems in everyday life (DES, 1985e).

*Topics in science activities*

In the 1982 and 1984 surveys the questionnaire included a list of topics, and schools were asked to indicate which of these the work of their 10/11 year olds during the current school year had concerned, responding separately for written work and for practical work. The list used in 1982 was based on responses to an open question about topics covered which had been included in the 1981 survey. Some changes, mainly additions, were made to the list between 1982 and 1984. Detailed results for 1984 are given in Table 2.14 (the corresponding data for 1982 will be found in Report No. 3, DES, 1984a).

**Table 2.14** *Topics encountered in science work of 10/11 year olds in the current year*
(Percentage of schools in 1984 indicating each topic for written and practical work)

| Topic | Written work | | | Practical work | | |
|---|---|---|---|---|---|---|
| | Eng | Wales | NI | Eng | Wales | NI |
| Life cycle of any animal | 63 | 68 | 61 | 47 | 39 | 44 |
| Life cycle of any plant | 61 | 58 | 67 | 55 | 47 | 60 |
| Structure of any animal | 47 | 40 | 26 | 31 | 19 | 10 |
| Structure of any plant | 51 | 53 | 55 | 47 | 40 | 55 |
| Life in a particular habitat | 62 | 68 | 62 | 60 | 55 | 48 |
| Food chains/webs and interdependence | 45 | 40 | 31 | 24 | 17 | 13 |
| Properties of air | 45 | 63 | 46 | 43 | 58 | 44 |
| Properties of water | 59 | 70 | 69 | 61 | 69 | 73 |
| Properties of materials | 43 | 41 | 26 | 46 | 38 | 26 |
| Forces | 43 | 47 | 27 | 47 | 46 | 28 |
| Movement | 37 | 49 | 48 | 37 | 40 | 34 |
| Time | 56 | 64 | 67 | 54 | 50 | 60 |
| Electricity | 46 | 47 | 39 | 47 | 46 | 39 |
| Magnetism | 41 | 49 | 43 | 46 | 50 | 51 |
| Light and vision | 43 | 42 | 36 | 44 | 42 | 36 |
| Sound and hearing | 35 | 47 | 36 | 36 | 44 | 32 |
| The sky (sun, moon, stars, etc.) | 42 | 59 | 67 | 25 | 31 | 36 |
| The weather | 53 | 70 | 78 | 49 | 60 | 71 |
| Rocks and soil | 28 | 34 | 26 | 26 | 26 | 28 |
| Human food | 46 | 40 | 52 | 36 | 19 | 28 |
| Number of schools | 435 | 274 | 116 | 435 | 274 | 116 |

Where comparisons can be made between the years there is generally consistency in the popularity of topics, the only exception being the increase in proportions studying *life in a particular habitat* in written work in all three countries.

In all countries some topics have been consistently studied more often through written work than practical work. These include *the life cycle and anatomy of any animal, life in a particular habitat, food chains or webs and interdependence of living things, the sky* and *human food*. These results may suggest that these topics have been studied mainly from written sources, but there may also have been some misunderstanding of the term 'practical work'. The topics in question do not lend themselves to *experimental work*, but their study need not exclude first-hand investigation, exploration, observation, recording and pattern seeking, all of which could be described as *practical work*.

Differences among the countries have appeared in relation to *animal structure, food chains, properties of materials, forces* and *electricity*, all of which have been more frequently included in England and Wales than in Northern Ireland. On the other hand Northern Ireland schools included work on *the sky* and *weather* more often than those in Wales, where it was in turn more common than in England. Schools in both Wales and Northern Ireland included work on *properties of water* more often than those in England.

Pupils' experience of science was not, of course, restricted to what they studied in the school year in which the survey took place, but extended back to their previous classes. In order to explore the inclusion of the various topics more widely in the school curriculum, the schools were asked (in the 1984 survey only) to indicate the year(s) in which each topic was normally encountered. The results, given in Appendix 2, indicate that many topics are encountered with equal frequency in all four years. Only three were more likely to be introduced in the earlier years rather than the later ones: *life cycles of any animal* and *of any plant* and *the weather*. Ten topics were more likely to be encountered in the upper two years than in the earlier two: *structure of any animal, interdependence (food webs and chains), properties of air, properties of materials, forces, movement, electricity, magnetism, rocks and soil* and *human food*.

Appendix 2 also gives the frequencies for the introduction of a topic *for the first time* and the proportion of schools not including each topic at all. Table 2.15 shows the most and least popular topics and the proportions of schools in each country where they were included.

Table 2.15 indicates that some of the most popular topics were less widespread in survey schools of Northern Ireland than in England and Wales and that the difference was even more marked for the least popular topics.

**Table 2.15** *Frequency of including the most and least popular topics in any of the four years of junior education*
(Percentage of schools in 1984 survey)

| | England | Wales | N. Ireland |
|---|---|---|---|
| **Most popular** | | | |
| Life cycle of any animal | 91 | 89 | 75 |
| Life cycle of any plant | 86 | 85 | 78 |
| Properties of water | 84 | 86 | 77 |
| Life in a particular habitat | 82 | 88 | 73 |
| The weather | 81 | 88 | 88 |
| **Least popular** | | | |
| Food chains and interdependence | 64 | 61 | 43 |
| Structure of any animal | 63 | 60 | 38 |
| Properties of materials | 62 | 64 | 42 |
| Forces | 60 | 72 | 45 |
| Rocks and soil | 59 | 56 | 44 |
| Movement | 58 | 66 | 59 |
| Number of schools | 410 | 133 | 113 |

11

## 2.4 Use of curriculum materials, television programmes and microcomputers

In the 1982 and 1983 surveys, information was collected in the questionnaire about the curriculum materials in the schools and in use in the science work of 10/11 year olds. The enquiry was not repeated in 1984 and thus there is nothing to add to the results given previously (DES, 1985a, pages 8–9). These have indicated that in all three countries the Science 5/13 Units were most frequently used of all materials and their popularity had increased between 1982 and 1983, when they were used by 54 per cent of the sample in England, 38 per cent in Wales and 23 per cent in Northern Ireland.

Information about the use of television programmes with 10/11 year olds was collected in the 1982 and 1984 surveys. The findings for the frequency of use with this age group were unchanged over the two years. Additional information was provided in the 1984 survey about the use of television programmes with other age groups in the school. The results are given in Table 2.16.

There is a steady rise in the use of television over the first three years of junior education in England and Wales where about three-quarters of schools make some use of television programmes in science. The use in Northern Ireland schools continues to increase in the fourth year

and four out of five schools use television programmes. Fewer Middle schools than other types make use of television in science. Catchment area appears not to be associated in any consistent way with difference in use of the medium.

A question about the use of microcomputers in schools was included for the first time in the 1984 survey. The enquiry covered various uses including the use of software packages relating to science. The results, in Table 2.17, show that 82 per cent of survey schools in England, 85 per cent in Wales and 76 per cent in Northern Ireland provided their 10/11 year olds with some computer experience. There is reasonable agreement between these findings and those from the pupils' responses to questions asking about their computer experience (see Chapter 3, page 17).

The present lack of software consistent with the general aims of primary science (as represented in, for example, the objectives of Science 5/13) means that it is likely that in the 20–25 per cent including science in the programs used, the proportion of computer usage in fact concerned with science is very small. Thus the two types of software usage could be combined, giving totals which are higher for Wales than both England and Northern Ireland. Use of the microcomputer in programming was greater in England than in the other countries. Within types of school in England microcomputers were more frequently used for programming in Independent and Junior schools than in Junior-with-infant and Middle schools, but were used less often with software in Independent than in other types of school. Use did not vary appreciably with school catchment area.

## 2.5 Summary

A school questionnaire has been used in each survey to collect information about various aspects of the provision of science in the survey schools. The results show that, using schools' own definition of science, the curriculum of almost all survey schools in England and Wales and 90 per cent of those in Northern Ireland has included some science for 10/11 year olds.

**Table 2.16** *Use of television science programmes in the four years of junior education*
(Percentage of schools in 1984 survey)

| | No. of schools | Use with years 7–8 | 8–9 | 9–10 | 10–11 | No use of TV |
|---|---|---|---|---|---|---|
| England | 442 | 17 | 25 | 41 | 43 | 23 |
| Wales | 139 | 19 | 24 | 47 | 42 | 26 |
| Northern Ireland | 120 | 12 | 23 | 37 | 53 | 19 |
| **School type in England** | | | | | | |
| Junior-with-infant | 270 | 18 | 28 | 44 | 46 | 20 |
| Junior | 82 | 21 | 27 | 45 | 48 | 20 |
| Middle | 54 | – | – | 30 | 31 | 35 |
| Independent | 36 | 17 | 28 | 28 | 33 | 28 |
| **Primary schools in England** | | | | | | |
| Inner city | 33 | 17 | 32 | 44 | 51 | 27 |
| Other urban | 200 | 17 | 23 | 39 | 38 | 22 |
| Rural | 100 | 17 | 31 | 46 | 52 | 22 |

**Table 2.17** *Use of a microcomputer by 10/11 year olds in the survey schools*
(Percentage of schools in the 1984 survey)

| | Eng | Wales | NI | England only J+I | Jun | Mid | Ind | Inner city | Other urban | Rural |
|---|---|---|---|---|---|---|---|---|---|---|
| Playing games only | 7 | 5 | 12 | 7 | 8 | 8 | 9 | 8 | 7 | 9 |
| Simple programming (only) | 20 | 10 | 11 | 17 | 28 | 15 | 32 | 15 | 20 | 21 |
| With software (excluding science) | 35 | 43 | 36 | 35 | 31 | 42 | 29 | 28 | 34 | 38 |
| With software (including science) | 20 | 27 | 17 | 20 | 24 | 19 | 9 | 26 | 20 | 17 |
| None | 18 | 15 | 24 | 21 | 9 | 15 | 21 | 23 | 18 | 15 |
| Number of schools | 430 | 137 | 118 | 266 | 78 | 52 | 34 | 33 | 200 | 100 |

There is evidence that the time spent on science in survey schools in England and Wales has increased slightly over the year of the survey; however it is still the case that the majority of schools spend about 5 per cent of total curriculum time on science. In England proportionally more rural schools than schools in other catchment areas spent 10 per cent or more of curriculum time on science. There were no consistent trends over time associated with school type, and Independent schools have always been found to spend proportionally more time on science than other types of school.

The proportion of schools having a post of responsibility for science increased in England and Wales up to 1983 but levelled off thereafter. The increase has continued up to 1984 in Northern Ireland, but there still remain posts in only one in five schools in that country compared with one in two in England. There has not been any appreciable trend in the proportion of schools where responsibility is assigned voluntarily, which remains at about one in five in all three countries. It may be that, if the number of special responsibility posts has risen as much as the available points will allow, it is only through urging voluntary acceptance of responsibility that the proportion of schools not allocating responsibility for science can be further reduced. In England responsibility for science is assigned either formally or informally more often in Middle, Independent and Junior schools than in Junior-with-infant schools and more often in urban and inner city schools than in rural schools.

The pattern of schools' policies in relation to how science is organised within the curriculum has remained stable over the years for schools in England and Wales but in Northern Ireland there has been a steady increase in the proportion of schools including science as a specified part of the curriculum and a related decrease in those having no policy or one of including science 'as it arises'.

The results relating to schools' policy documents for science show the same country differences as for curriculum organisation, with no consistent differences associated with catchment area or school type in England. When the nature of schools' written policy documents was considered it was found that only a minority took the form of a scheme of work. Independent and Middle schools were more likely to have a document of this form than primary schools.

Few trends were found in the size of class or group when science activities were undertaken. There has been a steady decrease over the years in the proportion of very small classes or groups in Wales and Northern Ireland and in classes of 30 or more in England. In more than half of the survey schools in England there have been more than 25 pupils undertaking science activities at the same time throughout the five years of surveys. The corresponding figure for Wales and Northern Ireland has been about 40 per cent.

Teachers' attendance at an in-service course in science of more than three days in total has remained at about one in ten, with 1 per cent in England and Northern Ireland and 3 per cent in Wales undertaking a more substantial course leading to an award.

Schools were asked to indicate the goals of science work which they considered most important. Consistently, schools in all countries have given more importance to goals relating to ability to observe carefully, enjoyment of science activities and development of a questioning attitude. Most emphasis in science activities has been given to observations, making notes and writing satisfactory reports, and following instructions. In both goals and emphases items relating to design of experiments, choosing problems and suitable forms of recording and reviewing work critically have been low in the order of priority. No consistent differences among countries have been found. Within the survey schools in England, the priorities of Independent and Middle schools have more often included some subject-centred goals and emphases in addition to the more general ones compared with the primary schools.

The topics encountered by 10/11 year olds in science work have been investigated in the survey, whilst topics introduced in earlier years were the subject of enquiry in 1984 only. The results indicate that the popularity with teachers of topics for the 10/11 year olds equates with the popularity across all four years of junior education. Biological and physical topics were in both the most popular and the least popular group.

The curriculum materials used by schools have covered a wide range of publications, but Science 5/13 has been the most commonly used, its lead increasing over the two years (1982 and 1983) when this information was collected. About three-quarters of schools also made some use of television science programmes, mainly in the upper two junior years.

Use of a microcomputer was included in the school questionnaire for the first time in 1984. Over 80 per cent of survey schools in England and Wales and slightly fewer in Northern Ireland made some use of a microcomputer, though the extent to which this included science activities was not clear.

# 3

## Pupils' experience, activities and interests relating to science

### 3.1  Introduction

The picture of children's performance in science drawn by the surveys places what children can do in the foreground. For interpretation, these data from the tests need a background of information about the opportunities which children have had to develop the skills and concepts assessed and about their disposition to become involved in science activities. In the context of a survey it is very difficult to obtain and to use information about children's exposure to various relevant activities and their receptivity to them. The importance of the information, however, has encouraged persistence and various attempts have been made which are brought together in this chapter.

The school questionnaire has been the mechanism for gathering information about general arrangements for science in the school which are a part of the pupils' background of exposure to science. Within the general provision of the school there are considerable differences for individual pupils which arise from the particular topics and activities chosen by their teacher, the children's own preferences – where choice is allowed – and the degree to which they may have engaged productively in an activity, which is likely to be affected in part at least by their interests and attitudes towards science.

The differences in children's out-of-school experiences are also known to have an important impact on performance of all kinds. Further, the sorts of activities in which children choose to spend their own time, or would like to spend their time, can be a strong indicator of their attitudes and interests.

For all these reasons, therefore, the background information about children's experience to be added to the foreground in the picture of their performance, has to go beyond the school level to concern the individual pupil.

In the APU science surveys at age 11 some information about children's experiences and interests has been gathered in four of the five surveys. A first small step in gathering this type of information was taken in 1981 with children involved in the individual tests of **Performance of investigations.** One of the investigations concerned a simple electric circuit. As it was considered more likely in this case than in other investigations that performance would be affected by previous experience, pupils were asked by the tester at the end of the session to say whether or not they had done anything similar, using bulbs and

batteries, at school or at home. The results were as follows for 606 pupils:

—yes, at school  13 per cent (16 per cent of the boys; 10 per cent of the girls)
—yes, at home  19 per cent (31 per cent of the boys; 7 per cent of the girls)

(DES, 1983a, page 53)

There was a possibility that the wording and context of the question led children to say 'yes' only if they had experienced something closely resembling the investigation they had just attempted. The figures could thus be underestimates, though probably the interesting sex differences would not have been affected. As will be reported later in this chapter, the proportion of children having done some work on bulbs and batteries in the 1984 survey was close to 50 per cent. The apparent massive increase in work on simple circuits between 1981 and 1984 may well be accounted for in part by the difference in the presentation and wording of the question, but it is unlikely that all could be explained away in this fashion.

In the 1982 and 1983 surveys information was gathered about pupils' liking of various science activities in school (DES, 1984a, Appendix 2, and DES, 1985a, Chapter 7). The 1982 study was to some extent a pilot investigation in which two versions of an assessment instrument were tried out. In one of these, pupils involved in individual practical tests were asked to look at coloured photographs showing a girl and a boy involved in various science-related activities. The activities were designed to illustrate use of process skills and use of equipment as well as particular topics. Referring to four 'faces' showing expressions ranging from enjoyment to dislike, children were asked to say how they would feel if they were doing what the two in the photograph were doing. In the second version similar questions were put to children in a purely written form, using line drawings made by an artist from the photographs. The results showed that proportions of children indicating moderate or great liking for the activities were higher in all cases for those who had responded in the one-to-one practical test, but the order in which activities were placed according to degree of liking was very similar. The results of this pilot exercise justified using the written version of the instrument with a much larger sample in the 1983 survey.

The 1983 findings from the 'liking of activities' instrument, to which responses were gained from 10,200 pupils, confirmed the pilot trial results. The two activities most liked were *doing an experiment* and *planning an experiment*. The activity least liked was *putting down results in a table*. These were the same for boys and girls, but the order in which other activities were placed reflected a sex difference which factor analysis helped to interpret. For both sexes the two main factors showed that liking for activities involving experimenting tended to go together, as did liking for the non-experimental activities. Whilst both boys and girls preferred the *'experimental'* to the *'non-experimental'* group of activities, there was a very large difference in preference for the boys, but only a small difference for the girls.

Information was gathered in the 1984 survey on a much broader base than attempted earlier. The questionnaires used and results obtained are described in the following sections. The questions are included as Appendix 3, 4, 6i and 6ii.

The full set of questions about topics, equipment and activities would have taken too much time for each child to answer as part of the written test packages. It was therefore divided into two parts. Half of the sample answered the questions about the topics and the other half answered the questions about equipment use and activities in and out of school.

As a check on children's answers, the questions were also administered as an interview with those in the sub-sample for **Performance of investigations**. Again half of the sample was asked about topics and the other half about equipment and activities. The testers were able to ask pupils for examples to substantiate a claim to have done some work on a topic; for instance, to probe their memory and to take care in distinguishing between 'a few times' and 'quite often' in response to the activities.

Some children gave both oral and written responses to the same questions, though there was no control over whether the written test was taken before or after the practical testing. As only half of the written sample and half of the practical sub-sample took any one set of these questions, the chance of answering the same questions in both versions was 1 in 4. In fact a complete set of answers to both forms was obtained from 99 pupils only. This was a lower figure than that theoretically possible because the extra questions were always at the end of a package and so would not be reached by some children; similarly if the practical tester ran out of time they were advised to omit these questions rather than leave other testing incomplete. For these 99 children, however, the percentage agreement was above 67 per cent for all but two items, and it was considered justified to use the data from the whole sample taking the written packages rather than the much smaller practical test sub-sample. (The questions were not in fact included in two of the written packages, so the numbers do not correspond with the full written test sample.)

## 3.2 Experience of science topics

Twenty-six items referring to the content of activities were drawn up to correspond closely with the nominated range of science concepts and knowledge identified within the assessment framework at age 11. (The concept list is reproduced as Appendix 9.) Titles were sought which would be familiar to children; some might well be titles of topics studies at school (*Our food, Floating and sinking, Growing seeds*). For each one an illustration was prepared by an artist so that the meaning was conveyed pictorially as well as in words (see Appendix 3).

Children were asked to indicate, by putting a tick or a cross in the appropriate box by each topic, whether they had done some work on it and whether they would like to know more about the topic. The first of these pieces of information might have been sought from the children's teacher, but it was the intention to discover whether the children had encountered activities on these topics at all in their experience, not merely with their present teacher. During pilot trials of this instrument (when the children's answers were probed in discussion to explore their reliability) it was impressive and encouraging to note how often an 11 year old would refer to experiences in previous years, often going as far back as the infants' school. Pilot

**Table 3.1** *Children's experience of science topics: those who have done some work and those who would like to know more*

(Percentage of whole sample, boys and girls)

|  | 'Done some work' | | | 'Like to know more' | | |
|---|---|---|---|---|---|---|
|  | All | Boys | Girls | All | Boys | Girls |
| Air and burning | 53 | 59 | 47 | 48 | 44 | 52 |
| Speed | 38 | 38 | 38 | 54 | 55 | 53 |
| Dissolving things | 55 | 55 | 55 | 45 | 41 | 49 |
| Electric circuits | 45 | 51 | 40 | 57 | 58 | 55 |
| Making sounds | 52 | 52 | 51 | 44 | 40 | 47 |
| Growing seeds | 63 | 62 | 65 | 40 | 37 | 42 |
| Reflection in a mirror | 62 | 61 | 63 | 35 | 35 | 35 |
| Shadows | 42 | 44 | 40 | 49 | 48 | 51 |
| Time | 50 | 49 | 50 | 45 | 46 | 43 |
| The sky | 32 | 33 | 31 | 62 | 61 | 63 |
| Forces | 21 | 24 | 19 | 58 | 58 | 58 |
| Parts of plants | 61 | 59 | 62 | 42 | 39 | 45 |
| Water in the air | 35 | 38 | 32 | 52 | 51 | 54 |
| The weather | 43 | 45 | 41 | 50 | 49 | 51 |
| Our food | 58 | 55 | 61 | 44 | 42 | 46 |
| Differences between living things | 43 | 43 | 43 | 54 | 54 | 55 |
| Rocks | 38 | 39 | 37 | 51 | 52 | 50 |
| Magnets | 62 | 64 | 59 | 36 | 37 | 35 |
| How different things live together | 31 | 33 | 29 | 58 | 57 | 58 |
| Air is everywhere | 48 | 50 | 45 | 41 | 40 | 43 |
| How animals have young | 32 | 32 | 33 | 58 | 56 | 61 |
| Testing hearing | 38 | 38 | 39 | 50 | 47 | 54 |
| Separating colours | 23 | 26 | 21 | 61 | 58 | 65 |
| Floating and sinking | 64 | 62 | 67 | 32 | 33 | 31 |
| What's inside an animal | 34 | 34 | 34 | 61 | 61 | 60 |
| How materials are different | 31 | 34 | 27 | 54 | 55 | 53 |
| Number of pupils | 4,572 | 2,322 | 2,250 | 4,572 | 2,322 | 2,250 |

trials also enabled the children's responses to be checked against teachers' records of what the children had done. It was found that invariably the children included all that their present teacher was aware of; records of additional experiences, in previous classes or different schools, were not available to the class teachers in the trials.

Table 3.1 (p. 15) shows the proportions of pupils indicating that they had done some work on each topic and that they would like to know more about it.

The evidence here suggests a varied experience of different kinds of topic across the sample as a whole. It is *not* the case that the most frequently encountered topics are all related to 'nature study' and the least common to the physical sciences. In descending order of frequency, the topics on which most children had done some work were (starting with the highest frequency):

| | |
|---|---|
| *floating and sinking* | 64 per cent |
| *growing seeds* | 63 per cent |
| *magnets* | 62 per cent |
| *reflection in a mirror* | 62 per cent |
| *parts of plants* | 61 per cent |

The most frequent topics were similar for boys and girls except that *magnets*, whilst at the top of the list for boys, was in sixth place for girls, being replaced in the top five by *our food*. The least frequently encountered topics were (starting with the least of all):

| | |
|---|---|
| *forces* | 21 per cent |
| *separating colours* | 23 per cent |
| *how materials are different* | 31 per cent |
| *how different things live together* | 31 per cent |
| *the sky* | 32 per cent |
| *how animals have young* | 32 per cent |

Again the same topics, with only minor differences in order, were the least experienced by both boys and girls.

Comparison with the data given by school staff in the School Questionnaire in the 1982 survey is difficult because of the possibility of different interpretation of items presented to the teachers and children. However there is some correspondence between the most and least frequent activities reported by the pupils and the popularity of science topics explored through *practical* activities as reported by teachers in 1982 (DES, 1984a, page 21). *Magnetism, properties of water, plant structure and plant life cycle* were among the top five in both lists, while *properties of materials, interdependence* and *the life cycle of any animal* were near the bottom of both lists.

The frequency of work on the topics does not indicate any patterns there may be in pupils' experience; individual children or classes may encounter different selections of the most frequently found topics in combination with other topics. Factor analysis was used to investigate patterns in the data about 'work done'. Although the data for boys and girls were analysed separately the patterns revealed were almost identical.

The main factor, accounting for 22 per cent of the variance, showed that there was a strong tendency for the following items to be linked in children's experience:

*differences between living things*
*how animals have young*
*how different things live together*
*what's inside an animal*
*parts of plants*
*our food*
*the sky*
*rocks*
*growing seeds*

Here is the evidence of the 'nature study' approach, but the fact that it is not predominant in schools is clear from the presence of three of the least frequently encountered topics. Thus, while the nature study approach represents a strong theme in the variations between schools' programmes, it does not represent anything approaching the majority of schools.

Five other factors were identified, each accounting for between 4 per cent and 5 per cent of the variance. These could be described as focusing on:

*selected physics topics*
*air and water*
*water, sound, food, plants*
*forces and properties of matter*
*electric circuits and magnets*

It was noticed that all the most frequently occurring topics were included in at least two factors, whilst the least often encountered were found in only one factor each.

The data in Table 3.1 on pupils' choice of topics to 'find out more about' compare in an interesting way with the data on what they have already done. The topics about which most would like to know more are:

| | |
|---|---|
| *the sky* | 62 per cent |
| *separating colours* | 61 per cent |
| *what's inside an animal* | 61 per cent |
| *how animals have young* | 58 per cent |
| *how different things live together* | 58 per cent |
| *forces* | 58 per cent |
| *electric circuits* | 57 per cent |

These include all the topics *least* frequently encountered, apart from *how materials are different*. The lists of most popular items were very similar for boys and girls.

The topics which children placed at the bottom of the list for wanting to know more about were:

| | |
|---|---|
| *floating and sinking* | 32 per cent |
| *reflection in a mirror* | 35 per cent |
| *magnets* | 36 per cent |
| *growing seeds* | 40 per cent |
| *air is everywhere* | 41 per cent |
| *parts of plants* | 42 per cent |

These include all the most popular topics, a finding which fits the pattern of children wishing to do something different from that which they have already done. This pattern was confirmed by looking at the relationship for each topic between having already done some work and wanting to do some more. For both girls and boys there was an overwhelming vote against doing more of what they had done. For all 26 topics over 70 per cent of pupils who had done some work on the topic said they did not wish to do more. The decision was equally clear for boys and girls, the only difference being that the 'rejection' figure was over 80 per cent for all except 6 topics in the case of boys and 13 topics for girls. The girls were, then, just a little more open than boys to pursuing familiar topics a little further.

Factor analysis indicated that the strongest grouping among topics that children wanted to 'know more about' linked a wide range of topics. The main factor, accounting for about 30 per cent of the variance, included 16 of the 26 activities and was identical in the separate analyses for girls and boys. It included topics about forces, speed, materials, air, sky, time, the weather and living things. Three other factors, each accounting for 4 per cent to 5 per cent of the variance, included smaller numbers of topics but a quite varied range in each. The similarity in the patterns for boys and girls was striking. There was little evidence in these data of girls who only wanted to know about living things and boys who were only interested in mechanical things.

The interpretation of these findings must take into account the interaction between the two questions posed about each topic. As already noted, the children generally ticked 'like to know more' for topics about which they had done *no* work and vice versa. They were, therefore, in a sense asking for information when they did not know anything about the topic already. This could have been in the hope that it would turn out to be more interesting than the topics they had already studied and did not want to know more about. This reaction could be both an advantage and a disadvantage to the teacher. On the one hand it

suggests a possibility of readily engaging children in investigation of all aspects of their environment; on the other it foreshadows the 'we've done that' reaction when a topic is revisited. There is, however, a sharp contrast between this apparent 'butterfly' approach and the wish to do more of activities which they choose themselves, as reported below (page 20).

## 3.3 Use of various items of equipment

One of the pupil questionnaires asked children about their experience of using 12 different items of equipment which might be encountered in science-related activities (see Appendix 4). These questions were primarily designed to give some idea of the level of familiarity with measuring and other equipment which could be considered against the results of assessing children's performance in using these things (see Chapter 6). However, some additional questions were asked to enlarge the range of information, in particular to include the use of a computer.

Children were asked to indicate whether they had used each item at school and whether they had used it at home or out of school. Items in the list were illustrated by line drawings where the pre-trials showed that ambiguity might exist when only the names of the equipment were given. In other cases drawings were not given since items such as thermometers, stop clocks and screwdrivers may be encountered in such variety that to show a single example might have brought uncertainty to children who had used a quite different example.

The proportions of children indicating that they had used each of the 12 items of equipment either in school or out of school are given in Table 3.2.

The two items about the computer attempted to distinguish between use in playing games and other use. It is difficult for children (or sometimes for adults) to distinguish between computer games and other uses of the

**Table 3.2** *Children's use of various items of equipment at school and/or out of school*
(Percentage of whole sample, boys and girls)

|  | At school | | | Out of school | | | Total experience | | |
|---|---|---|---|---|---|---|---|---|---|
|  | All | Boys | Girls | All | Boys | Girls | All | Boys | Girls |
| Used hand lens | 66 | 66 | 65 | 65 | 70 | 59 | 93 | 95 | 92 |
| Used thermometer | 58 | 59 | 57 | 51 | 53 | 49 | 85 | 86 | 85 |
| Used stopclock/watch | 71 | 73 | 69 | 59 | 66 | 52 | 92 | 94 | 90 |
| Used spring balance | 46 | 49 | 43 | 24 | 28 | 20 | 64 | 69 | 59 |
| Used computer (games) | 70 | 70 | 69 | 63 | 68 | 57 | 93 | 95 | 92 |
| Used computer (other) | 57 | 57 | 57 | 45 | 52 | 38 | 81 | 84 | 79 |
| Used dropper | 22 | 24 | 20 | 42 | 46 | 37 | 55 | 60 | 50 |
| Used compass | 61 | 60 | 63 | 58 | 69 | 48 | 88 | 93 | 83 |
| Used metre stick | 89 | 90 | 89 | 19 | 22 | 16 | 92 | 94 | 90 |
| Used measuring cylinder/jug | 74 | 76 | 73 | 68 | 65 | 70 | 95 | 95 | 96 |
| Used screwdriver | 19 | 25 | 14 | 92 | 94 | 90 | 94 | 97 | 91 |
| Used weighing scales | 75 | 76 | 73 | 78 | 75 | 81 | 98 | 98 | 99 |
| Used microscope | 44 | 45 | 44 | 41 | 49 | 34 | 71 | 76 | 66 |
| Number of pupils | 4,888 | 2,463 | 2,425 | 4,888 | 2,463 | 2,425 | 4,888 | 2,463 | 2,425 |

computer seen as more directly educational. Perhaps this distinction is clearer in out-of-school use, whilst in school many educational programs are presented to children as games. Table 3.2 also shows how home and school together provide a high proportion of children with experience of using the equipment. It shows, for instance, that over 90 per cent of 11 year olds have handled a computer, if only to play games, though 80 per cent have used a computer for other purposes. This finding may well have implications for many secondary schools.

Differences between in-school and out-of-school experience reflect the availability of different items in each location; spring balances and stop clocks or watches are more commonly found in school, whilst droppers and screwdrivers seem to be used more often at home. Although the overall experience with these items of equipment is high, there still remains a proportion of children of age 11 who have not encountered them. One-third have not used a spring balance, nearly one-half have not used a dropper, one in eight have not encountered a compass and almost a third have not used a microscope. Were it not for the home experience the position would be rather more serious, for over a quarter of the children had not used, at school, a stop watch or clock, a measuring cylinder or weighing scales, and over a half had not used a spring balance, dropper, screwdriver or microscope at school. The experience of a thermometer at home is likely to have been of a clinical instrument and therefore it is probable that over 40 per cent of 11 year olds have not used a room or laboratory instrument.

Differences between boys and girls in terms of use of instruments in school is large only in the case of the screwdriver. It is interesting that out of school this particular difference disappears, which is against the general trend for girls to have experienced less use than boys of all the items (apart from weighing scales, likely to be used often in cooking) out of school.

## 3.4 Experience of, and liking for, science-related activities in and out of school

Whilst the two lists discussed so far focused on experiences closely related to the content of activities at school, a further list of activities ranged more widely and included hobbies and use of facilities out of school (though these could still be part of the curriculum by virtue of visits and field work).

The items were chosen to include as many as possible of the informal experiences which children could have which might influence their development of scientific skills or concepts. They included *visiting a museum, making models from a kit, playing snooker* and *watching birds*. A few items were included which were expected to show up differences between boys and girls (*knitting or sewing, playing with electric toy sets* and *weighing out ingredients*

*for cooking*), so that any such differences in out-of-school experience could be compared with in-school experience.

The children were asked to go through the list of 22 items twice; for this purpose it was presented twice to avoid asking for too many responses at the same time. In the first place they were asked to indicate *how often* they had been involved in each activity at school and at home or out of school. The options were *never, a few times* or *quite often* (about once a month). Pre-trials helped in deciding the criteria of frequency and to find a form of words which was simple but unambiguous. The graded size of boxes helped to avoid confusion in answering (see Appendix 6i).

On the second reading of the list (see Appendix 6ii) the children were asked to say if they would like to try each one (if they had not done it) or to do more (if they had already done it). This question was asked in order to obtain some indication of the children's interest in these activities, just as the corresponding question about the science topics indicated further interest in various content areas.

The results in Table 3.3 (p. 19) show the percentages of pupils claiming to take part 'quite often' (about once a month) in these activities at school, at home and at either place.

Table 3.3 shows that, as expected, school and home provide different opportunities for regular involvement in these activities. The frequency of involvement implied in 'quite often' probably accounts for the large difference in proportions of children who said they had done some work on *growing seeds* (Table 3.1, p. 15) and the proportion often involved in *sowing seeds or growing plants* recorded in Table 3.3.

Sex differences in activities undertaken at school are small compared with those in activities out of school. This is brought out in Table 3.4 (p. 20) where the same information is presented with activities arranged in rank order of participation in schools and differences between percentages of boys and girls indicated. The school appears generally to provide similar opportunities for boys and girls, with minor differences in matters where presumably a choice can be made. So boys tend more often than girls to *read science fiction, play draughts or chess* and *decide for themselves how to solve a problem*. Girls tend more often than boys to *weigh out ingredients for cooking, knit or sew* and *collect, or look at, wild flowers*. They also claim to *watch a teacher or scientist do an experiment* slightly more than boys, which is less easy to interpret in terms of choice, unless teachers tend to demonstrate how to do experiments to girls more than boys.

Out-of-school, where choice and preference has a much larger determining effect on the way they spend their time, conventional differences between boys' and girls' activities

**Table 3.3** *Children's participating 'quite often' in various activities at school and/or out of school*
(Percentage of whole sample, boys and girls)

| | At school | | | At home | | | Total experience | | |
|---|---|---|---|---|---|---|---|---|---|
| | All | Boys | Girls | All | Boys | Girls | All | Boys | Girls |
| Watch a TV school science programme | 34 | 35 | 33 | 11 | 13 | 9 | 41 | 43 | 38 |
| Watch a TV programme about science (eg Tomorrow's World) | 6 | 6 | 5 | 39 | 45 | 33 | 42 | 47 | 36 |
| Watch science fiction on TV | 6 | 6 | 5 | 34 | 45 | 23 | 37 | 48 | 26 |
| Read an information book about science/scientists | 10 | 12 | 8 | 8 | 10 | 5 | 15 | 18 | 12 |
| Read a science fiction book | 12 | 15 | 9 | 20 | 25 | 14 | 23 | 29 | 17 |
| Read news about science in a paper or magazine | 4 | 4 | 3 | 12 | 12 | 11 | 13 | 14 | 12 |
| Watch a teacher or scientist do an experiment | 22 | 20 | 24 | 6 | 6 | 5 | 25 | 24 | 26 |
| Decide for yourself how to solve a problem | 41 | 42 | 39 | 34 | 35 | 32 | 49 | 50 | 47 |
| Look after small animals or pets (eg mice, fish, insects) | 13 | 12 | 14 | 55 | 52 | 57 | 59 | 57 | 61 |
| Grow seeds or grow plants | 8 | 7 | 8 | 32 | 30 | 34 | 35 | 33 | 37 |
| Take things apart to see inside them | 8 | 9 | 7 | 28 | 38 | 18 | 32 | 42 | 22 |
| Weigh out ingredients for cooking | 12 | 9 | 15 | 44 | 29 | 60 | 47 | 32 | 63 |
| Watch birds | 11 | 11 | 10 | 29 | 30 | 27 | 32 | 33 | 30 |
| Use parts from a kit to make models (eg Lego, straws) | 9 | 10 | 7 | 37 | 50 | 23 | 40 | 53 | 27 |
| Make up models from a kit (eg Airfix) | 3 | 4 | 1 | 24 | 42 | 6 | 26 | 4 | 7 |
| Play with electric toy sets (cars, trains on tracks) | 3 | 4 | 2 | 31 | 45 | 16 | 32 | 47 | 16 |
| Play pool/snooker/billiards | 5 | 6 | 3 | 45 | 59 | 30 | 46 | 62 | 31 |
| Knit or sew | 22 | 5 | 38 | 26 | 5 | 46 | 35 | 8 | 61 |
| Collect/look at wild flowers | 7 | 5 | 9 | 38 | 8 | 27 | 20 | 11 | 29 |
| Visit a museum or zoo | 11 | 10 | 12 | 25 | 22 | 27 | 29 | 26 | 31 |
| Go fishing or pond dipping | 3 | 4 | 2 | 22 | 30 | 13 | 23 | 31 | 14 |
| Play draughts or chess | 14 | 16 | 11 | 35 | 41 | 28 | 38 | 45 | 32 |
| Number of pupils | 4,888 | 2,463 | 2,425 | 4,888 | 2,463 | 2,425 | 4,888 | 2,463 | 2,425 |

are more in evidence. Boys do the following things more often than girls:

*watch TV science programmes (such as Horizon); watch science fiction on TV; read both non-fiction science and science fiction books; take things apart; make models both from specific kits and from parts of kits; play with electric toy sets; play pool, billiards or snooker; go fishing or pond dipping; play draughts or chess.*

Girls, on the other hand do these things more often than boys:

*look after pets; weigh out ingredients; knit or sew; collect or look at wild flowers.*

Table 3.4 shows that in all cases, except *watch a teacher or scientist do an experiment,* sex differences are in the same direction in school and at home but are greater for activities carried out at home.

The data indicate that the boys do indeed take part far more commonly than girls in science-related pastimes such as *model-making, playing with electric toy sets, watching science programmes on television,* whilst more girls spend time in domestic activities such as *looking after pets, needlework* and *cooking.* Possible reasons can be suggested, but are only speculations. One is that although out-of-school activities appear to be a matter of free

choice, this is in fact not the case. Girls may be constrained, by anything from the physical absence of opportunities (no electric car sets, no model kits) to the less tangible social expectations, from taking part in the activities traditionally accepted as more suitable for boys. Another possibility is that fewer girls are really interested in 'boyish' pastimes and prefer the domestic ones which they presently undertake more frequently. Some light was thrown on this matter by the further data now to be presented.

So far the results have concerned what children say they do, but they were also asked what they would like to do. The question was phrased as 'would you like to try these things or do more of them?' so as to cover the situations where children had or had not already taken part in the activity. The children could give a 'yes', 'no' or 'not sure' reply. Table 3.5 (p. 20) shows the proportions answering 'yes'.

Comparison of the data in Table 3.3 with those in Table 3.5 shows that for all activities there were significantly more children wanting to do them than had experience of them either in or out of school. *Knitting or sewing* were no exception for boys, neither was *playing with electric toy sets* for girls. The fairly uniform additional proportions wanting to try or to do more of each activity leave the relative proportions for different activities rather

**Table 3.4** *Rank order of children's participation in various activities at schools and at home with difference between percentage of boys and girls*

| Activity | At school All | At school % boys minus % girls | At home All | At home % boys minus % girls |
|---|---|---|---|---|
| Decide for yourself how to solve a problem | 41 | +3 | 34 | +3 |
| Watch a TV school science programme | 34 | +2 | 11 | +4 |
| Watch a teacher or a scientist do an experiment | 22 | −4 | 6 | +1 |
| Knit or sew | 22 | −33 | 26 | −41 |
| Play draughts or chess | 14 | +5 | 35 | +13 |
| Look after small animals or pets (eg mice, fish, insects) | 13 | −2 | 55 | −5 |
| Read a science fiction book | 12 | +6 | 20 | +11 |
| Weigh out ingredients for cooking | 12 | −6 | 44 | −31 |
| Visit a museum or zoo | 11 | −2 | 25 | −5 |
| Watch birds | 11 | +1 | 29 | +3 |
| Read an information book about science/scientists | 10 | +4 | 8 | +5 |
| Use parts from a kit to make models (eg Lego, straws) | 9 | +3 | 37 | +27 |
| Sow seeds or grow plants | 8 | −1 | 32 | −4 |
| Take things apart to see inside them | 8 | +2 | 28 | +20 |
| Collect/look at wild flowers | 7 | −4 | 38 | −19 |
| Watch a TV programme about science (eg Tomorrow's World) | 6 | +1 | 39 | +12 |
| Watch science fiction on TV | 6 | +1 | 34 | +22 |
| Play pool/snooker/billiards | 5 | +3 | 45 | +29 |
| Read news about science in a paper or magazine | 4 | +1 | 12 | +1 |
| Make up models from a kit (eg Airfix) | 3 | +3 | 24 | +36 |
| Play with electric toy sets (eg cars, trains on tracks) | 3 | +2 | 31 | +29 |
| Go fishing or pond dipping | 3 | +2 | 22 | +17 |

**Table 3.5** *Children wanting to try or do more of various activities*

(Percentage of whole sample, boys and girls)

| | All | Boys | Girls |
|---|---|---|---|
| Watch a TV school science programme | 59 | 61 | 56 |
| Watch a TV programme about science (eg Tomorrow's World) | 59 | 65 | 55 |
| Watch science fiction on TV | 58 | 68 | 47 |
| Read an information book about science/scientists | 31 | 33 | 29 |
| Read a science fiction book | 48 | 55 | 41 |
| Read news about science in a paper or magazine | 33 | 32 | 34 |
| Watch a teacher or a scientist do an experiment | 70 | 66 | 73 |
| Decide for yourself how to solve a problem | 69 | 69 | 68 |
| Look after small animals or pets | 80 | 75 | 84 |
| Sow seeds or grow plants | 63 | 53 | 72 |
| Take things apart to see inside them | 61 | 74 | 58 |
| Weigh out ingredients for cooking | 66 | 47 | 84 |
| Watch birds | 56 | 57 | 55 |
| Use parts from a kit to make models (eg Lego, straws) | 60 | 73 | 48 |
| Make up models from a kit (eg Airfix) | 50 | 73 | 27 |
| Play with electric toy sets (eg cars, trains on tracks) | 58 | 72 | 44 |
| Play pool/billiards/snooker | 75 | 83 | 66 |
| Knit or sew | 49 | 19 | 78 |
| Collect/look at wild flowers | 43 | 24 | 61 |
| Visit a museum or a zoo | 82 | 81 | 83 |
| Go fishing or pond dipping | 53 | 63 | 43 |
| Play draughts or chess | 68 | 74 | 61 |
| Number of pupils | 4,888 | 2,463 | 2,425 |

**Table 3.6** *Comparison of children's wish to do more of various activities with their experience of them either in or out of school. Items arranged in order of participation with difference between percentage of boys and girls*

| | Participation All | Participation % boys minus % girls | Wish to do more All | Wish to do more % boys minus % girls |
|---|---|---|---|---|
| Look after small animals or pets (eg mice, fish, insects) | 59 | −4 | 80 | −9 |
| Weigh out ingredients for cooking | 47 | −31 | 66 | −37 |
| Decide for yourself how to solve a problem | 49 | +3 | 69 | +1 |
| Play pool/billiards/snooker | 46 | +31 | 75 | +17 |
| Watch a TV programme about science (eg Tomorrow's World) | 42 | +11 | 60 | +10 |
| Watch a TV school science programme | 41 | +5 | 59 | +5 |
| Use parts from a kit to make models (eg Lego, straws) | 40 | +26 | 60 | +25 |
| Play draughts or chess | 38 | +13 | 68 | +13 |
| Watch science fiction on TV | 37 | +22 | 58 | +21 |
| Sow seeds or grow plants | 35 | −4 | 63 | −19 |
| Knit or sew | 35 | −53 | 49 | −59 |
| Take things apart to see inside them | 32 | +40 | 61 | +16 |
| Play with electric toy sets (eg cars, trains on tracks) | 32 | +31 | 58 | +28 |
| Watch birds | 32 | +3 | 56 | +2 |
| Visit a museum or zoo | 29 | −5 | 82 | −2 |
| Make up models from a kit (eg Airfix) | 26 | +37 | 50 | +46 |
| Watch a teacher or scientist do an experiment | 25 | −2 | 70 | −7 |
| Go fishing or pond dipping | 23 | +17 | 53 | +20 |
| Read a science fiction book | 23 | +12 | 48 | +14 |
| Collect/look at wild flowers | 20 | −18 | 43 | −37 |
| Read an information book about science/scientists | 15 | +6 | 31 | +4 |
| Read news about science in a paper or magazine | 13 | +2 | 33 | −2 |

as they were in Table 3.3. Thus there are still more boys than girls wanting to participate in activities in which more boys already participate, and vice versa, but the proportional difference between the sexes is less.

Examination of the relationship between having already taken part in an activity and wanting to do more of it, shown in Table 3.6, produced results entirely different from those for the topics (page 15) where a desire for novelty appeared to be the rule. For the girls, for 21 of the 22 activities, over 70 per cent of those who had already done an activity wanted to do more of it. For the boys over 70 per cent were sure of this for all but four of the activities. Significantly, perhaps, these included two activities most popular among girls (*knitting or sewing* and *looking at wild flowers*) as well as two involving reading (*information books* and *news about science in a newspaper or magazine*). So it emerged that the children were, by and large, content with the way they spent their time in these self-selected activities, in contrast with their reaction to the topics they had worked on.

Looking at those who did not already take part in an activity, it appeared that there were generally more who wished to than wished not to try it. However there were considerable sex differences in the activities which children did not want to try. Girls who did not already do these things did not wish to *read science in books or magazines, make models* or *go fishing*. Boys who did not already *knit or sew* or *collect wild flowers* or *weigh out cooking ingredients* did not want to start. Thus the large sex differences in participation seemed to reflect preference (which may well result from inequality in earlier experience and social pressure) rather than opportunity. Where differences were less there was more willingness to try activities more commonly undertaken by the opposite sex.

## 3.5 Summary and implications

Some attempts have been made in four of the five surveys to gather information about pupils' experience of, and reaction to, various science-related activities. A questionnaire designed to elicit reactions to various types of activity, as distinct from the subject matter of the activity, produced results indicating a preference among both boys and girls for activities related to their own experimentation rather than non-experimental activities. These results were indicated by a pilot investigation in the 1982 survey and confirmed in the 1983 survey.

New results reported in this chapter derive from questions asked in the written packages in the 1984 survey. They concern the pupils' experience of various topics, items of equipment and activities both in school and out of school. In terms of activities encountered it was found that the most commonly experienced topics include ones from both biological and physical science: *floating and sinking, magnets, growing seeds and parts of plants.* Similarly the least frequently encountered topics included biological topics, such as about *how animals have young* and *how animals live together,* and physical science topics such as *forces* and *properties of materials.*

Asking children to say whether or not they wished to do work on a topic revealed a striking pattern which was almost the inverse of their experience of topics. Those which they had encountered they did not wish to study further, whilst those which they had not studied were the ones they wanted to work on. There were no findings supporting the conventional expectation that girls mainly wanted to know about living things and boys mainly about mechanical things.

Questions asking about children's experience of using various items of equipment showed that at least two-thirds of 11 year olds had, *at school,* used a hand lens, a stop-clock or watch, a computer, a metre stick and measuring cylinder or jug and weighing scales. Items not used frequently at school tended to have been used at home, so that all items included in the inquiry had been used at some point by at least two-thirds of pupils and over 90 per cent had used all the items just listed plus a screwdriver and a compass. There were few large differences between the sexes in relation to using the items in school, but out of school girls made less use than boys of every item except for weighing scales.

Children were asked to say how often they had taken part in various informal activities or hobbies, mostly relating to science. These were mostly activities in which children chose to take part and much greater sex differences were found. For example, less than 25 per cent of girls had, either at school or at home, *read an information book about science, read science fiction, read news about science in a paper or magazine, taken things apart to see inside, made a model from a kit, played with an electric toy set* or *been fishing or pond dipping.* Less than 25 per cent of boys had *read an information book about science, read news about science in a paper or magazine, watched a teacher or scientist do an experiment, done knitting or sewing,* or *collected or looked at wild flowers.*

The most popular activities for girls were *looking after pets, weighing out ingredients for cooking* and *knitting or sewing;* for boys they were *looking after pets, making models* and *playing pool or snooker.* When asked whether they wanted to do more of an activity there was an overwhelming preference to do more of the things they already did. This contrasts strikingly with the preference for not doing more on the topics they had studied in school.

The extent to which there is any relationship between pupils' performance in science and their experience of topics at school or activities in or out of school, or their preferences with regard to these items, remains to be explored. Some contribution of this experience to performance seems probable, but as it is only one of several factors affecting performance the significance of the contribution cannot be estimated until further analyses of the data have been undertaken.

# 4

# Pupils' science performances

## 4.1 Introduction

As indicated in Chapter 1, the science surveys have been designed to monitor pupils' levels of performance in each of a number of different aspects of science activity. These aspects are articulated as the categories and subcategories of the assessment framework (listed in the introductory chapter and discussed fully with respect to the monitoring exercise at age 11 in DES, 1984a). Their assessment over the initial five-year period of the monitoring programme has involved more than 50,000 11 year olds in written and in practical work.

Early in the life of the assessment programme – before the first survey was undertaken – a number of important decisions had to be taken which would have far-reaching consequences for the shape of the future monitoring exercise. These included decisions about the kinds of questions which would be created, and about the ways in which these would be selected for survey use and, indeed, administered in surveys so that there might be some possibility of monitoring performance levels over time in a meaningful way.

One particularly important decision was to adopt a 'domain-sampling' approach to test construction wherever possible, rather than to proceed with the well-tried but often-criticised method of administering the same 'fixed' or 'standardised' test whenever a survey was conducted. The essence of the domain-sampling approach is that a large pool of questions is created to represent a particular subcategory, and questions are selected at random from this pool to be administered to pupils in a survey, in the same way that pupils are selected at random to be tested. The pupil sample which is administered test questions is assumed to be representative of all pupils of this age (the 'population' of such pupils). In a similar way, the set of questions selected to represent a particular subcategory in a survey (the 'test') is assumed to represent the totality of appropriate subcategory questions which do or which could exist. Full details of the technical approach underlying the assessment programme are given in the companion technical report (DES, 1988c).

Of course, the ideal in theory is not always possible – or perhaps even necessary – in practice, and there are instances where the kinds of questions produced and/or the administration method adopted have dictated a different monitoring strategy. In particular, for a few subcategories the questions which have been developed are either

necessarily expensive in terms of testing time (eg **Planning entire investigations**) or in terms of apparatus supply and tester travel (the practical **Use of apparatus and measuring instruments**) or both (**Performance of investigations**). Only a handful of questions have therefore typically been included in any one survey to represent these subcategories. Test scores, therefore, are not normally produced in these cases. Pupils' abilities are here discussed with reference to their performances on individual written questions and practical tasks. The loss of generalised test information is compensated by the gain of detailed information of a different kind.

For most subcategories it has been found possible to create fairly short (in terms of testing time) questions in sufficient numbers of the kind which could be administered at relatively low cost to large samples of pupils for domain-sampling to be a possibility. However, in every case it has taken some time to reach the criterion-pool size (150+ questions): up to five years for some domains. Indeed, in 1980 it was not possible to 'domain-sample' questions for survey use, and in recognition of this it was formally agreed that the 1980 survey be considered a pilot exercise. This should be borne in mind when performance scores over the five-year period are reviewed.

In this particular chapter we consider overall 'test' performances for those subcategories which are currently domain-sampled, beginning with the picture which has emerged in the 1984 survey and moving on to consider the stability or otherwise of these performances over the five-year period. It should be noted that whenever reference is made to statistical significance this will be at the 5 per cent level.

## 4.2 Pupils' subcategory performance levels in 1984

Six subcategories at age 11 were represented in the 1984 survey by collections of questions randomly selected from relevant question pools. These are (with the numbers of questions selected and the ways in which they were packaged shown in brackets):

| | |
|---|---|
| **Reading information from graphs, tables and charts** | $(42-6 \times 7)$ |
| **Representing information in graphs, tables and charts** | $(42-6 \times 7)$ |

**Making and interpreting observations** (36–2 × 18)
**Interpreting presented information** (70–5 × 14)
**Applying science concepts** (70–5 × 14)
**Planning parts of investigations** (70–5 × 14)

The testing time demanded of any individual pupil at this age in a single test session is usually restricted to about 45 minutes, in which time it has been established that around 14 or 15 questions can comfortably be attempted by most pupils. The 294 pencil and paper questions selected to represent the five subcategories in the list which are non-practical were sub-divided into 21 test packages containing 14 questions each (six test packages contained an even mixture of the two subcategories concerned with reading/constructing graphs, tables and charts; the other test packages contained 14 questions from a single subcategory).

The questions representing the practical subcategory **Making and interpreting observations** were divided between two practical 'circuses' (circuses are test sessions in which a number of pupils take part at one time working independently on individual questions; pupils circulate around a series of tables on which the practical tasks are set out).

Each of the 21 'written test' packages was administered to a different random sub-sample of roughly 500 pupils drawn from almost as many different schools. The practical circuses were each attempted by different sub-samples of more than 650 pupils from about 90 schools – 8 pupils involved in each circus, both circuses administered in most schools. *In total* around 1,200 pupils were involved in the practical testing, and between 2,500 and 3,000 were involved in the assessment of each of the other subcategories. (See Appendix 7 for further details of sample selection and test administration.)

During processing of the pupils' responses, each pupil is awarded a percentage score for each subcategory included in that pupil's test package (most packages contained questions from just one subcategory). Individual pupil responses to individual questions are usually marked on a 0–3 scale, except for multiple-choice questions on which pupils can gain a single mark for a correct response. Mean percentage subcategory scores for individual pupils are computed simply by averaging the pupil's series of question scores and expressing the result as a percentage of the maximum possible 'test score'.

Estimated group performance levels are produced by a procedure which weights these pupil percentage scores appropriately to compensate for imbalance in pupil sample representation (for details of the estimation procedure see Appendix 7 and the associated technical report – DES, 1988c). The performance level estimates produced for the 1984 survey are shown in Table 4.1.

As in previous surveys at this and the other ages we see immediately from Table 4.1 the generally higher performance levels for the two subcategories concerned with

**Table 4.1** *Pupils' subcategory performance levels in 1984\**

(Mean per cent scores – weighted population estimates)

| Subcategory | | All | Boys | Girls | Eng | Wales | NI |
|---|---|---|---|---|---|---|---|
| Reading information from graphs, tables and charts | mean | 62.2 | 62.5 | 61.8 | 62.0 | 63.1 | 65.4 |
| | se | 0.6 | 0.7 | 0.7 | 0.7 | 1.3 | 1.3 |
| Representing information as graphs, tables, charts | mean | 57.4 | 57.1 | 57.6 | 57.4 | 57.6 | 58.3 |
| | se | 0.7 | 0.8 | 0.8 | 0.8 | 1.5 | 1.5 |
| Making and interpreting observations | mean | 44.3 | 44.1 | 44.5 | 44.7 | 39.2 | 42.6 |
| | se | 1.1 | 1.0 | 1.2 | 1.2 | 1.7 | 2.3 |
| Interpreting presented information | mean | 34.0 | 34.9 | 33.2 | 34.0 | 32.9 | 34.1 |
| | se | 0.5 | 0.6 | 0.5 | 0.5 | 1.1 | 1.3 |
| Applying science concepts | mean | 30.4 | 31.5 | 29.3 | 30.6 | 28.9 | 28.1 |
| | se | 0.5 | 0.6 | 0.5 | 0.4 | 1.0 | 1.0 |
| Planning parts of investigations | mean | 32.4 | 31.6 | 33.3 | 32.3 | 31.8 | 31.9 |
| | se | 0.5 | 0.6 | 0.6 | 0.4 | 1.1 | 1.0 |

\*Sample size details given earlier.

communicating information through symbolic forms when compared with the other four. Also as in previous surveys at *this* age we see no evidence of any significant differences in the performances of boys and girls in these same two subcategories nor in the practical **Observation** category. As before we *do* find the girls' average performance level to be slightly higher than that of the boys' for **Planning**, with this picture reversed for **Interpreting** and for **Applying concepts** (in all three cases the differences reach statistical significance).

As far as national performances are concerned we see from Table 4.1 rather similar levels of performance shown by the pupils in each country. There are three instances where differences in national mean scores reach statistical significance – between England and Northern Ireland for **Reading information from graphs, tables and charts** and for **Applying science concepts**, and between England and Wales for **Making and interpreting observations**. As we see later in the chapter, none of these significant differences has emerged consistently in past surveys at this age; indeed they all reverse previous patterns.

As has consistently been the case within England, the mean scores of pupils in the South of the country were generally about two percentage points higher than were those of their peers in the North (the differences almost always reach statistical significance). Midlands' pupils either produced mean scores equal to those of pupils in the South or in-between the other two groups.

The greatest mean score differences have always emerged between those groups of pupils in schools drawing from distinctly different types of catchment area. Headteachers were, as usual, asked in the school questionnaire to indicate whether their schools drew predominantly from rural, inner city or other urban areas. The results of performance comparisons for these school groupings – shown in Table 4.2 (p. 24) – confirm previous survey findings at this and the other ages.

23

**Table 4.2** *Performance levels broken down by catchment area*
(Unweighted per cent mean scores for pupils in English primary schools)

| Subcategory | Inner city | Other urban | Rural |
|---|---|---|---|
| Reading information from graphs, tables and charts | 52 | 62 | 65 |
| Representing information as graphs, tables and charts | 49 | 57 | 61 |
| Making and interpreting observations | 36 | 43 | 47 |
| Interpreting presented information | 26 | 34 | 38 |
| Applying science concepts | 26 | 31 | 33 |
| Planning parts of investigations | 26 | 33 | 35 |

Pupils in primary schools in rural areas performed at consistently higher levels than those in primary schools in urban areas – within urban areas the lowest performance levels were consistently those of pupils in inner city primary schools (differences in mean scores reach statistical significance in every case). This catchment area performance pattern is a familiar one, and is probably attributable for the most part to socio-economic factors (see previous reports for fuller discussion).

Repeating practice in previous years, the possibility of connections between pupil performance and various school characteristics was again investigated, with similar results as remarked below. The variables investigated included many of those about which information was gathered in the school questionnaire (see Chapter 2).

In particular, it was of interest to know whether there might be a connection between pupil performance and school policy for science ('specified part of the curriculum', 'planned part of broader topics' or 'as it arises'), time spent on science ('less than 5 per cent', 'about 5 per cent', 'about 10 per cent', 'about 20 per cent') or class size for science work ('over 30', '25–30', '22–25', '12–21', 'under 12'). It was also considered of interest to investigate links with the goals held for science by the schools and with the specific kinds of emphases within their pupils' science activity. Since there are differences between the schools in England, Wales and Northern Ireland, and between those in the independent as opposed to the maintained sector, for all these features the investigatory analyses were restricted to primary schools in England.

As reported for previous surveys, there is no evidence in the survey data of any links between pupil performance and any of these science-specific school characteristics.

Of course, as Chapter 2 reiterates, primary schools actually vary little in terms of their general levels of resource for science or in terms of the kinds of science activity they provide for their pupils (at least as far as this can be ascertained from postal questionnaire enquiries). For example, the majority of schools devote about 5 per cent of the learning time of 11 year olds to science activity, there is little difference in the relative importance given to various goals for science activity by different primary schools, and so on. This general similarity between schools

might explain the lack of association with pupil performance levels.

In other words, the lack of evidence in this survey data of a connection between pupil performance and particular school features does not mean that no relationship in fact exists. It might reasonably have been anticipated, for instance, that pupils spending 20 per cent or more of their lesson time on science, equivalent to two afternoons a week, would produce higher performance levels in science tests than pupils spending 5 per cent or so of their lesson time (about an hour a week) in this area. Unfortunately, there are too few primary schools in the former group to allow sensible investigation of this matter.

Another relevant point to note is the general complexity in the school system, with the result that it is difficult, even impossible in some cases, to isolate one variable for investigation without the confounding influence of others. For example, a high level of resource of one kind is often offset by a low level of resource of another kind, and the picture is further confused by overlap with the socio-economic background of the pupil intake (see DES, 1983a, for a full discussion).

## 4.3 Reviewing performance patterns over time

The 1984 survey was the last in the initial series of five surveys, and it is therefore appropriate to review the cumulated test data for evidence of consistent performance patterns, and also for indications of trends or stability in pupils' general levels of performance over this period. There are two main kinds of trend that we might investigate: systematic movements in 'absolute' levels of performnce; and systematic changes in the size of performance level differences between pupil sub-groups, ie changes in 'relative' levels of performance.

By how much would the absolute values of mean score estimates from one year to another need to differ before we can infer a real change in the performance level of the pupil population over that period of time? Recent research has suggested that for an established domain-sampling programme of this kind, with about 60 or so questions selected to represent any particular subcategory in a survey and with 200 or more pupils attempting any particular question, a difference in performance estimates of about twelve percentage points or more would be needed (Johnson and Bell, 1985).

However, the crucial phrase here is 'established' domain-sampling programme with its implication that a large and relatively unchanging question pool had been available from the start of the monitoring programme. In practice, as mentioned earlier, the question pools in this survey programme have been in the process of creation throughout the initial survey period. The process-oriented assessment framework is still a relatively novel one, particularly in the context of national monitoring, and few suitable questions were available for adoption by the Science Team in the early years. Virtually all questions now available were specially created for this monitoring purpose. The constant growth was inevitably accompanied by a certain instability in the composition of each pool, and both factors will have given rise to test score fluctuations in the period. Comment will be made as appropriate when test data are presented later.

Another factor which is most important to bear in mind when reviewing the test data is the voluntary nature of school (and indeed LEA) participation in the survey programme, which gives rise to the problem of non-response. Theoretical ideas about significance levels are based on the assumption that all samples are selected by some formal randomised sampling procedure so that they either directly represent their populations or the detail of their non-representativeness is known and can be allowed for in estimation.

In this particular programme a formal sampling scheme is implemented to select the survey schools, and later the pupils. Unfortunately, not all invited schools have felt able to be involved. Table 4.3 provides details of the numbers of schools which actually took part in each of the surveys in England, Wales and Northern Ireland, and also shows these as percentages of the number originally invited to collaborate.

As Table 4.3 shows, the participation rates have fluctuated from survey to survey in all three countries, those for the first two surveys in the series being lower than in later years. For England and Wales the rates of participation have been reasonably high at between 80 per cent and 90 per cent. In Northern Ireland, however, the participation rates have always been much lower, with initially two-thirds and in later years three-quarters of invited schools finally taking part.

**Table 4.3** *Numbers of schools which participated in the surveys*
(Bracketed figures indicate percentage rates of participation)

| Year | England | Wales | Northern Ireland |
|------|---------|-------|------------------|
| 1980 | 596 (80) | 278 (84) | 223 (65) |
| 1981 | 552 (85) | 159 (83) | 123 (64) |
| 1982 | 567 (90) | 166 (91) | 137 (75) |
| 1983 | 439 (91) | 168 (90) | 152 (78) |
| 1984 | 460 (90) | 147 (85) | 128 (74) |

Schools which have declined to take part in particular surveys have sometimes done so because they had already been involved very recently in one or more previous ones (in Mathematics, Language or Science). However, the relatively small numbers of schools involved in any one survey in Wales and, most particularly, Northern Ireland in combination with these fluctuating participation rates might well be another factor contributing to test score variation over the period. This is not a factor peculiar to the science monitoring programme, but affects equally the

corresponding programmes in mathematics, language and modern languages.

In addition to pool growth/instability and school non-participation, script markers will be another contributing source of test score variation. Any one written test package is shared between at most two markers, each marker being responsible for marking around 300 scripts. Marker reliability studies carried out during the 1980 survey indicated that there was high agreement between the rank orders of pupils on the basis of the marks independently awarded to them by any two of three markers (a traditional measure indicating 'high' reliability). However, when the pupils' scores were averaged there was in some cases a difference of up to 6 percentage points in the three figures produced. In other words, if the same 'test' were marked independently by two or more different markers and population estimates were produced on the basis of the results, these performance estimates could differ by up to 6 percentage points. This has clear implications for a test score review over the five-year period.

All three of the factors discussed above will undoubtedly have contributed to fluctuations in the performance level estimates over the five years, creating variation over and above that attributable to pupil, school and question sampling effects and to 'real' changes in the performance levels of the pupil population. It will also mean that differences will need to be rather substantial before they can be adjudged to be statistically meaningful.

Bearing this in mind we move on to review the cumulated test data, considering each subcategory in turn and drawing together general points later. For ease of communication the mean percentage score estimates are rounded to the nearest percentage point. The random sampling of questions has ensured that the overall standard deviations of pupils' raw test scores have remained roughly similar from year to year for any particular subcategory, so that it has not been necessary to resort to any form of standardisation of scores when reviewing differences in the levels of performance of pupil groups; for instance, boys and girls.

## 4.4 Using graphs, tables and charts

The two subcategories **Reading information from graphs, tables and charts** and **Representing information as graphs, tables and charts** typically show highly correlated pupil performance levels (intercorrelations of 0.8 + based on individual pupil scores). This is perhaps to be expected given that any work with these kinds of symbolic representations will provide practice in and reinforcement of both skills, and much work across the curriculum in the primary school involves this kind of activity. It makes much sense, therefore, to consider for some purposes the combined subcategory **Using graphs, tables and charts**, as is reported at ages 13 and 15. Another reason for combining the two subcategories is to increase the reliability of the

**Table 4.4** *'Using graphs, tables and charts' – developmental history, 1980–84*

| Survey year | No. of questions in pool/selected | Packaging strategy | Pupils/schools per package | mean % scores England | Wales | Northern Ireland |
|---|---|---|---|---|---|---|
| 1980 | 48/36 | 2 × 18 | 800/110 | 56 | 57 | 58 |
| 1981 | 89/36 | 4 × 9 (m18)* | 800/350 | 57 | 58 | 59 |
| 1982 | 119/84 | 12 × 7 (m14) | 900/700 | 59 | 60 | 60 |
| 1983 | 214/40 | 4 × 10 | 700/600 | 63 | 58 | 63 |
| 1984 | 254/84 | 6 × 14 | 510/480 | 60 | 61 | 62 |

\* m18 indicates that these sets of 9 questions were each contained in mixed-category test packages of overall size 18 questions. A corresponding interpretation attaches to the indicator m14.

performance estimates. This is an important advantage in this particular case for a temporal review, since rather few questions have sometimes been administered in individual surveys; 1980, 1981 and 1983, for instance, when just 18 to 20 questions represented each of these two subcategories.

Table 4.4 presents in summary form the statistical history of this combined subcategory as it has developed since the start of the survey programme. As the table reveals, the number of questions available for survey use over the period has grown consistently, starting with just 48 in 1980 and finally reaching 254 by 1984. 'Test' size has varied rather less systematically from survey to survey, with 36 questions selected for use in each of the 1980 and 1981 surveys, and a more adequate 84 questions selected in 1982 (prompted by the evidence of associated research which suggested the need for an increase) and in 1984. The decision to select 40 only in 1983 was taken deliberately to save costs and to release team time for other development work.

There have also been differences in the ways the selected questions have been packaged together: in 1980 and in 1984 the questions representing this combined subcategory were mixed together in packages of 18 and 14 questions in length, respectively. In 1983 they were allocated to four packages of ten questions each, with **Reading** questions in two of these and **Representing** questions in the other. In 1981 and 1982 questions from this combined subcategory were distributed among a number of different packages containing similar numbers of questions from other subcategories. In the table under '1982', for instance, we see that the 84 questions representing the combined subcategory were distributed among 12 different test packages containing a total of 14 questions each, 7 of these questions being drawn from other question pools.

The number of pupils who attempted each test package has changed over the survey period, as also has the number of schools in which each package was administered. These changes will have contributed rather little to test score fluctuations in comparison with the influence of question sampling (see DES, 1988c), but approximate figures are shown for the record in Table 4.4 and corresponding tables later in this chapter.

Despite the degree of pool growth, and despite the large variations in the numbers of questions selected each time and differences in the ways these have been packaged,

Table 4.4 shows relatively little change in the performance level estimates over the period in any of the three countries. Neither is there in the table any evidence of national performance differences; none of the small numerical differences reaches statistical significance. The very slight overall increase in performance scores through the earlier years is likely to be merely an artefact of the very small size of the question pool along with the relatively small numbers of questions selected for administration in 1980 and 1981. It is unlikely to be a reflection of any real trend in the performance levels of pupils in the population over the period.

Overall performance score estimates for boys and girls (England, Wales and Northern Ireland combined) are in many ways less informative than they might be. It would be more useful to look instead at the performance figures within each country separately, since in some cases an overall difference might be traced to a difference in one country only. This information is given in Table 4.5.

As Table 4.5 shows, there is no evidence of any difference in the performance levels of eleven-year-old boys and girls in England or Wales when **Using graphs, tables and charts** (the difference in the 1980 estimates for Wales does not reach statistical significance). In Northern Ireland the consistency of the pattern of discrepancy favouring girls is of note. However, the 1984 difference is the only statistically significant one, and the low participation rates of Northern Ireland schools should not be ignored.

**Table 4.5** *'Using graphs, tables and charts' – the performances of boys and girls*
(Mean per cent scores – population performance estimates)

| | England | | | Wales | | | Northern Ireland | | |
|---|---|---|---|---|---|---|---|---|---|
| | Boys | Girls | Diff. | Boys | Girls | Diff. | Boys | Girls | Diff. |
| 1980 | 55 | 57 | -2 | 61 | 53 | 8 | 54 | 62 | -8 |
| 1981 | 55 | 56 | -1 | 59 | 57 | 2 | 57 | 62 | -5 |
| 1982 | 58 | 59 | -1 | 60 | 60 | 0 | 60 | 61 | -1 |
| 1983 | 63 | 64 | -1 | 58 | 59 | -1 | 62 | 64 | -2 |
| 1984 | 60 | 59 | 1 | 60 | 61 | -1 | 58 | 67 | -9 |

These general 'test' results actually mask performance differences between boys and girls when handling specific kinds of symbolic representation. In particular, as noted in Chapter 5, there is evidence that boys produce higher average scores than girls on questions involving coordinate graphs. On the other hand, where girls have achieved higher average scores than boys on individual questions

**Table 4.6** *'Making and interpreting observations' – developmental history, 1980–84*

| Survey year | No. of questions in pool/selected | Packaging strategy | Pupils/schools per package | mean % scores England | Wales | Northern Ireland |
|---|---|---|---|---|---|---|
| 1980 | 49/40 | 2×13,1×14 | 800/100 | 50 | 53 | 52 |
| 1981 | 49/26 | 2×13 | 800/100 | 51 | 57 | 51 |
| 1983 | 128/36 | 2×18 | 750/130 | 45 | 43 | 40 |
| 1984 | 116/36 | 2×18 | 650/85 | 45 | 39 | 43 |

these have featured tables, bar charts, pie charts or Venn diagrams (for the majority of such questions boys and girls perform similarly). These findings have emerged also in the performance data of 13 and of 15 year olds (see the two review reports for these ages, DES, 1988a, b; and also DES, 1986).

## 4.5 Making and interpreting observations

This is a subcategory which has undergone a number of changes over the years, some minor and others more substantial. The subcategory has been difficult to define, and modifications to the pool structure have taken place as test experience has been gained. Such modifications have affected the question pools at all three ages. In addition there have been changes in the format of question administration at this age during the initial survey series. Full details are given in Chapter 7, but a general outline is included below of those changes which have clearly produced discontinuities in test scores over the period.

In all surveys in which this subcategory has been assessed the selected questions have been administered to small groups of pupils at any one session, the pupils working independently on the individual questions. However, in the first two surveys (1980 and 1981) some questions were presented on film, with the children providing written responses in answer booklets, while in the last two surveys (1983 and 1984) the questions were administered in practical circuses, ie the various question resources are set up on tables. Pupils circulate around the tables working independently and for set times on the individual tasks.

There were a number of reasons for this change in administration format, including cost and logistic considerations (see Chapter 7 for details). Following the decision to change it was necessary to organise the provision of suitable resources for all questions previously illustrated on film. To allow time for this the subcategory was not included in the 1982 survey. The move to circus administration in 1983 was accompanied by an increase of 5 in the number of questions administered in a single test session. This reduced costs by enabling similar overall numbers of questions to be administered in the surveys with fewer school visits.

The combined effect of the change in question administration method with the accompanying modifications to individual questions, and of the increase in the length of

each test session, is clearly seen in Table 4.6. The result has been a drop in mean scores of 5 percentage points in England, and of up to 15 percentage points in Wales and Northern Ireland. The stability in the mean scores for the first two years and for the final two years, however, is remarkable given the relatively small numbers of questions used and the relatively small number of schools visited.

The picture of national performance differences given in Table 4.6 is a confusing one. Wales produced significantly *higher* mean scores than England and Northern Ireland in 1981, but a significantly *lower* score in 1984. Northern Ireland produced mean scores *similar* to those for England in most surveys, but a significantly *lower* score in 1983. The different school participation rates in the three countries must be relevant in explaining this lack of consistency, particularly given the very small numbers of schools involved in this practical testing, perhaps combined with the change in pool content and method of test administration.

**Table 4.7** *'Making and interpreting observations' – the performances of boys and girls*
(Mean per cent scores – population performance estimates)

| | England Boys | Girls | Diff. | Wales Boys | Girls | Diff. | Northern Ireland Boys | Girls | Diff. |
|---|---|---|---|---|---|---|---|---|---|
| 1980 | 50 | 50 | 0 | 52 | 54 | -2 | 51 | 52 | -1 |
| 1981 | 51 | 52 | -1 | 56 | 57 | -1 | 51 | 51 | 0 |
| 1983 | 45 | 46 | -1 | 41 | 46 | -5 | 40 | 40 | 0 |
| 1984 | 45 | 45 | 0 | 38 | 40 | -2 | 38 | 47 | -9 |

No statistically significant differences have been recorded between the overall test performances of boys and girls for this subcategory. Indeed, Table 4.7 indicates clearly the similarity in the performance profiles of boys and girls; the only statistically significant difference in their performances is that in favour of the girls in Northern Ireland in the latest survey.

Where statistically significant differences have emerged for individual questions these have usually been in favour of girls where the requirement has been to note similarities and differences between objects (most often biological specimens) and in favour of boys where explanations of observations have been demanded (predominantly physical science events). Again these tendencies appear also in the data for 13 and 15 year olds.

**Table 4.8** *'Interpreting presented information' – developmental history, 1980–84*

| Survey year | No. of questions in pool/selected | Packaging strategy | Pupils/schools per package | mean % scores England | Wales | Northern Ireland |
|---|---|---|---|---|---|---|
| 1980 | 55/42 | 3 × 14 | 1000/150 | 40 | 41 | 47 |
| 1981 | 90/42 | 3 × 14 | 800/350 | 35 | 35 | 37 |
| 1982 | 110/42 | 6 × 7 (m14)* | 900/700 | 32 | 32 | 33 |
| 1983 | 159/56 | 4 × 14 | 700/600 | 33 | 35 | 35 |
| 1984 | 196/70 | 5 × 14 | 510/480 | 34 | 33 | 34 |

\* Mixed-category test packages each containing 14 questions in total.

## 4.6 Interpreting presented information

This subcategory has something in common with both those previously described. For example, there is a dependence in many questions on an ability to use graphs, tables and charts, since the information to be interpreted is often displayed in one or other of these forms if not in prose. Often the 'interpretation' requires the child to perceive a systematic connection between two variables, demonstrating this perception by describing the relationship or by interpolating or extrapolating it. Such questions parallel many in the practical **Observation** category, the essential difference being that in the one case the observations are made at first hand while in the other they are provided. Descriptions of the structure of this subcategory and of the kinds of individual questions representing it are given in Chapter 8.

As Table 4.8 illustrates, there has been the usual expansion over the period in the numbers of questions available for survey use, the current pool size of 196 questions having grown from an initial 55 in 1980.

As a result of a recent rationalisation exercise (see Chapter 8) there have been some minor modifications to the structure of this subcategory, and also a degree of question exchange between the three age-pools. The effect of these changes was not expected to be noticeable at age 11 (as indeed it is not), since the numbers of questions absorbed into or rejected from this pool have been relatively small.

Indeed, Table 4.8 reveals a rather stable picture of performance, both over time and between countries; only the performance difference between England and Northern Ireland in 1980 reaches statistical significance. The scores vary little over the period 1981 to 1984 when at least twice the number of questions used in each survey were available for random selection.

There is evidence in Table 4.9 of an almost consistent tendency for boys to produce marginally higher performance levels than girls on this subcategory in Wales and Northern Ireland. However, the only performance difference which reaches statistical significance is that for England in 1984. Many fewer pupils are involved in testing in Wales and Northern Ireland compared with England, and this will account for the lack of statistical significance for the same size discrepancies in these countries. Statistically significant differences in favour of

**Table 4.9** *'Interpreting presented information' – the performances of boys and girls*
(Mean per cent scores – population performance estimates)

| | England | | | Wales | | | Northern Ireland | | |
|---|---|---|---|---|---|---|---|---|---|
| | Boys | Girls | Diff. | Boys | Girls | Diff. | Boys | Girls | Diff. |
| 1980 | 40 | 40 | 0 | 43 | 39 | 4 | 49 | 45 | 4 |
| 1981 | 35 | 35 | 0 | 35 | 35 | 0 | 37 | 38 | -1 |
| 1982 | 32 | 32 | 0 | 33 | 31 | 2 | 34 | 31 | 3 |
| 1983 | 34 | 33 | 1 | 35 | 34 | 1 | 35 | 34 | 1 |
| 1984 | 35 | 33 | 2 | 34 | 33 | 1 | 35 | 33 | 2 |

boys have emerged occasionally at age 13, and have appeared *persistently* at age 15 (see DES, 1986c).

There are differences from one age-pool to another in the proportion of questions featuring coordinate graphs, the proportion increasing with age. At age 11 there are just a handful of such questions, while at age 15 about a third of those in the pool are of this kind. As mentioned earlier the performance data indicate that boys generally produce better performances than girls at all ages when handling coordinate graphs. This is clearly relevant in explaining the emergence at the later ages of a sex-related performance difference for this subcategory when none has appeared at age 11. There are other differences between the performances of boys and girls *within* this subcategory which are also in evidence at the younger age – for details see Chapter 8.

## 4.7 Applying science concepts

At ages 13 and 15 there are three subcategories concerned with the application of science concepts, distinguished by the science subject area. Thus, pupils are assessed separately for their abilities to apply biology concepts, chemistry concepts and physics concepts.

At age 11, on the other hand, no distinction has previously been made at the test level in these terms. Any set of questions selected to represent the subcategory **Applying science concepts** at this age will therefore include those requiring some knowledge and understanding of biological concepts and facts along with others demanding knowledge and understanding of physical science concepts and facts (there are few 'chemistry' questions in the age 11 pool, and those which do exist are almost all concerned with 'change of state'). This should be borne in mind when the data in Table 4.10 (p. 29) are reviewed.

**Table 4.10** *'Applying science concepts' – developmental history, 1980–84*

| Survey year | No. of questions in pool/selected | Packaging strategy | Pupils/schools per package | mean % scores England | Wales | Northern Ireland |
|---|---|---|---|---|---|---|
| 1980 | 63/42 | 3 × 14 | 1000/150 | 40 | 42 | 44 |
| 1981 | 114/42 | 3 × 14 | 800/350 | 36 | 37 | 35 |
| 1982 | 162/42 | 6 × 7 (m14)* | 900/700 | 31 | 32 | 31 |
| 1983 | 211/64 | 4 × 16 | 700/600 | 32 | 33 | 29 |
| 1984 | 196/70 | 5 × 14 | 510/480 | 31 | 29 | 28 |

* Mixed-category test packages each containing 14 questions in total.

There have been about twice as many physical science as biological science questions in the surveys, reflecting the composition of the question pool. The actual ratio has varied slightly over the years, but the variation is not sufficiently great to account for the general decrease in absolute mean scores over the period 1980 to 1982, after which time the picture is rather stable. The growth in the size of the question pool is the most relevant factor here.

**Table 4.11** *'Applying science concepts' – the performances of boys and girls*

(Mean per cent scores – population performance estimates)

| | England | | | Wales | | | Northern Ireland | | |
|---|---|---|---|---|---|---|---|---|---|
| | Boys | Girls | Diff. | Boys | Girls | Diff. | Boys | Girls | Diff. |
| 1980 | 41 | 38 | 3 | 43 | 40 | 3 | 47 | 41 | 6 |
| 1981 | 37 | 34 | 3 | 37 | 37 | 0 | 36 | 35 | 1 |
| 1982 | 33 | 29 | 4 | 35 | 29 | 6 | 32 | 29 | 3 |
| 1983 | 34 | 30 | 4 | 32 | 33 | -1 | 31 | 28 | 3 |
| 1984 | 32 | 30 | 2 | 30 | 28 | 2 | 29 | 26 | 3 |

Differences between the performance scores of pupils in the three countries are generally small and not particularly consistent in direction. The only statistically significant differences are those between England and Northern Ireland in 1980 and between Northern Ireland on the one hand and England and Wales on the other in 1983. These are likely to be of little pedagogic significance.

The performance scores for boys and girls separately are given in Table 4.11. The main feature in this table is the preponderance of performance discrepancies in favour of the boys in every country.

It is worth noting that much of the overall difference in performance scores is attributable to performance differences in the physical science area. Scores separately produced for **Applying biology concepts** and for **Applying physics concepts** reveal a variable picture for the former, with small differences in either direction, but a very stable picture for the latter with statistically significant differences in favour of the boys appearing in every case and varying only in their size (see Table 4.12). On average the physical science score difference between boys and girls at this age amounts to about a third of the common standard deviation of raw scores. The 'physics' questions at this age are mostly concerned with concepts of force and energy.

Girls' lower level of achievement relative to boys' in physical science persists at the higher ages. Indeed, the

**Table 4.12** *'Applying physics concepts' – the performance of boys and girls*

(Mean per cent scores – population performance estimates)

| | England | | | Wales | | | Northern Ireland | | |
|---|---|---|---|---|---|---|---|---|---|
| | Boys | Girls | Diff. | Boys | Girls | Diff. | Boys | Girls | Diff. |
| 1980 | 44 | 38 | 6 | 47 | 39 | 8 | 52 | 44 | 8 |
| 1981 | 36 | 29 | 7 | 34 | 33 | 1 | 36 | 27 | 9 |
| 1982 | 33 | 26 | 7 | 35 | 28 | 7 | 34 | 29 | 5 |
| 1983 | 39 | 34 | 5 | 38 | 35 | 3 | 37 | 30 | 7 |
| 1984 | 34 | 29 | 5 | 31 | 26 | 5 | 31 | 26 | 5 |

discrepancy between the performance levels of boys and girls increases by age 15–probably as a result of the large drop-out from physics of girls at 13 + (see Driver *et al.* 1984, and the Age 15 review report – DES, 1988b). It is, moreover, a feature of pupils' science performance which seems to be firmly established world-wide (see Comber and Keeves, 1973; Hueftle *et al*, 1983; Erickson and Erickson, 1984; DES, 1986). There is no evidence to suggest that the *size* of the performance gap among 11 year olds has changed over the period of these surveys.

The fact that this particular gap exists so strongly by this early age invites speculation as to its causes, particularly since the gap persists throughout the secondary school and presumably beyond. Searching for school-based causes is unlikely to prove a fruitful exercise. 11 year olds spend rather a small proportion of their in-school learning time on science (Chapter 2 showed that the majority of primary schools allocate around 5 per cent of lesson time to science activity – roughly an hour a week); and not all of this will be physical science. Moreover, the findings discussed in Chapter 3 on children's activities in and out of school do not suggest that boys and girls receive markedly different treatment in their science lessons: rather, these findings suggest that it is in children's *out-of-school* activities and interests that clues might be found.

For instance, it is reasonable to speculate that the particular strong difference in the performances of girls and boys in electricity and mechanics (see Chapter 9) is connected with the strong differences in their electrical and mechanical experience gained through their hobbies and play activities. Similarly, the differences in the average performances of boys and girls when handling different measuring instruments (see Chapter 6) can plausibly be linked to their differential measuring experience out of school. For fuller discussion of these likely connections see Erickson and Erickson, 1984; DES, 1986c.

## 4.8 Summary and discussion

As regards changes in pupils' *absolute* levels of performance over the period of this first series of surveys, it can be inferred with some confidence that there has been no change in the period 1982 to 1984, and it is likely that there was no change either between 1980 and 1982. Between 1981 and 1982 the level of voluntary participation of schools in the surveys increased by 10 percentage points and then remained stable (90 per cent of the invited schools in England agreed to take part in the surveys between 1982 and 1984, 85 per cent to 90 per cent of those in Wales, and around 75 per cent of those in Northern Ireland). In addition it was 1982 by the time the question pools reached an adequate size of 100+ questions each. The performance estimates for these later three years can therefore with greater confidence be assumed to reflect the actual performance levels of the pupil population at age 11 than can those estimates for the first two years. These later figures present a picture of stability.

It has consistently been the case, over all five years, that pupils' performance levels when **Using graphs, tables and charts** are markedly higher than when they are **Making and interpreting observations, Interpreting presented information, Applying science concepts** or **Planning parts of investigations**. While this pattern of performance has emerged at all three ages it is not straightforward to deduce from this that **Using graphs, tables and charts**, say, is an inherently easier skill than is, say, **Planning parts of investigations**; nor does it follow that the first activity is necessarily better taught or more extensively practised in schools (although the latter is likely). It can only be said that pupils are in general better able to tackle successfully the kinds of 'data representation' questions administered in the surveys than the kinds of 'planning' questions which have been used. Whether the difference in their performance levels on the various subcategories might in future be reduced with a shift in teaching emphasis and consequent increase in relevant practice in the process skills pupils find more difficult is open to debate.

There have been only rare instances of statistically significant differences between the subcategory performances of pupils in the three countries, suggesting that those which *have* occurred have been merely aberrations attributable to sampling problems. The performance levels of pupils in England, Wales and Northern Ireland are in general rather similar at this age in science.

Greater performance differences have emerged between pupils in schools with markedly different types of catchment area in every year in which the relevant information has been gathered (1982–84). Those pupils in inner city schools produce lower average test scores than do those in schools located in other urban areas, and these in turn perform less well than their peers in rural schools. All these features of the performance of 11 year olds in science are present also at ages 13 and 15, and are also present in the performance data which has resulted from the partner survey programmes in mathematics and language. It has been suggested in previous reports that socio-economic factors must be relevant in accounting for this phenomenon.

As regards the performances of boys and girls, there have been only rare instances of statistically significant differences at age 11 when **Using graphs, tables and charts, Making and interpreting observations, Interpreting presented information** or **Planning parts of investigations**. However, there *are* tendencies for boys to be consistently, though only marginally, ahead of girls when **Interpreting presented information** and for girls to be marginally ahead of boys when **Planning parts of investigations**.

A review of all the questions administered in one or more of the surveys in this initial period has also suggested differences *within* subcategories which are neutralised in the global analysis. In particular, there is definite evidence that boys are on the whole more competent than girls in handling coordinate graphs and explaining scientific observations (usually in physical science), with girls performing equally well or slightly better than boys on questions involving other forms of data representation (pie charts, tables, bar charts, etc) and on questions requiring similarities and differences between objects and specimens to be noted (these tend to be biological). Again these differences appear also at ages 13 and 15.

A statistically significant difference in the performances of boys and girls which has emerged consistently over the period in all three countries is that in favour of boys for **Applying science concepts**. On further analysis this overall difference can be traced for the most part to the pupils' performances on the physical science questions included in the tests, although where differences have occurred on biological questions these have often also been in favour of the boys. This relative weakness on the part of girls in physical science is marked and very general; it applies across the range of concepts included in the assessment framework, and persists in the data for 13 and 15 year olds. It has been suggested that differences in the out-of-school activities of boys and girls of the kind described in the previous chapter must be relevant in explaining this phenomenon.

Explorations for links between pupil performance and any of a number of different science-specific school characteristics have consistently failed to reveal any evidence of association. The characteristics investigated include time spent on science, presence of special posts, goals for science activity, availability of a scheme of work, and so on. The general similarity between primary schools in terms of each of these variables might explain this result. For instance the majority of primary schools spend around 5 per cent of lesson time on science. It does not necessarily follow that, say, time spent on science has no influence on pupils' science performance levels.

# 5

# Use of graphical and symbolic representation

## 5.1 Introduction

The various skills which are assessed under the title of **Graphical and symbolic representation** are represented by two main subcategories, one concerned with **Reading**, the other with **Representing information**. In terms of what questions require pupils to do there is a clear distinction between these two areas. This distinction, which has been used as the organising feature in previous reporting, does not emerge clearly in pupil performance levels. Performance on the **Reading** and **Representing** subcategories when set against a range of background variables also tends to be similar. While the results for **Reading** and **Representing** will be reported separately in this chapter, after the overall performance summary, information will be provided within each of five major representational forms. Within each of these five forms a number of Question types, each posing slightly different demands, will also be discussed. This organisation is possible because the seven Question types which comprise the **Reading** subcategory and the eight which together make up the **Representing** subcategory can be identified as relatively discrete groups of skills, with obvious similarities and differences. (A summary of the Question types which make up the two subcategories can be found in Appendix 8, page 139.) The five representational forms around which the major part of this chapter will be organised are:

Tables ⎤
Bar charts ⎬ Coordinate forms
Graphs and grids ⎦
Pie charts
Other representational forms (Flow charts, Food chains, Venn diagrams, etc)

## 5.2 Subcategory performance estimates

Each subcategory is represented by a domain of questions from which a random selection is made for survey purposes. The **Reading** subcategory contains 137 questions, 88 of which have been used in surveys, while **Representing** has 118 questions, 83 of which have been used. Some questions have been selected on more than one occasion; others have only been exposed through question trials and do not contribute to the scores reported here. Table 5.1 summarises subcategory scores over the five years of monitoring.

**Table 5.1** *Overall subcategory estimates: 'Reading' and 'Representing'*

|      | Reading | Representing |
| ---- | ------- | ------------ |
| 1980 | 53      | 59           |
| 1981 | 54      | 62           |
| 1982 | 57      | 63           |
| 1983 | 62      | 64           |
| 1984 | 62      | 57           |

There has been a fairly consistent effect of girls performing at a slightly higher level than boys in both subcategories, but more so in **Representing**. This difference in performance was statistically significant only in the 1981 **Representing** sample of questions. This and other aspects of performance at the subcategory level were discussed in detail in Chapter 4.

In comparison with the other skills within the assessment framework, the questions and scoring criteria used result in relatively high levels of performance in these two subcategories with pupils experiencing more success than failure. This is in contrast with all the other domain-referenced areas of the framework, where performance estimates are well below 50 per cent of maximum possible scores. Rates of non-response also tend to be low.

The following analysis will concentrate on the particular groups of skills demanded by each of the five representational forms defined above.

## 5.3 Overall performance by representational form

When the division between **Reading** and **Representing** is ignored and all questions used are allocated according to

**Table 5.2** *Performance by representational form (1980–84 data)*

|                               | Number of questions surveyed | Overall mean score % | Range of means % |
| ----------------------------- | ---------------------------- | -------------------- | ---------------- |
| Tables                        | 34                           | 68                   | 41–92            |
| Bar charts                    | 40                           | 61                   | 36–81            |
| Graphs and grids              | 53                           | 55                   | 21–81            |
| Pie charts                    | 25                           | 65                   | 33–93            |
| Other representational forms  | 19                           | 65                   | 36–81            |

the particular skill they demand to one of the five representational forms, the performance summary presented in Table 5.2 (p. 31) emerges.

It is noticeable that performance on the three coordinate forms declines from Tables, through Bar charts to Graphs/grids. The other two forms have similar middling overall levels.

The following sections will present and discuss each of these question forms in turn and attempt to identify the operations which make a question more or less difficult. Three important points should be borne in mind as the evidence which follows is examined.

Firstly, to some extent the skills which have been assessed overlap the representational forms, particularly those forms concerned with coordinates. Within each form, it is probably more helpful to think in terms of a composite group of skills, not all of which are called upon in every question example, and some of which may be critical attributes or defining features of all questions within a group.

The second point which needs to be considered when looking at the evidence presented is that there are undoubtedly variables operating in addition to the targetted science processes of the questions. The wide range of mean scores within each form is not explicable in terms of demands of science activities alone.

The third point is related to the two above, and offers some justification for the method in which evidence is presented and discussed in the following sections. It is simply that a systematic examination of variables of question demand is not possible because the pool of items deliberately set out to explore the effects of nuances of presentational differences. The evidence referred to is not defined by a statistical inference following from a research design, but from a careful clinical sifting of results. With the structure of the item banks designed to meet the requirements of random sampling, this kind of attempt to interpret performance differences is the only strategy presently available. However, the salient factors which are hypothesised as influencing performance on the target skills of data communication will be useful in re-labelling the composite demands of existing questions. In time it may also be possible not only to re-label questions, but also to test whether or not the features labelled do affect performance with new items composed for this purpose. What follows is the best picture that can be drawn together from available fragments.

## 5.4 Tables

Within this group are two Question types. From the **Reading** subcategory comes Type 1 which requires pupils to read information as directed from a table of figures, representational symbols or non-representational symbols.

**Table 5.3** *Summary of performance on Tables (1980–84 data)*

| | Number of questions surveyed | Overall mean score % | Range of means % |
|---|---|---|---|
| Reading from tables | 20 | 67 | 46–84 |
| Adding data to tables | 14 | 69 | 41–92 |
| All tabular questions | 34 | 68 | 41–92 |

From the **Representing** subcategory are questions which require pupils to add further data to tables which are partially complete. Table 5.3 summarises results on the two Question types, and overall.

Of the five representational forms defined in the introduction to this chapter, Tables has the highest overall performance estimate. There are no significant sex differences associated with this Question Group, and no significant differences between **Reading** and **Representing** tabular data.

Six of the nine questions with relatively low mean scores involved handling numerical data. The lowest overall score of all (41 per cent) occurred in a question which required pupils to enter data in a table summarising the distance a truck rolled from a ramp set at different heights. (The data are not only numerical, but also impersonal, having a 'physics' flavour.) Yet the activity of constructing such a table during an investigation would be a realistic one for this age group. The lowest score on a **Reading** question (46 per cent) also involved numerical data, this time a railway timetable. It is less likely that this type of data table would be generated by children themselves, but once again, the data in Table 5.3 are real and relevant. To redress the impression of these remarks concerning numerical data, it must be added that there is not invariably an association with poor performance (see Example 28, page 167, DES, 1984a), though there is a clear tendency for those items which result in the lowest mean scores to be concerned with the tabulation of numerical data.

There are five questions with particularly high mean scores. The three **Reading** questions all have mean scores of 84 per cent. These are 'Mammals', 'Birds' eggs' and 'Butterflies'. The last of these has previously been reported in detail (Example Question 9, pages 167–169, DES, 1984a). As the names suggest there is a common faunal connection in the content of these questions which probably has an influence on performance; 'Birds' eggs' contains some simple numerical data ($2 \times 5$ values, small whole numbers). The **Representing** questions are both concerned with tables of symbols; in one case, simple geometric non-figurative symbols standing for various weather conditions to be added to an incomplete table, while the other has a similar format but uses figurative laundering symbols (see Figure 5.1, p. 33). In these questions, children are required to translate verbal descriptions into symbolic labels by reference to a key, and then locate

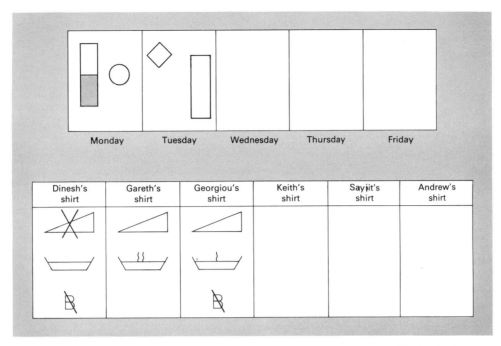

**Figure 5.1** *Non-figurative and figurative symbols used in Tables with the highest overall mean scores*

the label in the correct cell in the table. Pupils seem to manage this translation well and the apparently more abstract non-figurative symbols do not seem to deter them.

It was suggested in the detailed analysis of the 'Butterflies' question used in the 1983 survey that the particular operations required in using a table may make different demands. Examples of different operations are: given a row value locate a column value, (or vice versa); given row and column locate a cell; or compare cell values by given criteria. While having some effect within questions, the effect of logical complexity is not large and may be completely masked by the more powerful effects of content mentioned above. However, this analytical approach which attempts to define the particular operations of table reading may have some relevance to teaching strategies.

Clearly, table reading and construction has relevance to the design and organisation of investigations. It is salutary to compare the relatively high level of competence demonstrated in these pencil and paper questions with the perceived need to construct tables during the assessment of **Performance of investigations**. In the 1983 Survey, in the two questions where table construction was appropriate 2 per cent of pupils used a tabular form in the 'Sailboats' investigation and 1 per cent in 'Chopping board'. (Pages 96 and 121, DES, 1984a.) It is also interesting to consider where, if at all, the construction and reading of tables is taught in the curriculum. This is an area which may be easily overlooked. Socially, the skill of table reading is often extremely important. As vehicles for the organisation of data recording, tables can also be seen to have an important place in science activities.

## 5.5 Bar charts

Questions from four Question types are aggregated in this form one from the **Reading** subcategory and three from **Representing**. The **Reading** Question type asks pupils to read information as directed from a vertical or horizontal bar chart. The **Representing** Question types require pupils to: add data to a partially completed bar chart; draw axes, select a scale and construct a bar chart; construct a bar chart given data and labelled axes. (Types 113, 116 and part of 118 respectively in Appendix 8.) Table 5.4 summarises performance in questions involving bar charts.

**Table 5.4** *Summary of performance for Bar Charts (1980–84 data)*

|  | Number of questions used | Overall mean score % | Range of means % |
|---|---|---|---|
| Reading from bar charts | 16 | 58 | 26–83 |
| Adding to bar charts | 13 | 68 | 18–89 |
| Construct whole bar chart | 5 | 62 | 48–76 |
| Construct bar chart on labelled axes | 6 | 55 | 26–73 |
| All bar chart questions | 40 | 61 | 18–89 |

At 61 per cent, the overall mean score for questions involving bar charts is about 7 per cent less than the overall mean of questions involving Tables. It should be noted in interpreting these scores that the Question types are not exactly parallel. Where children are required to add information, the bar charts which they are asked to complete tend to be concerned with data and scales which they might themselves generate. The questions which ask children to read information in many cases use parallel stems. In addition, as **Reading** is likely to involve other data summaries, reading matter such as magazines, books and advertising material is utilised. Frequently this results in more complex information or scales, or simply more data to comprehend, and these factors are likely to depress performance. (Commercially produced bar charts tend to be a less useable source as they frequently omit grid lines or violate the conventions being assessed.)

Two of the questions requiring **Reading** had relatively low scores for this Question type. The first, 'Braking distance' (26 per cent) uses nested bars with a coded shading to present 'thinking distance' and 'braking distance' at various car speeds and a scale of 4 metres per division. The scale has to be deduced and used in order to answer the question, as did the shaded coding. The information is essentially that found in the Highway Code. The second question presents information about broadleaves and conifers as two adjacent horizontal bar charts and a scale of 100 trees per division which must be used in order to answer the question. The common factor in these more difficult questions seems to be the more complex nature of the presentation, each involving compound bars. (The first of these lower-performance questions uses interpolation between divisions for the value to be read, the second does not.) Four **Reading** questions had relatively high scores for the Question type. One, 'Litter size' (82 per cent) used a pictogram, one drawing representing one animal; a second 'Daysdoings' (83 per cent) presented information about the hours a boy and girl spent on various activities, using a scale of one hour per division with no interpolation; 'Cheese bar'

(76 per cent) presented nested bars and 'Metals' (80 per cent) horizontal bars but neither required the scale to be used, only bar lengths to be compared. The conclusion seems to be that simple 1:1 scales and comparison of bar lengths without necessarily referring to the scale are handled relatively well.

Turning to the **Representing** of data on bar charts, two questions had relatively low scores for the Question type. 'Flow rate' (33 per cent) concerns the total time various liquids take to drop from a squeezy bottle. The scale provided is 2 divisions per minute, and the data include parts of minutes (30 seconds and 15 seconds, which need to be represented as one division and an interpolation mid-way between divisions respectively). The second question found particularly difficult was 'London/Rhodes' (19 per cent) where a similar scale of two divisions per °C is used, plus the need to draw $\frac{1}{2}$°C on an unmarked division. It seems reasonable to infer that the difficulty is with the use of the scales presented. Completed relatively successfully were 'School dinner' (87 per cent) with a scale of two children per division, 'Shoe size' (90 per cent) and 'Car colour' (90 per cent). The two latter questions do not require any interpolation, only coordination of labels on the x and y axes. Again, the fact of whether or not there is a need to use a scale seems to have an important bearing on performance. It is also possible that the question content in these three instances is familiar to children and the data are found easier to manipulate as a consequence.

Table 5.4 includes information on the five questions in which children are required to construct a whole bar chart themselves, rather than just add information to one which is partially completed. These questions are much more

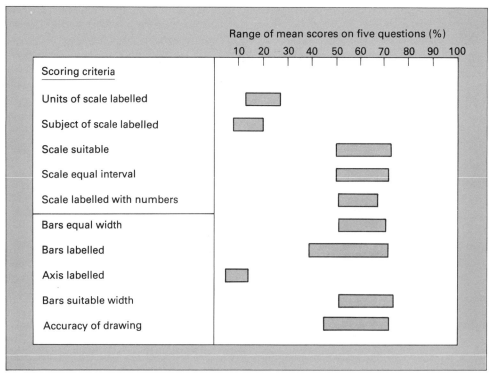

**Figure 5.2** *Summary of performance on five questions requiring pupils to draw entire Bar Charts (1982 data)*

34

time consuming both for children to complete and for markers to score and have been regulated to not more than one per test package. This Question type was discussed in detail following the 1982 Survey (pages 188-192, DES, 1984a). Figure 5.2 (p. 34) summarises performance on the five questions surveyed according to ten scoring criteria.

The scoring criteria used have intentionally liberal definitions appropriate to the age group. For example, a 'suitable' scale or bar width is one that is neither too small to show the data nor too large to fit on the graph paper provided. What emerges very clearly in Figure 5.2 is that while the logical demands of bar chart construction are being met at about a 60 per cent level of success overall, the labelling conventions which might be thought to be less demanding are neglected. Exact wording to match the data labels provided was not required: performance is not explicable in terms of excessively rigorous scoring criteria.

The bar chart questions in Type 8 of **Representing** provide children with labelled axes on which to draw their bar charts. They also require another step in that the data which they have to plot are more akin to 'raw' data. Data are not summarised, though they may be tabulated in some form. (See Question Example 10, pages 75-77, DES, 1981). In view of this extra step, the scales which are used in this type of question tend to be limited to the simpler 1:1 type. Nonetheless, the extra step of having to collate the information provided seems to have the effect of depressing the scores, on average.

## 5.6 Line graphs and grids

Six Question types are discussed under the heading of 'Line graphs and grids', three from **Reading** and three from the **Representing** subcategory. Under **Reading** are Type 5: reading information as directed from a graph; Type 6, which is concerned with naming the axes and describing what the graph represents; and finally Type 7 which requires children to read coordinates of designated points on a line graph or grid. Under **Representing**, Type 5 requires pupils to add further data to a partially completed line graph; Type 7 involves graph construction in its entirety and some questions from Type 8 require plotting on labelled axes. Table 5.5 summarises this information.

Of the three coordinate forms, tables, bar charts and line graphs, this particular group has the lowest mean score.

The **Reading** Question Type 6, which concerns naming axes and describing a graph will be discussed first for two reasons. Firstly, though only a small number of questions have been surveyed from this Question type, labelling of axes will be further illuminated. Secondly, this is the Question type with the lowest overall mean score. In fact,

**Table 5.5** *Summary of performance on Line Graphs and Grids (1980-84 data)*

| | Number of questions used | Overall mean score % | Range of means % |
|---|---|---|---|
| Reading from a graph | 14 | 52 | 24-69 |
| Naming axes and describing graphs | 4 | 33 | 21-49 |
| Reading coordinates | 12 | 59 | 36-81 |
| Adding data to a partially completed graph | 12 | 57 | 39-74 |
| Entire graph construction | 6 | 51 | 41-65 |
| Plotting on labelled axes | 5 | 67 | 56-65 |
| All graph/grid questions | 53 | 55 | 21-81 |

though included in Category 1, these questions have elements in common with the **Interpreting** subcategory (See Chapter 8) in that a more general and abstract view of graphs is called for than is generally the case in Category 1. In all questions, the graph presented on the question page is described in terms of the units used on each axis. Pupils are asked to provide labels and a title for the graph. A detailed qualitative remarking of one question 'Music box' (mean score 30 per cent) indicates that as described in the bar charts section, the labelling of axes is an area of relatively poor performance. In the example quoted (Example 10, pages 175-176, DES, 1984a), each axis tended to be described either by a variable name or by the name of the units used, but rarely both.

Moving on to **Reading** Question type 5 which demands reading from a line graph, the two questions which have the lowest scores also have affinities with the **Interpreting** subcategory. Both questions present time/distance graphs of cycle journeys. Rather than naming points by co-ordinates, these questions with mean scores of 24 per cent and 38 per cent require some interpretation of what the whole graph represents before it is possible to extract the information demanded by the question. Most questions in the Question type are of a more specific and directed nature, requiring little in the way of inference or overall understanding of the complete relationship presented in graphical data. For example, 'Class temperature' (68 per cent) asks children for temperature at a given time, time of maximum value and change in temperature between two given times, all values being read from marked divisions, both scales being 1:1. 'Rabbit growth' (mean score 67 per cent) and 'Rocket' (69 per cent) make similarly specific reading requirements which children seem more able to meet. These two groups of questions, the high performance and low performance, are separated by 30 or more percentage points. The difference seems to be between the demand for an integrated understanding of the information presented in the graph as opposed to following instructions to take a particular reading.

The **Representing** Question type 5 demands skills complementary to those discussed in the previous paragraph, children being required to add data to partially completed line graphs. Two questions had particularly low scores for this representational form. In 'Rabbit' (mean score 39 per cent) the difficulty is associated with the necessity to interpolate odd weeks between divisions on a scale of two weeks to five divisions on one axis, and the use of a decimal fraction on a scale of 5:1 on the other axis. 'Cooling curve' (45 per cent) indicates that there is some difficulty even with a one-to-one scale (°C in this case) when only every tenth division is labelled with a number; all coordinates were on grid lines, one set all being on labelled grid lines. The difficulty with 'Boiling water' (46 per cent) seems to be associated with the task of plotting minutes and seconds on a linear scale of five divisions to one minute, with the seconds given in multiples of 12. At the more successful end of performance, almost all the readings required of pupils are associated with number-labelled divisions on the grid. This type of reading avoids the complexity of interpolation between grid lines, or even use or understanding of the scale. Number labels on x and y axes simply have to be located and coordinated.

Two Question types, **Reading** Type 7 and **Representing** Type 8, contain questions based on grids and coordinates. (See Examples 27 and 30, pages 165 and 171, DES, 1983a and Example 12, page 179, DES, 1984a.) In these questions, the convention of the invariant order in which coordinates are expressed is always introduced via a question example. In **Reading** coordinates, lowest levels of performance were associated with the inclusion of one negative axis as in 'River scene' (45 per cent) or two negative axes as in 'Space scene', (mean score 36 per cent, see page 179, DES, 1984a), despite examples to convey the convention. Girls also seem to have more difficulty with negative values than boys. Incidence of correct reading of coordinates but reversal in expressing them ranges from 3 per cent to 37 per cent. At the more successful end of the performance scale, the three questions asked for straightforward reading of positive values all on labelled divisions of the grid presented. The five questions in the **Representing** subcategory show a very restricted range of only 9 per cent.

As with the construction of entire bar graphs, **Representing** Question type 7, which asks children to construct entire line graphs is a more time consuming type of question, bringing together all the aspects of graph construction that have been discussed as separate components in this section. Naturally enough, the same factors apply. Six questions have been used in surveys, and the aspect which adds to the above discussion concerns the type of graph children actually choose to construct. Only a minority of children actually acknowledge the distinction between continuous and discontinuous data by drawing a line graph when a bar graph would be more appropriate. When this occurs, their drawings are scored as for bar graphs. If only line graphs were scored, the mean score in this Question type would be drastically reduced.

The shift between the treatment of data as continuous rather than discontinuous/categorical may be of consider-able significance in terms of children's cognitive development. It implies a move from the treatment of the particular to the general, and from qualitative description to quantification and the use of measurement strategies. Consequently, this shift might be thought of as being significant in the development of a scientific orientation towards investigations. Teachers may well find that the move towards measurement and quantification, and the treatment of variables as continuous may need considerable support and encouragement within the age group under consideration.

## 5.7  Pie charts

There are two Question types contributing to the assessment of pie charts. Question type 4 in the **Reading** subcategory requires children to read information from pie charts; Type 4 in the **Representing** subcategory requires them to add further data to complete a pie chart. Children are not asked to construct a pie chart in its entirety as this would place a burden on mathematical skills which very few pupils would be expected to have mastered at the age of eleven. Table 5.6 summarises performance on pie charts.

**Table 5.6**  *Summary of performance on Pie Charts*

|  | Number of questions used | Overall mean score % | Range of means % |
|---|---|---|---|
| Reading information | 12 | 64 | 33–93 |
| Adding data | 13 | 65 | 40–84 |
| All pie chart questions | 25 | 65 | 33–93 |

Mean scores in the **Reading** and **Representing** Question types are very similar but the range in the latter is more restricted (spanning 44 per cent compared to 60 per cent). Both Question types were fairly extensively discussed in the report of the 1983 Survey (see Question Examples 1, 2 and 3, DES, 1985a, and Question Example 7, pages 67–68, DES, 1981). Much of the difficulty that children experience in this area seems to occur when they are required to work with fractions, percentages or proportions; ie when there is a mathematical skill intervening. The three **Reading** questions pupils found most difficult have this factor in common. For example, 'Vehicle damage' (overall mean score 33 per cent) presents a circle drawn and labelled with ten equal sectors. Children seem to be thrown by the fact that two sectors (totalling 20 per cent) are shared by labels referring to 8 per cent and 12 per cent. Another question with a low performance level refers to 'fraction', 'percentage' and 'proportion', while the difficulty in a third seems to be associated with nested pies (an inner and outer circle) with irregular regions labelled in percentages. By contrast, 'Rubbish pie' (mean score 93 per cent) asks for simple *identification* of sectors, given values or *comparisons* of values by comparing areas. The age 11 group is relatively successful with this level of demand.

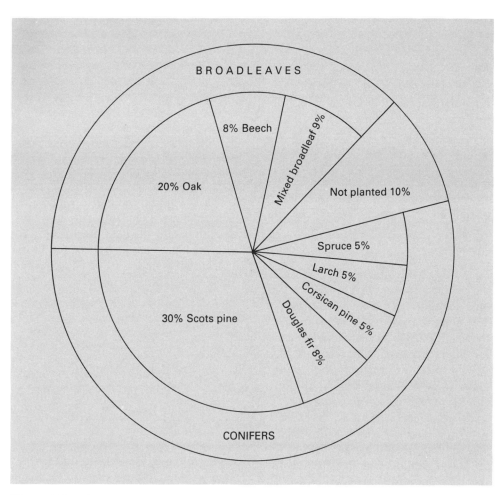

**Figure 5.3** *An example of a Nested Pie Chart*

Turning to **Representing information** as pie charts, similar characteristics are associated with performance levels as in the **Reading** subcategory. The question pupils found most difficult was 'Blackbird' (overall mean score 40 per cent) which was reported previously (Example 4, DES 1985a), in which two nested pie charts with values expressed in percentages are presented. Adding percentage values to a nested sector was found particularly difficult (see Figure 5.3). In another question (overall mean score 53 per cent) the difficulty seems to be more straightforwardly mathematical. It involves representing sums of 60, 20, 15 and 5 pounds sterling on a ten-sector pie chart. Both these performance levels are low. There are two questions with relatively high mean scores. The first (overall mean score 84 per cent) requires the use of the simple 2:1 ratio in adding elements to the eight marked sectors on the chart; the second (78 per cent overall mean) requires numerical values to be matched to different areas by collating numerical magnitude with a simple visual inspection of area magnitude.

## 5.8 Other representational forms

The last grouping is more heterogeneous than the previous four which have been described, encompassing flow charts, food chains, weather charts and Venn diagrams. The main distinction apart from the particular logic and conventions which apply is whether children are required to read information from that presented, or add further data. In the latter case, a partially completed version or an example is always included. Table 5.7 summarises performance.

**Table 5.7** *Summary of performance on other representational forms (1980–84 data)*

| | Number of questions used | Overall mean score % | Range of means % |
|---|---|---|---|
| Reading | 10 | 68 | 36–81 |
| Representing | 9 | 61 | 41–76 |
| All questions | 19 | 65 | 36–81 |

While pie charts are primarily devices to present descriptive data, like coordinate forms, Venn diagrams, flow charts and similar forms may contain elements which mirror or model the structure of investigations in science.

A total of 12 questions of those used in surveys have been based on flow charts, food chains or logic webs (eg A > B, B > C, C > D, etc), six each from the two subcategories. The **Reading** subcategory mean was 62 per cent, while for **Representing** the mean score was 58 per cent. Two examples of **Reading information** from flow charts were presented in the report of the 1983 Survey (Examples 6 and 7, DES, 1985a), with the cautionary comment that while some measure of the processing load may be gauged from the number of elements and the number of choice points in a flow chart, considerable latitude exists in the graphical possibilities (eg colour coding, three dimensional representation, etc). As with a railway timetable, it could be argued that the only acceptable way to read a flow-chart is with accuracy, since it is a form concerned with logical relationships rather than approximations or tendencies. It is difficult to draw a generalisation from children's performances other than to say that this accuracy is not in evidence. Only 2 per cent of children were completely accurate on the second example referred to above.

Most of the questions using Venn diagrams are based on three sets giving the opportunity for three single attribute regions, three double attribute regions and one triple attribute region. This format does vary, and being so clearly linked to the complexity of the information which can be presented, would be expected to have an effect on performance. Only four of ten existing questions have been surveyed to date, so generalisations based on the question parts within these lend only tentative support, though all in the expected direction. That is, the more attributes assigned to an element, the more difficult it tends to be to locate within a Venn diagram. Two of these surveyed questions, Question Examples 10 and 13 were included in the 1982 survey and reported in detail (DES, 1984a, pages 170–174 and 185–187). In both of these questions, the trend of performance was clearly linked to the number of attributes of the element in question. Question Example 5 in the report of the 1983 survey (DES, 1985a) added further support to the view that facility is linked to logical complexity. Two additional points are of interest. The first is that in Example 13 mentioned above, 16 per cent of children failed to score, despite being given examples of the location of single and double attribute elements in the introduction to the question. Secondly, in the same Question Example, 13 per cent of pupils were successful in placing a single attribute element, but double entered two attribute elements. (By 'double entry' is meant entering one element having two of the set attributes in each of the single set regions. That is, the element is entered twice on the diagram.) Clearly, their understanding of the logic of attributes was adequate for the task but they were unsuccessful in using the conventions of Venn diagrams.

Only two other questions have been used in surveys which are neither flow charts nor Venn diagrams. Broadly, the remainder of questions can be described as keyed diagrams, and indications are that they are found relatively less difficult than others in the group.

## 5.9   Gender-related differences in performance

Significant gender related differences in performance on individual survey questions occurred in 37 of a possible 171 instances (22 per cent of questions). Of those questions in which a significant gender difference occurred, 33 were in favour of girls, 4 in favour of boys. More of the differences in favour of girls were to be found in the **Representing** than the **Reading** subcategory (the exact ratio was 24:9).

The four questions in which boys performed significantly better than girls all concerned content of a non-living nature expressed in graphical form. Three of the questions expressed data in the form of line graphs, the fourth as a bar chart. Those questions in which girls performed significantly better than boys also appeared to show some association with the data presentation form used in the question. For example, half of the 14 questions used requiring information to be added to tables produced responses significantly higher for girls. This was not limited to tables containing verbal information. (See also the discussion on handling of categorical data in Chapter 8, pages 63–64.) Eight out of 18 questions used which were concerned with Other representational forms showed significantly higher levels of performance for girls. Six of 25 pie chart questions showed a significantly higher performance by girls. In summary, tables apart, it is in the non-coordinate forms that girls seem to be particularly likely to perform significantly better than boys.

Relating these gender-related differences to question content is a more tentative exercise; content and process are frequently related. For example, where verbal skills are called upon, girls are often found to perform at a higher level than boys. Flow charts are usually concerned with verbally presented information, so the two characteristics are confounded. When a content which appears to be attractive to girls, eg furry animals, is coupled with a verbal response mode, significant sex differences in performance appear to become more probable. The following information in this section must be understood in this light.

Forty-two questions were identified as having a clear 'animal' content. Girls performed at levels higher than boys on 33 of these questions, the differences reaching statistical significance in 14 instances. In the nine instances in which boys performed better than girls on an animal content, differences did not reach statistical significance.

Fourteen questions were centred on botanical content. Girls performed better than boys on thirteen of these questions, with statistically significant differences on two questions.

Questions having a content which was broadly social and domestic (eg based on food, household materials, social statistics, etc) also seemed to favour girls, on the whole. Of the 78 questions used, performance was higher for girls on 47, significantly so on eleven questions. Boys were ahead on 17 questions, the difference reaching statistical significance on one question. The remaining questions were tied.

On the 16 questions having an 'environmental' content, (weather, geography, solar system, etc.) girls were ahead on eleven, two of the differences being statistically significant. Boys were ahead with small differences on five questions.

Twenty-two questions were concerned with physical objects and events. Performance was equivalent on four questions, while of the remaining 18, half showed boys ahead and half showed girls ahead, the former with two significant differences, the latter with three.

## 5.10    Summary

The **Use of graphical and symbolic representation** has been assessed using a pool totalling 255 questions, 83 from the **Reading** subcategory and 83 from the **Representing** subcategory actually having been used in surveys. Pupils achieved relatively higher performance levels in this category than in other areas of the assessment framework. Results have been presented in terms of five representational forms which result in varying levels of pupil performance. These will be briefly summarised below.

The three coordinate forms show a gradual fall in mean performance from Tables, through Bar charts to Graphs/grids. Tables of *numerical* data are most likely to cause difficulties, though not invariably so since performance can be seen to be the result of an interaction of process and content throughout the category. Children appear to have more success manipulating tables of verbal or other symbolic elements. It was noted that very few children construct their own tables when it would be appropriate to do so when performing their own investigations (see pages 96 and 121, DES, 1984a), though when provided with a grid in an investigation, the proportion increases (page 150, DES, 1981). In using tables, performance differences between **Reading** and **Representing** are negligible.

In questions involving the use of Bar charts, complexity can be increased and pupil performance depressed by the use of compound or nested bar charts, perhaps requiring the use of a key. If the scale has to be deduced in order to make a reading, this will tend to make a question more difficult, especially where the coordinates are on unlabelled grid lines, or more difficult still, where interpolation between grid lines is required. The scale used to present data obviously affects performance when it has to be used; children are relatively successful when the task is more simply to read coordinates from labelled grid lines, or compare the relative height of bars without necessarily referring to the scale in order to make judgements of greater, lesser or equivalent value. Scales of 1:1 and 2:1 do not appear to pose difficulties for most children. In constructing complete bar charts themselves from given data, there is evidence that the construction and co-ordinating demands are met at a level approximately

equivalent to the mean for the category, but labelling conventions are neglected.

In questions involving Line graphs and grids, a picture very similar to that for Bar charts emerges, though with the overall mean score depressed. This is no doubt due in part to the fact that the difficulties associated with continuous data which are encountered on one axis on a bar chart may be encountered on both axes on a line graph. In using grids, the convention of the invariant order in which coordinates are presented is frequently ignored, even with examples given. The introduction of negative values on one or both axes, even in a semi-pictorial form, considerably depressed performance, significantly more so for girls than boys. The distinction between categorical and continuous data which determines the choice of bar chart or line graph to represent those data, does not seem to be widely recognised by pupils in the age group concerned.

It is interesting to see the extent to which children cling to labelled or unlabelled grid lines. Piaget's description of concrete operations is brought to mind. It is possible that there is a considerable gulf between the understanding of scales of which this behaviour is symptomatic, and the more complete and confident understanding which enables interpolations and extrapolations to be handled. What looks like a refinement may in fact be an enormous step in understanding.

The fact that Pie charts frequently refer to data in terms of fractions, percentages or proportions (sometimes all three) seems to be a source of difficulty with mathematical origins. Nested pie charts, where inner radii define subsets of outer sectors, tend to be found more difficult, possibly because they are less familiar. Children are most successful (80–90 per cent) when the task is simply to compare values by comparing the areas of the different sectors. It should be remembered that no questions require children to construct their own pie charts from scratch. Such an additional demand would be likely to have a significant effect on performance.

In questions presenting Other representational forms, the variety of presentational possibilities precludes firm generalisations. An *impression* of a lack of accuracy which may stem from unfamiliarity is apparent in children's responses to Venn diagrams. In both Venn diagrams and flow charts, performance is related to the variable logical complexity of the data presentation. Keyed diagrams are handled relatively well.

Sex differences on individual questions tended to be very markedly in favour of girls. Two influences can be identified. Firstly, data presentation form, secondly, specific question content. The questions on which girls scored significantly higher than boys were mostly in the question group concerned with Tables, Pie charts and Other logical forms. Girls scores on adding data to a table were likely to be significantly higher than those of boys, with a probability of 2:1. (There seems to be a common factor of greater facility in handling categorical data: see Chapter 8, pages 63–64.) The few cases in which boys performed at a significantly higher level than girls were in questions using graphs or grids to express information.

There are some indications of performance being influenced by specific question content and resulting in gender-related performance differences. Girls tended to be ahead on questions involving fauna, flora and social/domestic content. Questions concerned with the environment or physical objects and events did not show overall any clear gender-related advantages.

# Use of apparatus and measuring instruments

## 6.1 Methods of assessment used in the surveys

The range of measuring instruments and items of equipment which pupils of age 11 may need to use in science activities is quite modest compared with the range of laboratory apparatus which older pupils are expected to use. At age 11, therefore, this category has not been felt to justify a separate pool of test items and a sub-sample of pupils selected for its assessment in surveys. Instead the assessment has been associated with that of Category 6, the **Performance of investigations**, and pupils' ability to use various items of equipment has been carried out largely in contexts where these items were likely to be used anyway in the practical work. The individual practical investigations have provided a 'natural' context for the assessment of pupils' abilities to use measuring instruments, though the tasks set have required the use of specified equipment in standard ways.

An example is the use of a hand lens and a stop-clock in the practical investigation of the food preferences of mealworms (DES, 1981, page 122). Whilst introducing the equipment to the pupil, the tester placed a mealworm in a tray, passed the pupil a hand lens and invited the pupil to 'Look at this mealworm through the lens'. The tester observed and recorded the way the hand lens was used. Later, towards the end of the testing session and whether or not the pupil had used the stop-clock during the investigation, the tester asked the pupil to start the clock and then between one and two minutes later to stop it and read the dial.

All surveys which included assessment of the **Performance of investigations** (in 1980, 1981, 1982, and 1984) also included the assessment of the **Use of apparatus and measuring instruments** and the use of the following items has been tested in this way:

*tape measure, metre rule, measuring stick marked in arbitrary units, string and ruler to measure a curved line, stop-clock, hand lens, pipette dropper, measuring cylinder, spring balance, thermometer.*

In 1984, this information was supplemented by a set of questions designed to assess in greater depth performance in measurement of length, area, mass, time, temperature and volume. Some of the questions were based on those used in the assessment of use of measuring instruments at ages 13 and 15 (DES, 1985b). In cases where it was appropriate to use equipment and marking schemes for the younger pupils which were identical with those used for the older ones, some comparison of findings is possible (see chapter 13 in this report). Such comparisons must be guarded, however, since the questions were presented orally to the age 11 pupils, whilst at 13 and 15 pupils read instructions at a station in a circus practical.

These additional questions could not be placed in the natural context of the individual practical investigations and were presented to the pupils as a separate set of activities after the completion of the investigation. There were two sets of questions, each given to half the pupils in the individual practical sub-sample. The method of administration is illustrated by describing the set of questions relating to measurement of time, temperature and volume.

### Estimations

The pupil was first asked to estimate ('make a good guess'), in seconds, the time interval between a buzzer stopping and starting. Next a jug of water, slightly cooler than room temperature, was presented and the pupil put his or her fingers in it in order to estimate the temperature in degrees Celsius. Then the pupil was shown a small rectangular plastic box (translucent sandwich box) with about 300 ml of water in it and asked to estimate the amount of water in millilitres. The pupil wrote answers to these tasks in spaces on a paper where the appropriate units were already given.

### Measurements

The pupil's estimates (and the units) were covered over on the paper, whilst the pupil used instruments to measure the quantities. A stop-clock was provided to measure the interval between the stopping and starting of the buzzer and a thermometer to measure the temperature of the water (it was handed to the child in its case). Instead of measuring the volume of water in the sandwich box (which would have presented a tricky pouring problem) the child was given another container, some water in a jug and a 100 ml measuring cylinder. The task was to find out how much water would fill the container up to a given mark (the quantity was over 100 ml). In each case the pupil wrote down the measurement but this time no units were supplied.

### Reading

The pupil was asked to read the following instruments: a stop-clock showing 6 minutes 17 seconds; the temperature shown by the thermometer held in the air; a 100 ml measuring cylinder containing 42 ml of water. In each case the tester recorded the readings and any units given orally by the pupil, and noted the actual reading of the thermometer at the time.

The set of questions concerning measurement of length (straight and curved), mass and area were administered in a similar fashion. The particular tasks are indicated in the presentation of results in the next section.

Section 6.2 below describes the use of apparatus used for purposes other than measuring, and 6.3 examines performance on a variety of measuring instruments. Section 6.4 turns to a consideration of estimation; 6.5 discusses measurements of quantities which children had previously estimated. Section 6.6 is more narrowly focused on the skill of reading the scales of instruments; section 6.7 looks at gender-linked differences in performance; finally, 6.8 summarises performance in the category.

## 6.2 Children's performance in using non-measuring instruments

The use of a pipette dropper was assessed in the second and third surveys. The proportion of pupils using the dropper correctly was 68 per cent in the second survey (DES, 1983a, page 173a) and 67 per cent in the third survey (DES, 1984a, page 160). In both surveys considerably more boys than girls were judged to use the item correctly.

The use of a *hand lens* (approximately × 2 and 70 mm in diameter) was assessed in the first survey, when 78 per cent were judged as using it correctly (DES, 1981, page

157), and in the third survey, when the success rate was 75 per cent (DES, 1984a, page 160). In the fifth survey, 90 per cent of pupils were judged to be using the hand lens correctly. It may be recalled that Table 3.2 (page 17) shows that 93 per cent of children had used a hand lens either at school or out of school. The large difference between the performance of boys and girls in the first survey was much reduced in the third survey and was not found at all in the fifth survey.

## 6.3 Children's performance in using measuring instruments

The results of assessing the use of various measuring instruments within the setting of an investigation where their use was relevant are summarised in Table 6.1. In many cases details of the types of error in using and reading the instruments and in giving units for the measurement were noted, and can be found in the references quoted.

The results in Table 6.1 show that at least three-quarters of the pupils in the samples could read instruments for measuring length, temperature, volume and mass within generous limits of accuracy. There is some inconsistency in these results with regard to limits of accuracy and the notice taken of units, and it was to some extent to provide a more consistent set of results that the special tasks were incorporated into the fifth survey. These also provided the opportunity to assess pupils' ability to estimate quantities, an ability which had not previously been included in the testing at age 11. We begin with the results for estimation, Tables 6.2 and 6.4 (p. 43), and follow these with results for measuring given quantities, Table 6.5 (p. 44), and reading instruments, Table 6.6 (p. 45).

**Table 6.1** *Performance in using various measuring instruments assessed in the context of an investigation in the first five surveys*

| Instrument | Description | Survey | Reference | Criteria | % Pupils |
|---|---|---|---|---|---|
| Tape measure | 150 cm long, grad. in mm | 1980 | 1981, p 157 | ± 5 mm + units | 79 |
| Metre rule | Grad. in mm | 1982 | 1984a, p 162 | ± 5 mm + units | 60 |
| | | | 1984a, p 162 | ± 2 mm + units | 41 |
| Measuring stick | 120 cm long, 24 numbered divisions | 1981 | 1983a, p 172 | ± ½ division | 64 |
| Ruler and string | cm ruler, grad. in mm | 1981 | 1983a, p 174 | ± 5 mm (units ignored) | 60 |
| Stop-clock | 3-button clock, graduated in secs, numbered at 5 minutes intervals | 1980 | 1981, p 157 | ± 1 sec. (with units) | 68 |
| | | 1981 | 1983a, p 173 | ± 1 sec. (with units) | 62 |
| | | 1982 | 1984a, p 161 | ± 1 sec. (with units) | 57 |
| Thermometer | − 10°C to + 110°C mercury, 30 cm long | 1980 | 1981, p 157 | Removing from case | 17 |
| | | | | Holding in water whilst reading | 65 |
| | | | | ± 2°C (units ignored) | 85 |
| Measuring cylinder | 100 ml, graduated at 1 ml | 1980 | 1981, p 157 | ± 5 ml (units ignored) | 94 |
| | | 1981 | 1983a, p 173 | ± 1 ml (with units) | 43 |
| | | | | ± 1 ml (units ignored) | 72 |
| Spring balance | 100 g, graduated at 2 g intervals | 1982 | 1984a, p 161 | ± 2 g (units ignored) | 73 |
| | | | | ± 1 g (units ignored) | 41 |

## 6.4 Estimations

The ways in which pupils were asked to estimate time, temperature and volume have been outlined on page 78. In a similar way pupils were also asked to estimate the length of a straight wooden rod, the circumference of a metal ring, the mass of a small packet of rice and the area enclosed in the metal ring. Table 6.2 shows the proportions of pupils whose estimates fell within wide, medium and narrow ranges. In all cases units were supplied in the question and the pupils asked to answer in terms of the given units. In cases where the value may have varied from one occasion to another, the tester recorded the actual value at the time of each child's attempt and the result was scored in relation to that value.

**Table 6.2** *Performance in estimating various quantities in given units*

| Quantity | Actual value | Range of answer | % Pupils | % Pupils* (cumu.) |
|---|---|---|---|---|
| Length (straight) | 20 cm | ± 2 cm | 33 | 33 |
| | | ± 4 cm | 14 | 47 |
| | | ± 10 cm | 47 | 94 |
| Length (curved) | 22 cm | ± 2 cm | 13 | 13 |
| | | ± 4 cm | 12 | 25 |
| | | ± 10 cm | 47 | 72 |
| Mass | 33 g (approx.) | ± 3 g | 2 | 2 |
| | | ± 6 g | 3 | 5 |
| | | ± 15 g | 13 | 18 |
| Area | 39 cm$^2$ (approx.) | ± 3 cm$^2$ | 10 | 10 |
| | | ± 6 cm$^2$ | 6 | 16 |
| | | ± 15 cm$^2$ | 32 | 48 |
| Time | 10 sec (approx.) | ± 1 sec | 36 | 36 |
| | | ± 2 sec | 12 | 48 |
| | | ± 5 sec | 27 | 75 |
| Temperature | 10–15°C | ± 2°C | 7 | 7 |
| | | ± 4°C | 4 | 11 |
| | | ± 10°C | 23 | 34 |
| Volume | 300 ml | ± 30 ml | 3 | 3 |
| | | ± 60 ml | 3 | 6 |
| | | ± 150 ml | 10 | 16 |

\* % Pupils in this column are cumulative.

Table 6.2 shows that even allowing a very large range of values, pupils of age 11 have difficulty in estimating area, volume, mass and temperature. Some children may not have been formally introduced in school to these quantities and the concepts behind them and so would not be expected to have an idea of the meaning of the unit used in these measurements (though only small proportions, below 5 per cent, declined to attempt an estimate). In contrast most children have by the age of 11 done a considerable amount of work on time and length. It is worth noting, too, from Chapter 3, that under 60 per cent of children had used a thermometer at school, compared with almost 90 per cent who had used a metre stick and just over 70 per cent a stop-clock or watch. On the other hand three in four children had used weighing scales and a measuring jug or cylinder in school and higher proportions had used these either at home or school. So it is not simply a matter of exposure to use of the

instruments that is associated with ability to estimate the measured quantities.

School is not the whole of children's experience, and in daily life children are familiar with buying sweets and food in packets by mass and hearing the daily temperatures in weather forecasts. It may be significant, however, that they are unlikely to have measured these quantities themselves, judging from their out-of-school use of the instruments.

An interesting trend which does not emerge in Table 6.2 is that there was a consistent and strong tendency to *underestimate* the value of the quantity in all cases except for time. This was most striking in the estimates which were outside the ranges shown in Table 6.2. Table 6.3 summarises the direction of these 'wide of the mark' estimates.

**Table 6.3** *Proportion of estimates falling outside the wide range which were too high and too low*
(Percentage of pupils)

| Quantity | Estimates outside the wide range | |
|---|---|---|
| | Too high | Too low |
| Length (straight) | 2 | 5 |
| Length (curved) | 1 | 26 |
| Mass | 15 | 67 |
| Area | 8 | 42 |
| Time | 20 | 5 |
| Temperature | 10 | 49 |
| Volume | 8 | 73 |

For three of the quantities, length, mass and area, estimation was also assessed by asking children to separate a given amount from a larger quantity. They were asked to cut off 50 cm ('as near as you can') from a roll of paper tape, to make a lump of plasticine 100 g in mass and to cut 6 cm$^2$ from some squared paper. No measuring instruments were given; the paper was marked out in cm squares but the children were not told the size of the squares. Table 6.4 gives the result for these products.

The results in Table 6.4 contrast quite acutely with those in Table 6.2 for mass and area. It may seem that the pupils were more successful in producing an estimated quantity than producing an estimated measurement. However, certain other differences in the tasks have to be

**Table 6.4** *Performance in producing a given quantity from a large amount*

| Quantity | Required | Range of product | % Pupils |
|---|---|---|---|
| Length | 50 cm | ± 5 | 26 |
| | | ± 10 | 50 |
| | | ± 25 | 81 |
| Mass | 100 g | ± 10 | 19 |
| | | ± 20 | 31 |
| | | ± 50 | 72 |
| Area | 6 cm$^2$ | ± 1 | 66 |
| | | ± 2 | 67 |
| | | ± 3 | 73 |

considered at the same time. The quantity required for the plasticine was 100 g and it may be that this larger mass is easier to estimate than the smaller one of the rice. The different densities of rice grains and plasticine may also have been a factor. The rice occupied more volume for the same mass than the plasticine and was thus more 'spread out' in the hand when held, which may have accounted for the low estimates of its mass.

In the case of area there seems little doubt that the squares did guide the pupils and that a very different result would have been obtained had the paper been plain. One of the popular errors was to produce a piece of paper 36 cm² in area, which suggests that children were using the squares and, in this case, counting six along each side of a square.

The estimates outside the ranges reported in Table 6.4 tended to be overestimates rather than underestimates. This is consistent with the results in Table 6.3, for in both estimating products and measurements the findings suggest that the units pupils use tend to be larger than the standard ones (similar results have been found for pupils of age 13 and 15, see pages 53 and 54, DES, 1985b).

## 6.5 Measurements

A useful measurement includes a reliable number and a statement of the unit to which the number refers. In the tests the pupils were asked to measure the quantity they had estimated a short time before and although their estimate and the units were no longer visible to them, their attention had been drawn to the units. It is relevant to keep this in mind in looking at Table 6.5 which gives the results for these two components of the measurements. In the majority of cases pupils either gave the correct unit or no unit at all; there was only a small incidence of giving incorrect units.

The measurement of mass is not included in Table 6.5 as the administration procedures did not allow reliable measurements to be made using the spring balance provided. However, aspects of how the instrument was used by the children were recorded and are reported below. It should also be noted that non-response was confined to the use of the thermometer (children who just could not see the mercury) and to volume (a few who were baffled by the problem of using a 100 ml measuring cylinder to measure a quantity greater than 100 ml).

Further analysis of the data in Table 6.5 reveals some associations between accurate values and the stating of correct units. In the case of measuring time, for example, almost all of those who gave the correct unit also gave an answer within the closest range. Sixty-two per cent of those who timed within the closest range also gave correct units. For volume, 73 per cent of those whose answer was in the closest range gave the correct unit and 60 per cent of those giving the correct unit gave a value in the closest range. In the case of temperature, however, the association between accurate values and the correct unit was not apparent.

It appears from Table 6.5 that the quantities pupils could most readily measure with some accuracy were time and straight length. Volume, area and curved length were less

**Table 6.5** *Performance in measuring various quantities after estimating them*

| Quantity | Instruments provided | Accuracy | | Unit | |
| --- | --- | --- | --- | --- | --- |
| | | Range | % pupils (cumulative) | Type | % pupils |
| Length (straight) (20 cm) | Ruler | ±0.1 cm | 70 | cm | 70 |
| | | ±0.2 cm | 73 | mm | 4 |
| | | ±0.3 cm | 78 | other | 4 |
| | | | | none | 22 |
| Length (curved) (22 cm) | Tape, ruler, string, scissors | ±0.5 cm | 38 | cm | 74 |
| | | ±1.0 cm | 61 | mm | 1 |
| | | ±2.5 cm | 78 | other | 1 |
| | | | | none | 25 |
| Area (39 cm²) | 1 cm squared paper (no sub-divisions) | ±1 cm² | 20 | cm²/sq cm | 48 |
| | | ±2 cm² | 35 | cm | 9 |
| | | ±3 cm² | 46 | other | 8 |
| | | ±5 cm² | 63 | none | 35 |
| Time (10 sec) | Stop-clock | ±1 sec | 85 | sec/second | 59 |
| | | ±2 sec | 91 | other | 1 |
| | | ±5 sec | 95 | none | 39 |
| Temperature (10–15°C) | −10 to 110°C thermometer | ±1°C | 40 | °C (or in words) | 40 |
| | | ±2°C | 46 | °C (or in words) | 6 |
| | | ±3°C | 49 | other | 2 |
| | | non-response | 11 | none | 40 |
| | | | | non-response | 11 |
| Volume (135 ml) | 100 ml cylinder, container to fill to mark, water | ±10 ml | 51 | ml | 60 |
| | | ±20 ml | 68 | other | 2 |
| | | ±50 ml | 79 | none | 33 |
| | | non-response | 3 | non-response | 3 |

accurately measured and temperature presented the greatest difficulty. It is important to distinguish between simply reading an instrument and using it to make a measurement with some accuracy. The reading of instruments is reported later, but in the tasks presently under discussion the pupils had to decide how to use the instruments as well as to read them. These techniques were described by the testers and later categorised, forming the basis of the following reports.

In measuring the length of the circumference of the ring 59 per cent of pupils placed the string round the ring, marked the length needed in some way and then measured the length of string using the ruler. Three per cent began by cutting a measured length of string, put it round the ring and then estimated by how much it was too long or too short. Twenty-eight per cent used the tape measure, made up of 25 per cent who wrapped it round the ring and 3 per cent who rolled the ring along it. Four per cent measured the diameter instead of the circumference and the remaining 6 per cent used a variety of other methods.

In measuring the mass of the rice it was noted that only 10 per cent of the pupils adjusted the scale to zero or read it before placing the object to be weighed on the pan. This is exactly the same proportion as found in the third survey, when the spring balance was used in the context of an investigation: it was reported that 10 per cent read the scale both before and after placing the object on it (DES, 1984a, page 162).

When measuring the area enclosed by the metal ring all the pupils placed the ring on the squared paper. Twelve per cent drew round the ring and then began counting the squares. The remainder kept the ring in place and some of these (5 per cent of the total) appeared to guess rather than count. Altogether 34 per cent made a good job of counting whole and part squares. Eleven per cent counted the whole squares and 'added something on' for the part squares and another 11 per cent counted only the whole squares. Counting was described as unsystematic for 10 per cent of pupils and for the remainder the detail recorded was insufficient for them to be classified.

When asked to measure the temperature of the cold water the thermometer was handed to the pupil, still in its case. Eighty-five per cent of pupils placed it in the water as it was; 13 per cent only removed it from the case first. This can be compared with 17 per cent reported as removing the instrument from its case when the use of a thermometer was assessed in the first survey (see Table 6.1, page 42).

The problem of using a 100 ml measuring cylinder to measure a quantity of water of about 135 ml was overcome by most pupils (56 per cent) by pouring all the water into the cylinder at once and estimating the amount above the top of the scale. This was fairly accurately accomplished by many of them since 51 per cent gave an answer to the nearest 10 ml whilst only 18 per cent used the more accurate method of measuring the water in two parts using the cylinder scale. Five per cent poured the water from the cylinder into the beaker in stages but generally ended up roughly estimating how much more was needed to reach the mark after 100 ml had been poured in. Ten per cent used the cylinder as if it were a ruler, standing it by the side of the beaker and reading off the point on the scale level with the mark to which the beaker had to be filled. Since the cross-sectional areas of the beaker and measuring cylinder were quite different, children arrived at completely wrong answers by adopting this strategy.

## 6.6  Reading the scales of instruments

As described on page 41 pupils were asked to read the scales of three instruments showing pre-set measurements. The answers were given verbally and recorded by the tester. The results are given in Table 6.6.

Comparison of results in Table 6.6 with those in Table 6.5 shows considerable differences between pupils' performance in simply reading a scale and in using the instrument correctly to make a measurement. These differences vary from one quantity to another.

**Table 6.6**  *Performance in reading the scales of three measuring instruments*

| Instrument | Reading | Pupils' reading | | Units | |
| | | Range or value | % pupils | Type | % pupils |
| --- | --- | --- | --- | --- | --- |
| Stop-clock | 6 min 17 sec | 6 min 17 sec | 40 | min + sec | 58 |
| | | 17 sec only | 9 | min only | 9 |
| | | Incorrect min, 17 sec | 12 | sec only | 18 |
| | | Other | 38 | none | 13 |
| Thermometer | Air temperature | ± 3°C | 75 | °C | 36 |
| (−10°C to 110°C | (noted) | ± 2°C | 74 | degrees | 6 |
| mercury in glass) | | ± 1°C | 71 | C | 4 |
| | | other | 16 | none | 46 |
| | | non-response | 7 | non-response | 7 |
| Measuring cylinder | 42 ml | ± 3 ml | 95 | ml | 71 |
| (100 ml) | | ± 2 ml | 93 | other | 2 |
| | | ± 1 ml | 72 | none | 26 |

In the case of measuring time, a high proportion used the clock to measure a 10-second interval to within one second. It appears that reading a clock for such an interval presents no difficulty. When minutes *and* seconds have to be read, however, performance falls quite considerably. Indeed, comparing results for reading the stop-clock in Tables 6.1 and 6.6 suggests that the difficulty is greater the larger the number of minutes. There is another difference in the tasks from which these results derived which may be significant. The results in Table 6.1 were obtained in the context of the individual practical tests and the pupils watched the clock hands move round from zero, past one minute to the time to be read. The results in Table 6.6 refer to the set questions in which a clock already reading 6 minutes 17 seconds was presented to the child. It appears that reading the dial in this context was a more difficult task.

For temperature measurement, Table 6.6 suggests that reading the scale to ±2°C was achieved by three-quarters of the sample. In the first survey, 85 per cent of the pupils read the scale correctly. Again the results are not strictly comparable because of the different contexts of the tests. More noteworthy, perhaps, is the difference between the success rate in Tables 6.5 and 6.6. The result in Table 6.6 refers to reading a temperature which was steady, whilst in the task assessed in Table 6.5 the thermometer was being used to measure the temperature of cold water. The accuracy of the measurement required more than reading the scale; the instrument had to be kept in the water until the reading was steady and then read whilst still in the water. About a third of the pupils (a similar proportion to that reported in the first survey) removed the thermometer from the water in order to read it, which accounts for the difference in figures in Tables 6.5 and 6.6.

Similar comments apply to the measurement of volume. Table 6.6 shows that pupils could read the scale of the measuring cylinder to within 2 ml with some ease. The figures in Tables 6.6 and 6.1 show very similar proportions reading the scale correctly to within 5 ml and to within 1 ml in previous surveys. The lower figures in Table 6.5 reflect performance in using the measuring cylinder in the tasks of measuring a given quantity of water (greater than the range of the scale) as opposed to merely reading the scale.

## 6.7 Gender-related differences in performance

Noteworthy sex differences were found in favour of girls in the accuracy of measuring curved length and area. In both cases these measurements required some care for the measurement to be within the narrow range of accuracy. In the case of measuring area more boys than girls counted whole squares only and so ended up with a measurement considerably below the actual value. There was also a general tendency for more girls than boys to give correct

units, but this was not a large difference in any particular case.

Boys performed better than girls in several tasks relating to time and temperature. Boys were ahead of girls in estimating and measuring a time interval and in reading a fixed time on the stop-clock. Similar differences were found in measuring temperature and reading the thermometer scale. More boys than girls checked the reading before taking a measurement, or adjusted the scale to zero, and it is possible that this is associated with the greater use of this instrument by boys than by girls (Table 3.2, page 17).

## 6.8 Summary and implications

A more detailed assessment of children's use of equipment was undertaken as part of the 1984 survey than previously included in the age 11 surveys. The context in which the 1984 testing was carried out was less 'natural' than in the earlier surveys and therefore adds information of a different character to that gathered previously within the context of the individual practical investigations.

Two main themes emerge from the 1984 results. One, which has implications for assessment as well as for classroom practice, is the importance of distinguishing between being able to read the dial or scale of an instrument and being able to use it in making a measurement. Eleven year olds on the whole perform well at reading the scales of simple equipment for measuring length, volume, mass, temperature and time (though they have difficulty in reading minutes and seconds correctly from a stop-clock) but much less well, apart from the measurement of straight length, when they have to use the instrument to measure a given quantity. It is therefore important not to assume that if children can read an instrument showing a given amount that they can therefore use that instrument in practice. The implications for the curriculum emerge from considering this finding at the same time as the finding that children tend to avoid quantitative methods in their practical investigations (see Chapter 11). These findings together could make a case for encouraging children to use measuring instruments more in their practical work.

The second main theme is the difference in performance in aspects of measurement relating to time and straight length, which is generally high, and the much lower performance in relation to mass, area, volume and temperature. That the latter are more difficult quantities for children to grasp is perhaps not unexpected, given their complex and abstract nature. Indeed it may be a warning that we should temper the encouragement of more quantitative methods by attention to children's understanding of what it is they are measuring or comparing when they use measuring instruments.

# 7

# Observation

## 7.1 Introduction

Questions in this category attempt to assess pupils' ability to make and use observations. In defining the **Observation** question domain, two criteria have been of particular importance. The first is 'task', the subsidiary process pupils are required to deploy in any question, also referred to as 'question type'; the second is 'content', the material on which pupils deploy the various subsidiary processes. A restriction on the range of allowed question content in the **Observation** category is implied within the science assessment framework. Not only must the content be capable of a 'science' categorisation, but in any question the interaction between task and content must not of necessity require application of taught science concepts and knowledge. (Application of taught science concepts and knowledge is assessed in Category 4 ii—Chapter 9.)

Since all observations are made within a framework of one's conceptual understanding and experience, the above restrictions on content have led to two main problems for question writing. The first might be termed 'question pool validity' and the second 'individual question validity'.

Question pool validity refers to the problem of defining the science content domain appropriate to a national assessment of 11 year olds' abilities to make and use observations. Bearing in mind the restricted range of science experiences of some pupils, what was required before question writing began was a description of the conceptual knowledge and understanding 11 year old pupils use to make sense of the natural phenomena within their everyday experiences. Such a description has never been made explicit, the set of assumptions underlying this description lies embedded within the **Observation** question pool. In other categories of the science assessment framework a similar problem has been encountered and a solution sought by similar means.

In order to appreciate the problem referred to as 'individual question validity' it is first necessary to realise that in any given situation the number of correct (but not necessarily relevant to the task) observations that may be made is large, far larger than 11 year olds could be expected to write down. Since marks are only awarded for relevant observations made within a science interpretational framework, the problem translates into one of focusing pupils' attention sufficiently on the science aspects of the task-content interaction without reducing the question to a straightforward test of, for example, pupils' eye-sight or hearing.

**Observation**, as defined within the assessment framework, requires pupils to detect information about their environment through use of all the senses, not just sight alone. This in turn means that the assessments must be practically based and cannot be undertaken by use of pencil and paper tests. The latter requirement further restricts the range of possible question content and is the cause of the third main problem associated with question writing-equipment reliability. If any sense is to be made of the results obtained from the many tests used in each of the four surveys then the equipment (resource) on which pupils make their observations needs to be not only capable of sustained use by pupils with the minimum of servicing but also accurately reproducible.

The remainder of this chapter is organised in the following way. General background and history of the **Observation** category is described in the next section. This is followed by a brief description of test administration and tester training (section 7.3). Results for questions grouped by 'resource' and separately by 'task' are presented and discussed in detail in section 7.4. Non-response and differences in performance of boys and girls are described in sections 7.5 and 7.6 respectively. Finally, a summary of the main findings is given in section 7.7.

## 7.2 Background and history

The definitions set out in section 7.1 above were only arrived at after a long process of coping with, on the one hand, the requirements of the assessment framework and, on the other, the limited range of pupils' relevant experience. However, difficulty was not only associated with defining the set of assumptions underlying the selection of question content appropriate for 11 year olds to make observations on. It was also associated with devising methods of test administration which would not be intimidating to 11 year olds (some of whom may have had little first-hand experience of practical work in science) and yet would enable an educationally valid assessment to be made of pupils' ability to observe. Any solution had, of course, to be manageable within the constraints of a programme of national assessments. The history of this category, both in terms of question pool composition and mode of test administration, is one of continual modification and change in the light of feedback.

Changes in question pool size and category performance estimates 1980–84 are shown in Table 4.6 of Chapter 4.

Two factors are mainly responsible for the changes in this category. The first concerns changes in definition of the question domain and the second changes in test administration. The requirement that **Observation** be a practical-based assessment involving pupils interacting individually with, amongst other things, real objects and small experiments (known as 'events') produced problems in addition to those outlined in the Introduction to this chapter which were specific to the assessment at age 11. Because of 11 year olds' possible unfamiliarity and hence uncertainty with practical work in science, a method of small group test administration was adopted initially in which the seconded teacher testers administered questions orally one at a time. This method of administration further restricted the range of possible content since each pupil answered the same question at the same time and each tester therefore required a complete set of all the apparatus for every pupil in each test administration. The only exception to this was certain events which were shown on film by the tester, all the pupils making their observations at the same time. This form of test administration was adopted for the first two age 11 surveys (1980 and 1981).

During the time covered by the first two surveys changes to the question pool were minimal. The main change was the collapse of the two subcategory question pools, **Observing similarities and differences** and **Interpreting observations**, into one subcategory pool entitled **Making and interpreting observations**. These two subcategories had been described separately in the 1980 Report. The small group of hand-selected questions, **Using a dichotomous key**, because of the high logic and language demands, was described separately in both the 1980 and 1981 reports (DES, 1981 and 1983a)

The 1982 survey did not include any questions from the **Observation** category. This afforded an opportunity, after appropriate question trials, for the development of a fundamental change in the method of test administration from small group to 'circus' plus tester demonstrations. In a circus pupils move between a number of different activities so that at any given instant each pupil in the test is answering a different question. This facilitated extension of both the variety of tasks and range of question content which could be used. New circus-style questions were added to the question pool and existing questions were rewritten into circus-style format. In order to reduce both the logic and language demands associated with dichotomous keys, each one was rewritten into the corresponding branching format. This allowed them to be added to the main question pool.

The change to a circus-style administration was welcomed by pupils and teacher testers alike. During trials, groups of pupils responded to two similar tests, one administered as a group and one as a circus. These pupils much preferred the circus. In order to change questions they had to get up from their place, whereas the group test made them sit still for long periods of time. The testers preferred the circus because, although it was more demanding to administer, the expanded range of task and question content allowed the assessment to be more representative of 'observation' in the primary classroom.

The results of these changes were seen for the first time in the 1983 survey which comprised four circuses of activities (80 per cent of questions) together with films and tester demonstrations. Before this survey took place the question pool was re-defined in terms of the allowed question content. This resulted in some questions being deleted, including all questions of the high scoring type 'select the object which matches the written description'. The changes which took place during 1982–83 go a long way to explaining the observed changes in subcategory mean score. However, it seems unlikely that the change from 'small group' to circus-style administration is responsible for the apparent reduction in performance between the 1981 and 1983 surveys. Other factors, described below, such as changes in task (question type) and range of question content are more probable influences. Before the final survey in 1984 a further revision of the question pool was undertaken. Questions which could not be re-written so that they had a maximum mark of three or more were deleted as were all film questions which could not be re-written into either circus or tester demonstration format. During the survey period there has been a change of emphasis in the type of resource on which pupils made their observations. This change was from representations, either photographs or drawings of objects and films of events, to real objects and events. In the light of the above, it seems clear that any changes in performance should not be interpreted as evidence of changes over time in pupils' performance ability. This is discussed in more detail later on in this chapter.

## 7.3  Test administration and tester training

Tests in the **Observation** category were administered to pupils by specially trained teacher testers seconded to the project for the period of testing in schools. During the four surveys, tests were administered by a total of 98 testers, 51 in England, 24 in Wales and 23 in Northern Ireland. Training meetings which all testers attended were held prior to the start of testing in schools. These meetings were held in London and Leeds (South and North of England respectively), Llandrindod Wells (Wales) and Belfast (Northern Ireland). Testers also attended a feedback meeting after the testing had ended. More details of the training and the administration of tests can be found in the Research Reports of each survey and in the Science Report for Teachers No 6 (DES, 1985d).

## 7.4 Analysis of performance by type of question

The results from all five surveys are summarised in Table 7.1 below. Results are shown in terms of the different tasks given to pupils.

**Table 7.1** *Summary of survey mean scores by Question type*

| Question type (task) | No. of questions | Mean* | Range |
|---|---|---|---|
| Identify objects using a branching key | 9 | 59 | 35–73 |
| Identify and use the criteria on which objects have been classified or generate rules to classify given objects | 10 | 42 | 27–48 |
| State three similarities and three differences or state as many differences as possible | 14 | 46 | 29–57 |
| Make a record of changes in an event | 3 | 39 | 31–43 |
| Select the drawing which most closely matches a given photograph | 3 | 70 | 60–84 |
| Make a drawing of an object | 3 | 50 | 41–55 |
| Arrange drawings of an event in order and discard those which do not belong | 5 | 38 | 15–60 |
| Make a record of observations and give an explanation | 8 | 43 | 26–75 |
| Make a record of changes and make a prediction | 3 | 54 | 30–72 |
| Identify differences and select a prediction | 16 | 47 | 25–80 |
| Make a record of changes and describe patterns in them | 12 | 42 | 20–69 |

*Mean = average per cent mean score of all relevant questions.

For the purposes of this table, cell values were obtained by using the mean score of relevant questions the last time each question was used in a survey, irrespective of whether the question was administered within a small group or circus format. As described in the report of the 1983 survey, and subsequently verified in the 1984 survey, change in method of administration made little difference to individual question mean scores although it did affect rates of non-response. Questions administered within a circus had higher rates of non-response than the same questions administered within a small group.

No neat hierarchy was observed between mean scores and question types. This, coupled with the wide ranges of mean scores, makes any attempt at identifying patterns in pupil performance extremely difficult.

The different Question types described in Table 7.1 define the different tasks which pupils are required to perform as part of the assessment. Within each task, content and, where appropriate, resource type are allowed to vary in a largely unconstrained way. It has been suggested in previous survey reports that the observed performance results from an interaction between three main factors: task, content and resource type (eg DES, 1985a). However, classifying questions according to these criteria in order to describe pupils' performance raises problems. There may be a lack of congruence in perception between pupils and assessor and between one group of pupils and another. Classification of questions by resource type is likely to be less problematic. The distinction between representations—coloured photographs and drawings—and real, static objects and dynamic events is clear and pupils' perception of the resource is unlikely to be influenced by interaction with either the task or the content.

When attempting to classify questions by content in order to describe pupils' performance, difficulties may arise which become manifest in a number of different ways. When presented with the resource for a question, ie the content of the question, it may be that pupils' natural, possibly unconscious, step is to try to associate it with some particular context or setting with which they are familiar. This is the cause of the first difficulty. Some questions in this category present pupils with resources for which the context is unclear either because they have met nothing quite like it before or because the resource is in an artificial setting divorced from all contextual clues. For example, a question about a dropping pipette floating in a lemonade bottle full of water may to some pupils be associated with a domestic situation because the question asks them to squeeze a flexible lemonade bottle. To other pupils, who have done some work on floating and sinking, the question may be associated with school science because the dropping pipette sinks when the lemonade bottle is squeezed. The former group of pupils may centre their attention on the bottle whilst the latter group may be more concerned with the dropping pipette. Whatever the effect, pupils' previous experience acts as both a filter and a lens focusing their attention on specific aspects of the resources additional to that provided by the question and can act in very different ways for different pupils.

The above difficulty is independent of task. A second difficulty arises when content and task interact, as the following example illustrates. A question about classification of seeds may be seen by some pupils as a question about seeds (domestic) because they have focused on the content whilst other pupils may see it as a question concerned with classification (school) because they have focused on the task.

Because of the problems above concerning 'content' the following discussion will be mainly concerned with the nature of the task and its influence upon performance, although some discussion will consider the influence that the type of resource has upon performance. However, it should be borne in mind that task and resource type are alternative criteria used to classify the same group of questions. When describing performance on questions grouped by task, resource type varies and vice versa. Hence any observed change in mean scores may be attributable to task variation but it may also be attributable to interactions between changes in task and resource type. Performance on questions classified by resource type will be described first.

### Results for questions grouped by resource type

Results from questions grouped by resource type, 'drawings and photographs', 'objects' and 'events' are shown in Table 7.2. In this table Question type ranges across

**Table 7.2** *Analysis of mean scores by resource type*

|  | Number of questions | Overall mean % | Range |
|---|---|---|---|
| Drawings and photos | 29 | 52 | 27–84 |
| Objects | 16 | 43 | 27–65 |
| Events | 41 | 44 | 15–80 |

the three resource types, although it should be remembered that a combination of some question and resource types is not possible eg question type 'make a record of changes in an event' and resource types 'drawings and photographs' and 'objects'.

Overall pupils found it easiest to gain marks on questions which required observations to be made from either coloured drawings or photographs. Questions requiring observations of objects and events had similar (but lower) overall mean scores. These results may help to explain the apparent higher performance in early surveys since in the first two surveys there were many more questions in which pupils made observations based on representations (films, photographs and drawings) than in the last two. In similarities and differences, questions associated with coloured drawings and photographs had higher average mean scores than those associated with objects. However, this order of mean scores was reversed in questions where differences had to be identified and a prediction selected. This would seem to indicate some interaction between task and resource type.

However, a detailed examination of the questions for the effects of any task-resource type interaction is not possible since not only are the numbers of questions of any given question type but different resource type small, but the questions almost invariably relate to different content. For example, in the similarities and differences questions described above, the objects shown as photographs were not the same as the real objects given to pupils. Pupils generally found it easier to gain marks classifying coloured drawings of objects than classifying actual objects. However, four of the five drawings questions were of the type 'form own group' whilst the same proportion of objects questions were of the type 'add to groups'. Hence it is again possible that the observed differences in mean scores may be due to differential interactions between resource type and task.

A possible conclusion from the results presented in Table 7.2 is that a way forward for primary science is to place emphasis on pupils making observations from photographs and drawings. However, the natural environment in which pupils live comprises real objects and events, not their representations. If one adopts the view that primary science involves a study of the natural environment then the results in Table 7.2 suggest that making observations from real objects and events is one aspect of science work where pupils need additional experience, help and encouragement. Experiences derived solely from photographs would be deficient in, for example, both breadth and balance.

## 7.5 Matching items and selecting the correct answer

Two question types involved pupils in matching given items and selecting the correct answer. The first type required pupils to select from a number of similar drawings the one which most closely matched a given photograph. In the second type pupils were asked to identify items using a branching key (ie to select the series of statements which most closely matches the given item).

In working through a branching key pupils were required to note similarities and differences between the written statements in the key and the object to be identified. In effect, pupils were required to select YES or NO to a number of questions of the type 'is the object like this (the written statement)?' By making the correct judgements the most appropriate series of statements (observations) about the object was obtained.

The number of decisions to be made in each key question was three, one mark being allocated for each judgement correctly made. All key questions except one asked pupils to identify animals from coloured drawings. The one question which asked pupils to identify real objects had an above average mean score for this question group. It was also the only question about plants. There appeared to be no clear relationship between mean scores and key complexity in terms of the number of choice points (ie number of statements that had to be read). The most complex key question had a mean score only marginally below that of the least complex.

In the report of the 1980 survey it was stated that the mark distribution for dichotomous keys was U-shaped, the conclusion advanced being that pupils either could or could not work through the key (DES, 1981, page 49). A different shaped distribution was observed in branching key questions which can best be described as 'J-shaped'.

The two Question types described in this section had the highest average mean scores of all question types in this category. The type involving visual-visual matching (photograph to drawings) had an average mean score approximately 10 per cent higher than the type where the matching was verbal-visual (written statement to drawings or objects). It is perhaps worth mentioning that in the 1980 and 1981 surveys (DES, 1981, and 1983a), the now rejected 'select the object which matches the given written description' Question type also had relatively high mean scores. As Chapter 8 describes, pupils found it easier to identify relationships between data presented in the form of drawings than data presented in words. However, not only did all three question groups involve pupils in minimal writing (a factor known from previous reports to enhance mean scores, eg DES, 1983a), but also the nature of the task clearly focused pupils' attention on the type of observations that were required.

Although rates of non-response were low compared with other categories of the assessment framework, they were higher for key questions than for matching drawings to a photograph. As mentioned earlier, this may be attributable to pupils experiencing difficulties of language and/or logic when attempting to work through the key. For key questions there may be a direct relationship between complexity and rates of non-response, although caution should be exercised as the variation in non-response rates between individual questions was small.

## 7.6  Generating similarities and differences

A number of different question types will be discussed under this heading. Amongst other things, they differ in the extent to which the task specified in the question acts as a focus for the types of observations that are not only correct but relevant.

*Generating similarities and differences only.*  This question type required pupils to identify similarities and differences between objects, between photographs and between events. In each question the number of different items to be compared was two. (In the assessment of pupils aged 13 and 15 three items had on occasion to be compared.) Within this question type there were two question groups. One question group asked pupils to describe differences only whilst the other question group required both similarities and differences to be described. In the reports of the 1980 and 1981 surveys these two question groups were reported separately but were amalgamated from 1983 onwards. In 'differences only' questions, pupils were asked to describe as many differences as possible, whereas in 'similarities and differences' questions a specified number (three of each) was required. However, in responding to both groups of questions, pupils on average felt justified in writing down about two differences and two similarities. Most of these statements were about global features of the items being compared. There was little evidence to suggest that observations of fine detail had been made.

A common marking scheme was adopted within each question group and between question groups where appropriate. One mark was awarded for each correct similarity and difference stated in general terms and an additional mark for specific statements about the nature of the difference. (Report No 4, page 66 *et seq.*, explains this more fully—DES, 1985a). Hence 'similarities and differences' questions were marked out of a total of nine marks and 'differences only' questions out of a total of six marks. There was no difference in the average mean scores between 'differences only' and 'similarities and differences' questions. On 'similarities and differences' questions, although pupils found it easier to state differences, because of the marking scheme adopted proportionally more

marks were awarded for similarities than for differences. Mark distributions within 'differences only' questions consisted of a series of U-shaped curves with peaks at the even marks (including zero) and troughs as the odd. 'Similarities and differences' questions were characterised by a more uniform overall mark distribution. The average mean score was higher for questions where observations were made from photographs than for questions where observations were made from objects or events.

Girls were ahead on all questions belonging to either of the above two groups, even those normally associated with aspects of physical science, eg comparing an object with its image in a concave mirror. (See Chapter 9 for a description of pupils' ability to apply science concepts.) On just under a half of these questions the difference reached statistical significance.

The average mean score for questions in which similarities and differences had to be identified from scratch was, as one might suspect, lower than that for the types of questions described in the previous section ('Matching items and selecting the correct answer'), where the similarities and differences to take note of were more focused by the task. However, comparison is not straightforward since differences in other factors known to affect performance, such as the extent to which writing is required, exist between the two Question types.

In the questions so far described pupils were not required to apply the similarities and differences which they had identified in any way. Apart from the general setting of 'science' and the type of resources used, the task gave no clues as to what types of observations would be considered relevant and therefore mark-worthy. Any criteria as regards relevance (as opposed to correctness) pupils brought to the questions themselves. The following two question types discussed within the context of identifying similarities and differences offered some internal criteria for judging relevance. The first was concerned with classification and the second with selecting predictions.

*Classification.*  In forming a classification system the notion of relevance assumes paramount importance. Similarities and differences exist between elements within and between groups. Within groups, similarities between elements are of importance (relevance), the differences being of little importance. Between groups, it is differences between elements which now assume importance, the similarities now being of little importance. The relative importance of the identified similarities and differences, those which are taken note of and those which are discarded, only becomes apparent as the classification system begins to unfold. Classifying elements involves identifying relationships between salient similarities and differences.

Elements to be classified were of three basic types: (i) coloured drawings of animals; (ii) geometric and everyday objects (originally shown on film); (iii) common everyday materials such as wood, metal, cloth, etc. Tasks were of two types. Pupils were required to either (i) form their own classification system or (ii) identify the criteria used to classify objects and then to add more items to the groups.

The marking schemes for both tasks were similar in that pupils were awarded marks for stating a correct classification system. They differed in that in the former task marks were awarded for *any* grouping provided only that all the elements were grouped and there were no repeats. In the latter task, however, marks were only awarded if the element concerned had been placed in its *correct* group. The average mean score for the five questions which required pupils to form their own classification system was approximately 10 per cent higher than the group of five questions which required them to identify the criteria used to classify pre-grouped elements and add further elements to the groups. Apart from differences in the nature of the task and marking criteria, a further difference which might exert some influence upon performance was that 'form own group' and 'identify the criteria' questions were usually associated with two and three groups respectively. Averaged over all ten questions the mean score was 42 per cent of the maximum.

Three common errors were associated with 'form own group' questions. The first was where children produced a classification system in which the groups overlapped (ie individual elements could not be assigned unambiguously)—not that the pupils concerned realised this or if they did they chose to ignore this fact. The second type of error, and in a way the opposite of the first, was where a classification system was developed which was incomplete in that some elements (usually one) could not be assigned. The third error, normally associated with grouping coloured drawings of elements as opposed to the elements themselves, was where trivial presentational effects, eg the position of the dogs' tails, were used as the criteria for classification.

Fewer different errors were associated with 'identity the criteria' questions. The most common and in a sense the most easily understood error was to assign an element to its correct group, but then to give a correct though incomplete explanation for the assignment. (This is described more fully in Report No 2, page 144 *et seq.*—DES, 1983a.) Another less common error, associated with both types of question, involved pupils bringing everyday, personalised knowledge about the elements to the question and using this as a basis for classification—eg 'dogs people like as pets', 'fish found in shops'.

*Selecting predictions.* In these questions pupils were required to identify similarities and differences between objects or events and then to use their observations to select a prediction. Unlike classification questions where relevance assumes greater clarity the more involved one becomes in the task, the list of possible predictions acts as a powerful focus for defining relevance right from the start. It is not too surprising therefore that 'select a prediction' questions had an overall mean score higher (5 per cent) than that of 'classification' questions, the only

surprise being that this difference was not larger since, in addition to differences in 'focus', answers to the latter questions required a much higher language demand.

Before making a prediction pupils were expected to take note of differences between elements. In some questions the necessity to note differences was implied, in others it was made more explicit. In the former type of question pupils were presented with a list of possible predictions prior to making their observations; in the latter type of question the situation was reversed and pupils were directed to make their observations prior to being presented with the list of predictions. This is not to suggest that pupils saw the component parts as being more independent in the latter type of question, although of course this is possible. The group of six questions where the list of predictions was presented first, all of which involved senses other than sight, had an average mean score 18 per cent higher than that of the group of ten questions, all of which relied on sight alone.

Not all questions in which predictions had to be selected asked pupils to make their observations explicit. It was possible to divide those which did into two groups. The first group consisted of six questions in which the question order was prediction followed by observations. In the second group (seven questions) the question order was reversed. The overall mean score for both groups was similar—45 per cent for the former and 41 per cent for the latter. This result would appear to suggest that the overall mean score difference described in the previous paragraph is mainly attributable to the use of different senses in the two types of questions rather than differences in order within the two question groups. The percentage of pupils who scored no marks on questions in this section (which required observations to be made explicit), either because they did not respond or because they selected an incorrect prediction, ranged from 1 per cent to 42 per cent.

Unlike questions in other subcategories of the assessment framework, in particular **Application**, most pupils who selected the correct prediction in questions in the **Observation** category went on to gain marks for the justification for their selection.

## 7.7 Describing events and objects

Questions to be discussed in this section asked pupils either to describe an event by writing or by sequencing a series of drawings/photographs or to describe an object by drawing. In describing an event those features which change with time act both as a focus, drawing the observer's attention to them, and as a criterion of relevance. No equivalent focusing mechanism operates when static objects have to be described. The common stem for all questions which asked pupils to describe objects by drawing contained the phrase '. . . to show the details which you think important'.

*Describing events*.   Three questions asked pupils to describe (in writing) the changes which took place during an event. Their overall mean score (39 per cent) was approximately the same as that of the equivalent question type (five questions) where an event had to be described by selecting the correct sequence of time-lapsed drawings/ photographs. The near equivalence in average mean scores is difficult to explain, since in other categories an inverse relationship between writing demand and mean score has been postulated. It may be that 'task' difficulty overrides difficulties associated with language demands and that pupils do experience problems when attempting to sequence time lapsed drawings of an event. Evidence for this may be borne out by the observation that 'sequencing' questions were characterised by relatively high percentages of pupils selecting a totally incorrect sequence (over 50 per cent in some instances), whereas in 'writing' questions far fewer pupils (less than 5 per cent in some cases) did not state at least one correct observation.

However it should be stressed that it is the question types which are 'equivalent' and not the events being observed. One event only was common to both question types. This event concerned getting a hard-boiled egg into a bottle—DES, 1981, page 52, gives more details of the event. The mean score of the 'sequencing' question was higher (by 77 per cent) than that of the 'writing' question. In the latter type of question an extensive numerical marking scheme was adopted with upwards of nine separate mark-worthy observations being possible. This would probably have the effect of reducing question mean scores relative to a less extensive marking scheme. In 'writing' questions most pupils tended to score in the mid-range of the marks, whereas in 'sequencing' questions the mark distributions tended to be much more uniform. It seems likely that differences in response style coupled with consequent differences in mark schemes are responsible for the observed differences in mark distributions.

*Describing an object*.   Three questions asked pupils to describe an object by making a drawing of it. These questions had an average mean score 13 per cent higher than that of the group of questions where events had to be described by writing. Apart from obvious differences in response style between the two question types, other differences associated with the two different types of resource—such as the constancy of the features being observed and the facility to repeatedly check observations—may exert some influence on pupils' performance.

A common marking scheme, divided up under headings of 'shape', 'proportion' and 'detail', but adopting different criteria within each heading, was employed for all drawing questions. One mark was allocated to each heading described above. In order to be awarded the mark a drawing had to display all the features (or a specified number) in the mark scheme under that heading. Consequently, some drawings, although recognisable, were awarded no marks.

About a third of the drawings were awarded marks for 'shape' only; about the same proportion were awarded marks for both 'shape' and 'proportion'. The proportion gaining full and no marks was more variable. This, it would appear, is further evidence that pupils' observations lack fine detail. Making and recording *detailed* observations should be a fundamental part of all pupils' *scientific* experiences in primary schools.

No marks were awarded for artistic merit. The general 'science' setting, made explicit by the administrators at the beginning of the test session, directed pupils' attention to the type of drawing that was required.

The question which asked pupils to draw a sycamore wing had the lowest mean score. In view of the emphasis that some primary schools place on a study of nature, this result may be a little surprising. In the question which asked pupils to draw an open, but wired-up, square-pin mains electrical plug the mean score for boys was statistically higher than that for girls.

## 7.8   Describing patterns

Twelve questions asked pupils to identify and describe patterns of changes in events. In seven questions pupils performed the events themselves as part of a circus of activities. In the remainder they watched the tester do a demonstration. (All events associated with pattern description questions were shown on film in the first two surveys.)

Intuitively one would anticipate that performance on individual questions would be influenced by the extent to which the variables to be associated had been identified in the question stem. Before pupils are in a position to describe patterns in data, they are of course required to collect sufficient and relevant data. The need to collect data is one feature which distinguishes **Observations** and **Interpretation** pattern description questions. A major problem associated with writing pattern identification questions was to focus pupils' attention on to the salient variables (so that they could collect the necessary data) in such a way that the question does not reduce simply to a test of auditory or visual discrimination. An initial solution was to identify the independent variable with letters of the alphabet. This had to be abandoned since the majority of pupils described relationships in terms of the letters of the alphabet and appeared, it would seem, to ignore changes in the independent variable. The solution eventually adopted was to treat each question on its merits and to vary the degree of explicitness so that some questions, for example, simply asked 'What do you notice?', others asked 'What do you notice as X changed?' and others 'How did changes in X affect Y?'.

Most questions did not ask pupils to record their observations as they went along. It seems likely that question mean scores would be influenced by whether data have to be recalled from memory to enable an overall 'relationship' to be identified or whether the data are constantly or simultaneously present. For example, the manner in which various materials burned, the associated smells, and so on, need to be individually recalled in order to make comparisons. The phenomena would not be present contemporaneously. The requirement to recall data from memory is another feature which distinguishes **Observation** and **Interpretation** pattern description questions, since in the latter, results are recorded, and interpretations are based on those records. Results from the 12 pattern description questions in the **Observation** category seem to indicate that 'memory' rather than 'degree of explicitness' is the more important determinant of mean scores. The question with the lowest mean score asked pupils to identify a relationship between the size and shape of six bubble frames and the size, shape and number of bubbles produced. (Pupils were directed to make notes as they went along, but not everything can be recorded or appears relevant at the time.) The question with the highest mean score, some 15 per cent above its nearest neighbour, required little use of memory. All observations could be made simultaneously and checked as often as necessary. This question asked pupils to identify a relationship between the length of thin pieces of metal rod and how far they bent when equal masses were hung on the end.

Three questions asked pupils to make observations through senses (hearing) other than sight alone. In all three, pupils had to rely on memory, which may help explain why mean scores were below the average for pattern description questions. However it should also be remembered that questions where data were gathered through the sense of hearing were characterised by relatively high numbers of pupils stating correct observations based upon aesthetic, as opposed to scientific, frames of reference for which they were awarded no marks (see Report No 4—DES, 1985a). It would appear that experiences in music lessons provide a very powerful interpretative framework.

A common mark scheme was adopted for all pattern description questions. Marks were progressively awarded as the number of data pairs correctly associated increased (Report No 4 gives more details). In most questions pupils were required to associate in some way three or four discrete sets of data pairs. The percentage of pupils associating different numbers of data pairs was very question-specific, as was the percentage of pupils whose statement referred to only one of the variables to be associated. Most pupils either gave a series of statements specific to all the data gathered or else gave a statement restricted to one or both extremes. Relatively few pupils associated all data pairs in the form of a generalised statement. Given the need to focus pupils' attention onto the salient variables in such a way as not to invalidate the questions, the relatively low occurrence of answers containing a generalised relationship may be more a reflection of the way the questions were phrased than of pupils' ability to perceive an overall relationship.

## 7.9  Supplying explanations

Two problems were associated with writing questions requiring explanations to be supplied. The first related to the assessment framework and the need to restrict explanations in the **Observation** category to the application of 'everyday' science concepts. The second, similar to that described in the previous section, was concerned with directing pupils to the type of explanation required and at the same time ensuring that the data gathering task that preceded it was not a trivial exercise. Performance can be expected to be dependent upon the extent to which the question makes explicit the type of explanation required.

Eight questions asked pupils to supply an explanation for observations which they had made. The overall mean score was 43 per cent (range 26 per cent to 75 per cent). No generalised mark scheme was adopted although the mark scheme for each question did allow marks to be separately awarded for observations and explanations. Although most pupils were awarded marks on these questions, mark distributions indicate that most pupils gained more marks for their observations than for their explanations. With the exception of one question, less than 10 per cent of pupils gave a complete explanation of their observations.

Three very similar questions about the contents of a small match-box required pupils to use senses other than sight. The mean score for two of these questions was above the average for the question type.

As mentioned earlier, pupils generally experienced little difficulty in gathering data. What distinguished low scoring from high scoring questions was the difficulty associated with the explanation part of the question. This was particularly evident in the question which asked pupils to explain why a clenched fist displaced more water than a lump of plasticine (most pupils gave an explanation in terms of mass rather than volume) and in the lowest scoring question of this type, which asked pupils to explain why an empty sample tube rolled down a slope quicker than a similar tube partially filled with sand, but slower than a tube full of sand. In the latter question pupils' main difficulty was in finding appropriate language with which to explain what they had observed, whilst in the former their main difficulty was associated with the application of an inappropriate concept.

## 7.10  Gender-related differences in performance

Girls were ahead on more questions than boys. In the case of girls most of these questions were concerned with either *photographs* or *drawings of animals*. For boys most of the questions were to do with *rotational movement of objects*. The only difference which persisted over the whole period of monitoring was the previously described higher mean scores of girls on all questions where either similarities and differences or differences only had to be described. This may be attributable to the high language demand of these questions relative to other **Observation** questions. Mean score differences in favour of girls are often found in questions in other categories of the assessment framework where the writing demand is high.

As one might anticipate, given the relatively low overall rates of non-response which characterise **Observation** questions, there was little difference in the rates of non-response of boys and girls. Any *small* differences that were observed were invariably due to the higher non-response of boys. Given the greater willingness of boys to engage in practical work in science (DES, 1985a), this result may be a little unexpected.

## 7.11 Summary

Results from 86 different questions attempting to assess pupils' abilities to make and use observations have been described in this chapter. Questions have been grouped by Question type (task) and type of resource. Grouped by either criterion, questions did not fall into a neat hierarchy of difficulty. This, coupled with the wide range of question mean scores, makes the identification of patterns in performance difficult.

Rates of non-response were low; lower than that generally found for questions in other categories of the assessment framework.

There is evidence from pupils' responses, both written and drawn, that observations are not systematic and lack fine detail.

On questions requiring observations to be interpreted, most marks were gained for making the necessary observations rather than for using them to, for example, identify relationships or supply explanations.

The questions pupils found easiest to gain marks on required them either to match a photograph to the most appropriate drawing or to identify items using a branching key (Question types 5 and 1 respectively). Both question types required minimal writing. The most difficult questions required pupils to describe events, either by writing (Question type 4) or by sequencing time-lapsed drawings (Question type 7). Within the limitations of the questions set, pupils generally found it easier to set up their own classification system than to identify rules used to group elements (Question type 2).

Generally, pupils found it easier to gain marks on questions requiring observations of representations (coloured drawings and photographs) rather than real objects or events.

Pupils were able to use their observations to make correct predictions. However, most justifications for predictions were incomplete. On questions requiring identification of a relationship between observations most pupils described their observations one at a time rather than in the form of a generalised relationship.

The performance of boys and girls was similar. The only persistent difference (in favour of girls) was in similarities and differences questions, which tend to have a high language demand. On about half of these questions the difference in performance was statistically significant.

# Interpreting presented information

## 8.1 An overview of the assessment of 'Interpreting presented information'

Before embarking on a description of performance in the **Interpreting** subcategory, the context of the whole category will be outlined. It may be recalled from Table 1.1 (page 2) that Category 4 comprises five subcategories. These five subcategories are divided into two separate groups by the crucial distinction of whether or not a *question* demands any science concept recall on the part of the pupil. Each of these two groups includes a major subcategory which is domain-sampled. The remaining subcategories are represented by a small number of hand-selected questions. Table 8.1 summarises the relationship between these five question groups.

**Table 8.1** *Sub-divisions within 'Interpretation' and 'Application'*

| | Pupils' source of information | |
| --- | --- | --- |
| | All necessary information included on the question page | Response necessitates science concept recall and application |
| Domain-sampled questions | 4.1 **Interpreting presented information** | 4.4 **Applying science concepts to make sense of new information** |
| Hand selected questions | 4.2 Judging the applicability of a given generalisation | 4.5 Generating alternative hypotheses |
| | 4.3 Distinguishing degrees of inference | |

This chapter will be concerned only with those questions in which all the necessary data are presented on the question page, while Chapter 9 will be concerned with questions requiring science concept recall and application. This main division through the five subcategories has much in common with the distinction between a requirement for inductive reasoning processes (4.1, 4.2 and 4.3) and deductive processes (in 4.4 and 4.5). Sections 8.2 to 8.8 of this chapter will be concerned with **Interpreting**, subcategory 4.1. Section 8.9 discusses the subcategories 4.2 and 4.3, while section 8.10 presents a summary.

## 8.2 'Interpreting presented information': history and development

As discussed in the introductory chapter, domain-sampling requires a group of questions to be constructed within an overall definition which embraces the full variety of the universe of such possible questions. As the number of questions exploring this variety has grown through additions of questions to the bank so has the understanding of the nature of the interactions between question characteristics and pupil responses. This in turn has led to a clearer and more precise overall subcategory definition as a result of a refinement of the nature and range of the question types.

The changes which had taken place in the **Interpreting** subcategory were documented in the 1983 survey report (pages 76–77). In summary, two decisions were implemented. Firstly, it was decided that all questions in the **Interpreting** subcategory must present data in which there is an unequivocal pattern. This decision arose out of *post hoc* efforts to label the various Pattern types (see section 8.6 below) in order that any possible relationship with performance levels might be explored. All questions incorporating equivocal data or equivocal statements about data were moved to the subcategory, **Judging the applicability of a given generalisation**; all remaining questions contain data which can be described in terms of one of nine Pattern types. The second refinement was at the Question type level, where it was felt that demanding a *description* of a pattern (where dependent and independent variables are named) is not the same as requesting a *justification* for a prediction which does not specifically refer pupils to the data. This realisation led to the splitting of these two types, which had previously been treated as equivalent. The final refinement in 1983 was to separate from the 'Select a prediction' Question type those questions which might more accurately be described as demanding the selection of a Description. This minor change also served to balance the structure of demands in the subcategory.

Technical details apart, the global aim in the **Interpreting** subcategory has remained constant since the initial development of the framework. Essentially, children are presented with the kind of interpretable information from which generalisations may be inferred. They are required to impose an order on the data such that a more concise generalisation can be described (or a prediction based on that generalisation can be offered). Pupils are invited to use their powers of induction in order to generate a general statement from the information presented on the question page. This contrasts with the logical operation of deduction, which pupils are invited to deploy in the **Applying science concepts** subcategory. That is, in the latter case, from a known concept having some generality, children are invited to reveal their knowledge through specific applications. This distinction between the **Interpreting** and **Applying** subcategories is clear to question writers. There is no reason to assume that the distinction is apparent to pupils at the age of eleven. Indeed, it is frequently clear from their responses that children may view an **Interpreting** question as a call upon their knowledge base. The result may be seen directly in the importation of knowledge or belief as the basis for a response, or may be inferred indirectly (eg by low success rates or high non-response) from performances where the question contexts are likely to be less familiar. The identification of the factors which are more or less likely to elicit the desired inductive or inferential production of generalisations is of particular interest. However, these factors can only be discussed incidentally, where they arise and are relevant. A systematic investigation was not an objective and was not built into the structure and composition of the bank.

No significant differences between the performance estimates for boys and girls were detected. Readers are referred to Chapter 4 for a discussion of subcategory estimates.

## 8.3 Structure of the subcategory

The eight Question types which constitute the **Interpreting** category can be described in terms of three kinds of question demand and two general response modes. The question demands may be presented singly or in combination as composite questions, and are defined as follows:

Describe (D): a verbal generalisation about presented information most frequently cued by a focused attention on dependent and independent variables.

Predict (P): by means of extrapolation or interpolation, a value of y for a given value of x (or vice versa) must be identified.

Justify (J): used only in combination with a request for a prediction, this type of question demand requests the reasoning behind the prediction to be made explicit. There is no direct focusing on dependent and independent variables, as in Describe.

The essential distinction in response forms is between:

Generate (G): where the pupil must invent the response, in words, drawing or numerical form.

Select (S): where a coded answer format, most frequently calling for a tick in the appropriate box, is requested.

Table 8.2 summarises the entire pool of **Interpreting** questions in terms of these demands and response forms, which singly or in composite form comprise the eight separate question types. As Table 1.2 (page 3) made clear, the number of questions available in each domain has increased considerably over the five-year span reviewed here. Since question selection in any survey was randomised, not all questions have been used in the assessment procedures.

**Table 8.2** *Performance by reference to the eight Question types*

| Question demand | Number of questions used | Overall mean % | Range of means, % |
|---|---|---|---|
| Generate description | 31 | 30 | 3–58 |
| Generate description & generate prediction | 13 | 30 | 15–51 |
| Generate description & select prediction | 6 | 36 | 9–49 |
| Generate prediction | 19 | 46 | 14–81 |
| Select prediction | 9 | 35 | 11–59 |
| Select description | 12 | 39 | 18–66 |
| Generate prediction & justification | 15 | 33 | 13–52 |
| Select prediction & justification | 10 | 34 | 11–55 |

One hundred and fifteen of the 196 available questions have been used in surveys (some of these on more than one occasion). The results for the questions used suggest that there is no statistically significant difference in performance attributable to question type. There is no overall sex difference in performance and no sex differences in performance within each of the eight question types.

It is difficult to extricate the particular question demands for comparison due to the composite demands and modes of response which are likely to interact in the various question types. Given the interaction between 'select'/ 'generate' and 'predict'/'describe', there is no clear-cut difference between 'predict' and 'describe'. There is no difference in performance between 'select', 'prediction' and 'describe'. There is a significant difference between 'generate prediction' and 'describe' in favour of the former. There are no significant sex differences associated with these question groupings. How are these results to be interpreted? Logically, it seems correct to assume that a prediction is only possible after a generalisation (description) has been formulated. Thus a prediction entails the same processing as a description, plus a little more: the formulation of a novel data pair. This might lead us to the conclusion that predictions should be more difficult, which the evidence contradicts. The explanation might be that a description is more difficult to verbalise in a way that gains marks than is a prediction; that competence is arriving at a generalisation with sufficient grasp to make an accurate prediction is not matched by linguistic explicitness. When this linguistic burden is removed to the extent that a response has only to be selected, the performance differences between 'predict' and 'describe' become insignificant.

The experience gained from category coding of responses to many questions suggests, not unexpectedly, that the 'justify' demand is of particular interest in terms of the qualitative information it tends to elicit about the way pupils are treating particular sets of data. (See Examples 17 and 18, DES, 1984a.) There is an impression that pupils regard an invitation to explain how they decided their predictions (in Question types 7 and 8) as an opportunity to reveal their knowledge base rather than their logical processes, but this hypothesis cannot be tested with available questions. (Matched pairs of 'justify' and 'describe' questions would inform this issue.)

In order to explore other possible dimensions of difficulty, all questions were labelled and results analysed in terms of three other characteristics which were considered to be possibly relevant. These three characteristics were:

—Information noise level
—Pattern type
—Variable presentation

These labels were applied to the pools of questions after a validation exercise conducted with the assistance of a group of science teachers/teacher educators. These validators accepted that the complete pool of questions which they were shown was a fair representation of the process purported to be measured. The application of a new set of labels was a *post hoc* attempt to label what might be salient question characteristics. They evolved as the result of the experience of developing questions and the attempts made to interpret the pupil/question interactions.

## 8.4   Information noise level

An aspect of question presentation, which experience has shown influences performance, is the level of 'noise' in which each regularity is embedded in the question presentation. Three variables, each dichotomous, are used to describe each of eight possible cells in which a question can be located. These dimensions are indicated in Table 8.3. In interpreting the values in this table it is essential to bear in mind that Information noise level is a more arbitrary property of questions than is Pattern type or Variable presentation. As such, it is more likely to be adjusted by question writers in an effort to achieve the balance within and across questions which is considered appropriate to the age group. Table 8.3 is, as a consequence of this consideration, probably best viewed as providing another perspective on the inbuilt structure of the **Interpreting** domain of questions. In order to provide

Table 8.3   *Number of questions at different noise levels* (1980–84 data)

| | Presented information | | | |
|---|---|---|---|---|
| | Contains irrelevant or unrelated data | | All relevant to the target relationship | |
| | Clean Idealised | Perturbed | Clean Idealised | Perturbed |
| Information is disordered | 4 | 0 | 25 | 5 |
| Information is ordered (not disordered) | 5 | 1 | 60 | 15 |

a full range of experience of data, the more embedded presentations might be incorporated into otherwise more manageable questions as a deliberate policy.

The first distinction to be considered in Table 8.3 is whether a question contains irrelevant or unrelated data, or, alternatively, whether the information presented is only that which is relevant to the establishment of a relationship. An example of irrelevant information occurs, for example, in a question in which children are asked to describe a relationship in data concerning pollen count, humidity and temperature. In this case, pollen count is inversely related to humidity and temperature is not a related variable. The 'irrelevant' information may act as a distractor when an assumption is made that it *is* a variable. As children in this age group have difficulty enough handling straightforward data, the more embedded variety of question is greatly outnumbered. Questions containing irrelevant or unrelated data have accounted for less than 10 per cent of survey questions.

The second dichotomy concerns the order of presentation of data pairs. In some cases data were arrayed according to magnitude, while in others they would be randomised, with the effect of imposing another step in the information handling. More than twice as many of the surveyed questions presented data in an ordered series than in disorder. The overall mean scores for questions containing disordered data and ordered information are not significantly different (39 per cent and 33 per cent based on 34 and 81 questions respectively), but in reverse of the expected order of difference had all other factors been equivalent. It seems fair to conclude that the more complex presentation may be associated with questions which are easier on some other dimension(s).

The third dichotomy concerns whether presented data are 'clean' or 'perturbed'. In Examples 8.1 and 8.2 (p. 59), the data presented to pupils show no sign of having been affected by confounding variables or measurement errors. All the balls are recorded as having taken exactly two seconds to reach the ground; the readings of all thermometers are exactly 20°C. The readings are not only identical; they are neat, rounded values. Since 'real-life', even 'real-laboratory-life' data are not usually so clean and idealised, some comment is appropriate. The essential

## Example 8.1 'Galileo's Spheres'

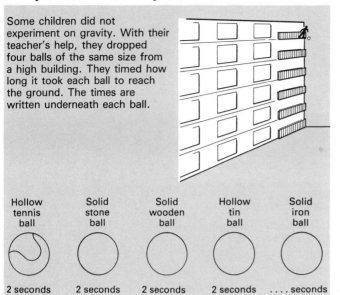

Some children did not experiment on gravity. With their teacher's help, they dropped four balls of the same size from a high building. They timed how long it took each ball to reach the ground. The times are written underneath each ball.

| Hollow tennis ball | Solid stone ball | Solid wooden ball | Hollow tin ball | Solid iron ball |
|---|---|---|---|---|
| 2 seconds | 2 seconds | 2 seconds | 2 seconds | .... seconds |

a) Write in how long you think it took the solid iron ball to reach the ground.

b) How did you decide your answer?

....................................................................

....................................................................

....................................................................

....................................................................

....................................................................

### Mark scheme

(a) 2                                                                    1

(b) All the others took 2 seconds/the same as the others    1

Mass/weight/material makes no difference           1

## Example 8.2 'Beaker Temperature'

Some pupils had been finding out about temperature. When they returned to school the next day, none of the things they had been using had been moved.

The thermometer on the wall gave a reading of 20°C.

a) Write in what temperature the thermometer *in the jar of cotton wool would show*. The other readings they found have been put in for you.

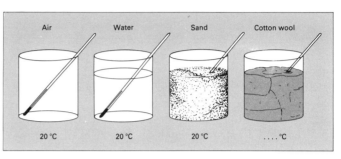

| Air | Water | Sand | Cotton wool |
|---|---|---|---|
| 20 °C | 20 °C | 20 °C | .... °C |

b) How did you decide your answer?

....................................................................

....................................................................

....................................................................

....................................................................

....................................................................

### Mark scheme

(a) 20                                                                   1

(b) All the others are at 20°C/Room temperature        1

Material makes no difference, so cotton wool will also be at 20°C           1

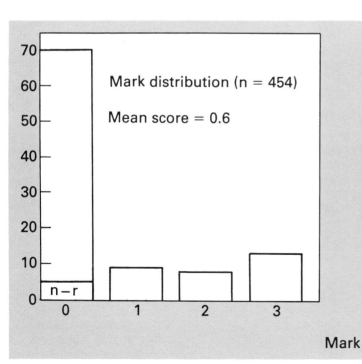

Mark distribution (n = 454)

Mean score = 0.6

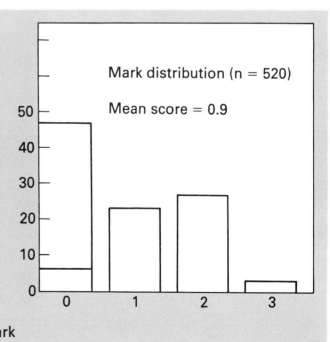

Mark distribution (n = 520)

Mean score = 0.9

Mark

point is that the focused burden of question demand in the **Interpretation** domain is the generation of generalisations and predictions from data. Pupils in the age group concerned are easily hindered in this task by circumstantial information processing demands. The use of decimal fractions in numerically presented data would be just such a distraction, which would prevent many children from tackling the central problem. Furthermore, the language demand when pupils are required to describe 'noisy' data is likely to require conditional clauses which increase the language burden. Despite these considerations, as full a range of data characteristics as possible is provided, and about 22 per cent of questions used contained data complete with perturbations. There is not a significant difference between the mean scores of questions presenting clean data and those in which the data are perturbed (35 per cent and 34 per cent based on 94 and 21 questions respectively).

As suggested in the introduction to this section, Information noise level is closely related to question complexity and hence to difficulty levels. As a consequence, the three factors described above have been carefully regulated in the degree to which they are represented on the question bank and balanced with other question characteristics, so as not to overwhelm children. The distribution of questions reported in the cells in Table 8.3 above reflect this deliberate management. There are more questions based on relevant, ordered and clean information than in all the other cells combined. Pattern type and Variable presentation, which are reported in the following sections, being intrinsic qualities of data, are more broadly distributed, and offer a better opportunity for insight into the ways in which question characteristics influence performance.

## 8.5　Pattern type

Nine different patterns of relationship within the presented information contained in questions have been identified. These patterns are, where possible, defined in terms of the functional relationship between independent and dependent variables. The nine patterns identified are given in Table 8.4 along with summary performance data.

Performance is highest on the Pattern type in which data are concerned with dynamic spatial regularities such as occur in the use of pulleys and gears (see DES, 1981, page 85, and DES, 1984a, pages 216–218, for examples). Overall mean performance is relatively low on the group of questions featuring more complex relationships between x and y than the simple direct or inverse (eg Examples 15 and 16, 1984a). It is perhaps to be expected that more complex relationships in the presented information should depress performance levels. Although only four questions have been used where pattern is a constant value of y for any x, all four have low mean scores. Questions representing this Pattern type have not been previously reported. In view of the insights which

**Table 8.4** *Performance by reference to the nine Pattern types*
(1980–84 data)

| Pattern type | Number of questions used | Overall mean % | Range of means, % |
|---|---|---|---|
| Constant value of y for any x | 4 | 27 | 21–34 |
| Direct trend between x and y | 38 | 33 | 11–70 |
| Inverse trend between x and y | 12 | 34 | 18–50 |
| More complex relationship, eg irregular, Gaussian curve etc | 17 | 27 | 3–66 |
| Simultaneous relationship between x and y, and z and y, eg height/ width and stability | 3 | 30 | 11–45 |
| Discontinuous or categorical variables, eg 2×2 or x by y matrix | 18 | 42 | 11–66 |
| Cyclically repetitive series, eg seasonal order of events | 3 | 39 | 27–47 |
| Dynamic spatial regularities, eg gears, pulleys | 11 | 49 | 30–81 |
| Static spatial regularities, eg symmetry | 9 | 30 | 9–66 |

responses to these questions afford into the nature of intellectual functioning in the subcategory as a whole, two examples will be discussed in some detail at this point.

In the introductory comments to this chapter it was mentioned that the **Interpreting** subcategory can be thought of as demanding inductive reasoning. Pupils have to impose a generalisation on the array of particulars on the question page; the presented data must be capable of being ordered, while nonetheless making some demand on children themselves to impose that order. It has proved to be the case that the question stem which asks, "What do you notice . . .?" or "What pattern do you notice?" is unnecessarily circumspect. The intention was to be non-directive, but where, for example, geometric elements occur in the data, 'pattern' is readily misinterpreted as refering to a part of, rather than being inherent in all, the data. This realisation led to a shift to a more directed demand, of the form, "What do you notice about x and y?" This more favoured demand still leaves a considerable question burden for children. The quality of pattern type deemed suitable has shown what can be thought of as a parallel shift from the more disembedded and circumspect, to the more explicit. In terms of inductive reasoning, the first pattern type is the most direct, being of the form $f(y_1) = f(y_2) = f(y_3) = f(y_n) = x$.

In Example 8.1, the data concern the time four balls of similar size but different materials take to reach the ground. The data are 'ideal': a tennis ball and others made of stone, wood and tin (two hollow, two solid). Each is said to have taken two seconds to reach the ground. A prediction of the time taken for the fifth (solid iron) ball is required. Example 8.2 follows a similar format. Four beakers are described as having been left with thermometers in the various materials which they contain. The readings of the thermometers containing air, water and sand respectively are all 20°C. A prediction of the reading of the thermometer in cotton wool is requested. Although framed as questions for assessment purposes, these data might be seen as having some parallels with instructional techniques where a series of outcomes are highlighted to demonstrate a general principle.

Responses to Question Examples 8.1 and 8.2 convey an impression that the atheoretical and open-minded reception of information which is implied by the description of intellectual processes as 'inductive', is not the exclusive mode of functioning in **Interpreting presented information**. Only 30 per cent of pupils made the correct prediction of two seconds in 'Galileo's Spheres'. When the responses offering the alternative of a greater or lesser value than two seconds are examined, it is immediately apparent that the selection of these is not randomly distributed. Overall, three times as many pupils tend to markedly *under*estimate the time taken. These responses seem likely to stem from a belief that greater mass = greater acceleration under gravity = heavier objects fall faster. There is a significant difference between the score distributions of girls and boys, as Table 8.5 indicates.

**Table 8.5**  *'Galileo's Spheres'. Estimates for duration of fall of iron ball*
(1984 data)

|  | Boys (n = 212) | Girls (n − 242) | All pupils (n = 454) |
|---|---|---|---|
| Two seconds (correct response) | 34 | 25 | 30 |
| More than two seconds | 6 | 25 | 15 |
| Less than two seconds | 51 | 45 | 48 |
| No response | 8 | 6 | 7 |

Boys offer more correct responses and more strongly favour the shorter fall for the iron ball. Four times more girls than boys predicted that the iron ball would take longer than two seconds to reach the ground.

Example 8.2 shows a slightly higher overall performance level, with 53 per cent making a correct prediction. Only 3 per cent gain the full marks for a complete explanation. Once again, the alternative responses of a greater or lesser value than the given series is not randomly distributed. While 33 per cent estimate that the reading of the thermometer in cotton wool will be higher than those immersed in air, water or sand, only 6 per cent predicted that it would be lower. There is no significant sex differences in the distribution of choices on this occasion.

## 8.6   Variable presentation

The third method used to divide questions for re-analysis in the **Interpreting** subcategory was in terms of the nota-

tional form in which the data were presented. Four varieties of Variable presentation were defined on the grounds that (a) they appear relatively discrete and identifiable to a question writer, and (b) that they seem to imply different modes and densities of information handling on the part of pupils. The four types combine in seven pairings which uniquely label any combination of dependent and independent variables, as shown in Table 8.6.

**Table 8.6**  *Variable presentation labels*

| Modes of Variable presentation | | Question labels derived from modes of Variable presentation | |
|---|---|---|---|
| (P) Pictorial, | including diagrams, and maps | pictorial –pictorial | (p–p) |
|  |  | pictorial –verbal | (p–v) |
| (V) Verbal, | either single word or longer descriptions | pictorial –numerical | (p–n) |
|  |  | verbal –verbal | (v–v) |
| (N) Numeric, | quantitatively expressed data in tables, etc | verbal –numerical | (v–n) |
|  |  | numerical–numerical | (n–n) |
| (G) Graphical, | including bar, point or line graph | graphical | (g) |

Variable presentation and Pattern type should not be thought of as independent. They represent two methods of sorting the same group of questions using categories which in some cases have a degree of correspondence between the two sets. For example, the Pattern types which describe cyclically repetitive series, dynamic and spatial regularities are more likely to have at least one variable presented pictorially. Complex relationships are more likely to be presented graphically because of the density of information which can be managed in this mode.

Table 8.7 summarises performance on this dimension, the connection of which with performance has proved to be statistically significant. It could be argued that moving from the first grouping through to the seventh is to shift along a dimension of increasing abstraction, and perhaps increasing difficulty. Clearly other factors (subject matter, 'noise level', for example) have a confounding effect. If this concrete to abstract representation has any validity, it does not show clearly in the mean scores, though the means of the first four groups are higher than those of the last three. As ever, interpretation is made problematic by the large ranges in means.

**Table 8.7**  *Performance by reference to seven Variable presentations*

| Variable presentation | Number of questions used in surveys | Overall mean % | Range of means |
|---|---|---|---|
| Both pictorial | 21 | 38 | 9–81 |
| Pictorial/verbal | 10 | 44 | 16–58 |
| Pictorial/numerical | 21 | 44 | 11–70 |
| Both verbal | 4 | 50 | 35–66 |
| Verbal/numerical | 8 | 29 | 11–53 |
| Both numerical | 31 | 27 | 3–46 |
| Graph | 20 | 30 | 4–66 |

**Example 8.3** *'Mouth Acid Ticks'*

**Question Type:** Generate Description/Generate Prediction

**Information Noise Level:** Some irrelevant data ordered/idealised

**Pattern Type:** Discontinuous Variables

**Variable Presentation:** Verbal–Verbal

Girls perform significantly better than boys

The moisture inside your mouth is sometimes acid and sometimes not acid.

This is how the inside of Pamela's mouth changed one day:

| Time | What Pamela was doing | Mouth not acid | Mouth acid |
|------|------|------|------|
| 7.00 | Getting up | ✔ | |
| 8.00 | Eating breakfast | | ✔ |
| 9.00 | Arriving at school | ✔ | |
| 10.00 | Reading | ✔ | |
| 11.00 | Eating a snack | | ✔ |
| 12.00 | Playing | ✔ | |
| 13.00 | Eating dinner | | ✔ |
| 14.00 | Painting | ✔ | |
| 15.00 | Writing | ✔ | |
| 16.00 | Eating tea | | ✔ |
| 17.00 | Watching TV | ✔ | |

a) What pattern do you see in this information?
   The pattern I see is ......................................................
   ...............................................................................
   ...............................................................................

b) Fill in ticks to show what you expect the changes in Pamela's mouth to be during the evening:

| Time | What Pamela was doing | Mouth not acid | Mouth acid |
|------|------|------|------|
| 18.00 | Playing ball | | |
| 19.00 | Reading a book | | |
| 20.00 | Having a biscuit and hot drink | | |
| 21.00 | Asleep | | |

**Mark scheme**

| | |
|---|---|
| (a) mouth acidity when eating | 1 |
| not acid when not eating | 1 |
| (b) 1, 2 + 4 acid, 3 not | 1 |

Mean Score Boys   47%
Mean Score Girls   55%

**Example 8.4** *'Hoop Ball'*

**Question Type:** Select Prediction

**Information Noise Level:** Only relevant data ordered/realised

**Pattern Type:** Dynamic Spatial

**Variable Presentation:** Pictorial–Pictorial

Boys perform significantly better than girls

Mary rolled a steel ball round the inside of a hula hoop. The hoop was flat on a smooth floor, so the ball could roll fast. While it was rolling, she lifted the hoop and watched to see which way the ball went.

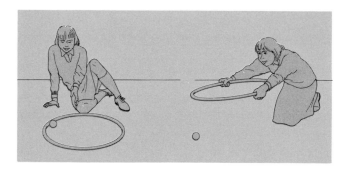

She did this four times and made these drawings to show what happened:

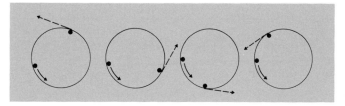

⟶    shows the direction the ball was going *inside* the hoop.
•    shows where the ball was when the hoop was lifted.
- - -→    shows the direction of the ball when the hoop was lifted.

Mary rolled the ball again. *One* of the drawings below shows how the ball really rolled when she lifted the hoop. *All* the drawings above are correct. Use them to help you decide which *one* is correct below.

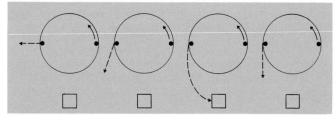

Put a tick in *one* box under the drawing which is correct.

**Mark scheme**

4th option correct: max 1

| | | | | | |
|---|---|---|---|---|---|
| Boys | % | 4 | 24 | 23 | 39 |
| Girls | % | 6 | 32 | 31 | 24 |

62

The Variable presentation with the highest overall mean score and the most restricted range is the fourth, where both independent and dependent variables are presented in words. Only four questions are represented in this group, but it is interesting to note that in three out of these four questions, the performance of girls is significantly higher than that of boys. This is particularly interesting in consideration of the fact that there are only nine questions altogether in the **Interpretation** domain where girls perform significantly better than boys. (Two of these questions, 'Zood' and 'Infection', were reported as Question Examples 17 and 18 in the 1984 Survey report, DES, 1985a. The third is Example 8.3 on page 62.)

The next highest overall mean scores all involve a Pictorial Presentation of at least one variable (see Example 8.4, page 62). The lowest overall mean score occurs in the Numerical-numerical group, ie both variables presented numerically. In six of the 31 questions surveyed with this Variable presentation, boys significantly outperform girls; this is from a total of 19 questions in the subcategory in which boys' results are significantly higher than those of girls. However, the overall mean scores of boys and girls in these numerical questions are not significantly different. It seems probable that the Numerical data presentation may more likely be associated with a *content* which boys favour (planets, boats, bridges and burning candles in the instances where significant differences occur: See Question Examples 17 and 18, DES, 1984a).

## 8.7 Gender-related differences in performance

Neither the overall subcategory estimates nor any of the question characteristics discussed above suggest any significant differences in performance related to gender. However, there are significant gender-related performance differences on 28 (24 per cent) of the 115 questions surveyed, 19 of these (67 per cent) favouring boys, 9 (33 per cent) favouring girls. While acknowledging that none of the pattern types or variable presentations as a whole are associated with this type of difference, it is interesting to see how the individual questions where gender differences do occur are distributed across these categories. The information for Pattern type is summarised in Table 8.8.

In the pattern types concerned with direct, inverse or complex relationships any significant difference occurring favours boys at a rate of one in 13–25 questions. In pattern type, 'Dynamic spatial regularities' (see Example 8.4, page 62), boys perform significantly better than girls in 5 of the 11 questions used. Seven of the nine instances of girls performing at a significantly higher level than boys occur in patterns involving 'Discontinuous variables'.

When the same questions are examined in terms of variable presentation, the most interesting point is that in the

**Table 8.8** *Distribution of questions showing significant sex differences by Pattern type*

| Pattern type | No. of questions used | Boys signif. higher | Girls signif. higher |
|---|---|---|---|
| Constant value of y for any x | 4 | | |
| Direct trend between x and y | 38 | 5 | |
| Inverse trend between x and y | 12 | 3 | |
| More complex relationship, eg irregular, Gaussian | 17 | 3 | 1 |
| Simultaneous relationship | 3 | | |
| Discontinuous or categorical variables, eg 2×2 or x by y | 18 | 1 | 7 |
| Cyclically repetitive series, eg seasonal order | 3 | 1 | |
| Dynamic spatial regularities | 11 | 5 | |
| Static spatial regularities, eg symmetry | 9 | 1 | 1 |
| All questions | 115 | 19 | 9 |

Numerical–numerical group, six of the 31 questions surveyed produced significantly higher results for boys. Five of these questions were associated with 'Direct' and 'Inverse' trends as shown in Table 8.8 above.

This subcategory shares with **Using graphs, tables and charts** the characteristic of having an intended emphasis on information handling, rather than concept recall. Nonetheless, it is accepted that children perceive the presented question content in the light of their own experience, rather than as neutral information to be manipulated. Questions were allocated to the same broad content headings as described in section 5.9 of Chapter 5, and examined for any associations between question content and gender-related performance differences. As previously, the picture is complicated by the contribution of so many different factors, but some associations do seem to be revealed.

Twenty-six questions were based on a content concerned with *animals*. Boys were ahead of girls on 18 of these. On three of these questions, the difference was statistically significant. These particular questions all concerned invertebrates: ants, woodlice and various fossil forms. Girls were ahead by small margins on six questions, mostly concerned with birds and mammals. Two questions were tied.

Ten questions had a *botanical* content. Girls were ahead on six of these, by statistically significant margins in three. Boys scored ahead of girls by small margins on four questions.

Nineteen questions were allocated to the *domestic/social* content area, where girls were ahead on 12 (significantly so on 5). Boys scored higher on five questions, while two scores were tied.

*Environmental* content (weather, geography, etc) formed the subject matter of eleven questions, in ten of which boys were found to have scored higher than girls. In four cases the differences were statistically significant.

*Physical objects and events* was the heading under which almost half of the questions used in this subcategory were subsumed. Boys were ahead of girls on 36 of the 49 questions in this group. The margins were statistically significant on 12 of these questions. Girls scored higher than boys on 12 questions, including one statistically significant margin.

## 8.8 The minor subcategories

Table 8.1 makes reference to the two minor subcategories in the **Interpretation** subcategory: **Judging the applicability of a given generalisation** and **Distinguishing degrees of inference**. No new questions representing these subcategories were included in the 1984 survey. The following comments summarise information gained from earlier surveys.

A detailed analysis of responses to questions in the subcategory **Judging the applicability of a given generalisation** was presented in the report of the 1983 science survey (DES, 1985a, pages 101–5). The important distinction between questions in this subcategory and the major subcategory discussed above is that in the former either the data presented, or statements about the data, may be equivocal. Using a multichoice format, children were required to evaluate statements about data as being 'true', 'not true' or 'not possible to tell'. Analysis of 800 responses to 28 statements presented in 7 questions indicated that successful evaluation of 'true' and 'not true' generalisations were at approximately equal mean levels, (59 per cent and 56 per cent respectively). The overall mean performance for successful recognition of statements unsupported by the facts was considerably lower at 40 per cent. Even incorrect responses to 'true' and 'not true' statements were biased against the equivocal 'not possible to tell'. It was suggested that willingness to select 'not possible to tell' has much in common with what is generally known as an ability to 'tolerate lack of closure'. This contrasts with the everyday context where decisions based on insufficient or inconclusive information must be made frequently, with the support of personal experience. This contrast might be thought of as similar to a distinction between objective or scientific reasoning on the one hand and imaginative use of common sense on the other. The distinction does highlight a possible tension between the generalist tradition in primary education, and the specific formal rigour required in scientific thinking.

Questions drawn from the subcategory **Distinguishing degrees of inference** were discussed in the reports of the 1980 and 1981 surveys (Examples 16 and 17, DES, 1981, pages 90–93, and Example 19, DES 1983a, pages 133–135). Where these questions have been used in surveys, they have been hand selected and individually reported without any attempt at aggregating scores or generalising about pupils' responses. What this subcategory attempts to assess is pupils' ability to identify which of a given selection of statements makes least assumptions about a situation presented pictorially on the question page. It is not maintained that scientific observation should be (or even can be) inference-free. The more defensible position adopted in this subcategory is that even if complete objectivity is not a possibility, some descriptions of situations make fewer assumptions than others. These comments perhaps give some hint of the interest and discussion which has surrounded the development of this subcategory, which is so appealing on first consideration, yet so fraught with problems in its implementation.

On the six questions which have been used in surveys, the highest overall mean score achieved was 50 per cent. The rate of violation of the question rubric by multiple response has been extraordinarily high in comparison with questions in other areas of the framework using a similar format. This high rate of multiple response seems to reflect the difficulties which pupils have in rejecting descriptions which are very reasonable and of fairly high probability in everyday terms (eg a dog being described as 'thirsty' or 'panting' etc., rather than simply having 'its tongue hanging out'). Once again, a difference between what is appropriate in a 'science' as opposed to an 'everyday' frame of reference is highlighted.

## 8.9 Summary

Just over half of a pool of almost 200 questions representing the domain **Interpreting presented information** have been used during the five annual surveys. These questions contain data from which generalisations and predictions are required to be inferred by pupils. Pupils are required to Generate or Select descriptions or Predictions, or Justify predictions in a variety of response modes including drawing, short or extended writing, multi-choice or numerical responses. As the pool of questions attempts to reflect a wide variety of data characteristics, the demands made on pupils are, not unexpectedly, multi-dimensional. The analysis of question results presented in this chapter attempts to explore the salient aspects of demand revealed in differential performance levels.

*Overall performance*. The overall mean scores suggest that it is difficult for children in this age group to produce responses that satisfy all the requirements of the marking system in the **Interpreting** subcategory. This does not imply that children actually experience the questions as posing difficulties. In the context of the whole framework, the skills involved here would appear to be among the more demanding.

*Information noise level*. Questions in which the embeddedness of data in arbitrary and extraneous 'noise' has risen to unmanageable levels will have been rejected during question trials. The structure of the bank has been managed to limit factors such as redundant information, ordering of data, and inclusion of interferences such as measurement error. Were it not for this management, there is no doubt that overall performance would be lower than the current estimates.

*Describing and predicting.* While significant differences in performance by Question type are not discernible, a significant difference between 'Describe' and 'Predict' questions in favour of the latter is detectable. Since prediction is only possible when the generalisation in presented information required by the 'Describe' demand has been formulated, this difference is not interpretable in terms of the differing logical demand of the two types. It is possible that a description is found more difficult to express, which might point to a discrepancy between competence and performance. This conclusion can only be tentative since the 'Describe' and 'Predict' questions are not matched on all characteristics, but has been reproduced in the assessment of older pupils also.

*Pattern type.* The particular pattern or regularity which the presented data expressed has a significant effect on performance. Complex relationships between x and y tend to produce an overall low mean score. Higher mean scores tend to be associated with Dynamic spatial regularities and Discontinuous variables.

*Content.* Although the **Interpreting** domain was designed primarily with a process demand in mind, there is evidence to suggest that pupils frequently engage data at the level of content. This is not necessarily incompatible with moving to an abstraction, but there are clearly occasions when pupils do not see the need to take a view any broader than their personal experience of particular content. To be able to view data in abstract terms and generalise from the particular is an important scientific skill. Many pupils fail without knowing they do so in the **Interpreting** subcategory because they respond by reference to personal experience rather than to the evidence presented in any given question and the formal demands which refer to it. This raises the issue of whether the 'personal' rather than 'scientific' response is symptomatic of a general response to science, or an unfamiliarity with novel question demands.

*Variable presentation.* The factor of whether variables are expressed in Pictorial, Verbal, Numerical or Graphical form has a significant effect on performance. The questions in which all data are expressed verbally tend to have the higher overall mean scores, but only four questions are represented in this form. Generally, those questions in which at least one variable is expressed in Pictorial form tend to have higher overall mean scores.

*Gender related performance differences.* Almost one-quarter of the questions give rise to significant gender-related differences in performance, twice as many in favour of boys than girls. None of the major question groupings shows a significant difference by gender; there are suggestions that girls do better on verbal presentations, boys better on numerical, boys better on Spatial dynamic patterns, girls better with categorical data. The individual questions on which boys seem to do better than girls tend to have non-human physics and technology contexts, or creepy-crawlies; girls do better with people and plants.

In the subcategory in which equivocal data or statements about data are presented, pupils are attracted to and have more success with categorical 'true' or 'false' responses than when they are required to suspend judgement or tolerate lack of closure. Experience may be used to supply missing information in a way which is necessary in everyday life, but which is, formally speaking, 'unscientific'. The same thing probably occurs when pupils are asked to select statements making least assumptions about a situation.

# 9

# Applying science concepts to make sense of new information

## 9.1 Introduction

Questions in this subcategory attempt to assess pupils' ability to recall and apply relevant science concepts and knowledge. It must be stressed that pupils are not required to recall and simply state specific learned concepts, knowledge or science experiences but to go one stage further and apply them in usually familiar but novel situations. The concepts and knowledge thought appropriate to ask 11 year olds to apply were identified after discussions by the monitoring team with groups of teachers, advisers and members of the APU Steering Group in Science. The list of concepts and knowledge finally agreed is described in Appendix 9. It was intended that questions in the **Application** subcategory would require application of ideas stated on this list at a level appropriate to 11 year olds. Most of the concepts and knowledge on this list are likely to be acquired at the necessary level by pupils through teaching strategies which set out to include some *planned* science work either as a separate study or as work in science integrated within other broader topic areas of the primary curriculum. The pool of questions was designed to survey the range of pupils' conceptual understanding in science rather than as a systematic in-depth probe into pupils' understanding of specific concepts. Therefore only a few questions were written to any single statement in the concept list.

Questions in this subcategory are of two types:

**Applying science concepts**
**Generating alternative hypotheses**

All five APU surveys in science of pupils aged 10/11 years have included questions of the first type randomly selected from a question pool which in 1984 contained around 200 questions. Questions of the second type are much fewer in number and are hand-selected for inclusion in surveys. Only questions in the **Applying science concepts** pool contribute to the overall **Application** subcategory score. Although allowed Question types in the **Applying science concepts** question pool had been agreed prior to the first survey (and have remained unchanged throughout the whole five-year period that monitoring has taken place, subject to minor re-definitions) the total number of questions has in general steadily increased. This is the net result of new questions being added and other unsatisfactory ones being either modified or deleted. Therefore some questions available for inclusion in early surveys were not available for later surveys and vice versa. The final agreed list of different question types at all three survey ages, defined in terms of the different processes and outcomes pupils are expected to deploy, is shown in Table 9.1. The number used to identify the different question types in this table will be used in the remainder of this chapter.

**Table 9.1** *Subcategory 'Application': Question types*

1 Supply a prediction based on data and accepted concepts

2 Supply a prediction and give a reason based on data and accepted concepts

OR

Describe a pattern based on data and accepted concepts and make a prediction

3a Select one prediction from four and give a reason based on data and accepted concepts

3b Select one prediction from two and give a reason based on data and accepted concepts

4 Select a prediction based on data and accepted concepts

5 Supply an explanation consistent with the data and accepted concepts

6 Assess the validity of explanations in relation to data and accepted concepts

7 Select the best explanation in relation to the data and accepted concepts

8 Select all explanations which are consistent with the data and accepted concepts

9 Re-order drawings of stages in a life-cycle according to accepted concepts

In the following sections survey results will be described and pupils' performance discussed. A simple 'input–output' model to describe and explain pupils' performance in the **Application** subcategory might be expected to identify the following important factors, some of which are pupil-related and some of which are question-specific:

(i) mode of data presentation, eg prose, pictorial, numerical, tabular, graphical, etc

(ii) nature of concept to be applied and the depth of conceptual understanding required

(iii) experience and ability of pupil answering question

(iv) response style, eg extended written, short written, multiple-choice, etc

For any question the observed mean score is the product of all these and other interactions. Therefore in any detailed discussion of results it is necessary to consider the influence of each of these factors in turn whilst all the others are held constant. Such a discussion, were it possible (bearing in mind (iii) above), would require a large number of questions – far larger than that of the present **Application** question pool. Consequently the following discussion will, as in previous survey reports, focus on one factor at a time, but it must be remembered that the remaining factors are not held constant in the question.

Within the science assessment framework two of the above factors, namely (ii) nature of concept to be applied and (iv) question type (including response style), have been major descriptive and reporting labels. However, it should be remembered that 'concept' and 'question type' are not mutually exclusive labels. They simply represent alternative ways of describing the same group of questions. In Table 9.2 questions are tabulated by both concept region

**Table 9.2** *Analysis of questions according to Question type, concept applied and maximum mark*

Number of different questions used in the surveys*

| Question type | 'Living things' | 'Force & energy' | 'Materials & their characteristics' | Total |
|---|---|---|---|---|
| 1 | 1 (2) | 17 (25) | 1 (1) | 19 (28) |
| 2 | 2 (6) | 8 (19) | 8(10) | 18 (37) |
| 3a | 10(15) | 9 (14) | 3 (3) | 22 (32) |
| 3b | 2 (2) | 2 (2) | 0 (0) | 4 (4) |
| 4 | 3 (5) | 10 (14) | 0 (0) | 13 (19) |
| 5 | 21(25) | 18 (28) | 9 (9) | 48 (62) |
| 6 | 2 (2) | 0 (0) | 1 (2) | 3 (4) |
| 7 | 1 (1) | 1 (1) | 0 (1) | 2 (3) |
| 8 | 2 (2) | 0 (1) | 0 (0) | 2 (3) |
| 9 | 4 (4) | 0 (0) | 0 (0) | 4 (4) |
| Totals | 48(64) | 65(104) | 22(26) | 135(196) |

* Figures in brackets indicate the number of questions in that cell which were available for selection in the 1984 survey.

– 'Living things', 'Force and energy' and 'Materials and their characteristics', – and Question type as described earlier in Table 9.1. (See Appendix 9 for more details.) No suggestion should be inferred from the use of 'Living things', 'Force and energy' and 'Materials and their characteristics' in this report that science in primary schools should be taught or even described under these labels. They act simply as readily identifiable criteria for grouping questions by concept (eg DES, 1983a, and DES, 1985a). They should be seen as concept regions, rather than either curriculum content (eg topic work) or teaching labels. In Table 9.2 the total number of questions in each cell available for selection in the final survey, together with the total number of these questions used in the five surveys, is shown. Random selection of questions has understandably left some questions as yet unused.

## 9.2 Performance related to Question type

This section discusses how the observed interaction between the information presented in questions and pupils' conceptual understanding is influenced by Question type; in particular, pupil response mode.

Mean scores for all questions of each type used in the five surveys are summarised in Table 9.3 below.

**Table 9.3** *Summary of mean score by Question type* (1980–84 data)

| Question type* | Number of questions used | Overall mean % | Range of means |
|---|---|---|---|
| 1 Supply a prediction | 19 | 42 | 11–78 |
| 2 Supply a prediction and give a reason OR Describe a pattern and make a prediction | 18 | 36 | 9–68 |
| 3a Select one prediction from four and give a reason | 22 | 31 | 7–54 |
| 3b Select one prediction from two and give a reason | 4 | 20 | 11–32 |
| 4 Select a prediction | 13 | 53 | 28–89 |
| 5 Supply an explanation | 48 | 24 | 6–59 |
| 6 Assess validity of explanations | 3 | 29 | 13–40 |
| 7 Select the best explanation | 2 | 35 | 32–37 |
| 8 Select all explanations consistent with data | 2 | 54 | 50–57 |
| 9 Re-order drawings of stages in a life-cycle | 4 | 77 | 49–95 |

* See Table 9.1 for fuller description of each Question type and Appendix 8 for a complete description.

Of the 135 different survey questions that have been used in the survey programme just under a half (67 questions) were selected for use in more than one survey. Where this occurred, the most recent mean score was used to calculate cell values in the above and subsequent tables of performance details; similar values were obtained when mean scores for individual questions averaged over the surveys were used to calculate cell values.

All questions in which pupils had to re-order drawings of stages in a life cycle required application of the same concept and virtually all had mean scores higher than that of all other questions in the **Application** subcategory. It is for these reasons that they have been excluded from the remainder of the discussion in this section. The average Question type mean scores were in the range 20–54 per cent. Question types do not fall into a neat hierarchy of difficulty, with individual questions of any given type occupying a narrow range of mean scores discrete from the range of mean scores for individual questions of any other question type. In virtually all Question types the mean score of the majority of individual questions was within the range 10–60 per cent of the maximum. Questions with mean scores above this range were generally associated with either *supplying* or *selecting predictions* only; questions with mean scores below this range were generally associated with *supplying explanations*.

Questions requiring a prediction only to be *selected* had overall mean scores greater than the corresponding type of question where the prediction had to be *supplied* However, those questions where the prediction had to be *supplied* and a reason given had a marginally higher overall mean score than that of the corresponding group of questions where the prediction had to be *selected* and a reason given. Marks were awarded for correct predictions only in the former Question type. (In the latter Question type no marks were awarded for selecting the correct prediction since pupils had a 50 per cent chance of guessing the correct answer.) It may be that selecting one prediction out of four is easier than supplying a prediction from scratch. However forcing pupils to supply a prediction either motivates or makes them see the necessity to explain the reasons for their prediction more than when selecting the prediction. Pupils may take the view that in selecting a prediction there is no need to give an elaborate reason as the person who will read their answer (the question writer) already knows the 'correct' reason since it was (s)he who was responsible for supplying the prediction in the first place. Whether this explanation is true or not, pupils *as a rule* were more successful on questions where predictions only had to be either supplied or selected, than on questions where written reasons for predictions were required.

Most pupils who were awarded marks in questions requiring reasons for predictions gained most of their marks for the 'predict' part of the question. Furthermore, most reasons were incomplete and frequently stated in specific rather than general terms. Hence, it would appear that pupils were able to apply appropriate concepts successfully but experienced difficulty in making the concept explicit in their reasons. Although this interpretation may be true, it should be tempered by the observation that in some 'predict and reason' (composite) questions the 'predict' part can be answered by recall of everyday experiences (eg Example 29, DES, 1984a, Example 20, DES, 1985a). For questions where this is true, it is only the 'reason' part which requires application of science-specific experiences. However, everyday experiences do not automatically lead to the correct prediction (see Example 17, DES, 1983a).

There are likely to be exceptions to the generalisations described in the previous two paragraphs. Because factors other than Question type influence mean scores, there are instances of individual 'prediction and reason' questions with mean scores in excess of those of 'prediction only' questions.

For questions requiring explanations only, those which required explanations to be *selected* had a higher overall mean score than the corresponding group of questions where the explanation had to be *supplied*. However, it should be remembered that, because of the difficulty of supplying plausible alternative explanations at a level appropriate for 11 year olds, the number of questions requiring explanations to be selected was very small, two in fact. For the same reason, the conclusion that questions which require pupils to *assess* the validity of alternative explanations had an overall mean score approximately half that of questions which required pupils to *select* all the explanations consistent with the data and accepted concepts, should be treated with extreme caution.

### Concept applied

In this section results are discussed in relation to the concepts and knowledge which have to be applied to answer questions. No account is taken of the changes in question type, mode of data presentation and other performance-related variables which are not uniform or systematic between one concept and another. It is proposed to compare and discuss pupils' performance on groups of concepts in general terms, rather than to attempt a detailed discussion of performance on individual concepts as in previous reports. Of course, not only is type of concept an important determinant of performance, but so is the detail of conceptual understanding required. The influence that 'detail' exerts on mean scores has been briefly described in connection with questions about food chains and food webs (DES, 1981, page 100, and DES, 1983a, page 124). However, no comparisons of the levels of detail of conceptual application will be attempted here. It is as well to remember in the ensuing discussion that it should be possible to alter performance on one group of questions relative to that of another group simply by changing the level of detail at which the same concepts have to be applied.

Two types of marking have been employed in this subcategory. The first involving numerical marking schemes, has been used to mark all questions. The second involving qualitative marking schemes, has been used less frequently, being restricted to those questions discussed in more detail in reports. The purpose of the qualitative marking schemes has been to give detailed information about pupils' performance additional to that provided by numerical marks. General results from qualitative marking will be described first.

Because survey questions were randomly selected from the **Application** question pool, questions for qualitative marking were selected for their individual intrinsic interest and not as part of an overall plan spanning the five surveys. Because content and context influence pupils' responses in, at present, largely unknown ways, pupil response category profiles may have a restricted utility. Response profiles may be different for questions which, although requiring application of the same concept, use different content and/or contexts.

Two possible explanations for the relatively low mean scores on certain Question types are (1) pupils' believing they have supplied more information in their answers than they can actually be given credit for and (2) pupils' superficial understanding of the relevant concept to be applied. The former explanation has also been mentioned when describing responses to a number of questions in previous reports. Answers which illustrate this point are clearly seen in Example 18 (DES, 1983a), a question about explaining why salt disappears when water is added to it and in Example 30 (DES, 1984a), a question about explaining how the pollen from hazel catkins is spread. The latter example question clearly illustrates the problem for markers in deciding whether an answer simply displays evidence of superficial conceptual understanding on the part of the pupil or whether the pupil concerned understood the concept but simply did not know how to answer the question (page 244 op. cit.). Example questions 28 and 29 in the same report illustrate further instances where pupils may have thought that they had implied more in their answers than they could be given credit for. Distinguishing between superficial understanding and insufficiently explicit responses is a particular problem associated with marking the 'reason' part of 'predict and reason' questions. However, answers to many of the questions mentioned below display conclusive evidence of pupils' partial understanding of the relevant concepts, as for example, migration (Examples 24, 25 and 26, DES 1985a).

Qualitative marking has also shown evidence of pupils' conceptual misunderstandings. Because the number of questions subjected to category marking is relatively small and because no overall strategy for category marking could be adopted, evidence of 11 year olds' conceptual misunderstanding is less extensive than it could be. Results of surveys by (inter alia) APU and HMI give clear indications of where schools are or where they should be with respect to science and the primary school curriculum. (See, for example, the results from school questionnaires described in APU Science survey reports, DES, 1978; DES, 1985b; DES 1983d.) However, not enough is presently known of where pupils of primary school age are with respect to their conceptual understanding in science. More work in this area will be required if the philosophy of 'starting where the pupils are' is to be extensively applied to primary science curriculum initiatives.

Conceptual misunderstandings identified as a result of qualitative category marking which has taken place in the APU surveys includes misunderstanding between:

—energy and speed (Example 20), dissolving and melting (Example 18) - both described in DES, 1983a;

—pollen distribution and seed/fruit dispersal, agent and mechanism (Example 30, DES, 1984a);

—migration and hibernation (Examples 24 and 25), the nature of heat and how heat differs from temperature (Examples 20 and 22) - both described in DES, 1985a.

There is also evidence of the application of inappropriate concepts, eg:

—differences in particle size, colour and mass (usually referred to as 'weight') to explain why salt dissolves in water but soil does not (Example 18 – DES, 1983a);

—pollen distribution agents and mechanisms (Example 30 – DES, 1984a).

The various misconceptions highlighted above may be less widespread than the relevant pupil response profile leads one to believe. As cautioned in previous reports, words take on idiosyncratic meanings and pupils may in some cases be applying the correct concept but using an incorrect label (eg 'emigrate' for 'migrate', Examples 24 and 25, DES, 1985a, and 'disappear'/'disintegrate' for 'dissolve', Example 18, DES, 1983a). Because of the purposes for which APU surveys were conducted it was not possible to determine more accurately the extent to which this occurs.

With regard to the science assessment framework, 'content' may influence the processes pupils deploy in one very important way. If the content is very familiar, pupils may be able to answer the question by *recall* of specific knowledge rather than the *application* of a generalised principle. Of course *recall* and *application* are not discrete, unrelated processes but represent stages in the development and deployment of pupils' conceptual understanding. Some pupils may be able to answer certain questions by *recall* of specific facts or experience whereas other pupils have to *apply* a generalised principle. The proportion of pupils able to answer by *recall* will be, of course, question–specific. Evidence of how moving from *recall* towards *application* affects mean scores has been presented in previous reports (eg DES, 1981, and DES, 1984a). For example, three questions (DES, 1981) asked pupils to apply the same concept in order to re-order drawings of stages in a life-cycle. Although questions of this type are characterised by relatively high mean scores, the percentage of pupils who selected the correct sequence decreased (by 20+ per cent each time) in the order frog, butterfly, horse-chestnut. This order probably represents the decreasing order of pupils' familiarity with the three organisms concerned. (The same type of question, but this time involving a bean plant, was used in the 1984 survey. This question had a mean score mid-way between that of the frog and butterfly.) It would be interesting to investigate what the effect on mean score would be if the life cycle of a named species of frog, unfamiliar to most 11 year olds, was substituted for the familiar one used in the question discussed above.

Discussion now turns to an analysis of the results from numerical marking of questions. A framework consisting of concept regions (3), concept areas (6) and concept groups (16) has been developed to classify the science concepts thought appropriate for 11 year olds to apply. (Appendix 9 gives more details.) How the six concept areas relate to the more broadly defined concept regions is shown below.

| Concept region | Concept area |
| --- | --- |
| Living things | A Interaction of living things with their environment |
| | B Living things and their life processes |
| Force and energy | C Force |
| | D Energy |

*Continued overleaf*

| Materials and their characteristics | E | The classification and structure of matter |
|---|---|---|
| | F | Chemical interactions |

Taken together there is broad agreement between the ideas embodied within the above framework and statements by, *inter alia,* DES and HMI concerning the nature of the science content thought appropriate for children of primary school age (DES, 1983d, and DES, 1985f). Because of their important role in defining science in the primary school a description of pupils' performance by concept region and concept area is given first. This is followed by a description of performance on selected concept groups.

Average mean scores of questions grouped by concept region are shown in Table 9.4 below. Reference to this table shows little apparent difference in the overall mean scores of the three concept regions although individual question mean scores have a more restricted range for Materials and their characteristics than for either Living things or Force and energy. Any differences that can be discerned are probably opposite to those expected given the (over) emphasis on studies of living material, both plant and animal in some primary schools (DES, 1984a). However the observed near equivalence of mean scores across the three concept regions may not result from any positive outcomes of primary school science curricula. It may simply be a measure of pupils' conceptual understanding in science resulting from 11 years of experience restricted to the 'everyday'. Possible corroborative evidence comes from the surveys of pupils aged 15 years. Equivalence of mean scores across the three concept regions was noted for the lowest ability group of 15 year olds (DES, 1986c). These pupils are the least likely of all 15 year olds to have received either a sustained or balanced course of science experiences. The possibility that the observed near equivalence of mean scores simply reflects an unconscious attempt on the part of question writers to make the three question groups of more or less comparable difficulty also needs to be considered.

**Table 9.4** *Summary of mean scores by concept region* (1980–84 data)

| Concept region | Number of questions | Overall mean % | Range of means |
|---|---|---|---|
| Living things | 48 | 32 | 6–95 |
| Force and energy | 65 | 35 | 6–89 |
| Materials and their characteristics | 22 | 36 | 8–68 |

It is evident from Table 9.2 (page 67) that the total number of questions in each concept region and the composition by Question type across concept regions is different. It is possible to identify three factors which contribute to these observed differences:

The different extent to which pupils have been exposed, both in school and out of school, to experiences which

aid development of concepts within each concept region.

The breadth and depth of these experiences in relation to the underlying concepts.

The extent to which it is possible to write questions appropriate to 11 year olds within other imposed constraints such as language demand, both reading and writing, question length etc.

In order to give a more detailed description of pupils' performance it is necessary to sub-divide the broad-based concept regions into more closely defined concept groupings. In the subsequent discussion each concept region has been broken down into two concept areas which in turn have been sub-divided into small groups of closely allied concept statements. (See Appendix 9 for more details.)

Question results for each concept area are shown in Table 9.5 below.

**Table 9.5** *Summary of mean scores by concept area* (1980–84 data)

| Concept area | Number of questions | Overall mean % | Range of means |
|---|---|---|---|
| Interaction of living things with their environment | 37 | 30 | 6–59 |
| Living things and their life processes | 11 | 39 | 7–95 |
| Force | 45 | 35 | 6–78 |
| Energy | 20 | 34 | 11–89 |
| The classification and structure of matter | 18 | 39 | 8–68 |
| Chemical interactions | 4 | 26 | 19–31 |

Reference to Table 9.5 indicates that the apparent similarity between overall mean scores across the three concept regions (Living things, Force and energy, and Materials and their characteristics) is only superficial. Pupils were most likely to gain marks on the group of questions which asked either about 'Living things and their life processes' or the 'Classification and structure of matter'. They were least likely to gain marks on the group of questions which asked about either 'Chemical interactions' (though this group is represented by only four questions) or the 'Interaction of living things with their environment'. It is stressed that the above statements refer to groups of questions and not to individual questions. It will be obvious from a study of the range of individual mean scores shown in Table 9.5 that it is possible to pick *small* groups of questions where the above generalisations are reversed. It would seem evident that the concept regions 'Living things' and 'Materials and their characteristics' are characterised by each comprising a concept area which pupils found relatively easy and another which pupils found relatively difficult. The concept areas 'Force' and 'Energy' pupils tended to find of intermediate difficulty.

As mentioned previously, the six concept areas can be sub-divided into a number (16 in the case of surveys at age 11) of closely allied concept groupings. The number of questions within each concept grouping varied from one to twenty-two. One must therefore be wary of comparative statements at this level since effects due to possible bias (eg question type, question content) cannot be discounted. Results for the nine concept groupings where five or more different questions were used in the surveys are shown in Table 9.6 below.

**Table 9.6** *Summary of mean scores for selected concept groupings*

| Concept grouping | | Number of questions used | Overall mean % | Range of means |
|---|---|---|---|---|
| Ai | Interdependence of living things | 22 | 33 | 9–57 |
| Aii | The physical and chemical environment | 14 | 26 | 6–59 |
| Bii | Reproduction | 5 | 63 | 12–95 |
| Ci | Movement and deformation | 14 | 38 | 7–68 |
| Cii | Properties of matter | 21 | 33 | 9–70 |
| Civ | The Earth in space | 8 | 37 | 21–59 |
| Dii | Electricity | 8 | 32 | 11–89 |
| Diii | Waves | 8 | 38 | 21–53 |
| Ei | States of matter | 14 | 32 | 5–55 |

In Survey No. 3 schools were asked to state which of 14 specified topics had been (or were to be) explored in their 11 year olds' written and/or practical work in science. Results are shown in Table 2.6 of Report No 3 (DES, 1984a, page 18, *et seq*). Hence it is possible to compare *in a very rough* fashion the level of pupils' competence to apply science concepts and the likelihood that they have been exposed to school-based science experiences which aid development of relevant concepts. Not surprisingly perhaps, such comparisons appear to suggest a direct association between competence and exposure. However, given the nature of the data in Table 9.6, this point is made, only very tentatively, in the nature of a hypothesis worthy of further exploration.

It is possibly the case that by the end of their primary schooling pupils have, for one reason or another, developed a conceptual understanding in science which demonstrates an inherent imbalance both between and within the groups of science concepts as defined by the APU. If this were true, then there would appear to be a case for primary school science to take compensatory action to redress the balance. This is not to suggest that the imbalance results solely from any lack of balance in pupils' primary science experiences. Powerful everyday experiences may channel development along a narrow band of concepts to the detriment of others. The net result may be that pupils' science conceptual understanding of the world is not only restricted and superficial but may also lack balance and progression. This in itself indicates avenues for possible future developments in primary science.

*Mode of data presentation*

The question stem exerts influence upon pupils performance in a number of ways. These include (a) the extent to which pupils are able to perceive the nature of the task being posed by the question; (b) the ease with which pupils are able to internalise *relevant* data; and (c) the extent to which the question focuses pupils' attention on the concept or knowledge to be applied.

All questions in the **Application** subcategory are presented to pupils on a single sheet of A4 paper, and nearly all contain a drawing of some form or another. In some questions this drawing describes essential data or information, in others it is simply illustrative, either giving the question a more appealing visual impact, so enhancing pupils' motivation, or acting as an *aide-mémoire*. The mere fact that a drawing is present enables pupils to glean some information additional to that presented by the prose part of the question. It is usually assumed that this additional information is helpful but this is not necessarily so for all pupils (see Example 22, DES, 1985a). Furthermore, visual data in the form of drawings convey irrelevant as well as relevant information to pupils to an extent which, because of its greater impact, may be far larger than that of the written word.

A few questions did not include a drawing in some form or another. Of these questions, most included either a graph or a table of numbers instead. Such questions tended to have relatively low mean scores, frequently less than 10 per cent of the maximum. Questions in which *all* essential data or information are conveyed in the form of drawings frequently have high mean scores, sometimes in excess of 90 per cent of the maximum (see Example Question 18, DES, 1981). However, this is not a hard and fast rule and, as mentioned earlier, other factors are important in determining overall mean scores. The mode of information presentation is not an area in which clear data exist within this subcategory, as to present matched questions based on similar conceptual demand would distort the question pool. It may be assumed that the issues discussed in the previous chapter relating to data presentation also apply when the assessment burden is on concept application.

## 9.3 Gender-related differences in performance

Differences in the performance of boys and girls will be described in relation to two factors only: Question type and concept to be applied.

Considering Question type first, overall mean scores for boys and girls were similar across all response styles. Generally differences were less than 3 per cent (but in favour of boys) except for the Question types 'supply a prediction' (19 questions) and 'select a prediction' (13 questions) where the differences were 8 per cent and 4 per cent respectively. This finding is in agreement with that described in previous reports of performance in this and other subcategories; a short written response tending to favour boys, an extended written response tending to result in a small performance difference between the sexes.

However, differences were small and any such conclusions should be tempered with caution. Across all questions, the average mean score for boys was higher than that for girls by just under 3 per cent.

Differences in the performance of boys and girls in relation to the concept applied were equally small. Only in the concept region 'Force and energy' was any difference in mean score observed (6 per cent in favour of boys based on a sample of 65 questions). The difference was marginally higher for questions about 'Energy' than for questions about 'Force'. Within the concept region 'Force and energy' the *difference* in performance was largest (9 per cent) on the eight questions about 'Electricity' and smallest (4 per cent) on the 8 questions about 'Gravity and its effect on objects' (the Earth in space). However, five of the eight 'Electricity' questions required pupils either to supply or to select a prediction only, a response style identified previously as tending to favour boys.

## 9.4 Generating alternative hypotheses

Questions in this subcategory attempt to assess pupils' ability to suggest possible alternative explanations for given observations or events. Unlike questions in the **Application** subcategory, where only one answer is assumed correct, these questions are concerned with both creative and selective applications of science concepts. Questions are written so that there is no one best explanation. Pupils are asked to be divergent in their thinking and to select from their experiences and apply appropriate science concepts in order to give two possible explanations for the presented information. [Example Questions are given in Reports Nos 1 (Examples 22, 23 and 24), 2 (Example 20) and 3 (Examples 35 and 36) – DES, 1981, 1983a and 1984a.] The assessment focuses on three areas of interest:

The extent to which the age group under consideration is capable of accepting that more than one explanation for a given situation may be possible.

The diversity of explanations which 11 year olds as a group give and hence the range of concepts applied.

The type of concepts pupils choose to apply.

Although a generalised numerical marking scheme has been adopted for all questions, no attempt has been made to aggregate scores across questions since it was realised that any description of performance in terms of the above foci of interest would be specific to the context and content of individual questions. However, it is possible to give some qualitative generalised statements about pupils' performance with respect to the three areas of interest, bearing in mind that only nine questions have been used in the surveys.

Averaged across questions, about 85 per cent of pupils gave two explanations for the presented information. For each statement two marks were awarded if it was consistent with the presented information and gave an explanation of how the effect was caused. One mark was awarded to suggestions which were reasonable but which included no explanation. This made a total of four marks for each question. However, as one might anticipate, the quality of answers from those pupils who did give two explanations was generally lower for the second explanation than for the first. For all questions, a similar mark distribution was observed. For the first explanation the mark distribution was characterised by the number of pupils awarded zero, one and two marks decreasing in the order mark 1 > mark 0 > mark 2; the second explanation was characterised by the order mark 0 > mark 1 > mark 2. Therefore most pupils who were awarded marks gained them for a partial explanation for the given observations or events, usually an outcome in specific rather than general terms (see Report No 2, Example 20 and 3, Examples 35 and 36 – DES, 1983a, and DES, 1984a). Explanations were frequently a simple application of everyday experiences. Marks tended to be higher on questions where pupils could apply their everyday experiences directly rather than have to apply a generalised principle.

In addition to the generalised numerical mark scheme, question-specific, qualitative (categorical) marking schemes were also developed. In order to describe adequately the full range of explanations pupils gave it was usual for the qualitative mark scheme to consist of more than twenty discrete categories. Some indication of the diversity of the explanations which 11 year olds gave, both as a group and as individuals, is given in Report No 2 (Example 20 and 3, Examples 35 and 36 – DES, 1983a and 1984a).

As might be expected, the types of concepts and experiences pupils applied were very question-dependent. For example, science-specific concepts and knowledge were more frequently applied in questions where the links with pupils' experiences were through science-based work in schools. However, where the context was less well known and the links with experience less direct, then pupils frequently either applied incorrect or inappropriate concepts and knowledge or assumed information beyond that given in the question. Although the number varied from question to question, relatively few pupils applied appropriate 'commonsense', everyday, non-science experiences in their answers to questions in this subcategory. The statement, 'they have not been pruned', given by one pupil to explain why one set of rose bushes was taller than the other (Example 20, page 137, DES, 1983a) illustrates the last mentioned category of answer.

## 9.5 Summary

Results from all five surveys have been incorporated into a discussion of performance in the **Application** subcategory. In total, results from 135 different questions have been included.

Questions have been grouped by Question type and concept to be applied. Grouped either way, questions did not fall into a neat hierarchy of difficulty. Mean scores for most questions lay within the range 10–60 per cent of the maximum. Questions above this range were usually associated with supplying or selecting predictions only; questions below this range were usually associated with supplying explanations. Pupils found questions requiring answers to be selected generally easier than questions where the answer had to be supplied. Questions requiring predictions only were generally easier to gain marks on than questions where in addition reasons for predictions had to be supplied.

Pupils found questions requiring application of concepts about either 'Living things and their life processes' or the 'Classification and structure of matter' easiest to gain marks on.

Average mean scores of boys and girls were similar across all Question types. Differences were largest (in favour of boys) on questions requiring predictions to be either selected or supplied. Differences were equally small when questions were grouped by concept. The difference was largest (again in favour of boys) on questions requiring application of concepts about 'Force and energy', in particular those about 'Electricity'.

Most pupils were able to supply alternative explanations for a given set of observations. Answers to each question encompassed a wide range of applied concepts, most of which were classified as scientific rather than everyday, 'common sense'. This was particularly true in questions where the link between question content and pupils' experience is likely to be through school-based work in science. In unfamiliar situations, where links with experience are less direct, pupils often assumed information beyond that given in the question. Most pupils gained marks for stating explanations in specific rather than general terms. Marks were highest on questions requiring direct application of everyday experiences rather than application of a generalised principle.

# 10

# Planning of investigations

## 10.1 Background

The assessment of ability to plan investigations is an area where little work had been done prior to the APU's science surveys. It was recognised that a considerable amount of exploration, of trial and revision, would be needed to reach a useful structure for a bank of questions for this category and for this reason its assessment was not included in the first survey (1980) at age 11. Development and trials took place in 1979 and 1980 in preparation for including the assessment of **Planning** in the second survey (in 1981). However the number of questions included in the survey for this category in 1981 was rather small (see below) by the standards adopted later, and the bank from which they were drawn was also small. As reported at the time (DES 1983a, page 91) it had been found difficult to produce satisfactory questions and many had been rejected at the trial stage. The results obtained in the 1981 survey have, therefore, to be treated with considerable caution.

A major review of the nature of **Planning** was begun after the 1981 survey. The decision was taken not to include the assessment of **Planning** in the 1982 survey, apart from a few selected questions on the planning of whole investigations. These were designed to explore the effect on performance of planning as a purely written exercise, compared with planning in the context of carrying out an investigation (DES, 1984a, Chapter 3). This gave time during 1982 for the structure of the category to be revised and for a substantial number of questions to be written. Few of the original questions were retained and therefore the surveys in 1983 and 1984 were carried out effectively from a new base-line. The Category structure now outlined is the one which emerged from the major revision and was used in the fourth and fifth surveys.

The two subcategories of **Planning** are:

> **Planning parts of investigations**
> **Planning entire investigations**

The first of these is represented by a pool of short questions (206 in number) and the second by a small number of extended answer questions (14 in number). Random sets of questions have been computer-selected from the pool for **Planning parts of investigations** and subcategory score estimates have been based on the results. For **Planning entire investigations** a few questions have been hand-picked and reported in full; no subcategory score has been calculated.

In **Planning parts of investigations**, as the title suggests, the questions ask about a particular part of the planning process and present necessary information about other parts. For example, to focus a question on what is to be measured or compared to determine the outcome of an investigation, it is necessary to state the problem in general terms and to describe the way the investigation was set up. Different types of question have been identified, focusing on different parts of the process. The types are summarised in the next section.

In **Planning entire investigations** the questions present a problem, expressed sometimes in very general terms and sometimes being more specific (as in the example on page 79). Answering these questions fully demands a description of how an investigation might be set up, which variables would be changed, which kept the same, which measured or compared, how steps might be taken to ensure a reliable result and how the results would be related to the initial problem. These aspects of answers are assessed separately using a detailed system of qualitative marking categories and performance can be related to performance in the corresponding parts of investigations when these are presented as separate questions.

The **Planning** category also contains a few additional short questions which assess **Identifying or proposing testable statements**. This prior ability in the process of planning involves distinguishing problems which can be tackled by investigation from those which cannot, either because they are insufficiently defined or are matters of value judgement. These questions have been reported individually (as, for example, in DES, 1985a, pages 189–193).

The numbers of questions of various kinds used in the surveys is summarised in Table 10.1.

**Table 10.1** *Summary of assessment of 'Planning of investigations' in the five surveys*

| | Number of questions used | | | | |
|---|---|---|---|---|---|
| | 1980 | 1981 | 1982 | 1983 | 1984 |
| Planning parts of investigations | – | 13(43*) | – | 56(124*) | 70(206*) |
| Planning entire investigations | – | 2 | 4 | 3 | 2 |
| Identifying or proposing testable statements | – | 4 | – | 4 | – |

\* Size of pool at time of survey

## 10.2 Planning parts of investigations

The pool of questions is structured in terms of seven types of question which are described in Table 10.2. Table 10.2 also gives numbers of questions available and range of means for each type, the information being restricted to the 1983 and 1984 surveys when the revised category structure was implemented.

The numbers of questions used reflects the number of questions of each type in the pool. There are two reasons for the much greater number of the first type of question. When the revised structure was designed there were two question types focusing on the variables to be controlled, one in which operational details of the given investigation were supplied and the other in which the investigation was expressed only in general terms. Both types were heavily represented in the age 11 bank since they reflect the attention given to 'fair testing' in primary school science. Approximately twice the number of these questions as of other Question types were produced. Trial results showed, however, that the distinction between the questions with and without operational details was difficult to sustain. Questions could not always be unambiguously categorised as being of one type or the other and there were no systematic differences in performance which were associated with presence or absence of operational details in the given question. Thus the two types were combined and the total number of questions of this type was consequently about four times that of any other.

It is evident in Table 10.2 that there is a considerable difference in performance between the first four question types and the last three. The difference in the kind of question demand between these two groups which seems the most probable explanation of this difference in performance, is that the last three types all concern in some way the variable to be measured. It appears from evidence derived from other parts of the surveys (see Chapter 11, for example) that children have particular difficulty with aspects of investigations concerning measurements, taking steps to make measurements reliable and using their measurements. These parts of an investigation are carried out in practice towards the end of a set of procedures, by definition, but if they are to be carried out effectively they need to be planned at the same time as the control of other variables.

It is not unexpected that children might have difficulty thinking through a number of steps in an investigation and 'tail off' before they reach the end. This would explain poor performance in these later aspects of an investigation plan when planning a whole investigation. It does not explain the poor performance in the context of planning parts of an investigation, where the Questions fill in the earlier steps in planning so as to focus only on particular later ones. Further light is shed on this problem by examining the children's answers, and particularly their incomplete or inaccurate answers, to the individual questions. The following brief comments on each Question type summarise what has been found from such analyses.

*Type 1: identifying the variables to be controlled*

Questions of this type had the highest mean scores of all types, taking the picture across the fourth and fifth surveys together. Values of question facility clustered relatively closely round the mean, varying mainly between 23 per cent and 67 per cent. The questions were all of open response format, in which pupils had to supply the names of variables which would have to be kept the same in a given investigation for the test to be fair.

It was not easy to discern any pattern relating certain features of questions to facility. One possible factor explored in a special set of questions included in the 1983

**Table 10.2** *Mean scores for different types of question used in assessing 'Planning parts of investigations'* (1983 and 1984 data)

| Type | Given by question | Focus of question | Number of questions used | Overall mean score % | Range of means % |
|---|---|---|---|---|---|
| 1 | A statement of an investigation with or without experimental details | The variables to be controlled | 43 | 45 | 13 – 80 |
| 2 | A statement of an investigation with or without experimental details | The variables to be changed and controlled | 10 | 36 | 5 – 80 |
| 3 | A statement of an investigation with experimental details | Operational details concerning the variables to be changed and controlled | 9 | 38 | 14 – 65 |
| 4 | A description of a procedure specifying the variables changed and measured | The statement of the problem being investigated | 8 | 39 | 32 – 53 |
| 5 | A statement of an investigation with details of the variable being changed | Operational details concerning the variable to be measured | 12 | 17 | 9 – 26 |
| 6 | A description of an investigation including the variable to be measured | Procedures for ensuring valid measurements | 11 | 18 | 8 – 29 |
| 7 | A description of an investigation including the kind of measurements taken | How the measurements can be used to answer the question under investigation | 9 | 19 | 8 – 32 |
| Overall | | | 102 | 35 | 5 – 80 |

survey was the effect of the contextual setting of the question. Comparing facilities of pairs of items, differing as far as possible only in regard to whether they were set in an everyday or a school context, showed no systematic relationship of context with facility. Several questions with very low facilities concerned problems which people might tend to decide by methods other than a scientific test (which carrier bag is stronger, whether paint peels more quickly if the wood is not cleaned before repainting, whether brown bread toasts more quickly than white), but nevertheless there were others of higher facility where this was equally true, so it was not the only factor involved.

In the two random selections of questions for the 1983 and 1984 surveys there were ten questions which were included in both. There was a close correspondence between the facilities for these questions in the two years and no systematic trend in their mean scores.

### Type 2: defining what is to be changed and what kept the same in general terms

These questions, which were sometimes presented in open response and sometimes in fixed answer format, described the first steps in an investigation and focused on what variable to change or keep the same as the investigation proceeded. Whilst interest was in whether the independent variable would be correctly identified, in order to find this out it was necessary to ask about what would not be changed as well as what would be changed.

The average facility for these questions was slightly lower than that for questions of the first Question type. Analysis of patterns of response showed that the limiting factor in performance was the ability to identify the independent variable. In general, those who did this also correctly identified the variables to be kept the same, whilst those who identified the variables to be controlled did not necessarily give the independent variable correctly. This fits in with the relative facilities of types 1 and 2. One of the common errors could be described as an 'all change' syndrome; a tendency to change more than one correct independent variable. This was found to a considerable degree also in the next type of question.

There were few gender-related differences of note in this type of question; the small ones which were found were more often in favour of the girls.

### Type 3: defining what is to be changed and not changed (the independent and controlled variables) in operational terms

The focus of three questions was the same as for those discussed above, but the problem of the independent and controlled variables had to be considered at a more detailed level. The difference can be illustrated by a question about bouncing balls asking how to find out if the surface makes a difference to how the balls bounce. In the general form (type 2) the question would be asked

in terms of the names of the variables – the surface to be changed, whilst the ball and height of drop were to be kept the same. In the operational form the question might be posed in terms of which ball, which surface and which height should be chosen after a particular ball, surface and height had already been used.

Pupils generally found questions posed at the operational level easier than those at the general level. This was despite a rather more stringent marking scheme applied to questions of type 3 than to type 2, according to which no marks were given unless the independent variable was changed. In type 2 questions it was theoretically possible to obtain some marks for controlling variables even if the independent variable was not identified, although as already noted this was not a common pattern of answer. Thus it appeared that pupils were more able to plan how to set up an investigation in terms of specific actions to be taken rather than through considering the actions at a more general level.

### Type 4: identifying the problem under investigation from the procedures used

Questions of this type at age 11 used a common format. Each consisted of an account of a set of procedures which had been conducted, illustrated by a drawing. The independent, controlled and dependent variables were identified implicitly in the procedures. The problem was to decide whether or not each of four given questions would be answered by the procedures. Generally, but not invariably, two of the statements were questions which would be answered and two were not. Pupils were asked to put a tick or a cross by each one. The chance of success by guessing was to some extent taken into account in the mark schemes.

A prominent pattern in answers to these questions was the greater success pupils had in ticking correct statements as compared with marks gained by disagreeing with incorrect ones. Invariably the highest proportion of marks was gained from ticks rather than crosses. There seemed no obvious reason why correct answers should be more easy to spot than incorrect ones; indeed the incorrect ones seemed, at least to an adult, rather too obviously false. Part of the explanation might be that the form of question is unfamiliar to children, who are generally given problems where the emphasis is upon the right answer rather than weighing up all types of answer. Perhaps a certain reluctance to disagree with a printed statement results from this experience.

### Type 5: defining what is to be measured or compared (the dependent variable)

For this and subsequent Question types performance was consistently found to fall to below half the level for the Question types so far discussed. This change is accompanied by an increase in non-response rate to about 11 per cent as compared with about 5 per cent for the first four Question types in Table 10.2. Questions of Type 5 were of an open response format. The question gave a description of a problem and of how an investigation was set up to tackle it, including details of equipment used. Pupils were then asked to suggest what should be measured or compared to find the result of the investigation.

Less than 5 per cent of pupils scored full marks on any of the questions of this type in either of the surveys under discussion. In no case in 1984 did the mean performance level for a question exceed 20 per cent. (This happened in one question in 1983, where a mean of 37 per cent was reported for a question about measuring change in rate of heart beats. This question was also included in the 1984 survey, where its mean score was found to be 20 per cent. The difference was traced to a systematic error in the application of the mark scheme in 1983.)

Typical score profiles for these questions showed between 60 per cent and 80 per cent gaining no marks, between 15 per cent and 30 per cent gaining one mark, 5 per cent to 15 per cent gaining two marks and under 4 per cent gaining full marks. Translated into characteristics of answers this means that by far the majority of answers were so vague, imprecise or irrelevant that no mark could be awarded. Up to 30 per cent gained their one mark generally by an answer which was relevant in vague terms but did not specify the quantities to be measured. The most common expression in these answers was along the lines of 'see how many/how much/which is most', without further elaboration. However, there was some evidence, in the number of irrelevant answers or ones which answered a different question from the one posed, that these questions were of an unfamiliar type (the unfamiliarity being possibly not so much with the form of question as with the task of specifying this part of a plan). There were perhaps only 25 per cent whose zero scores could be explained in this way (including non-respondents). Thus a further 35 to 55 per cent attempted an answer but failed to produce one worthy of a mark.

## Type 6: procedures for ensuring valid measurements

These questions described a problem and a way of tackling it, invariably in the form of an account of actions taken by some children involved in an enquiry. To focus on the way the measurements were made, pupils were asked in some cases to give possible reasons why certain procedures were adopted (why measurements were repeated, for example, as in the question in Figure 10.1), in others to say what was wrong with the measuring procedures used or to suggest ways of achieving more accurate results. Scoring levels were uniformly low for these questions (close to the average of 20 per cent) and not noticeably affected by whether the demand was to identify the inaccuracies in a given procedure or to propose a more accurate procedure. Non-response rates tended to be high (11 per cent and 15 per cent in 1983 and 1984 respectively) but there was little evidence in the non-scoring answers that children did not understand the question. Their answers appeared to derive from not recognising the procedures

that would make measurement more accurate. Thus, for example, they suggested that the problem of trying to measure a small difference in volume with a measuring cylinder should be solved by reading the scale more carefully (rather than increasing the difference, as was possible within the problem).

The answer given in Figure 10.1 also illustrates a common misunderstanding of the reason for repeating measurements. In this and in other questions children indicated that repetition would make sure the measurement was right or would tell you whether or not it was right. There is an indication here that simply ensuring that pupils repeat measurements is not necessarily adding to their understanding of the inherent errors in any measurement.

**Figure 10.1** *A common misunderstanding of the reason for repeating measurements*

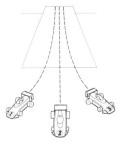

Winston had three toy cars. *He wanted to find out which one would travel furthest if thery were all given the same chance.* He set up the experiment below:

- He rolled each car down a ramp
- He used the same start position for the cars
- He marked the final position of each one
- He measured the distance each car travelled

The diagram shows the final position of each car.

After looking at his results he decided to repeat the experiment before reaching a conclusion.

Why do you think he repeated his experiment?

*To make sure the cars could travel the same distance again.* . . . . . . . . . . . . . . . . . . . . . .

## Type 7: using the results

Questions of this type took the child right through an investigation, to the point at which measurements (assumed reliable) or comparisons had been made. The focus was then on how the results would be used to decide the answer to the investigation. Drawings helped to convey what was inevitably quite a large amount of information to take in for these questions. However there was undoubtedly a problem of communicating a question about how an answer would be found as distinct from what the answer would be. A very common type of error is illustrated by the answer in Figure 10.2 (p. 78). Other patterns of error across these questions were to repeat or criticise features of the procedures given. Answers addressed to the question posed were given by about one-third of the sample and the majority of these were incomplete. They mentioned comparison of measurements but generally did not link these back to the problem under investigation. It was not possible to know from the results whether this was because the link was possibly seen as too obvious to mention or whether pupils do tend to lose sight of the initial problem by the time they reach the end of an extended set of actions.

**Figure 10.2** *A common error in the use of results*

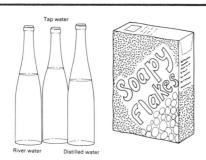

Tap water

River water    Distilled water

After a school journey to a river, Ann's class did some experiments with the water they brought back. One thing they did was to see how easily they could make a lather with the water compared with tap water and distilled water.

This is what they did:

1. Put equal amounts of the three kinds of water in three bottles.
2. Added soap flakes one at a time to each one.
3. Shook the water up with the soap flakes.
4. If the lather disappeared when they stopped shaking they added another soap flake.
5. They went on doing this until the lather did not disappear and counted the number of soap flakes needed for each one.

How would they use these results to find out how easily the river water lathered compared with the tap water and the distilled water?

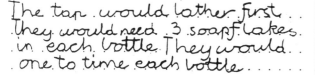

## 10.3 Planning entire investigations

In contrast with some of the questions assessing performance in preparing parts of an investigation plan, those assessing the preparation of a whole plan can be briefly posed but require a lengthy answer. The understanding of the question is thus not a large problem, but the generally high non-response rate (around 20 per cent) is probably accounted for by the writing demand which is signalled by the space provided for answering as well as by the nature of the question. A few questions only have been included in any one survey (Table 10.1), and there is no attempt to form an overall score for this subcategory.

Whilst the results clearly show that the particular subject matter of the investigation to be planned has a considerable influence on the adequacy of the answers, there are nonetheless patterns in responses across different questions which enable certain general statements to be made about children's performance in written plans for scientific investigations. These patterns are brought out by the use of mark schemes which have as far as possible a common structure relating to various components of a plan. Categories of response within each component are specific to each investigation. Examples of these mark schemes are provided on pages 79–81 relating to the two questions from this subcategory included in the 1984 survey. Schemes with this structure were not used in the 1981 survey and therefore the results of the questions used in that year are not included in this summary.

Performances in the various questions in the last three surveys are summarised in Table 10.3 in terms of the main generalised components of planning. The proportions for each component are found by summing frequencies for the appropriate categories in the marking schemes. The percentage scores included in Table 10.3 are derived from those categories to which marks are awarded (these are indicated for the two examples in the schemes on pages 79–81).

**Table 10.3** *Summary of performance in 'Planning entire investigations' in questions used in the 1982, 1983 and 1984 surveys*

(Percentage of pupils, including non-responders)

| Year of survey: | 1982 | | | | 1983 | 1984 | |
| --- | --- | --- | --- | --- | --- | --- | --- |
| Question name | Chopping board | Paper towels | Mealworms | Swing-boards | Bouncing balls | Snails | Shadows |
| Response attempted | 84 | 78 | 83 | 76 | 84 | 82 | 79 |
| Investigation proposed | 66 | 58 | 67 | 59 | 59 | 75 | 38 |
| Independent variable: | | | | | | | |
|   identified | 61 | 52 | 55 | 38 | 40 | 40 | 31 |
|   operationalised | 19 | 39 | 33 | 9 | 34 | 10 | 6 |
| Variables controlled (any) | 5 | 14 | 12 | 1 | 11 | 8 | 3 |
| Dependent variable: | | | | | | | |
|   identified | 52 | 31 | 52 | 30 | 22 | 39 | 8 |
|   operationalised | 45 | 24 | 28 | 9 | 13 | 26 | 4 |
| Results interpreted | 24 | 18 | 20 | 4 | 7 | 8 | 0 |
| Number of pupils | 904 | 904 | 909 | 898 | 135* | 127* | 260 |
| % mean score | 23 | 21 | 25 | 14 | 19 | 15 | 6 |

* Numbers refer to sub-sample marked in detail.

**Example 1** *'Snails' question and sample answer*

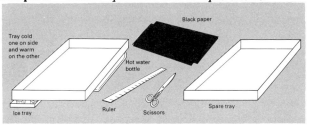

Suppose you have some snails and you want to find out something about the conditions they prefer. You have a tray which can be made cold on one side and warm on the other, and all the other equipment shown in the drawing above. (You don't have to use all of it)

What would you do to find out.

> Which of these places do the snails prefer if they are given a choice?
>
> cold and dark
> cold and light
> warm and dark
> warm and light.

Make sure you say:
- which things you would use
- what you would do with them
- how you would find out the result

*I would use The tray with a warm and cold side, 2 strips of black paper, scissors and ruler. I would put 1 strip of black paper over half of the cold side and put the other black strip over half of the warm side. Then I would put the snails in the tray and leave them for an hour. After an hour I would look where the snails had gone.*

Category codes for this answer:

1. A
2. A (1)
3. C
4. A (2)
5. B (1)
6. B (1)
7. C (1)
8. D

Score = 6

## Mark scheme and results

Each answer receives 8 category labels, one from each of the headings. Marks out of 7 are composed from those categories where a mark is indicated in brackets.

|  |  | % pupils (n = 127) |
|---|---|---|
| **1. Interpretation of question demand** | | |
| Plan attempted to investigate given problem | A | 62 |
| Describes investigation previously done | B | 0 |
| Describes alternative investigation | C | 0 |
| Supplies answer and gives investigation plan | D | 13 |
| Supplies answer, no investigation plan | E | 5 |
| Statement not relevant to problem | F | 2 |
| No response | N | 18 |
| **2. Equipment used—given** | | |
| Warm and cold tray only + black paper | A (1) | 20 |
| One tray only (not identified) + black paper | B | 11 |
| Spare tray only + black paper | C | 9 |
| Both trays + black paper | D | 7 |
| Tray(s) but no black paper mentioned | E | 17 |
| No reference to equipment given | F | 10 |
| Not relevant (no investigation) | G | 7 |
| Black paper only | H | 2 |
| **3. Equipment used—not given** | | |
| Reference to equipment not given in addition to that given | A | 5 |
| Reference only to equipment other than that given | B | 5 |
| No reference to equipment not given | C | 65 |
| Not relevant (no investigation) | D | 7 |
| **4. Independent variables set up** | | |
| The four different conditions set up as choice in one tray | A (2) | 5 |
| Two different conditions only available as choice | B | 18 |
| The four conditions set up but in different trays | C (1) | 5 |
| One condition only provided— warm and dark | D | 12 |
| One condition only provided— other | E | 15 |
| Conditions not specified | F | 29 |
| Not relevant (no investigation) | G | 7 |

*Continued overleaf*

## 5. Variables controlled

| | | | |
|---|---|---|---|
| Initial position of snails + equal areas of conditions + time of exposure | A | (1) | 0 |
| Any two of above | B | (1) | 0 |
| Initial position of snails only | C | (1) | 6 |
| Equal areas of conditions | D | (1) | 2 |
| Time of exposure only | E | (1) | 0 |
| No reference to controlled variables | F | | 67 |
| Not relevant (no investigation) | G | | 7 |

## 6. Number of snails

| | | | |
|---|---|---|---|
| Specified number >5 | A | (1) | 0 |
| Specified number >1 <5 | F | (1) | 5 |
| Snails (plural) but number unspecified | B | (1) | 26 |
| One snail only implied or stated | C | | 26 |
| No reference to number | D | | 17 |
| Not relevant (no investigation) | E | | 8 |

## 7. Measurements or observations made

| | | | |
|---|---|---|---|
| Find/count number of snails in each part | A | (1) | 1 |
| Measure how far snail(s) had moved/time movement | B | (1) | 5 |
| 'See' where snail(s) are/what they do | C | (1) | 20 |
| See which snail(s) like/prefer (if choice) | D | | 3 |
| See if snail(s) like it (no choice) | E | | 2 |
| See what happens | F | | 2 |
| Other effects observed (e.g. whether they live or die) | G | | 8 |
| No reference to observing a result | H | | 34 |
| Not relevant (no investigation) | I | | 7 |

## 8. Use of results

| | | | |
|---|---|---|---|
| Use positions to indicate what they most like/prefer | A | (1) | 6 |
| Use other evidence or effects to decide which they prefer | B | (1) | 2 |
| Direct observation of preference (as in 6D) | C | | 2 |
| No reference to using results obtained | D | | 30 |
| No results observed | E | | 34 |
| No relevant (no investigation) | F | | 7 |

---

## Example 2   *'Shadows' question and sample answer*

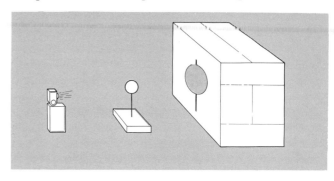

Suppose you have a torch, a ball on a stand and a box, as shown in this drawing. When you switch on the torch there is a shadow of the ball on the side of the box.

What would you do with these things to find out:

> How does the size of the shadow change when you move
>> the torch
>> the ball
>> the box

Make sure you say:
- which things you would use
- what you would do with them
- how you would find out the result

*Moving the torch. I would use all three things, and first put the torch in the position illustrated. I would draw around the shadow. I would move the torch back 5 cm and draw around the shadow again then I would move it 5 cm forward from it's first position and draw around the shadow for a third time. I would then calculate how the area of the shadow changed per 5cm. I would move the ball & box forward and back 5cm and calculate the shadow in the same way.*

Category codes for this answer:

1. A
2. A (1)
3. A (1)
4. A (2)
5. C
6. B (1)
7. B
8. A (1)

Score = 6

(*Example 2*) **Mark scheme and results**

Each answer receives 8 category labels, one from each of the headings. Marks out of 7 are composed from those categories where a mark is indicated in brackets.

| | Category | % pupils (n = 260) |
|---|---|---|
| **1. Interpretation of question demand** | | |
| Plan attempted to investigate given problems | A | 23 |
| Describes investigation previously done | B | 0 |
| Describes alternative investigation | C | 7 |
| Supplies answer and gives investigation plan | D | 8 |
| Supplies answer, no investigation plan | E | 30 |
| Statement not relevant to problem posed | F | 8 |
| No investigation plan | G | 3 |
| No response | N | 21 |

| | Category | % |
|---|---|---|
| **2. Use of equipment** | | |
| Use of given items made explicit | A (1) | 12 |
| Use of given items plus measuring instrument | B (1) | 1 |
| Reference to given items, no explicit use | C | 17 |
| Reference to some, not all, items | D | 15 |
| No reference to any of given items | E | 1 |
| Reference to other equipment not given (apart from measuring instrument) | F | 2 |
| No investigation | G | 33 |

| | Category | % |
|---|---|---|
| **3. Independent variables** | | |
| Movement of torch, box and ball independently | A (1) | 6 |
| Movement of torch (or equivalent) only | B | 11 |
| Movement of ball (or equivalent) only | C | 6 |
| Movement of box (or equivalent) only | D | 2 |
| Movement of torch and ball | E | 3 |
| Movement of torch and box | F | 2 |
| Movement of box and ball | G | 1 |
| No mention of moving any item to find effect | H | 15 |
| 'Movement' interpreted as moving out of the way | I | 1 |
| No investigation | J | 33 |

| | Category | % |
|---|---|---|
| **4. Range of variation** | | |
| Direction and range of movement of object specified (e.g. closer and further away) | A (2) | 4 |
| Movement specified in one direction only | B (1) | 8 |
| Movement, without range or direction, mentioned | C | 18 |
| No movement specified for finding effect (other than moving out of the way) | D | 16 |
| No investigation | E | 33 |

| | Category | % |
|---|---|---|
| **5. Variables controlled** | | |
| Control of position of two variables whilst third changed | A (1) | 3 |
| Position of one variable made explicit whilst other changed | B | 0 |
| No mention of other variables whilst one changed | C | 27 |
| Not relevant (no movement or no investigation) | D | 50 |

| | Category | % |
|---|---|---|
| **6. Observation of dependent variable** | | |
| Size of shadow on box measured | A (1) | 3 |
| Size of shadow on box observed | B (1) | 1 |
| Look at the box | C | 1 |
| Look at the shadow | D | 3 |
| 'See' what happens | E | 4 |
| No mention of any observations when objects moved | F | 15 |
| Not relevant (no movement or no investigation) | G | 52 |

| | Category | % |
|---|---|---|
| **7. Repetition** | | |
| Mention of repetition to check | A | 0 |
| No mention of repetition | B | 47 |
| No investigation | C | 33 |

| | Category | % |
|---|---|---|
| **8. Use of results** | | |
| For each variable find how size of shadow was affected by the movement | A (1) | 0 |
| See how the shadow changed | B | 1 |
| Find result by looking at shadow | C | 3 |
| No reference to using results | D | 10 |
| Not relevant (no results or no investigation) | E | 66 |

Table 10.3 shows a considerable variation from question to question apart from the first two steps of making a response and proposing some sort of investigation. The independent variable was more readily identified for 'Chopping board', 'Paper towel' and 'Mealworms' (see DES 1984a, pages 31 to 66) where it took the form of different physical objects of the same type (wood, paper, food) which had to be compared. The other questions involved investigation of either combinations or variations of conditions which appeared to present greater difficulty. Describing the way in which the independent variable was to be manipulated (operationalised) presented particular difficulty in the case of 'Swingboards', 'Snails' and 'Shadows'. In the first two of these there were two properties to be considered at the same time and in 'Shadows' the problem was of mentioning the variation of all three variables. Together these findings suggest that pupils had greater difficulty in planning the set-up for investigations where there were two or more different conditions to be considered or two conditions to be combined. Planning to set up straightforward comparisons between objects was found much easier.

Identifying the variable to be measured was found to be easier in the case of 'Chopping board', 'Mealworms' and 'Snails'. In these problems the choice of what to measure was more open than in the other investigations and could be chosen by the child to suit the particular tests they had planned. Performance was low for all investigations in operationalising the measurements and particularly so for 'Swingboards' and 'Shadows' where deciding what measurements to make involved interpreting the meaning of 'how fast it swings' in the former and the 'size of the shadow' in the latter case. These interpretations were clearly influenced by children's conceptual understanding of rate of swinging and size. The sample answer for 'Shadows' on page 80 is one of only 3 per cent which were explicit enough to indicate whether linear dimension or area was taken as the measure of size.

Certain regularities exist in the data for all the investigations, however. Performance is uniformly low in mentioning control of variables. Very few even mentioned keeping any one condition the same for a fair test, let alone mentioning all of the variables that might appropriately have been controlled. Also, performance in relation to the dependent variable is uniformly lower than that

relating to the independent variable. Again for every question very few children discussed the interpretation in terms of what the investigation was designed to find out.

Some comparisons can be made between these findings and the results for the corresponding Question types in **Planning parts of investigations**. It is quite striking that the Question type where performance was highest in planning parts, stating variables to be controlled, was the component of the whole plans where performance was lowest. This seems to suggest that pupils omit from their plans any mention of controlling variables not because they do not realise what is required for a fair test but perhaps because they do not realise that these points should be included in plans for investigations. The performance of pupils in carrying out some of the same investigations in practice lends support to the interpretation, since in practice a much greater proportion of pupils pay attention to controlling variables. The suggestion that pupils are unfamiliar with writing plans, and therefore with what should be included in them, may account for other areas of low performance indicated in Table 10.3, which should not therefore be interpreted as indicating what pupils are capable of doing but only what they do at present. Such evidence as there is from other work suggests that experience of extended planning is quite rare for most children (Galton, Simon and Croll, 1980).

The fall in performance in the Question types of **Planning parts** which were concerned with the dependent variable and use of results (Types 5, 6 and 7, Table 10.2) finds a parallel in the lower performance in these components of the whole investigation plans in Table 10.3. However, the drop in performance is much less, in Table 10.3, for the dependent variable than it is for the interpretation of results. A better comparison with the figures for **Planning parts** can be obtained by taking into account that not all pupils even attempted an investigation. Table 10.4 expresses the findings in Table 10.3 as proportions of those who proposed an investigation of any kind. A crude comparison can be made by averaging across all the questions in Table 10.4. For operationalising the independent variable, the figure obtained is 35 per cent, which compares with an average across questions of type 3 in Table 10.2 of 39 per cent.

**Table 10.4** *Performance in the components of 'Planning entire investigations' expressed as a proportion of those who attempted to propose an investigation*
(Percentage of pupils)

| Question name | Chopping board | Paper towels | Mealworms | Swing-board | Bouncing balls | Snails | Shadows |
|---|---|---|---|---|---|---|---|
| Independent variable: | | | | | | | |
| identified | 92 | 90 | 82 | 64 | 68 | 53 | 82 |
| operationalised | 29 | 67 | 49 | 15 | 58 | 13 | 16 |
| Variables controlled (any) | 8 | 24 | 18 | 2 | 19 | 11 | 8 |
| Dependent variable: | | | | | | | |
| identified | 79 | 53 | 78 | 51 | 37 | 52 | 21 |
| operationalised | 68 | 41 | 42 | 15 | 22 | 35 | 11 |
| Results interpreted | 37 | 31 | 30 | 7 | 12 | 11 | 0 |

For the operationalised dependent variable, Table 10.4, there is an average of 33 per cent, compared with 18 per cent for the comparable Type 5 in Table 10.2. The figures for interpreting results are 18 per cent from both tables. There is a suggestion in these results that pupils may be better able to identify what to measure in the context of a plan of their own rather than within a partially complete one presented to them. One reason may be that in type 5 questions the child had to read, understand and 'take on' the problem posed without having thought through it from the start as he/she does when planning the whole investigation from the start. This suggests that the results of type 5 questions underestimate children's ability in relation to identifying what to measure.

In both contexts the performance is low in stating specifically how results would be interpreted. The evidence of misunderstanding of these questions when presented as parts of an investigation (Type 7) suggests that children are not familiar with being asked to think in these terms. Following the same argument they may omit reference to the use of results in their own plans because of not recognising this as something which should be included. The otherwise excellent answer to the 'Snails' question, shown on page 79, demonstrates the point. The evidence from both planning parts and planning whole investigations suggests that in this case, unlike the measurement of the dependent variable, the lower performance cannot be explained in part by the form of the question.

## 10.4  Identifying or proposing testable statements

Questions assessing ability to distinguish scientifically testable statements from those which cannot be decided by investigation were included in the 1981 and 1983 surveys. In both, some questions were multiple choice, where a statement that was not testable had to be selected from others which were, and some asked for an open response. In all cases, and for both surveys, performance levels were close to 40 per cent.

The main errors in the fixed answer questions were ticking more than one statement; in every case the proportion of pupils giving a multiple response (often over 20 per cent) was greater than for any single wrong answer. As in other categories, this is evidence of the severe limitations of this response format. In the open response questions the main reasons for not giving marks were vagueness in describing testable properties rather than proposing statements about non-testable properties.

## 10.5  Gender-related differences in performance

A review of those questions administered in the 1983 and 1984 surveys shows a relative strength on the part of girls in the **Planning** category. Girls produced higher mean scores than boys on around three-quarters of the 103

questions which have been used to represent **Planning parts of investigations**, and on most or all of the fewer numbers of questions which have represented the sub-categories **Identifying or proposing testable statements**, and **Planning entire investigations**. While 'higher' here refers to anything from a single percentage point higher to statistically significant differences of ten percentage points or more, the pattern is clear.

The girls' relative strength is very broadly based, and is reflected in the statistically significant difference in domain scores in their favour for **Planning parts of investigations** (see Chapter 4).

## 10.6  Summary and implications

Some questions in the **Planning** category have been included in all surveys at age 11 since 1981 but it was only in 1983 and 1984 that one of the main subcategories, **Planning parts of investigations**, has been adequately represented. The initial pool of questions for this subcategory was largely replaced following a redefinition of the sub-category to reflect sub-processes of planning and a pool of over 200 questions now exists. Questions assessing **Planning entire investigations** have always been few in number and hand-selected for the surveys; there is no large pool. Development of analytical mark schemes, reflecting the same sub-process structure, enables results for **Planning entire investigations** to be related to those for **Planning parts of investigations**.

The initial step in planning is expressing a problem in a testable form. A few questions assessing this ability have been included in two surveys. Although score levels have been about 40 per cent, errors have not generally been in failing to distinguish testable properties but in other aspects of providing an adequate answer. Thus it appears that this first step does not present a great difficulty to 11 year olds.

In producing a whole plan, clearly success in later parts depends on the earlier parts and so a 'tailing off' in performance in proceeding through a plan is to be expected. The extent of this tailing off and the levels of performance in various parts of the plan vary considerably from one problem to another and any general statements made about performance have to be interpreted against this background. The variation due to the subject matter of the question has been found to be very large. Although reasons for this variation in performance have been discussed, there are many interacting influences and it would be unwise to attempt to predict performance on planning other whole investigations from the results of the questions used in the surveys.

A general pattern in all 'entire investigation' plans is that pupils have often omitted operational details of how variables will be manipulated or measured, whilst mention of controlling variables as required for fairness in testing was mentioned by a small proportion of pupils. Hardly any pupils mentioned taking steps, such as repeating readings, to increase the accuracy of results. Performance was also low in describing how results obtained would be used in answering the initial problem.

In the 'entire investigation' questions only a little guidance was given to pupils as to what they should include, though a reminder to mention what things they would use, what they would do with them and how they would use the results (see pages 79–81) was given. Pupils therefore decided for themselves what to include and the results indicate what they saw as relevant to the task of planning rather than necessarily their ability to tackle various planning tasks. In other words low performance may have reflected a restricted appreciation of requirements of a written plan rather than low ability in the process of planning.

The results for the subcategory **Planning parts of investigations** helps to sort out these alternative interpretations of performance. In this subcategory questions were focused on to specific parts of the plan of an investigation and pupils asked directly about each part. Performance was higher in questions where the focus was on the parts of planning which logically came earlier in developing a plan and tailed off rapidly on questions focusing on obtaining and using results. Thus the general trend in results for the 'entire investigation' plans was confirmed, but there were some important differences. Performance on questions about controlling variables was the highest of all types of question, suggesting that the low performance on the whole plans was less a matter of inability than of recognising this aspect as something which should be included in producing a plan.

Performance was relatively higher in dealing with the measurement of the dependent variable in whole plans than in parts of plans, though levels were extremely variable from one investigation to another. There was some indication that where pupils were left free to decide for themselves what to measure then they were more likely to give adequate operational details. The 'part' questions were particularly restrictive in this respect. In both whole plans and in 'part' questions, however, performance was below 20 per cent, on average, in describing how results would be related back to the initial problem.

These results point to some implications for assessment of planning skills. A balance between providing too much and too little freedom for the pupil to decide what kind of answer to give to a question is difficult to find. Closely focused questions provide guidance about what aspect of the problem to address but make it difficult for pupils to enter the problem in a way which engages their creativity and critical thought. So, for example, rather than being taken through an investigation by being told how it was set up, then asked what should be measured a child might give a more adequate answer if he or she had decided

how to set up the situation and so was in a better position to think about relevant measurements.

Leaving the situation more open, as in the planning of a whole investigation, has the opposite advantages and disadvantages. Pupils may not include details which they are quite capable of producing because they do not know that these are expected. Suggesting a list of things to include is not always effective, as some pupils tend to ignore it, and for others it can restrict freedom in the design of an investigation. As for many dilemmas arising in assessment, there is no perfect solution which removes all ambiguity in the interpretation of results. It remains essential that the interpretation of performance is made in the light of the kinds of questions used, and variations in performance associated with the content, context and form of the questions.

The relevance of these results for the curriculum depends on the case for the importance of planning as a part of science activities. Planning is the thinking part of 'doing'. Planning may not always be carried out before 'doing' begins, which is yet another factor to be kept in mind in the interpretation of purely written plans, as produced by the children in the surveys, and applying the results to planning in normal classroom conditions. Whenever it occurs, however, planning should help children in thinking ahead, imagining results of actions not yet undertaken, considering alternative actions, and assessing the feasibility of suggested procedures. It is thus important for children to learn how to plan and to know what should be included and the kinds of details to work out. There is evidence in the results presented in this chapter that planning performance is low at age 11 but, more importantly, that in many cases it appears that it may be low due to lack of experience of planning and of realisation of what is involved.

Performance levels in the initial steps in planning, at about 50 per cent, suggest that many children already have a basis for extending their planning skills to later steps in the planning process. Others may need help to make a start. Experience of carrying out investigations is a necessary basis for planning, for primary children cannot think about a series of actions if they have had no experience of what is involved and no knowledge of why certain steps, such as controlling variables, are required. Teachers might well consider, therefore, the extent to which their pupils are familiar with carrying out a whole investigation, before placing emphasis on planning. Discussion of various parts of investigations actually carried out, particularly where procedures were found to be inadequate, provides a useful precursor to thinking about possible actions before they are carried out. Once planning has become an established part of science activities the experience of translating plans into actions, while performing investigations, can become the means to improving planning and performance hand in hand.

# 11

# The performance of investigations

## 11.1 Overview of the assessment of 'Performance of investigations'

The assessment of children's ability to carry out practical investigations or to solve problems through active enquiry has been regarded as an essential part of the assessment framework. The other five categories of science activity assess processes which may be involved in carrying out an investigation but the sum of these parts does not necessarily make the whole. Furthermore, in other categories, even in the practical assessment of **Observation**, there is a strong dependence upon pupils' ability to read questions and to produce written answers. For all children, but particularly those in the age 11 sample, the assessment of what they can *do* as against what they may be able to convey through writing, makes a most important contribution to the picture of their scientific ability.

Not that assessing practical performance is without its problems, both in terms of logistics and validity. The approach adopted in the surveys has been to assess pupils individually carrying out an investigation in the presence of a trained tester. During the surveys testers visited schools staying in one school for a whole day and assessing five children one after another. The testers brought all the equipment needed, presented it according to instructions received during training, and recorded on check-lists the way pupils carried out the investigation. At the end of the investigation the testers asked pupils structured questions in order to probe features of their performance which were not entirely observable (for example the children's intentions in the way certain actions had been carried out).

Assessing children in this way has provided detailed accounts of how they tackle investigations in the test context, but it must be stressed that this is not the classroom context in which children would generally be working. The main differences are that the subject matter of the investigation and the particular problems to be solved have been presented 'out of the blue', the equipment may be unfamiliar, they have to work alone rather than in a group and they have to work in the presence of an unfamiliar teacher. While steps have been taken to reduce the impact of these circumstances, by providing a 'play period' with the equipment before the investigation begins, for example, their influence has to be borne in mind.

These cautions apply to the use of the results, but they were not at the time perceived as negative influences on the children. The evidence of the testers was that the children, with very few exceptions, enjoyed the testing and indeed gained a great deal from it. The testers, too, found the experience valuable, for rarely do teachers have the opportunity to watch individual children closely and to do this for eight to ten days increased their insight into the way children approach practical problems. These by-products were largely due to careful selection of testers by the local authority advisers. The advisers facilitated the release of experienced head teachers or assistant teachers for the duration of the training, the testing and the feedback meeting.

The number of investigations used in a survey and the number administered to each child in the sample varied from year to year according to the length of the investigations and on whether other questions were included in the testing session (the extended Category 2 questions in 1984, for example.) Table 11.1 lists the titles of the investigations used in the four surveys in which **Performance of investigations** was included and gives the number of pupils assessed in each investigation.

**Table 11.1** *Summary of 'Performance of investigations' and numbers of pupils assessed in each investigation*

| Investigation | 1980 | 1981 | 1982 | 1984 |
|---|---|---|---|---|
| Caterpillar | 561 | | | |
| Mealworms | 559 | | | |
| Sugar lumps | 555 | | | |
| Circuits | 555 | 610 | | |
| Paper back | 559 | 609 | | |
| Snails | 553 | 608 | | |
| Paper towels | | 606 | | |
| Woodlice | | 606 | | |
| Bouncing balls | | 606 | | |
| Paper towels* | | | 513 | |
| Mealworms* | | | 980† | |
| Chopping board | | | 980† | |
| Sail boats | | | 468 | |
| Swingboards | | | 981† | |
| Snail | | | | 385 |
| Shadows | | | | 320 |

* These were modified versions of the investigations of the same name included in earlier surveys.
† Two forms of administration were used in these cases; the figure given is the total of those performing after planning on paper and those performing without first writing a plan.

Each investigation was a real situation which differed in a number of respects from any other. Depending on the subject matter and the type of question posed, some parts of the investigation process were represented to a greater degree than others. For example, in 'Paper towels' (where the problem was to find which of three types would hold most water) there was a considerable burden upon deciding how to compare or measure the dependent variable (the amount of water a piece of paper towel would hold). In contrast, the investigation of circuits (where a bulb had to be lit in a simple circuit in which there were two faults) the decision about the dependent variable was trivial, and indeed made explicit in the question posed; the burden in this case was on controlling variables whilst one variable at a time was systematically changed. There was no attempt to make the investigations similar to each other in their demand for investigative skills; they were designed to differ in their demands so that between them skills across the range required in scientific investigations were well represented.

The investigation of 'Shadows' was designed to provide for more interaction between tester and pupil than in other investigations so as to give opportunity to probe the extent to which children were able to apply the result they had found in an initial enquiry to solve further short practical problems posed by the tester. This investigation was more structured than others which had been used and the children's actions and responses could readily be recorded using a check-list. 'Snails', by contrast, was more unstructured than any other investigation, being highly dependent on the ideas and choices of the pupils at the time of testing. The record of most of each child's performance had to be in the form of notes made at the time, giving an account of the observations made, questions asked and the way the child carried out the investigation. However, for all of the investigations a check-list was used for recording certain common features, such as whether the child made any records during the investigation and whether the result obtained was consistent with available evidence.

The results unique to the 'Snails' and 'Shadows' investigations will be described after the general findings arising from children's performance of investigations have been summarised.

## 11.2 Summary of findings

As already mentioned, each investigation has a number of unique features and the best way of reporting results is to describe the children's performances in some detail, as has been done in the full survey reports (DES, 1981, 1983a, 1984a). At the same time certain components of the process of investigation can be identified in most problems; these can be used to summarise performance and enable comparisons to be made both within and across investigations.

Quantifying performance in these components was helped by the statistical analysis which led to their identification. The method has been described in the reports of the

second and third surveys (DES, 1983a, and DES, 1984a) and full details can be found in Qualter (1985). The five components found in most investigations (but not necessarily all) can be described in terms of the check list items (check-points) as follows:

'General approach' – comprising check-points relating to setting up a situation in which the independent variable can be investigated.

'Control of variables' – action which ensured that the independent variable was the only effective difference between events or experimental conditions when measurements or comparisons were made.

'Measurement of the dependent variable' – including check-points referring to what was measured and how it was measured.

'Record of findings' – information about whether any records or notes were made during and/or at the end of the investigation without a reminder being given.

'Nature of result' – derived from check-points referring to whether results were consistent with evidence (as observed by the tester at the time – no 'correct result' criteria were imposed) and whether or not they were quantitative in nature.

Table 11.2 (p. 87) brings together the percentage performance figures for these components for all the investigations. It must be emphasised that the check-points used in defining a performance level for a particular component varied both in number and nature and the figures therefore provide for only the roughest of comparison across investigations. Where no figures are given the check-lists did not contain check-points relating to the component.

The wide variation in the 'profiles' of the investigations shows that pupils' response to the demands made on various skills depended very much on the particular problem. The investigation of 'Sailboats' has the most uniform profile across components but in all other cases pupils had considerably less success in some parts than in others.

Looking at performance component by component, across investigations, a similar variation is found. It appears that pupils adopted a satisfactory general approach, enabling the independent variable to be put into operation with some ease, except for 'Swingboards', 'Mealworms' and 'Woodlice'. Two of these three involved combining two variables in order to tackle the problem–the length and width of the swinging boards, and the conditions of light and dampness for the woodlice. Mealworms required pupils to operationalise the notion of choice, so that the food preferences of the mealworms could be investigated, not merely whether they would or would not eat each food. It was noted in Chapter 10 that the performance in planning of 'Swingboards' and 'Mealworms' was found low in regard to the operationalisation of the independent variable (Table 10.3, page 78).

**Table 11.2** *Rough estimates of performance in various components of 'Performance of investigations'*
(Percentage of maximum scores)

| Investigation | General approach (Independent var.) | Control of variables | Measurement of dependent variable | Record of findings | Nature of result |
|---|---|---|---|---|---|
| Caterpillar | 78 | 47 | 67 | 91 | 84 |
| Sugar lumps | 77 | 51 | 50 | 64 | 78 |
| Circuits | 84 | 73 | – | 61 | 60 |
| Paperback | 93 | 50 | – | 89 | 67 |
| Snails | 80 | – | 58 | 73 | 66 |
| Woodlice | 65 | 30 | 65 | – | 39 |
| Bouncing balls | 87 | 74 | 58 | 85 | 62 |
| Paper towels | 78 | 61 | 45 | 75 | 61 |
| Mealworms | 64 | 56 | 79 | 69 | 50 |
| Chopping board | 75 | 62 | 78 | 73 | 47 |
| Sailboats | 75 | 68 | 68 | 78 | 57 |
| Swingboards | 40 | 52 | 52 | 78 | 38 |
| Snail | – | – | – | 69 | 61 |
| Shadows | 84 | 93 | 49 | 77 | 71 |

The control of variables in the various investigations presented a variety of demands. Performance was high in this component where the variables were limited in number and had a fairly obvious effect, as in 'Bouncing balls' and 'Shadows'. Whether or not variables are controlled when their effect is less obvious depends to some extent on pupils' knowledge of what may affect the result. This could account for the low performance in 'Woodlice', where a large proportion of pupils failed to equalise the areas set up with different conditions. 'Mealworms' and 'Swingboards' also caused problems, perhaps because pupils did not expect the distance of the mealworms from the food to be important or the size of swing to matter in swinging of the boards. The control of variables was also low in 'Caterpillar', an investigation with a clockwork toy, where children's performance was often characterised by lack of care in such things as preventing unwinding of the spring, and starting the toy to control for the effect of its variable length. Similarly in 'Paperback', an investigation which involved comparing types of paper under tests devised by the pupils, the testing was carried out in a somewhat rough and ready manner without apparent regard to ensuring fair treatment of the papers. Interestingly 'Paper towels', also involving comparing paper, was carried out with rather more regard for fairness. This could have been because 'Paper towels' involved using equipment and measuring instruments which suggested that a scientific approach was appropriate, whereas the 'everyday' equipment provided for 'Paperback' suggested an 'everyday', less controlled, approach. (The equipment is shown on pages 57 and 60 of DES, 1983a.)

Measurement of the dependent variable was low in 'Shadows', 'Swingboards' and 'Paper towels'. Deciding what to measure in *planning* these particular investigations was mentioned in Chapter 10 (page 82) as presenting difficulty, possibly because of the conceptual demand in deciding what to measure to find 'how fast', in the case of 'Swingboards', 'how big' in the case of 'Shadows' and which will 'hold more water' in the case of 'Paper towels'. It appears that these demands may have also affected performance in practice in these investigations. Of the three other investigations with relatively low performance

in this component, 'Snails' involved the concept of speed but 'Bouncing balls' and 'Sugar lumps' were probably low for the reason that pupils failed to make measurements and instead just looked superficially at what happened.

The performance levels in recording notes and results show that most pupils generally wrote down something on their paper during the investigation. The lowest figure was for 'Circuits', where there were no measurements to make and pupils tended not to put down the result of each attempt to make the bulb light; even at the end many were content to have succeeded and needed prompting to put down the reasons why the bulb did not light at first. The high figure for 'Caterpillar' was due to a ready-made table being provided on the pupil sheet. It was noted that, whilst pupils would use a table if provided, very few would produce one for themselves when it was appropriate to tabulate results (DES, 1984a, page 96).

The component relating to the nature of the result referred to the consistency of what the pupil wrote with the evidence as seen by the tester. Performance was very variable and in some cases depended on the pupils' choice of dependent variable. So, in 'Swingboards', those pupils who judged the speed of swinging from which board stopped moving first, were unlikely to give a correct interpretation of the evidence. In the case of 'Woodlice', the main problem was that the pupils used too few woodlice to be a basis for any result and so the result they gave was not supported by evidence. Similar remarks apply to 'Mealworms' where in many cases the children were judging from evidence which was not related to preference. Low performance in 'Chopping board' arose because pupils had generally carried out several tests and then found difficulty in combining the results into an overall judgement consistent with the evidence.

In each investigation testers were asked to give general ratings to two aspects of the pupils' performance. One was based on pupils' willingness to be involved in the investigation. The criteria for assigning ratings 0, 1 or 2 were as follows:

|  |  | Rating |
| --- | --- | --- |
| —evidence of real interest in investigation, looking carefully and intently at what happens, actions deliberate and thoughtful | | 2 |
| —willing to carry out investigation but no sign of great enthusiasm or special interest | | 1 |
| —carries out only the minimum necessary, may look bored, uninterested or scared | | 0 |

The other was based on responses to a question posed at the end of every investigation, as follows:

*'If you could do this investigation again, using the same things that you have here, would you do it in the same way or change some things that you did, to make the experiment better?'*

Follow-up questions probed the reasons for any claim that a change would be an improvement. Again a rating of 0, 1 or 2 was assigned, using the following criteria:

|  | Rating |
| --- | --- |
| —shows awareness of variables which were not controlled, procedures which turned out to be ineffective, the need to repeat measurements or criticise other factors which are central, not merely peripheral, to the investigation | 2 |
| —shows awareness of alternative procedures but unaware of particular deficiencies of those used (does not have very good reasons for suggesting changes) | 1 |
| —uncritical of procedures used, can suggest neither deficiencies nor alternative approaches | 0 |

Table 11.3 gives the average ratings for these two aspects of performance for the whole sample and for boys and girls. Willingness to take part was rated highly for all investigations. There was a consistent gender-related performance difference, with boys apparently showing more enthusiasm than girls. This was particularly marked in the investigations involving living things ('Snails', 'Snail', 'Mealworms' and 'Woodlice'). Further evidence of girls' reactions to animals was revealed in the ratings of pupils' care in handling them. About 34 per cent of the girls, compared with about 12 per cent of the boys, were reported as being unwilling to touch the snails and rather higher proportions of both sexes unwilling to touch woodlice and mealworms. Few pupils (7 per cent or less) handled the creatures with lack of care for them as living things, but this proportion included about twice as many girls as boys.

The results for critical reflection show the average rating below 1 in all cases with no consistent gender difference. Thus in general pupils did not recognise the inadequacies of their procedures after seeing the result of them. They

**Table 11.3** *Average ratings of 'Willingness to take part in the investigation' and of 'Critical reflection on procedures' for all investigations* (1980–84 data)

| Survey | All | Willingness to take part: (maximum, 2 marks): | | | Critical reflection: (maximum, 2 marks): | | |
| --- | --- | --- | --- | --- | --- | --- | --- |
|  |  | Boys | Girls | All | Boys | Girls | |
| Caterpillar | 1 | 1.4 | 1.5 | 1.3 | 0.7 | 0.7 | 0.7 |
| Sugar lumps | 1 | 1.4 | 1.5 | 1.3 | 0.8 | 0.7 | 0.9 |
| Circuits | 1,2 | 1.5 | 1.6 | 1.5 | 0.8 | 0.8 | 0.8 |
| Paperback | 1,2 | 1.4* | 1.5 | 1.3 | 0.8 | 0.8 | 0.8 |
| Snails | 1,2 | 1.4* | 1.5 | 1.3 | 0.9 | 0.9 | 0.9 |
| Woodlice | 2 | 1.7 | 1.7 | 1.7 | 0.9 | 0.9 | 0.9 |
| Bouncing balls | 2 | 1.7 | 1.8 | 1.6 | 0.9 | 0.9 | 0.9 |
| Paper towels | 2,3 | 1.8 | 1.8 | 1.8 | 0.9 | 1.0 | 0.8 |
| Mealworms | 1,3 | 1.4 | 1.5 | 1.3 | 0.9 | 1.0 | 0.8 |
| Chopping board | 3 | 1.3 | 1.4 | 1.2 | 0.6 | 0.6 | 0.6 |
| Sailboats | 3 | 1.4 | 1.5 | 1.3 | 0.7 | 0.7 | 0.7 |
| Swingboards | 3 | 1.4 | 1.4 | 1.3 | 0.7 | 0.7 | 0.7 |
| Snail | 5 | 1.5 | 1.6 | 1.4 | – | – | – |
| Shadows | 5 | 1.5 | 1.5 | 1.4 | – | – | – |

* These are the ratings given in the first survey. Those given in the second are consistently 0.3 higher, suggesting that there was a systematic tendency for testers to rate more highly in the second survey. This would account for the high ratings for 'Woodlice', 'Bouncing balls' and 'Paper towels'. The average rating for 'Mealworms' was the same in the first and third surveys.

may have been unused to thinking about ways of improving methods used in investigations or lacking knowledge of more effective procedures which could have been used. One particular feature of their performances which was notably absent was the repetition of measurements. Except in 'Bouncing balls', where 25 per cent of pupils dropped the same ball more than once, less than 10 per cent of pupils repeated measurements where this was advantageous. When invited to reflect on how to improve their investigation so as to be more sure of the results, only a handful of pupils who had not repeated measurements indicated that this should have been done.

Analyses carried out on data in the 1982 survey showed that a high rating for critical appraisal was associated with high levels in performance in various components of the investigation (DES, 1984a, pages 99 and 143, for example).

## 11.3 Additional information from the 1984 survey

*'Snail'*

The focus of this investigation was a Great African Land Snail. The specimens were large (between 15 cm and 25 cm in length when extended – except for those used in Northern Ireland where only immature ones could be obtained), strikingly different in other ways from common garden snails, and active. Few children had seen one before and it was expected that the snail would stimulate curiosity.

The first phase of the administration was to give the child time to look at the snail, using a hand lens if he or she wished, and then invite any questions the child wanted to ask about the snail. The tester wrote down the questions verbatim as far as possible, responding with 'anything else?' until no more questions were raised. Table 11.4 summarises the frequency of various types of question which were asked.

**Table 11.4** *Frequency of various types of questions raised by pupils during first phase of 'Snail' investigation*
(Percentage of questions asked, 1984 data)

| Questions | All | Boys | Girls |
|---|---|---|---|
| About food | 12 | 13 | 11 |
| About growth, size, weight | 10 | 11 | 8 |
| About origin, where it lives, what condition: | 6 | 6 | 7 |
| About age and life span | 5 | 6 | 3 |
| About speed of movement | 5 | 5 | 5 |
| About the purpose and use of its tentacles | 5 | 5 | 4 |
| About how it is attached to and fits in its shell | 4 | 5 | 2 |
| About pattern, shape, colour of shell | 4 | 4 | 3 |
| About shell growth, thickness, material & whether it is renewed | 3 | 4 | 2 |
| About 'slime' or trail left and why it is moist | 3 | 3 | 3 |
| About how it is 'born' and reproduces | 3 | 3 | 2 |
| About how it moves | 3 | 3 | 2 |
| About the colour and pattern of the skin/foot | 3 | 2 | 5 |
| About location of named parts (where is its . . .?) | 3 | 2 | 5 |
| Request for names of parts (what's this . . .?) | 2 | 2 | 3 |
| About how it carries out named functions (how does it . . .?) | 2 | 1 | 3 |
| About its sex | 2 | 2 | 2 |
| About its sight and eyes | 2 | 2 | 3 |
| About preference for warm or cold surroundings | 2 | 2 | 1 |
| About retraction of tentacles | 2 | 3 | 1 |
| About its enemies/predators | 2 | 2 | 2 |
| About why it has a shell/carries shell around | 2 | 2 | 2 |
| Function of parts (what's this for?) | 1 | 2 | 1 |
| About occurrence/rarity/evolution | 1 | 2 | – |
| About whether it can smell | 1 | 0 | 2 |
| About its hearing | 1 | 1 | 1 |
| About sensitivity to touch/ability to feel things | 1 | 1 | 1 |
| About whether it is edible | 1 | 1 | 1 |
| About its sleep pattern | 1 | 1 | 1 |
| Where this particular one came from | 1 | 1 | 1 |
| Other | 7 | 3 | 13 |

Roughly half of the questions were ones which could have been answered by the children by observation or investigation. They were not necessarily expressed in the form of an investigable question but could have readily been turned into one, in a classroom context. It is seen in Table 11.4 that only a very small proportion of questions were ones asking for names and the wide range of subjects of the questions is testimony to the children's expansive curiosity.

The number of questions raised by any one child ranged from none (4 per cent overall, but a higher proportion of girls than of boys) to 11. Boys asked, on average, 4.1 questions each and girls 3.3 questions. Other differences between the questions of boys and girls were the slightly higher proportion of non-investigable and naming questions asked by the girls. Also girls asked more questions falling into the 'other' category, which covered anything from 'What is his name?' to 'Is his mother back in Africa?' and 'Why has it got a long neck?'

When the child asked no further questions the tester provided answers to purely factual ones, but not the ones to which the child could find the answer by investigation. The child was then shown a list of ready prepared questions, which may have included several already raised, and was asked to choose just one to work on there and then. This could be either a new item from the list or a question of his or her own. The list, compiled from questions asked by children during development trials, was provided mainly to give ideas to children who had not raised investigable questions of their own but was shown to all pupils so that administration procedures were the same in all cases. The questions were as follows:

> Can it hear?
> Can it see?
> Does it notice a light?
> Can it smell?
> Can it feel a touch?
> How fast can it move?
> Does it move faster on some surfaces?
> What food does it like best?
> How hard can it pull?

During the time when questions were being raised and selected, the equipment provided for the possible investigations was concealed from the child's view so as not to suggest enquiries. Once the child had chosen a question, the equipment was revealed and the child told to select from it whatever was needed.

Table 11.5 shows the frequency of choosing different questions. All except 'what food will/does it eat?' and 'does it like light or darkness?' were ones included on the list shown to the children. However, the question may have been the child's own even though it was on the list. Analysis showed that 11 per cent of questions investigated by children were ones they had suggested themselves, 85 per cent chose a question from the list different from any they had asked and 4 per cent had not suggested a question of their own.

The interest in food and speed of movement, indicated in Table 11.4, is reflected in the popularity of questions, chosen as shown in Table 11.5. However, Table 11.5 is no more than a rough guide as to what the children actually investigated. It is based on the children's selection

**Table 11.5** *Frequency of choice of different questions ('Snail' investigation)*
(Percentage of pupils, 1984 data)

| | |
|---|---|
| What food does it like best? | 20 |
| Does it move faster (better) on some surfaces than others? | 19 |
| Can it hear? | 13 |
| How fast can/does it move? | 11 |
| Does it see/notice a light? | 10 |
| What food does/will it eat? | 7 |
| How hard can it pull? | 7 |
| Can it see? | 6 |
| Can it feel a touch? | 4 |
| Can it smell? | 4 |
| Does it like light or darkness? | 1 |

of a question when asked to choose one, but what they did often bore little relation to this choice. Frequently testers reported children exploring many other things besides, or sometimes instead of, their chosen topic. One child told the tester, in explanation after the practical phase, that she had used the equipment to find out as much as she could about the snail. In a large proportion of investigations the snail was given some food, sometimes as a bait to encourage it to move, but often when the relevance of giving food was far from clear. (See examples of testers' accounts of pupils' investigations/actions in Appendix 10.)

Whilst the investigation was being carried out the tester wrote down an account of what was done, giving details as suggested during training. These reports provide much more lively accounts of the children's performances than are captured by a check-list and some examples are provided in Appendix 10. The performances in the various components were, however, similar to those already summarised in the previous section and will not be presented.

Additional information was gathered when the child had finished the investigation by asking a series of structured questions. Four questions probed the children's experience relevant to the 'Snail' investigation. These questions and the answers are summarised in Table 11.6.

**Table 11.6** *Children's experience related to the 'Snail' investigation*

(Percentage giving a positive answer, 1984 data)

| Question | All | Boys | Girls |
|---|---|---|---|
| Done anything with any snails before? | 23 | 21 | 26 |
| Looked at other small creatures before? | 77 | 77 | 77 |
| Used equipment to find something out (about anything) before? | 41 | 40 | 42 |
| Ever decided for yourself how to do an investigation before? | 30 | 32 | 27 |

A further two questions were not directly related to the investigation but were using the topic and the opportunity to present a problem orally to the children in order to compare performance in this context with performance on the same question in a pencil and paper package. One question was of the pattern identification type used in assessing the subcategory **Interpreting presented information**. The other was the type of question used to assess ability to set up a situation in which the effect of the independent variable can be tested, in the subcategory **Planning parts of investigations**. In both cases the written form of the question was included in the probe packages (ie not part of the random sample of questions). In the interview the questions were presented using large scale versions of the same diagrams reproduced in the written questions, with the tester explaining the situation in the words given on page 91. The pupil responded to both questions orally and the tester recorded the answer verbatim. Later, answers to the written and interview versions

were scored and categorised using the same marking scheme.

*'Snail preference'*

The two versions of this **Interpreting presented information** question are shown on page 91, together with the mean scores. The rate of success was considerably greater in the case of the individually administered question than in the purely written form. The slightly higher score by girls over boys in the written version (girls 1.8; boys 1.6) was reversed in the oral version (boys 2.4; girls 2.3).

Table 11.7 shows how the answers differed qualitatively. Proportions giving correct answers making reference either to the position of the snails or their preference were 50 per cent higher for the oral presentation sample than for the written test sample. In both samples the majority of pupils gave a summary interpretation, rather than a description of the result in terms of the numbers of snails in each place. Additionally, if attention was given to only one set of conditions, it was always the light and dark conditions, for both test samples. This is probably because the difference between light and dark is easier to portray in the drawings than the difference between hot and cold. In the oral presentation there was less difference in the attention given to the light and dark and the hot and cold conditions.

**Table 11.7** *Categories of answers to 'Snail preference' when presented as a written question and orally to individuals*

(Percentage of pupils, 1984 data)

| Categories of response | Mark | Written (n = 260) | Oral (n = 385) |
|---|---|---|---|
| Correct answer in terms of position (most went to warm and dark place) | 3 | 12 | 17 |
| Correct answer in terms of preference (they liked the warm and dark place best) | 3 | 23 | 37 |
| Correct comparison of numbers in more than one place | 3 | 4 | 6 |
| Statement that 'all' were in or preferred the warm and dark place | 3 | 4 | 3 |
| Separate statements of relative numbers relating to warm-cold and light-dark places | 2 | 2 | 4 |
| Separate statements of preference for warm-cold and light-dark | 2 | 8 | 5 |
| Correct statements referring to warm-cold only | 1 | 1 | 5 |
| Correct statements referring to light-dark only | 1 | 21 | 13 |
| Incorrect judgement of preference | 0 | 6 | 2 |
| Other | 0 | 7 | 6 |
| No response | 0 | 11 | 1 |

It is not surprising that there is a large difference between the non-response rates for the two samples, but the results in Table 11.7 do suggest that many more children can attempt, and succeed in, this question when the additional demands of decoding a written version and writing an answer are removed. Performance may also have been enhanced by more focused attention provided by the context and by the presence of the tester.

**Example 1**  *'Snail preference'*

*Written version*

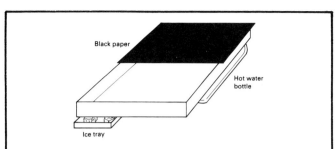
Black paper
Hot water bottle
Ice tray

Sophie and Bobby were finding out about the conditions that snails prefer. They used a deep plastic tray and covered half of it with black paper. They also made one side cold and one side warm.

1. When they had set up their tray it looked like this from the top:

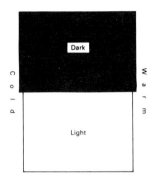
Dark
Cold
Warm
Light

2. They put 10 snails in the tray like this, and watched to see where they went:

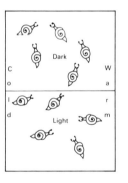
Dark
C o l d
Light
W a r m

3. After 20 minutes this is where the snails were:

What do you notice about how the snails' position is affected by the conditions in the tray?

..........................................................

..........................................................

..........................................................

*Oral presentation*

Tester used A4-sized versions of illustrations to point out the various features as they were mentioned:

*Let me show you what some children did to find out some conditions that snails like and don't like. They had this large plastic tray and made one side of it cold by putting ice trays under it and the other side of it warm with a hot water bottle. They also put black paper over half of the tray, like this. Then they put 10 snails in the tray all in different parts, like this. They waited for 20 minutes and then looked to see where the snails were. The result was like this. What do you notice about how the positions of the snails are affected by the different conditions in the tray?*

n = 260   Max. = 3        Mean score 1.7

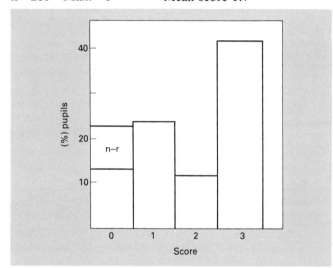
(%) pupils
n–r
Score

n = 385   Max. = 3        Mean score 2.3

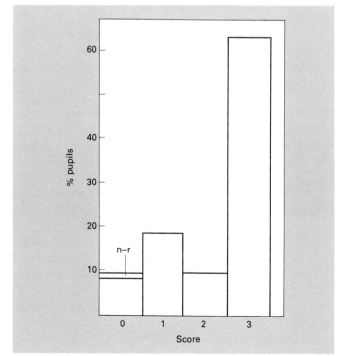
% pupils
n–r
Score

91

**Example 2** *'Choice conditions'*

*Oral presentation*

Sophie and Bobby were finding out about the conditions that snails prefer. They wanted to know which of these places the snails would go to if they had a choice:

> cold and dark
> cold and light
> warm and dark
> warm and light

This is what they did. They used two deep plastic trays and set up different conditions like this:

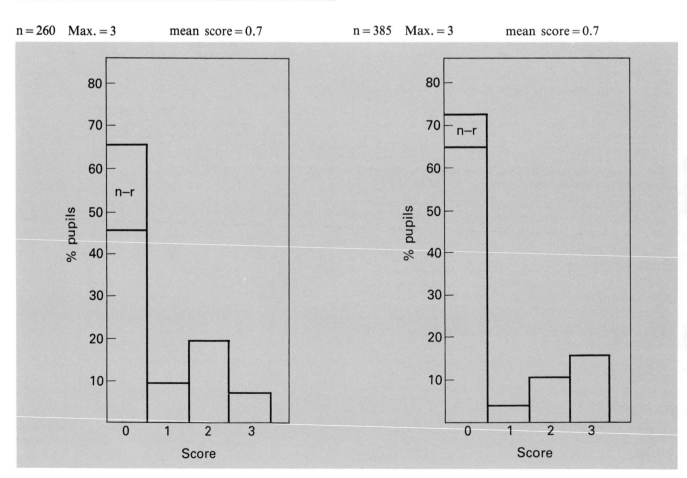

Dark

Light

Cold    Warm    Hot water bottle

Ice tray

There is something wrong with this way of setting up the conditions. Look carefully at what they did and write down why they would not be able to find out what they wanted to know.

....................................................................

....................................................................

....................................................................

....................................................................

....................................................................

This followed on from 'Snail preference':

*Now some other children wanted to find out about some other conditions that snails might prefer. They wanted to find out which of these conditions snails would prefer if given a choice: damp and dark, damp and light. This is what they did to start with. (Show and describe the two trays.)*

*Do you think there is anything wrong with this way of starting the investigation?*

*What do you think they should do to make the investigation better?*

n = 260   Max. = 3          mean score = 0.7

n = 385   Max. = 3          mean score = 0.7

**Example 3** *'Shadow graph'*

*Written version*

Janice and Sihan made a shadow of a ball using a torch, like this:

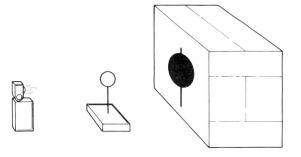

When they moved the torch to different distances from the bulb, the size of the shadow changed. They measured the size of the shadow when the torch was at different distances from the ball. They used their results to draw this graph:

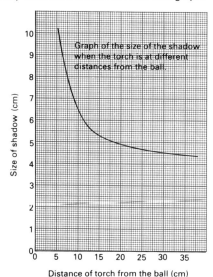

Graph of the size of the shadow when the torch is at different distances from the ball.

Size of shadow (cm)

Distance of torch from the ball (cm)

Use their graph to answer these questions.

a) How did the size of the shadow change when the light was moved?

..............................................................................

..............................................................................

b) How big was the shadow when the light was 30 cm away?

..............................................................................

c) How far away was the light when the size of the shadow was 5 cm?

..............................................................................

*Oral presentation*

Referring to the equipment used in the 'Shadows' investigation, the tester said:

*Let me show you what one girl/boy did. She/he kept the ball and the box in the same places and moved the torch. She/he measured the sizes of the shadow when the torch was at different distances from the ball. Then she/he drew this graph.*

(She/he used to match the sex of the child.)

The tester then showed the child a full A4 drawing of the graph (as on the written version) and asked:

*Have you ever drawn a graph like this?*

and continued after the answer:

*There is a different kind of graph where you draw blocks and sometimes colour them in, like this one.*

(The tester showed an A4 block graph.)

*Have you ever drawn one like that?*

Turning back to the line graph:

*Have a look at this one again. What does it tell you about the way the size of the shadow changed when the torch was moved?*

The tester wrote down what the child said, then asked:

*Can you tell me from the graph how big the shadow was when the torch was 30 cm away?* (Answer recorded)

*Can you tell me from the graph how far the light was when the shadow was 5 cm in size?*

The tester then asked about whether the child had used a line graph and a bar chart before to find out information.

*Per cent Mean scores*

|  | Written | | | Oral | | |
|---|---|---|---|---|---|---|
|  | All | B | G | All | B | G |
| (a) | 16 | 18 | 14 | 29 | 33 | 24 |
| (b) | 46 | 45 | 48 | 39 | 39 | 39 |
| (c) | 38 | 35 | 43 | 45 | 45 | 46 |
| Total | 29 | 29 | 30 | 36 | 38 | 33 |
| n | 258 | 137 | 121 | 345 | 164 | 181 |

## 'Choice conditions'

This problem was designed to assess one aspect of **Planning parts of investigations.** As with 'Snail preference', there were two versions, one presented as part of a written test and one presented during the individual interview after the 'Snails' practical investigation. Both are shown on page 92 together with the mean scores.

It should be noted that these questions were given to the same samples as the two versions of 'Snail preference'. In the case of the practical sample, 'Choice conditions' was presented immediately after and so there was the potential for pupils to transfer ideas directly from the drawing seen just a few minutes earlier. The small proportion (14 per cent) giving a fully acceptable answer shows that this transfer did not occur to any large degree. In the case of the sample taking the written test, the two questions were placed at opposite ends of the package, and roughly half would have found 'Choice conditions' before 'Snail preference' and the other half would have encountered the questions in reverse order (due to the practice of giving two versions of each written package with the questions in one in the reverse order to those in the other). Again, given the chance to compare the diagrams in the two questions, it is surprising that only 7 per cent of this sample obtained maximum marks.

By contrast with 'Snail preference' there is no large difference in scores overall for the two versions, though there are considerable differences for boys and girls separately. The boys' performance was higher in the practical question, the reverse being the case with the girls.

The types of response given are summarised in Table 11.8. An important difference in wording of the two questions must be borne in mind, as it may account for some part of the differing patterns of response. In the oral presentation the question was put in two parts; first 'Do you think there is anything wrong with starting like this?' and then 'What do you think they should do to make the investigation better?' If the answer to the first part was 'No' (as it was from 47 per cent of the sample) the second part was not asked. In the written question, however, it was stated that there was something wrong and so there was no option to deny this. What appears to have happened is that those who could find nothing wrong in terms of the conditions set up turned their attention to non-relevant details, or declined to respond. Thus the non-scoring responses are differently distributed in the two samples but amount to somewhat similar proportions overall (72 per cent of responses for the oral sample and 65 per cent for the written sample). As in the case of 'Snail preference', the proportion of the oral sample giving a fully acceptable answer was considerably greater than that of the written sample. However, since these proportions were in any case low and the written sample obtained more marks from incomplete answers, the difference does not show in the mean scores.

The demands of this question are no doubt difficult for 11 year olds to meet. Two features may account for this:

the need to combine two variable quantities to provide for conditions, and the notion of providing choice. In a previous survey, pupils were set the problem of providing a choice of four conditions, by combining dampness and light, to test the preference of woodlice (DES, 1983a, page 36). Just less than half the pupils (46 per cent) managed to set up all the conditions at one time, even though the four were described for them. In other investigations, such as those concerning the food preferences of mealworms (DES, 1981, page 122, DES, 1984a, page 99) providing choice has appeared as a major obstacle. However, the comparison of performance in the theoretical problems, as in 'Choice conditions', with the practical investigations suggests that more pupils can succeed in these problems when they are able to manipulate the variables physically themselves as compared with a situation where they can only talk about (or write about) what might be done.

**Table 11.8** *Categories of answers to 'Choice conditions' when presented as a written question and orally to individuals*

(Percentage of pupils, 1984 data)

| Categories of response | Mark | Written (n = 260) | Oral (n = 385) |
|---|---|---|---|
| Statement indicating that snails have only two things to choose from, not four | 3 | 5 | 2 |
| Detailed indication of how experiment should be set up with all four conditions | 3 | 2 | 12 |
| Incomplete statement recognising that some element of choice is missing | 2 | 9 | 7 |
| Suggestion for extending choice but not to the four conditions required (eg connect boxes together) | 2 | 5 | 1 |
| Some indication that the conditions of heat and light have to be combined but not how | 2 | 5 | 2 |
| Suggestion for altering conditions (incomplete) | 1 | 9 | 3 |
| Statement that there is nothing wrong | 0 | – | 47 |
| Criticism of other features of set-up but not range of choice | 0 | 27 | 5 |
| Statement of answer to problem (what snails prefer) | 0 | 5 | 5 |
| Other statement not relevant to question | 0 | 15 | 8 |
| No response or 'not sure' | 0 | 18 | 7 |

## Shadows

As already mentioned, this was a much more structured investigation than any other; the equipment provided was just that which was needed (whereas in other investigations a range was provided from which pupils had to select) and the problem indicated the independent variable and the dependent variable in general terms. The apparatus consisted of a torch (which was self-standing, throwing a diverging beam in a horizontal direction), a 3 cm ball supported on a short metal rod in a wooden block (the centre of the ball being at the height of the centre of the torch beam), a box with squared paper on one vertical side (acting as a screen for the shadow) and a tape-measure. The tester showed the pupil how to throw the shadow of the ball on the side of the box and demonstrated that the size could be changed by moving the torch, ball and box. The problem was then introduced: 'Find out how the size of the shadow changes when you move the torch, the ball and the box.'

The usual time was allowed for the child to ask questions, to be introduced to the equipment, to the sheet for writing notes and the result and to check that the problem had been understood. The tester used a check-list to record what the child did. The check-list, results and notes used to guide the testers are given in Appendix 15. Most pupils completed the investigation quite quickly, in about 8 to 10 minutes, since few took any measurements (only 4 per cent took measurements of the size of the shadow as it changed), the others basing their results on visual judgement of the shadow size as they moved the pieces of equipment. When the investigation had been finished, the interactive part of the testing began by the tester asking the pupil to 'Make a shadow that is twice the size of the ball'. More pupils (12 per cent) used measurement to help with this task, the others again judging by eye. Fifty-seven per cent succeeded in producing a shadow which was within 1 cm of being twice the diameter of the ball. For the others, the tester made some adjustments to make the shadow diameter closer to twice the ball diameter.

It was important for the later questions that all the pupils saw the arrangement of torch, ball and box operating when the shadow size was twice the ball size. The tester then moved the *ball* nearer to the box so that the shadow was no longer twice the size of the ball and the child was asked to restore it to twice the size by moving the *torch* only. The torch was switched off before the child moved it so that (s)he had to use knowledge of the relationship of the torch position to shadow size in deciding which way to move the torch. Seventy-three per cent of pupils moved it in the correct direction and 41 per cent to approximately the correct position (making the distances between torch and ball and between ball and screen equal). The torch was switched on to check the result after the child had decided where to put it.

Performance in predicting from the perceived relationship was again tested by moving the *torch* so that the shadow was not twice the size of the ball and asking the pupil to restore the size by moving the *box* only, again with the torch off. The proportions succeeding were very similar (74 per cent for the correct direction and 51 per cent for the correct position). The child was again invited to check, turning on the torch. If the size was not correct, the tester made it so and then asked the pupil directly 'Did you notice anything about where the torch, ball and box were when the shadows were twice the size of the ball?' Responses showed that 44 per cent noticed the equal distance relationship.

In all of these prediction parts of the testing where action or oral responses were given there were noteworthy gender differences, with boys ahead of girls. Such differences were not found, however, in the pupils' written results from the earlier part of the investigation. These responses were categorised after the practical testing had been completed, using a system of categories similar to that used in marking written questions involving pattern identification in the subcategory **Interpreting presented information**. The results, given in Table 11.9, show a

proportion of pupils writing statements which describe the relationship between two variables which is far higher than found when pupils are asked to describe relationships in given data (eg 23 per cent for the example described in Report No. 3, DES, 1984a, page 200). The following is an example of one of the more comprehensive answers, but is not atypical of the way in which the relationships were expressed:

'If you move the torch forward then the shadow grows larger but if you move the light back then the shadow shrinks. The opposite happens when you move the ball because when you move it back the shadow expands and if you move if forward then the shadow diminishes. Also just moving the box back the shadow expands but moving it closer to the ball diminishes the size considerably.'

**Table 11.9**  *Types of pattern statement included in pupils' written results of the 'Shadows' investigation*
(Percentage of pupils, 1984 data)

| Category of response | per cent pupils |
|---|---|
| Correct statement of relationship connecting the size of the shadow with the movement of ball, torch or box (any one of these) | 78 |
| Incomplete statement (eg shadow got smaller when the torch was moved) | 6 |
| Separate statements of linked data points | 1 |
| Indication of relationship but not of direction | 6 |
| Reference to one variable only | 3 |
| Incorrect relationship | 2 |
| Pattern not relating to size of shadow | 2 |
| Non-pattern statements | 2 |

The striking differences between performance in describing patterns in the practical and written test context suggests that when pupils have seen a relationship in action they can describe it quite adequately.

An interview with the pupil was added after the 'Shadows' investigation as it was for the 'Snail' investigation. Some questions asked about children's previous experience relevant to the abilities tested in 'Shadows'. Other questions enquired about children's experience of line graphs and bar charts, after they had been shown one in the course of administering 'Shadow graph', described below. The questions and a summary of responses are given in Table 11.10.

**Table 11.10**  *Children's experiences related to the 'Shadows' investigation*
(Percentage of pupils giving a positive answer in each case, 1984 data)

| | All | Boys | Girls |
|---|---|---|---|
| Done work on shadows before? | 38 | 39 | 37 |
| Used equipment to find something out (about anything) before? | 49 | 54 | 46 |
| Drawn a line graph yourself? | 47 | 44 | 50 |
| Drawn a bar chart yourself? | 94 | 94 | 95 |
| Used a line graph to get information? | 38 | 37 | 40 |
| Used a bar chart to get information? | 88 | 91 | 86 |

Table 11.10 shows a proportion of children claiming to have done some work on shadows which corresponds quite well with the proportion claiming the same in the written science topics questions (Table 3.1, page 15). It also shows clearly that pupils of age 11 have far more commonly drawn and used bar charts as compared with line graphs. Comparison with table 11.6 shows that the gender-related performance difference in favour of boys with regard to the proportions claiming to have found out something before by practical investigation, apparent in relation to 'Shadows', was not found for 'Snail'. The most likely explanation of the difference is a context effect of the question, despite children being asked to answer 'about anything'.

### 'Shadow graph'

This question was presented to children in a written form in one of the written test packages and to individual children during the interview following the practical investigation. The two forms of the question are indicated on page 93, together with the mean scores for the three parts of it. The comparison of results, which overall favours the oral presentation, must be considered against the different test contexts. Children answering the written question encountered it in a package of other questions of completely different subject matter, whilst the children interviewed had just spent upwards of 30 minutes in practical investigation and discussion of the same subject matter as described in the question.

The mean scores on page 93 show two points of interest. Firstly, the differences in performance in the two contexts reside mainly in the first part of the question which required a statement of the relationship shown in the graph, rather than in the second and third parts which involved reading from the graph. Secondly, with oral presentation boys' performance was higher than girls' particularly, but not only, in the description of a relationship.

The oral responses recorded by the testers and the written responses were categorised using the same scheme. The results can be compared in Table 11.11.

**Table 11.11** *Types of pattern statement in pupils' written and oral responses to 'Shadow graph'*
(Percentage of pupils, 1984 data)

| Category of response | Written | Oral |
|---|---|---|
| Correct statement of relationship (eg the closer the torch the larger the shadow, or vice versa) | 11 | 24 |
| Incomplete statement (eg shadow became shorter when torch was moved) | 8 | 4 |
| Indication of existence but not of type of relationship | 8 | 6 |
| Statement about graph but not about relationship (eg it tells you how big the shadow is) | 1 | 12 |
| Statement about change in size of shadow only | 17 | 21 |
| Incorrect statement of relationship | 5 | 9 |
| Other non-pattern statements including attempts to give explanation | 23 | 6 |
| No response | 27 | 17 |

In the written form there were less than half the proportion of correct and complete pattern statements found in the oral responses. There was also a much greater proportion of unclassified 'other' answers which were non-relevant statements showing misunderstanding of the question. The proportion of complete pattern statements by the interviewed children was very much less than the proportion who made such statements in describing their own results, as indicated in Table 11.9. This seems to suggest that the experience of seeing the effect of changing one variable on another is highly significant in children's grasp of a relationship. When represented on paper only, the meaning in terms of real things changing in relation to one another is grasped by rather a small proportion of pupils. The sophistication of the written expression of the patterns found in their own practical investigation strongly suggests that the low performance by expressing patterns on paper is not a matter of vocabulary or writing demand but of grasping the nature of a relationship.

Categorisation of the answers to the questions to parts (b) and (c) of 'Shadow graph' showed that the main reason for lower scores of the oral group was the omission of units, which was penalised in the mark scheme. The accuracy of reading (disregarding units) was at a similar level (about 50 per cent) for both groups, with no gender differences.

## 11.4 Summary and implications

Individual practical investigations have been included in four of the five surveys at age 11. Each child in the sub-sample for these practical tests has been asked to carry out up to three investigations in the presence of a trained tester. The child's performance has been recorded using a check-list, with clarification of some aspects provided through a discussion at the end of practical work. Each investigation has been distinct in its demands and the problems have been chosen so that, between them, a wide range of skills of investigation have been called upon. In the fifth survey two investigations were devised so that the skills assessed included question raising in one and describing and using patterns in a practical context in the other.

The results have shown that it is hazardous to attempt to generalise about children's performance in the various investigations. The particular subject matter of a problem has a very strong influence on performance, introducing a number of variables whose influence cannot easily be disentangled. This is borne out both by the detailed accounts of performance in an investigation as a whole, which have been given in the full survey reports, and the analysis of results in terms of various component parts of the investigations. The analysis has shown, for example, that children have generally set up a situation which enabled the effect of the independent variable to be investigated (adopted a good general approach, in other words) except where this involved a combination of two variables or conditions. Variables which had to be controlled for a fair test were kept unchanged if they were obvious and limited in number, but in many problems a 'rough and ready' treatment of variables characterised the children's performance.

Unless the problem specifically suggested measurement, pupils tended to judge results by eye rather than by more accurate means. They did not set up situations so that quantitative methods could be used to find a result. Very small proportions of children repeated measurements to check results. Generally the pupils made some record of their work or results but it was notable that they rarely used diagrams, tables or other conventional forms to record observations or measurements unless a structure was provided for this.

Invariably the children reached a conclusion from their practical work, being prepared to give an answer to the problem posed even when the evidence they had obtained was insufficient to sustain it. It was remarkable that no child decided that he or she could not give an answer or said 'I can't tell', when this would in fact have been the most scientific conclusion from the evidence provided by their investigation.

There were no consistent gender differences in the performance of the investigations, but boys were given higher ratings than girls in willingness to undertake the investigation. Both sexes were, however, given a high rating in their general attitude to the practical work; the average for boys being 1.6 and for girls 1.4 from a maximum rating of 2. Another feature of performance rated, using criteria which were the same for all investigations, was the pupils' critical comment on their procedures when the work had been completed and discussed. The average rating in this case was 0.8 from a maximum of 2, with no gender differences.

Additional information gathered in the 1984 survey came from presenting orally, during the individual administration, certain questions which were also presented to other children in a purely written form. Not surprisingly, perhaps, this showed that higher performance was associated with oral presentation. There were much lower levels of children not responding, or saying they did not know, and of non-relevant answers in the oral presentation. This suggested less misunderstanding of the question when presented by a tester and leads to the conclusion that more children may be able to give better answers to these questions than do so in the written tests.

Perhaps of greater significance was the result of categorising the statements children made of their findings in the 'Shadows' investigation. The proportion of pupils expressing these results as a relationship (78 per cent) was very much above the proportion expressing their interpretation of given data (in which a pattern existed) as a relationship. This result suggests that it is the visualising of the relationship rather than finding a way to express it which is the main reason for the much lower proportion of children

(generally under 25 per cent) who express a pattern in given data as a relationship between the variables.

The implications for assessment arising from the findings of **Performance of investigations** confirm, on the one hand, the importance of including this particular form of testing in the framework but, on the other hand, indicate the difficulty of interpreting the results. Each investigation as a whole presents a unique set of demands which vary widely from those of other investigations depending on the subject matter and the type of question posed. Thus an 'average' performance across all investigations has little meaning; the important information lies in the way pupils have responded to the different demands presented by the problems.

The position is not unlike that created by the difficulty of drawing conclusions from case studies in educational research. Some claim that conclusions must be drawn by the reader, whilst others have developed methods of meta-analysis for combining the results from separate studies (Glass, 1981). The approach used here, of reviewing the investigations in terms of a set of components, has much in common with case-study review and represents something of a half-way position. The components have been chosen by a combination of statistical analysis and informed judgement.

The importance of assessing **Performance of investigations** in the surveys is seen not only in the information it gives about how children tackle whole problems but also in the light thrown on the results of assessing other categories of the framework. Because of the freedom of action in the whole investigation context it is possible to find out whether children *will* use certain skills where they are appropriate and not only whether they can use them. So, for instance, it is found in the **Reading** and **Representing** subcategories that children can with ease use information in the form of tables, but **Performance of investigations** shows that they rarely tabulate data out of choice. The opposite situation is also revealed, where children will operate more effectively in the practical context (as in describing patterns and using results) than they do in a written question which is focused on a particular skill.

All this adds up to saying that the assessment of practical investigations provides information which is essential to the interpretation of information from other categories and which does not duplicate it, in addition to yielding data which cannot be obtained in any other way.

There are curriculum implications in several of the above points. Practical investigations provide the concrete experiences which enable children to use, and so to develop, skills without the barrier of having to visualise a situation at second hand. But activity and investigation is not *per se* scientific. Much evidence has been presented which shows that children's investigations lack the features which make an enquiry scientific; moreover the children appear not to realise this, for they are generally uncritical of the way they have tackled a problem. Whilst there is a great deal to be said for allowing children to try things their own way and learn from mistakes, there will be no learning if they do not recognise 'mistakes' or if they do not realise that there is room for improvement in the procedures they have used. There seems to be a case, therefore, once children have confidence in their ability to tackle problems by practical enquiry, for introducing more discussion of what they have done, how they have done it and what alternative courses of action could have been taken.

In such discussions there are several worthwhile points of focus. Children may have controlled only the most obvious variables, as they did in the surveys; can they suggest other things which should be kept the same during the investigation to make a more fair result? They may have made decisions about what to measure or compare; did they consider other possibilities? They may have made rather rough observations of the result; would measurements have helped? They probably based their result on one set of observations or measurements; what would happen if they repeated the observations? The survey suggests that it is worth checking whether the results were recorded in a systematic and ordered fashion; what ways would be most appropriate?

The enthusiasm and enjoyment which children showed in their practical work suggests that there would be interest in discussing better ways of doing it, especially if these discussions were carried out in the practical context and not at a theoretical level.

There is some evidence of differences between the experience and enjoyment of girls and boys in practical investigations. Alerted to this, teachers might take steps to ensure the participation of girls in both action and discussion. The surveys show that the abilities of girls in practical enquiry are no different from those of boys but their attitudes may well be less positive. Attention to this is important if girls are to share equally with boys enjoyment in continuing science activities in their later education.

# 12

# A summary and exploration of links across science activity categories

## 12.1 Introduction

It was stated in Chapter 1 (p. 1) that a particular view of science is implicit in the assessment framework and operationalised in the form of the Science Activity Categories. The emphasis of the framework can be more explicitly stated as a particular perspective viewing the scientific activities of pupils as a range of operations, procedures or processes applied to the objects and events of the physical world. There is an emphasis on the active, investigatory nature of scientific behaviour. Although implemented within a framework developed for assessment purposes, its claims for validity rest on a view of science learning as an actively participatory endeavour. The emphasis is not on reception learning, rote memorisation and recall (though memory is certainly involved in the processes described). The focus is the assessment of children's behaviour, their performance when required to function scientifically, bearing in mind that 'science is to be regarded as a mode of thought and activity which may be encountered in a number of subjects appearing in the school curriculum' (DES, 1978a). The tensions and discrepancies which may arise in practice between this 'generalist' view of primary education and the occasional 'specialist' demands of scientific thinking will receive more attention later.

The division of science into the assessment categories was a necessary exercise, ensuring that assessment might be both manageable and meaningful. Although the monitoring of changes requires a stable measurement instrument, feedback from practice has led to modification in some areas. The fact that few changes have been necessary reflects the success of the Science Steering Group in producing a coherent and workable structure, rather than a commitment to inertia on the part of the development teams. However, domain-sampling requires enormous efforts to develop item pools which are large enough to operate reliably. The annual survey reports have frequently issued caveats against hasty conclusions, due to the need for further evidence, but with data from five years of surveys, some more definitive commentaries have been attempted and advanced within the Category chapters. It remains for this chapter to explore how these divergent strands may link one with another. The science activity categories represent science in pieces. Is it possible to fit the pieces back together again in any sensible fashion?

One method of obtaining something approaching a coherent picture in reviewing performance across the categories is to start with the **Performance of investigations.** This category has had a special role in the assessment programme. The features of individual practical assessment, the requirement for the integration of a variety of scientific activities and the goal-directed investigatory or problem-solving nature of the tasks presented to children result in tasks which derive validity from being recognisably close to what might be happening in primary classrooms. This in-depth assessment on a small range of tasks ideally complements the much greater breadth of context, content and discrete skills which it is only possible to approach via the much larger numbers of domain-referenced questions. Since a discussion of children's **Performance of investigations** makes frequent reference to some common factors in the design and implementation of investigations, it will help to have these in clear focus before considering specific results from other areas of the framework.

The following chapter will firstly summarise the main points arising from the **Performance of investigations,** and then move on to explore how results from each of the other areas of the framework relate to those findings. The categories will be discussed in turn in sections 12.3 to 12.7 inclusive. **Applying science concepts** is not treated in the same way as the other assessment categories, but is discussed in section 12.8, together with some comments on 'content' and 'context'. *This organisation is in recognition of the crucial importance of viewing all outcomes of the assessment exercise as a product of the interaction between the demands of process and content.* Section 12.8 thus spans the other categories as well as looking specifically at some concept demands. The more general vantage point is maintained in section 12.9 which examines children's response to demands for divergent thinking in various aspects of the framework. Section 12.10, again looking very broadly across the results of the assessment exercise, identifies some areas of gender-linked differences in performances.

## 12.2 Summary of 'Performance of investigations'

Fourteen investigations is a relatively small number despite the huge expenditure in time and resources and the enormous amount of in-depth information which has resulted.

It has become evident that, depending on the particular content employed to frame an investigation, the burden of particular process demands has varied. These differences in emphasis were deliberately exploited rather than suppressed, question differences being maximised so as to provide evidence across the range of science processes. The detailed reporting of each investigation offers considerable insights into children's performance. However, it has also proved possible to make valid comparisons across investigations by re-analysis of check-lists. A combination of statistical association, logical connection and educational relevance has led to the postulation of five components of the process of investigation, each not necessarily present in every investigation. Performance characteristics on each of the components will be discussed in turn.

The first component, *General approach,* embraces the setting up of a situation in which the independent variable can be investigated. Where the problem *defines* the independent variable performance levels are high. Naturally enough, where some redefinition is required, levels are lower; sometimes very much lower, as when two variables have to be manipulated in order to tackle the problem. (An example is 'Swingboards' where length *and* width of boards affect the period of swing.) It should be remembered that the independent variable may vary continuously along a given physical dimension, eg mass, or length or time. Alternatively, rather than being formulated as a *continuous variable,* it may in other cases consist of a series of discrete physical states or objects. An example of the latter would be an investigation to find out which of three given kinds of paper is best to use for covering a book. In this case, the variety in the nature of the paper, a *discontinuous variable,* itself constitutes the independent variable, and performance on *General approach* is relatively high. Primary children have more familiarity with discontinuous variables in other areas, such as in drawing bar charts. This point will be developed under the section 'Use of graphs, tables and charts'.

*Control of variables* was well managed when variables were obvious in their effects and few in number. Advance knowledge of the outcome of certain actions implies that conceptual understanding is important in knowing what may interfere with the isolation of the independent variable. The concept burden inherent in a task and the knowledge base possessed by the investigator may be important factors in an investigation. Whilst the specifically learned-science conceptual background required within any task was kept to a minimum in most problems, in some investigations in which it was inherent there was evidence that it depressed performance on this component. A different kind of shortcoming was more readily identifiable as procedural. This was the 'rough and ready' lack of care and control which was occasionally in evidence, particularly in the problems set in more everyday contexts. (By contrast, the presence of equipment and measuring instruments may have cued children to use more rigorous controls in some other investigations.) Lack of attention to the finer points may be evidence of lack of familiarity with the normal procedures adopted in an investigation.

*Measurement of the dependent variable* shows evidence of two distinct factors influencing performance. Firstly, there is the problem which children must resolve of *what* it is that must be measured in order to gather information relevant to the investigation. Secondly, a decision must be taken as to *how* the measurements are to be made, if at all. Where a conceptual burden existed, problems in deciding *what* to measure were more likely to occur. In other investigations, although children may have been perfectly clear about the outcome to be heeded, poor performance was due to a superficial qualitative gathering of 'results', frequently a casual visual inspection, when a quantitative treatment would have been more appropriate.

Performance in the fourth component, *Recording of findings,* was frequently disorganised and descriptive but was enhanced when a ready-made table was provided in appropriate cases. It would appear that children felt little obligation to record the results of their own investigations, and did not deploy skills in the context of tackling these practical investigations which performance in other categories of the framework suggests that they have available, eg the use of tables to organise their results.

The fifth component, *Nature of result,* refers to the consistency between results and evidence, and obviously has a logical connection with the dependent variable selected as addressing the solution to the problem. A child's selection of an inappropriate dependent variable might imply that a problem other than that presented was investigated, with consequent difficulties of interpretation. Children also encountered difficulties due to insufficient evidence being collected to justify or support the conclusion drawn. There was also evidence of difficulties in drawing together the separate pieces of data into an overall result.

These are the broad points emerging in **Performance of investigations.** They complement the more richly detailed points drawn out in the individual reports of investigations. A number of the points mentioned may be amplified or elaborated by reference to other areas of the assessment framework. The following sections will briefly summarise the findings in each of the categories or subcategories, and refer back to the **Performance of investigations** where relevant.

## 12.3  Use of graphs, tables and charts

In this review, the two subcategories, **Reading** and **Representing,** have been reported in combination. Performance levels in this area have been consistently higher than in other areas of the framework. This category has often been regarded as embracing activities on the fringes of science, or as posing a 'hurdle' to be crossed in some other question types. This is probably as a result of affinities with mathematics, and of the discrete technical skills which can be identified. However, it can be argued that skills in this area, particularly those involving co-ordinate forms, may be the closest formal representation to the structure of an experimental procedure to which children at ages 10/11 are exposed. A line graph not only represents a set of data points; it also implies a relationship between two variables and a methodology in setting one variable against another. It is not suggested that this is the way in which graphs are introduced to primary pupils. Rather, that if we search the experiences contributing to a schema relating to experimental procedures, it is on the *reading* and *representing* of data as graphs and tables that we find the closest formal representation, particularly for those pupils whose lives are touched by science only incidentally. Evidence suggests that there is a considerable gulf between the ability to manipulate the representation and the ability to see the implicit relationship and rationale behind various coordinate forms.

In summarising results it was found that a convenient way through the complexity was to trace five Question groups: Tables, Bar charts, Graphs and grids, Pie charts and Other logical forms (Venn diagrams, flow charts, etc).

The three coordinate forms have the most obvious link with **Performance of investigations**. Performance declined from Tables, through Bar charts to Graphs/grids, with a significant difference between the first and the last of these groups. This age group shows a greater familiarity and competence when handling discontinuous variables, and the progression of declining facility through bar charts and line graphs possibly parallels the learning exposure of most children. The greater success with physically discrete independent variables when performing investigations also no doubt reflects this experience.

It is salutary to compare performance on 'Tables' (mean score 67 per cent), when assessed as a focused and discrete skill, with pupils' use of tables in an investigation on an occasion when it would be appropriate to do so. (In the 'Sailboats' investigation, only 2 per cent used tabulation to record the progress of three different hull shapes combined with three different sail shapes: DES, 1984a, page 96). Such discrepancies do not invalidate pencil and paper assessment procedures, provided clear distinctions about the situations in which the skills are deployed are borne in mind. In this instance pupils have a competence which, for unknown reasons, they fail to use to their advantage.

This failure to deploy an apparently available skill calls for a very careful consideration of the range of possible explanations. The simplest level of explanation might hypothesise a lack of familiarity with investigations, and a failure to recognise an opportunity to use a skill at a particular juncture. Such omissions might be amenable to correction by more experience of investigations. On the other hand, a view of the use of tables (or, as touched upon earlier in this section, graphs) as organising struc-tures has quite different implications. The latter view is describing a way in which a scientific investigation sets about imposing order, rather than the incidental deployment of a skill. The evidence from the **Planning** category does not support the view that pupils at age 11 use such well defined organising structures in their plans for investigations. Whether they are capable of doing so is an open question. However, it would seem to satisfy both logic and common sense to conclude that tables and graphs, like plans, are most meaningfully approached by reference to real data, within broadly defined 'investigations'. Primary mathematics has made great strides in emphasising the understanding which must accompany mathematical operations. There are undoubtedly lessons in this history for the use of data communication forms in primary science. A number of questions based on graphs were used by the APU Mathematics team (DES, 1985c). A summary and discussion of performance on graphical forms is included in the independent appraisal of the mathematics monitoring, where the point is made that pupils' increasing access to computer software which encourages the storage and sorting of data by reference to rows and columns may serve to increase the fund of experience relevant to the use of coordinate forms (DES, 1985e, Chapter 7).

Performance on Bar charts was depressed by the use of compound or nested bars, sometimes requiring the use of a key. If the scale had to be operated in order to make a reading, the question was made more difficult (compared with a simple comparison of bar lengths, for example). Where coordinates were on unlabelled grid lines, or, more testing still, where interpolation between grid lines was required, performance levels tended to be further depressed. A very similar picture emerged in the Graphs/grids Question group, but with a trend of lower scores. The difficulties of interpolation encountered on the measured variable of a bar chart become possible on both axes of a line graph, where both axes represent continuous variables. In using bar graphs and line graphs, it has been noted that it is the labelling conventions which are most frequently neglected or ignored. As Figure 5.2 (p. 34) clearly shows, labelling of the axes to indicate the identity of the variable and measurement units is very incomplete. Again, it is tempting to draw parallels with the lack of operationalisation and casual regard for quantitification of the dependent variable which are in evidence both in **Performance of investigations** and in **Planning**. As the next section shows very clearly, it should not be assumed that children have a very clear idea of physical quantities. Their omission as labels on a graph may be more than mere oversight.

## 12.4 Use of apparatus and measuring instruments

For children at age eleven, the approach to the identification, quantification and measurement of a dependent variable during an investigation will be limited to the existing repertoire of understanding of physical quantities. In most cases, this range will derive from experience (probably gained through activities in mathematics) of standard measures of length, area, volume, mass, time and perhaps temperature. Many children will also have experience of inventing and using non-standard measures. The science-specific units and the related measuring instruments which are more familiar to pupils at the secondary stage, will not yet be available. As well as increasing the measurement repertoire at the secondary stage, the units are closely linked to concepts and consequently specifically tied to a science context. The contextualisation of the more general measurements assessed at age 11 has been provided by associating them wtih the **Performance of investigations.**

The only non-measuring instruments introduced into the assessment procedures—a pipette dropper and a hand lens—were used relatively successfully, the former by two-thirds, the latter by at least three-quarters of those assessed.

When the tasks were presented within investigations, at least 75 per cent of pupils were able to read instruments for measuring length, temperature, volume and mass (within fairly generous criteria of acceptability). Children found much more difficulty in *estimating* area, volume, mass and temperature, all values being markedly under-estimated except for time. In addition to estimating a given quantity, a variation on the estimation task was to require a specified amount to be separated from a larger quantity. This task difference resulted in marked performance differences for both mass and area estimates. Though the virtue of standard measures is that they permit comparisons across materials and contexts, it was very apparent that for children at age 11, the task, the particular magnitude and the specified material may all have a significant influence on performance in *estimation*.

In assessments involving measuring instruments, the distinction between simply reading a scale and using the instruments to make a measurement with some accuracy is a crucial one. This point is brought clearly into focus with the information that only 10 per cent adjusted the spring balance to zero before starting to make a reading—exactly the same percentage as did so in the context of an investigation. When handed the thermometer in its translucent plastic case, only 15 per cent removed it from the case before placing it in the water. (In the first survey, 17 per cent removed the thermometer from its case.) Only 18 per cent of children measured 135 ml of water in two steps when provided with a 100 ml measuring cylinder. Ten per cent used the measuring cylinder as if it were a ruler, placing it beside the beaker of water. The quantities which pupils could readily measure with some accuracy were time and straight length. Volume, area and curved length were less accurately measured and temperature presented the greatest difficulty. When asked to read the pre-set scales of a stop-clock, thermometer and measuring cylinder, performance differed considerably from results

*using* an instrument. For example, reading a stop-clock dial was performed less accurately, probably because minutes and seconds were involved and the passage of the minute-hand had not been witnessed. For temperature scale reading, accuracy of $\pm 2°C$ was achieved by 75 per cent of pupils. The major difference in *use* (once it has been indicated that the thermometer should be removed from its case) is the movement of the thermometer liquid level. Volume was read to $\pm 2$ ml by 95 per cent of the sample, a very much better level of performance than in *use*.

It may be of particular significance that all children who named units correctly also gave a response within the closest range in their use of measuring instruments for time and for volume. (This association was not apparent for temperature measurements.) Certainly, performance on **Use of apparatus and measuring instruments,** limited in scope though it is for this younger age group, offers an interesting perspective on children's handling of the dependent variable in the **Performance of investigations.** If performance in taking measurements is as tied to specific content as the evidence presented in Chapter 6 suggests, it is tempting to conclude that a more general usage and understanding will only be achieved through a wider experience of using, estimating and measuring physical quantities of all kinds. That wider experience may in turn give children insights into applications of measurement strategies of which the great majority seem at present to be unaware. Quantification is such a fundamental strategy in scientific decision making that it seems quite wrong to regard measurement as a mere 'hurdle' to higher level skills. Measurement strategies are central to most investigations. Present evidence suggests that they are neglected by pupils at age 11.

## 12.5 Observation

This category has encountered more fundamental problems of definition than any of the other science activity categories, perhaps because the word itself is widely used in educational contexts, but also because psychological and philosophical interpretations may vary. The receptivity to sensory experiences tends to be the general educational emphasis in usage. In a science context, it is accepted that perception is theory-laden, but some attempt has been made to avoid a burden on learned-science conceptual knowledge in the **Observation** questions. Instead, *focused* demands are made for sensory-based information handling, using procedures such as *matching,* using *branching keys,* finding *similarities and differences, classification, sequencing, drawing* and finally *describing patterns.* The ability to make free-ranging observations by reference to personal criteria is not what is being assessed. Rather, there is an aggregation of activities, all closely constraining pupils towards the particular kinds of observation required.

The administration of practical as opposed to written questions of itself would be insufficient to define **Observation** as a discrete and identifiable 'Science activity category'. The distinction between practical and written presentations is anyway not absolute, since many resources in **Observation** are in the form of drawings or photographic representations, rather than physical objects. This is an important point in view of the finding that the nature of the resource appears to have an important bearing on performance. The point was made in the introduction to this chapter that all performance outcomes should be interpreted as the product of an interaction between process and content (where 'content' implies theory-laden assumptions about the subject-matter, if not an actual learned science burden). The problems of avoiding a science conceptual knowledge burden in **Observation** questions might be deemed insurmountable, in view of this position. What happened in practice was that 'everyday' knowledge was not excluded as a requirement in some questions; other questions adopted an 'information-processing' stance. This distinction may help to clarify the relationship of **Observation** to other categories in the assessment framework.

The **Observation** questions which have an obvious concept burden require children to impose some kind of classification system on materials. For example, seeds may have to be sorted into groups according to criteria imposed by the children themselves. The criteria may be size, shape, smell, texture, porosity, hardness, etc. Assumptions about what are the important characteristics of seeds will govern the choice. Decision making about the important qualitative distinctions between seeds, clearly a theory-laden activity, is analogous to the decision which must take place in any investigation about the nature of the more important variables which might be operating. It would make little sense to attempt to describe these decisions without reference to the particular subject matter involved. There is an implicit concept burden.

The 'information processing' viewpoint is not so closely tied to considerations of content. Two levels of sensory information processing can be distinguished in the **Observation** category. The first can be described as being concerned with generalisations about data, while the second is concerned with specifics.

The questions which call for generalisations to be made about data in the **Observation** category would seem to be posing a demand similar to that posed in the **Interpretation** subcategory when children are asked to describe a relationship between x and y. Questions can be set in each category, the only difference being the mode of presentation (ie practical or written). Clearly some data which can be presented in written form are totally unsuitable for practical administration on grounds of cost, scale or the dangerous nature of the materials described. Another constraint on **Observation** questions is that with quantification, the process of observation gives way to *measurement,* which could be described as formalised observation having external and quantified criteria. To avoid this quantification, pattern-description questions in **Observation** tend to be limited to data of a categorical nature.

The second type of information-processing demand in the **Observation** category is related to the specific nature of elements within data. Rather than requiring an overall pattern, questions require children to focus on elements and make comparisons, seek identities, describe differences, etc. The range, acuity, accuracy and perhaps speed of information handling in various modalities is assessed. These skills are relevant to the collection of qualitative data in an investigation. While the type of demand described here would appear to have a much reduced concept burden, it may not be negligible. For example, drawing could be described as primarily a matching task in a science context. It was interesting to find that boys performed significantly better than girls when required to draw a 13 amp plug. The established finding that boys perform better than girls on questions centred on electricity (DES, 1984e) extends even to activities including drawing. In this one question is found a striking example of how process and content may interact.

When performance in the **Observation** category is examined by reference to the type of resource employed, it emerges that questions using representations in the form of drawings and photographs have a higher overall mean score than those presenting actual objects or events. There has been a gradual shift in the pool of questions to favour real objects and events, with a consequent depression in the overall category score. No doubt the selectively focused nature of a drawing or photograph offers children something of a pre-digested task. In school and in their everyday lives it is real objects that children encounter. The constraints of reliability and reproducibility of resources occasionally dictate the use of these substitute representations, but the better levels of performance resulting certainly would not justify the advocacy of similar materials for teaching purposes.

As mentioned earlier, it is possible to present matched questions which meet the definitions of the **Observation** category in their practical form, while in written form they fall within the definitions of the **Interpreting** subcategory. A small number of such questions were exposed during the 1983 survey and briefly reported (DES, 1985a, Appendix 9, pages 250-254). The expectation that the age group might be better able to abstract a general pattern when using real objects rather than written and diagrammatic representations was not upheld. Children tended to have slightly more success on average when responding to written versions of questions. Possibly this is related to the inevitably more focused and organised nature of the written data presentation, where to some extent decisions about selection of relevant data have already been made. This is another important consideration to be borne in mind in any attempt to translate the lessons learned from assessment into possible implications for teaching.

## 12.6 Interpreting presented information

Most questions in this subcategory actually name the independent and dependent variables, present data pairs relating to them, and require children to *describe* the relationship, make a *prediction* based on an inferred relationship or *justify* a prediction. In the context of components of **Performance of investigations** described in section 12.2, there is clearly some connection with the last component which includes a consideration of whether results are quantitative, and whether the conclusions drawn are congruent with the data collected. Not all presented information in the **Interpreting** subcategory is quantified, but the necessity for imposing an order consistent with that information is a constant factor. The pool of almost 200 questions has permitted a much broader exploration of the conditions influencing children's ability to interpret presented information than is possible within the small range of practical investigations. The **Interpreting** subcategory further extends the range of relationships which children are required to consider by virtue of the fact that they have not had to generate the data themselves. A possible sense of commitment to the data may therefore be missing, but responses generally show a sense of involvement, and rates of non-response are low.

The overall mean scores for **Interpreting** suggest that the scoring criteria are difficult for this age group to meet. This does not imply that children experience a sense of difficulty. Many energetic, confident responses are non-scoring, but in the context of the whole framework, performance is within the lower three of the six domain-referenced areas. A significant difference between *describe* and *predict* questions in favour of the latter has been detected, but this must be viewed with caution as the two groups are not matched on all characteristics. This paradoxical finding (which has echoes at other ages and in other parts of the framework) draws attention to a basic assessment problem. The paradox is that a prediction (in practice by means of interpolation or extrapolation) is only possible *after* a relationship has been established. It appears that pupils find it more difficult to gain marks for their descriptions of relationships, these requiring a lengthier and more precise verbal expression than do predictions. It seems that pupils' competence in establishing relationships as revealed by their ability to make predictions based on them is not matched by their performance in accurate verbal expression. To describe a relationship accurately carries a certain expressive language burden, including the use of comparative adjectives (rather than the often-favoured absolute form) and sometimes, as when there are perturbations in the data, conditional clauses. It is possible that children are experiencing similar difficulties in the **Performance of investigations** in expressing the relationship between collected data and conclusions drawn. The effects of verbal as opposed to written communications are not known in this context. It seems likely that many children need educating to the fact that, for example, 'The *higher* the ramp, the *further* the truck rolls' and 'The truck rolls *furthest* when

the ramp is *highest*' are not interchangeable and equivalent statements. Once again, we see the particular precision and attention to detail required in a science, as distinct from an everyday context. This problem of distinguishing what pupils believe they have implied, in contrast to what they have objectively stated, is encountered throughout the assessment framework.

These considerations of language apart, there are other, more science-specific comments which can be made about children's performance on **Interpreting** questions. The first point to make here is backed not so much by survey performance outcomes as by experience of developing and managing the pool of questions. This relates to the degree of 'embeddedness' of the presented information. Where extraneous 'noise' has risen to unacceptable levels, questions will have been rejected during trials. Without this kind of management, the subcategory estimate would be even lower than it is. Pupils at age 11 have enough difficulties describing an uncluttered relationship that has been drawn to their attention.

More clearly based in actual performance characteristics is the effect of the particular pattern of regularity contained in the presented information. Nine different patterns of relationship have been identified, and defined where possible in terms of the functional relationship between independent and dependent variables. It has been found that Pattern type so defined has a significant effect on performance. Performance tended to be higher on average on those questions in which data were concerned with dynamic spatial regularities, such as occur in the use of pulleys and gears. This association is *not* independent of the mode of data presentation, another variable having a significant effect on performance. The Pattern types causing children most difficulty appear to do so for two quite different reasons. In the first type it is because a subjective view or personal knowledge overrides any hypothetical inductive process; in the second, it is apparently due more directly to the complexity of the information presented. These two types of difficulty are by no means restricted to the **Interpreting** subcategory.

The matter of whether independent and dependent variables are expressed in Pictorial, Verbal, Numerical or Graphical form also has a significant effect on performance. Seven combinations of these notational forms were possible. The highest overall mean score was obtained in the group of only four questions in which both variables were presented in words. This implies the presence of categorical data and discontinuous variables. (In three of these four questions, the performance of girls was significantly higher than that of boys.) The other three combinations of notation associated with higher scores all included the pictorial or diagrammatic presentation of information. The use of numbers and graphs in presenting information was associated with lower mean scores, and performance favouring boys. Of course, more complex information presentation is often possible in numerical or graphical form. It is also more probable that this mode will be used to express a physical science content, which tends to favour boys.

In the discussion of the **Observation** category, reference was made to a finding that on average, children had greater success in describing a pattern when presented with written data than when physical objects were presented. This may be because the written task is more focused. A rather different situation was described in Chapter 11 in the context of **Performance of investigations.** A typical set of data about the distance of an object from a screen and the size of the shadow which it cast was represented by a line graph. In this situation, where the data were accompanied by the actual apparatus used to plot the relationship, success rates in describing the relationship were higher than in the written version of the **Interpreting** question. Although a solitary instance, this question does suggest that the presence of the relevant physical materials may help children to interpret a set of data which would otherwise be problematic; the burden of envisaging the physical set-up has been removed, the data have been selected, and the question has been clearly focused. This may be in contrast to some questions in the **Observation** category where the burden on selection of data may not be completely eliminated.

## 12.7  Planning of investigations

In the **Planning** category the connections with the **Performance of investigations** are self-evident, but the assessment problems are entirely different. Two subcategories are represented. **Planning parts of investigations** uses domain-sampling from a pool of about 200 questions, while **Planning entire investigations** has used 14 hand-selected questions requiring written responses to tasks parallel to those in the **Performance of investigations.** A few additional questions assess **Identifying or proposing testable statements.**

In **Planning parts of investigations,** questions attempted to focus children's attention on just one particular aspect of the planning process, other necessary information being given. The balance of the question pool reflects the attention given to 'fair-testing' in primary science. Questions which required the identification of *variables to be controlled* had the highest overall mean scores. This was in an open response format, pupils being asked what needed to be kept the same in a given investigation for the test to be fair. It was not possible to relate any particular features to facility. Questions concerned with whether the *independent variable* could be correctly identified asked children to say what would be changed *and* what would be kept the same, ie would not be changed. Those children who successfully identified the *independent variable* tended to identify what would be controlled as well, but the reverse was not the case. When the same type of problem had to be considered at a more focused and specified operational level, pupils tended to have greater success.

That is, children were better at suggesting specific actions relating to the independent variable than with general considerations.

Approaching **Planning parts of investigations** from a different perspective were those questions which required pupils to assess the possibility of addressing each of four stated questions by means of the common set of procedures which were described in words and pictures. (The independent, controlled and dependent variables being implicitly identified in the procedures.) Results on this type of question indicate that children had greater success in accepting those questions which *could* validly be answered by the procedures described than they had in rejecting those questions which could not. (A similar difficulty in rejecting unsubstantiated conclusions is also strongly in evidence in the subcategory **Judging the applicability of a given generalisation.**) This type of question is one of the three concerned with the *dependent variable,* all of which are associated with lower levels of performance. Performance was at levels half or less of those concerned with controls and the independent variable.

In those questions in which children were asked to define what was to be compared or measured, the majority of answers were characterised by vagueness, imprecision or irrelevance. Rather than providing precise specifications of what they would measure, children tended to describe a general intention to 'see how many/how much/which is most'. The lack of detail and specificity which has been remarked upon in so many other areas eg **Applying science concepts, Observation,** was again noticeable. The next question type described how an investigation had been conducted and asked children to justify or criticise the procedures adopted. As with the previous question type discussed, overall mean scores were low and rates of non-response high, children showing little recognition of procedures which would make measurement more accurate. Finally, attention was focused on how results would be used by presenting a whole investigation with procedural details. Children were asked to say how the results could help to solve the problem being investigated. Many children were drawn to offering particular solutions and specific procedural criticisms, rather than commenting on the logic of solving the problem. As described in the **Interpreting** subcategory discussion, the resort to personal knowledge is a strategy which is frequently seen.

In **Planning entire investigations,** presenting the task to children unambiguously is less problematic, but a higher rate of non-response is probably due in part to the greater writing demands. Particular question content appears to affect performance markedly, but some comparative comments are possible as the mark schemes used had a common structure within which eight components were identified.

The great majority of pupils *attempted a response* of some kind to all questions, with most of these responses having an *investigation proposed,* (rather than, for example, a comment on a possible result). These two components apart, there was considerable variation in mean scores for the other components across questions. The *independent variable* was identified more readily when it comprised discrete physical objects than when the investigation required combinations or variations of conditions. A description of how the *independent variable* was to be *operationalised* caused more difficulty in every question. *Control of variables* received very little attention in the complete plans.

Turning to a consideration of the dependent variable, scores were higher for its *identification* in those cases in which the investigation was open to a range of different strategies. *Operationalisation* of the *dependent variable* was in all cases at a lower level of performance than was its identification alone. *Interpretation* of results was poorer still. Of course, identification, operationalisation and interpretation of measurements of the dependent variable are inter-connected, and some attenuation of performance is perhaps to be expected on this basis. Where interpretation of results also involved some conceptual underpinning, performance was particularly poor.

What the plans of entire investigations have in common is a uniformly low reference to the necessity for controls, poorer performance in relation to the dependent variable than the independent variable, and lack of specificity in operationalisation and interpretation. It would appear that the imposed focus of the **Planning parts** questions led to the control of variables being the area of best performance in that subcategory, while in **Planning entire investigations** it was the worst. It could be that controls are regarded as implicit in the whole plans, so that what is known is unstated. This might easily happen if requirements of the questions are unfamiliar and unrecognised. It may also be that children have little experience of producing plans and do not appreciate what they should contain. (This unfamiliarity might be relevant to the interpretation of performance on other components also.) An alternative interpretation might be that children have no recognition of the need for controls, implicit or explicit, until such need is directly drawn to their attention, in which circumstances they perform relatively well. It was noticeable that children paid more attention to the control of variables in the actual **Performance of investigations** questions which are parallel to the **Planning** questions. Both **Planning** subcategories revealed attenuated performance related to the dependent variable. It is tentatively suggested that pupils may be marginally better able to identify what to measure in the context of their own plans rather than in partly completed ones. As with the failure in nominating variables to be controlled, pupils lack of comment on how results are to be interpreted possibly occurs simply because they do not recognise this step as an integral part of the planning exercise.

The overall evidence is that performance in **Planning** is not well developed in the age 11 population, and that there is reason to infer that this is due in part at least to a limited appreciation of what is required, rather than the intrinsic difficulty of the task alone. Since a rigorous

plan will include more formal scientific procedures (controls ensuring that only the independent variable varies, repeated measurements, etc), those pupils who have brushed against science as only an incidental 'across-the-curriculum' experience will be unfamiliar with the possibilities for the elaboration of their responses. What has been assessed, quite legitimately, is *performance* in planning; this must not be read as pupils' *ability* to plan investigations.

It is perhaps opportune to make another important point about the implications of assessing **Planning** at this point in the discussion. Children's experience in planning investigations must in practice be tied to the experience of investigations themselves, so that the requirements of plans as actual prescriptions for actions which are carried out becomes a fundamental assumption. What was appropriate as an assessment strategy does not translate directly into classroom practice. This point can scarcely be overstated. During the 1982 survey (DES, 1984a) when **Planning** questions were introduced prior to investigations, the plans actually seemed to have a stultifying effect on performance, reducing flexibility and responsiveness to experimental feedback. In assessment terms, **Planning** questions have provided valuable insights. While plans could be used to help children to organise and focus their activities, the indications are that in practice, this might best be approached interactively, with the teacher (see 'Planning investigations at Age 11', DES, 1986a).

## 12.8   Concepts, Content and Context

All questions within the framework incorporate a particular question content or specific subject matter having some variable influence on performance. In the subcategory **Applying science concepts** it is the learned-science conceptual burden within the questions presented to children which is the actual assessment focus. The place of this subcategory within a framework which attempts to define predominantly the processes of science is justified by the emphasis on *applying* concepts rather than their recall alone. (Retrieval from memory can nevertheless be assumed to be part of the task of **Applying science concepts**.) The discussion in this section will firstly summarise performance on the taught-science concepts assessed in **Applying science concepts** followed by a consideration of the incidental influence of question *content* of a more general nature throughout the assessment framework. This will inevitably raise issues of question *context* which will also be briefly considered.

A science concept can be defined in terms of its unique attributes. Previous reporting has explored the understanding of some of the unique attributes of a few specific concepts, for example, energy and speed (DES, 1983a), pollen distribution (DES, 1984a), migration and hibernation (DES, 1985a). This type of detailed concept reporting from APU Science questions has also been a major component of the 'Children's Learning in Science Project'

(Bell and Driver, 1984). This project itself reflects the current widespread interest in the science education community in children's conceptual development (see, for example, Driver, 1983). A problem encountered in attempting a full and systematic reporting of any concept area has been that a domain-referenced item bank is not specifically constructed to meet such a need. Questions have been marked in detail to record the frequencies of various categories of response, but this has been for individual questions rather than batteries of questions exploring a particular concept. The general lessons learned from the assesment of **Applying science concepts** to be discussed here relate to the broader performance characteristics of a question pool containing considerable variety of content, concepts and modes of assessment.

Nine Question types have been used in the assessment of **Applying science concepts.** A variety of demands including generating, selecting and assessing predictions and explanations is embraced. A requirement for an explanation to be generated is by far the most common demand. No systematic effect of Question type on performance is discernible, though there is some indication of higher mean scores occurring in questions in which responses had to be selected rather than generated. This difference in performance levels between questions requiring Selection and those calling for the generation of responses has some parallel in the **Interpreting** subcategory, where an interpretation in terms of differing expressive language demands has been hypothesised earlier in this chapter. A rather similar problem associated with the written expression of ideas is found in the **Applying science concepts** questions. It is frequently difficult to distinguish, particularly in the briefer and more cryptic responses offered by children, whether the limited nature of their answers is attributable to a superficial understanding on their part or an insufficiently explicit response. Although to some extent it can be meaningful to discuss performance in relation to particular concepts, the point is stressed that increasing the requirement for *detailed* descriptions or explanations tends to make all concepts more difficult.

The list of science concepts developed for use with pupils at age 11 is organised into three main divisions or *concept regions:* 'Living things', 'Force and energy' and 'Materials and their characteristics' (see Appendix 9). Little difference in performance is in evidence at the level of concept region. In view of the apparent emphasis on living things in much primary education, this may be considered to be a surprising result. However, everyday experience can be an important source of information in responding to the particular style of questions used. Certainly, the precise source of pupils' knowledge will be indeterminate. There is also the possibility that questions have been tailored to make the more difficult concepts at least approachable to a reasonable number of pupils.

Each of the three *concept regions* is further divided into two *concept areas* which in turn encompass sixteen *concept groups.* This concept organisation is used at all three ages, though some concept groups are not used for the youngest age group, and the range and details of the concept application required also vary as appropriate. Nine of the sixteen concept groups were represented by five or more questions in surveys at age 11. Since the ranges of question scores were large, results cannot be conclusive. The group having the highest overall mean score (63 per cent) was concerned with *Reproduction* (life cycles). (This concept group is associated with a particular response mode, the re-ordering of drawings, so this performance must be interpreted with caution.) With overall mean scores of 37–38 per cent were *Movement and deformation* (speed—distance—time relationships), *The Earth in space* (gravity and astronomy) and *Waves* (light and sound). Dropping another five or six percentage points in overall mean scores, at 32–33 per cent were found *Interdependence of living things, Properties of matter* (pressure, water-levels, displacement) and *Electricity* (simple circuits). The lowest overall mean score (26 per cent) occurred in the question group concerned with *The physical and chemical environment* (seasonal cycles, air, water, soil).

As mentioned above, the source of children's knowledge is indeterminate, but some background information was provided by schools' reports during the 1982 survey on which of fourteen specified topics had been (or were about to be) explored during school science work. *Life cycle studies* were the most popular, followed by *Habitat studies. Interdependence, Properties of materials* and *Forces* and *Movement* were the least popular choices. Although there were differences by country in the popularity of the fourteen topics, there does seem evidence of a general trend of correspondence between exposure and competence. These are not necessarily cause and effect. It is possible that activities favoured in school science are deliberately those in which children have some interest and consequently wider experience.

Having briefly reviewed performance in **Applying science concepts,** attention will now be turned to the influence on pupil performance of question *content,* across the assessment framework. The distinction between 'concept demand' and question 'content' (or subject matter) carries a set of assumptions which need to be made explicit before the discussion may proceed. While the APU Science assessment framework is characterised as having a *science process* orientation, these processes cannot be presented and assessed in isolation. While it is possible to discuss science processes in abstract terms, in practice, every process is realised within a particular content. Although questions are written in such a way as to focus the demand on the given target process, this demand is inevitably expressed within a form, a subject matter, which to some extent interacts with and defines the particular nature of the process. In the practical business of assessment, pupils respond to all aspects of presented questions as they perceive them. Although they have not been systematically investigated, effects of particular content have been noted in several areas of the framework. The distinction between *content* and *concept* implicit here is that between the particular and the general. A science concept, for example, 'hibernation', may be explored by reference to mammals, or invertebrates. The choice of whether squirrels or butterflies are used as exemplars may have some impact on children's performance. This also applies to areas other than concept application. Two questions from the **Interpreting** subcategory having a similar structure and demand expressed in terms of different question content were reported from the 1983 survey (DES, 1985a) as producing significantly different results. The discussion of this interesting outcome examined the issues of the *implicit attributes* of question content inferred by children and the possibility of their operating on a level of personal knowledge gained through experience and familiarity, rather than with the more formal, 'objective' properties of the question. This line of reasoning is also relevant to the 'general versus science-specific skills' issue. Familiarity with question content often inspires children to impart additional subjective information. This sense of identification with material introduced into the primary classroom is precisely the kind of personal link sought and exploited in good general primary practice. While there is undoubtedly a place for this variety of personal involvement within some aspects of primary science, other facets, for example, **Distinguishing degrees of inference** and other questions in the **Interpreting** category call for some distancing from a personal viewpoint and a more literal and parsimonious treatment of information. The personal response to content is difficult to assess in any absolute sense except where questions are matched in all other respects. Very few such matched questions have been written. However, evidence from questions used with pupils at age 13 suggests that pupils' response to question content is a significant factor even in graph interpretation, a task which by its nature might be thought to encourage a shift from the particular to a more generalised, abstract response. However, when similar curves plotted with similar values on similar scales have been used to represent different content, differences in performance have resulted. In the absence of systematically matched questions on the age 11 item bank, the effects of content have been more noticeable as the result of gender differences in performance. These are discussed in the section on sex differences below.

In the discussion of the **Performance of investigations** it was mentioned that the particular *content* around which an investigation is based to some extent determines the science processes which are likely or possible to be deployed. To some extent, *content* also defines the *context* of an investigation. Depending on the assumptions made about *context,* the pupils' psychological set will vary. For the purposes of science assessment at age 11, the important distinction in *context* is between 'science' and 'everyday'. It was noted that those investigations presenting some apparatus usually associated with science activities tended to elicit a more rigorous approach. 'Everyday' materials tended to elicit an 'everyday' response; whereas in daily decision making, insufficient information on which to draw conclusions is the norm, in a 'science' context the 'everyday' approach is frequently inappropri-

ate. The practice of offering children the support of familiar everyday materials around which to deploy their science processes may incur some definite disadvantages, unless teacher expectations are clearly articulated.

## 12.9 Divergent science

The APU Science assessment framework embodies the implicit view that actively conducted investigations are important science experiences for children. This chapter has used the detailed analysis of such investigations as an organising structure. However, no assumption is made that the **Performance of investigations** is the *only* science in which children of this age group should be involved. While investigations require some rigour and discipline, their effective design may call for a creative approach. The logistics of mobilising an assessment of investigatory skills on a national scale requires some focusing of task and resources if comparability of results is to be approached. In the classroom, the time limitations are quite different, and unique resources and conditions can be imaginatively turned to account.

As described in Chapter 11, **Performance of investigations,** efforts were made in the 1984 survey to engage children in a more open-ended approach to carrying out an investigation. Children were invited to ask questions about the active (and to them probably novel) Great African Land Snail. Ninety six per cent of pupils were able to frame at least one question, and on average boys suggested 4.1 and girls 3.3 questions. About half of these questions were investigable by observation or experimentation. However, after having nominated a particular question for investigation a range of apparatus was revealed and this frequently led children into pursuing other questions. It was found that the orientation of curiosity and exploration was in many cases maintained during the investigation itself (see Appendix 10). It is possible that the nature of the content, Great African Land Snails, was a contributory factor in childrens' exploration of other things beside their chosen topic. It was mentioned earlier that particular question content may elicit a particular emphasis from children in the spectrum of science processes. It would seem quite appropriate that an active creature should be largely observed, perhaps with limited interventions, in order to establish its behavioural repertoire before a more sustained investigation. The message might be that an encouragement towards diversity and open-endedness in the formulation of an investigable problem on the one hand, and a more focused, goal-orientated investigation on the other, is a distinction which may not be obvious to children.

Among the written forms of assessment, the subcategory **Generating alternative hypotheses,** while asking for the application of learned-science concepts, is more open-ended than the **Applying** subcategory discussed above. Domain-referencing has not been used in this group of questions: nine selected questions have been used during the five surveys. A detailed qualitative assessment of the categories of response was deemed to be more informative than quantitative scores in this area. Though represented by few questions, the subcategory is important in calling for imaginative and creative applications of learned science. Questions require children to give two possible alternative explanations for a presented situation, there being no single best explanation. Pupil's ability to accept alternative explanations as a possibility, as well as the specific notions which they apply, are both of interest.

When responses are averaged across questions, about 85 per cent of pupils are found to have provided two explanations for the presented information. Although quantitative scoring revealed that the second responses offered tended to lack explanatory value, the extent to which the age group demonstrated flexibility of thinking (admittedly in response to directed questions assuming the possibility of alternatives) was revealing. Although the concepts which children called upon in their explanations were frequently of the 'everyday' variety, this was not exclusively the case. Some indication of the range and diversity of knowledge application which emerged has been indicated in previous reports. (See DES, 1984a, pp. 270–280, for example.) An important aspect which remains to be explored in a more systematic investigation is the effect of the context in which a question is framed on the range and type of explanation offered. For example, 'everyday' contexts, as in other areas of the framework, appear to lead pupils to make more unjustified assumptions based on personal knowledge than do questions based in more obviously science contexts. (See DES, 1985a, Chapter 4, for example.)

It is interesting to speculate on the extent to which the question form encouraged (or was responsible for) divergent thinking as a result of the explicit request for two or more explanations in **Generating alternative hypotheses.** Would pupils otherwise have been inclined to a single explanation? There is no direct evidence to inform this question, either to support it or to challenge it. There is strong evidence from two other subcategories of a sensitivity to question form in pupils' responses. In **Judging the applicability of a given generalisation** and **Identifying or proposing testable statements** a common element was the requirement for pupils to evaluate statements presented in the questions. Children were much more successful at identifying valid or true statements than they were at rejecting false or untrue statements. A possible explanation for this discrepancy is in terms of conformity or suggestibility to printed statements from a perceived authority, and a corresponding reluctance to challenge or reject such statements. In the first of these subcategories, there was also a clear aversion to equivocal statements, and a preference to achieve 'closure' despite insufficient data being available. In the **Performance of investigations,** children showed a similar tendency to be content with conclusions drawn from insufficient evidence. This desire for closure, or unique conclusions, contrasts with the acceptance of multiple solutions in **Generating alternative**

**hypotheses.** It would seem that children at this age are able and willing to be divergent on demand. Unless they entertain the possibility of alternatives, children are unlikely to be critical of the procedures they have adopted. Yet when the possibility of alternatives is made clear, children respond positively.

## 12.10   Gender differences in performance

Examples of gender-linked differences in performance can be found in most aspects of the assessment framework. These differences cannot often be described in terms of aetiology. What is clear is that gender differences are to be found in experiences and interests, in activities and operations, and in response to subject matter. They are to be found in cognitive, affective and social functioning and very often any particular influence is inextricable from the others. Despite this problem in identifying sources of difference, some attempt will be made to impose a structure on the discussion in this section. It also needs to be said that in the absence of clear determinants of sources of difference, strategies for dealing with differences by gender are not self-evident. No *a priori* assumptions are made in this discussion as to whether differences are to be interpreted as gender-linked deficiences best tackled by direct compensatory action, or to be avoided in favour of neutral alternatives. There is certainly a growing concern and awareness of the fact that females are underrepresented as participants in secondary science subject groups (see Johnson and Murphy, DES, 1986, for example). It is consequently of interest to explore the nature of these differences occurring as the as they do before exposure (for the great majority of pupils) to formal science.

*Differences in experience*

The degree of exposure or previous experience of a topic, whether at school or at home, may in many cases have some impact on pupils' performance when assessment is organised around that topic. It was this consideration which prompted the gathering of information about pupils' prior experiences of batteries and bulbs during the 1981 survey, as a background to performance on the 'Circuits' investigation. Striking gender differences in experience were revealed both at school and at home. While 31 per cent of boys reported some experience of something similar to batteries and bulbs at home, the proportion of girls was only seven per cent. This difference in exposure is indirectly matched by significant differences in performance on questions with a content of 'electricity' throughout the assessment framework (see DES, 1984e).

A more extensive attempt to gather information on experience of science topics, use of equipment and preferred activities was undertaken by means of questionnaires attached to all written test booklets used in the 1984 survey.

Generally it would appear that there is little difference in the exposure to topics on the concept list experienced by boys and girls. This is perhaps to be expected in an almost completely co-educational system, though small differences do occur where childrens' own choice of activity is a possibility. The same tendency applies to topics about which children express an interest in finding out more, though here girls are less reluctant than boys to re-visit topics. This finding is in contrast to their own selection of activities out of school where the desire for novelty vis-à-vis school topics already studied is replaced by a tendency to want more of the same.

Frequencies for out-of-school use of twelve items of equipment by girls were consistently lower than for boys where the more technical, science-specific apparatus was concerned (see Table 3.2, page 17). Only in the use of the measuring cylinder/jug and weighing scales was this position reversed, and these pieces of apparatus may well be associated with cooking.

The science-related activities selected by children as being those in which they participated 'quite often' (about once a month) also revealed some differences in the reported frequencies for boys and girls. In sixteen of the twenty-two activities conducted at home, boys were more frequent participants than girls. This difference was most markedly biased towards boys on the items: 'Watch science fiction on TV'; 'Take things apart to see inside them'; 'Use parts from a kit to make models (eg Lego, straws)'; 'Make up models from a kit (eg Airfix)'; Play with electric toy sets (cars, trains on tracks)'; 'play pool/snooker/billiards'. (These choices resulted in differences in frequency of reported participation of at least 20 per cent in favour of boys.) Equal or greater differences of frequency in favour of girls were found in response to the items: 'Weigh out ingredients for cooking'; 'Knit or sew' and 'Collect/look at wild flowers'. Lesser differences of bias towards girls were found with the items: 'Look after small animals or pets'; 'Sow seeds or grow plants' and 'Visit a museum or zoo'. (This issue of domestic/social/floral/faunal content favouring the girls will be discussed further below.) The fact that both boys and girls would tend to prefer to indulge in more of the same activities than increase their range of experience suggests that some definition of appropriateness of interest has already taken place by this age. Of course, expressed preferences may themselves be an expression of social conditioning. No suggestion of 'inherent inclination' is intended. Indeed, the activities under consideration are so strongly socially contextualised that the very concept of 'natural predisposition' to certain activities is of dubious validity.

Another attempt at the assessment of science-related preferences was the 'Liking of activities' instrument. The prototype was used on a small scale in the 1982 survey and more widely in 1983. The later version consisted of line drawings of a boy and girl involved in various science related activities. Both sexes preferred activities which were identified as having some commonality as 'experimental' situations. These 'experimental' situations were preferred to 'non-experimental' situations by both girls

and boys, the difference in preference being large for boys, but only small for girls.

Childrens' social preferences for engagement in science activities—whether as individuals, within small groups, in whole classes, and whether or not mixed gender interactions are acceptable—remains to be systematically investigated.

### Gender differences and the science activity categories

It has been stressed throughout this review that pupil performance inevitably represents a response to the combined effects of process and content. However, this section will examine possible occurrences of consistent gender differences in process performance across a range of content and concepts. The following section will then examine consistent gender-related responses to content across processes. Both, being incidental expressions of gender differences, can be related to the more explicit statements of preference elicited by the purpose-built instruments described in the above section.

In the **Use of graphical and symbolic representation,** when a broad division of questions is made, a fairly clear (but not invariable) association with gender becomes apparent. Where questions are concerned with coordinate graphs, boys tend to perform at a level higher than girls. This effect becomes particularly marked in questions using negative values on one or both of the axes. (See DES, 1984a, pp178–180.) Girls have tended to achieve higher average scores on individual questions, particularly in the **Representing** subcategory, and particularly with non-coordinate forms. The general superiority of girls in presenting written responses which is in evidence throughout the assessment framework may be a factor operating here, since verbal categories are commonly used. In Northern Ireland, overall scores for the combined **Reading** and **Representing** subcategories have consistently favoured girls, though only in the 1984 survey did this difference achieve statistical significance.

The category **Use of apparatus and measuring instruments** revealed girls to be performing at higher mean levels than boys in the *accurate* measurement of curved length and area, and tending to be more likely to give correct units.

The measurement and estimation of time and temperature was better accomplished by boys. The difference does not appear to be linked to experience, though the fact that more boys adjusted the spring balance scale to zero before taking a reading could be related to exposure. The cases of gender-linked differences thus summarised might be interpreted as favouring girls in the general skills, and boys where the situation is more science-specific.

The **Observation** category did not produce much in the form of gender-linked differences in performance; where these did occur, they are interpretable as a greater willingness on the part of girls to engage in questions having a relatively extended writing demand, rather than as a difference in observation skills *per se*.

Questions in the subcategory **Interpreting presented information** often have at least superficial similarities with those in the **Use of graphical and symbolic representation,** since tables, graphs etc are often used to present the information which is to be interpreted. No statistically significant differences in overall performance have been revealed at age 11, though boys tend to perform at slightly higher levels than girls. (This tendency is more marked at age 13 and is a persistent outcome at age 15.) Where data are presented in discontinuous form, with categorical variables and consequently an increased likelihood of a verbal medium, girls tend to perform better than boys. Numerical or graphical data and spatial-dynamic patterns tend to result in higher performance on the part of boys.

The subcategory **Applying science concepts** has shown fairly consistent differences in favour of boys which are statistically significant and are in evidence in each of the participating countries. Many of these gender-linked differences can be traced to differences in performance in questions concerned with concepts relating to physical science. This will be treated in further detail in the next section.

The **Planning** category shows a tendency for girls to produce slightly higher overall scores than boys. In the 1984 survey this trend reached statistical significance in Northern Ireland but, confusingly, was in the reverse direction in Wales. The general trend in favour of girls may be explicable in terms of the greater writing demands of questions in this subcategory.

In the **Performance of investigations** boys' mean ratings for willingness to undertake the investigations were higher than those of girls. This point may be elaborated by reference to the four of the fourteen investigations used which involved living things. While 34 per cent of girls were unwilling to touch the snails, the figure for boys was only 12 per cent. (The general tendency for girls to respond favourably to flora and fauna will receive further comment below.)

*Gender-linked responses to question content*

Most questions present children with multiple demands. Question writers decide on the particular burden being imposed, and confirmation of this judgement by another expert opinion has been used to validate such judgements. Since question content is not of itself a focused question burden, its effects are only seen incidentally. Content effects are apparent only when not masked by other demands, and when they recur in different contexts and activities. The discussion in this section is thus tentative, since a systematic investigation has not been possible.

In the Category **Using graphs, tables and charts,** girls tended to score at higher levels than boys on questions concerned with a content centred on *animals* and *plants,* as well as *domestic/social subject matter (food, household materials, social statistics,* etc). Questions with an *environmental* content did not markedly favour either sex. Where

*physical objects and events* was the focus, there was no clear gender-related pattern. In the **Interpreting** subcategory, boys tended to perform better than girls on questions about animals perhaps because of the kinds of associations between data pairs with which questions were concerned. There were statistically significant differences in favour of boys on three questions concerned with *living or fossil invertebrates.* The animal questions on which girls performed better than boys tended to be concerned with *mammals* and *birds.* As in the **Performance of investigations,** it seems that girls do not perform as well as boys where animals of the creepie-crawlie variety are concerned. However, the tendency towards higher performance levels of girls on *botanical* content was maintained in the **Interpreting** subcategory, as it was also where *social/domestic* content was concerned. In **Using graphs, tables and charts** girls and boys had performed overall at similar levels, although differently on particular questions, where the content was *physical objects and events.* In the **Interpreting** subcategory, this type of impersonal non-living material tended to favour boys.

Effects of question content seem very powerful on occasions. There is an impression that it is at what might be regarded as an experiential level of specific question content that pupils make their decisions about how to engage questions.

## 12.11   Conclusion

Some fairly clear threads linking various aspects of the framework have been indicated. Although various divisions and demarcations were imposed for the purposes of assessment some coherence between the various effects does emerge. This is not to suggest that the picture is either complete or unidimensional. Work in the **Performance of investigations** has quite understandably attracted a great deal of interest. The investigations included in this category have the great assessment strength of ecological validity. They provide the opportunity for the detailed exploration of science-related behaviour in a context which should be comfortable for, if not always totally familiar to children, under expert guidance and observation. The investigations, perhaps the more innovative aspect of the assessment exercise, are complemented by the pencil and paper item bank. This bank, by now fairly massive, comprising over 1,000 questions, adds to the close and detailed focus of the investigations the quality of diversity. Diversity of question form and demand, of concept, content and context, extend the range of sensitivity of the assessment exercise. These two aspects have developed side by side, each constantly informing the other. Additionally, there have been the unforeseen and incidental discoveries which were not formally and systematically built into an assessing framework which was geared to domain-referencing. The implications of all these for educational and assessment practice, the way forward, will be considered in the final chapter.

# 13

# Performance across ages

## 13.1 Introduction

The framework which serves to structure the assessment of pupils at ages 11, 13 and 15 has a great deal in common at the three ages. Naturally enough, in the interests of an age-appropriate assessment reflecting the different activities and emphases in the span of school years, there are also differences. During 1983/84, considerable efforts were invested by the teams aimed at rationalising the question banks at the three ages. Rationalisation implied checking the structure of the domain-referenced question pools to ensure that the same definitions of question demands, pupil response requirements and mark scheme criteria were used at all three ages. Since questions had been developed with a particular age group in mind, it was possible that divergencies might have arisen inadvertently or deliberately. It was also possible that definitions might have been interpreted in different ways, or that as an outcome of survey experience, slight organisational adjustments to the composition of the bank were required. While the motivation for this exercise was to check and where necessary re-establish correspondence of pool definitions between the three age-specific question banks, there were clearly implications at the individual question level also. A secondary objective of the rationalisation exercise was to iron out trivial differences in otherwise identical questions and mark schemes used at more than one age. A close perusal of questions and performance data guided by experience of age-appropriateness led to those questions which were not already used at more than one age being accepted for such use. Thus the degree of question overlap was enhanced in some categories, while in others, differences in definition or administration were made explicit and question overlap was minimal. Whatever the degree of question overlap, those question domains which are used in common are applied with common definitions. Consequently, comparisons of performance on the same domain and comparisons of profiles of performance across domains at different ages, can be contemplated.

The consideration of performance across age will focus particularly on the progression between ages 11 and 13. Comments on performance at age 15 are not precluded where they are of particular interest, but are discussed more fully in 'Science at, age 15: a review of APU survey findings, 1980–84' (DES, 1988b).

Discussion will proceed from two perspectives. Firstly, at the macro-level, a broad overview will be presented of performance in the domain-referenced categories, including a comparison of profiles at ages 11 and 13 across the assessment framework. The second perspective will examine the characteristics of children's performance in more detail, in order to examine how the aspects described in the Category chapters may be informed by a developmental viewpoint.

## 13.2 Profiles of performance at ages 11 and 13

Summaries of performance estimates for the domain-referenced question pools on which this discussion is based are presented in Table 13.1 (p. 113). **Reading and Representing** are combined as **Using graphs tables and charts** at ages 13 and 15 on the grounds that performance outcomes have a high degree of correlation. The category **Applying science concepts** is divided into three separate question pools, Physics, Biology and Chemistry for the purposes of assessing the two older age groups, while for pupils at age 11, no such division is imposed. While the concept list defining admissable concept demands is identical, the range and details of concepts exposed is restricted by considerations of age-appropriateness at the youngest age. While **Reading, Representing** and **Intepreting** have considerable question overlap between the two younger groups assessed, this is not the case for **Observation, Applying** and **Planning**. Details of these differences will be considered in section 13.3 and following.

It has consistently been the case at all three ages that the peak in the profile of domains as measured has been in the first category, **Using symbolic representation**. While the **Observation** category at age 11 formerly occupied a position in the middle ranges of obtained peformance estimates, the move to circus administration and increasing use of physical resources (as compared with representations in the form of drawings or photographs) has tended to reduce the difference between it and scores on **Interpreting, Applying** and **Planning**. Consistently producing the lowest performance estimates at all ages has been the **Applying** category. Table 13.2 (p. 113) summarises features of performance worthy of note between performance at ages 11 and 13.

At age 11, no differences in performance estimates between countries reached statistical significance. At age 13, it was noticeable that the scores of pupils in Wales were lower than those of pupils in both England and

**Table 13.1**  *Pupils' subcategory performance levels in 1984 at ages 11 and 13*

| Subcategory | | Age 11 All | Boys | Girls | Age 13 | All | Boys | Girls |
|---|---|---|---|---|---|---|---|---|
| Reading information from graphs, tables and charts | mean | 62.2 | 62.5 | 61.8 | | | | |
| | s.e. | 0.6 | 0.7 | 0.7 | | | | |
| | mean | | | | Using graphs, tables and charts | 65.8 | 64.6 | 67.0 |
| | s.e. | | | | | 0.6 | 0.8 | 0.7 |
| Representing information as graphs, tables and charts | mean | 57.4 | 57.1 | 57.6 | | | | |
| | s.e. | 0.7 | 0.8 | 0.8 | | | | |
| Making and interpreting observations | mean | 44.3 | 44.1 | 44.5 | | 37.2 | 36.1 | 37.9 |
| | s.e. | 1.1 | 1.0 | 1.2 | | 0.7 | 0.8 | 0.6 |
| Interpreting presented information | mean | 34.0 | 34.9 | 33.2 | | 42.4 | 43.1 | 41.9 |
| | s.e. | 0.5 | 0.6 | 0.5 | | 0.5 | 0.7 | 0.6 |
| Applying science concepts | mean | | | | Biology | 27.0 | 27.5 | 26.6 |
| | s.e. | | | | | 0.4 | 0.6 | 0.5 |
| | mean | 30.4 | 31.5 | 29.3 | Chemistry | 27.9 | 27.4 | 28.3 |
| | s.e. | 0.5 | 0.6 | 0.5 | | 0.5 | 0.6 | 0.5 |
| | mean | | | | Physics | 29.0 | 30.6 | 27.4 |
| | s.e. | | | | | 0.4 | 0.5 | 0.5 |
| Planning parts of investigations | mean | 32.4 | 31.6 | 33.3 | | 32.0 | 31.2 | 32.9 |
| | s.e. | 0.5 | 0.6 | 0.6 | | 0.5 | 0.6 | 0.6 |

**Table 13.2**  *Subcategory performance: comparisons of age 11 and 13 results*

| Subcategory | Age 11 | Age 13 |
|---|---|---|
| **Reading and Representing** | Generally higher levels than any other category. Little evidence of gender-related performance differences at subcategory level, but differences apparent within the sub-category. | Generally higher levels than any other category. |
| **Observation** | Performance estimate occurs in middle range of performance profile; slightly lower in 1984. No gender differences, except NI girls significantly higher than boys in 1984. | Overall performance estimate in lower range of profile (minimal question overlap 11/13 may contribute to differences in domain estimates). |
| **Interpreting** | Stable score over time and between countries. Boys tend to perform at a slightly higher level than girls especially in Wales and NI. | Statistically significant differences in favour of boys occasionally at 13, persistently at 15 (which could be related to the increased use of graphs as data presentation forms). |
| **Applying** | Performance discrepancies in favour of boys in each country, attributable particularly to differences on questions concerned with physical science. Consistently lowest sub-category estimates obtained in this area. | Relative weakness of girls in physical science persists, boys performing at a significantly higher level in 'Applying physics concepts'. This discrepancy extends to 'Applying chemistry concepts' at 15. Consistently lowest sub-category estimates in this area. |
| **Planning** | Girls' average performance slightly better than boys'. This difference is more pronounced in NI while the evidence from the Welsh sample is conflicting. | Girls tend to produce slightly higher mean scores than boys at 13 and 15. |

Northern Ireland on all categories except **Observation**. Performance estimates were similar for English and Welsh samples except that the former group was slightly ahead on **Observation**.

A consistent regional difference within England has been in evidence at all ages, with pupils in the South scoring about 2 per cent higher than pupils in the North and Midlands. This difference shifts slightly at age 13, with the South and the Midlands performing slightly ahead of the North.

The difference in performance between rural and urban samples was 10 per cent across the board at age 11, and as high as 20 per cent in **Use of symbolic representation**. The same trends are apparent at age 13; non-metropolitan samples ahead of metropolitan and inner city samples producing lower performance estimates than samples from all other catchment areas. There is little doubt that these disturbing findings related to region and catchment area are related to social class and inner city deprivation.

## 13.3   Using graphs, tables and charts

More overlap questions exist in this category than in any other. This is in part because some questions are scored by reference to a composite set of criteria, as in the complete graph construction questions. These criteria span a range of skills, some of which are accessible to the younger children (eg plotting points on labelled divisions) while others discriminate abilities within the older age groups (eg interpolation and drawing a curve of best fit). However, this possibility of spanning the three ages assessed breaks down if the question content is inappropriate, either because it is below the dignity of the older pupils or unfamiliar and anxiety-provoking for the younger children.

The evidence from question trials suggests that younger children may reject questions because the content does not strike them as being within their range of competence, even though the information handling demands certainly would be. For this reason, the question pools for ages 13 and 15 have a more obviously scientific/technological appearance, while at eleven, the across-the-curriculum style prevails. It is also the case that the balance of questions in the question types changes across the three ages, moving towards increasing representation of numerical data and line graphs, and decreasing verbal and pictorial representation and bar charts. There are also more subtle changes in the balance of numerical values which are required to be handled, such as decimal fractions, though at all three ages a policy of minimal requirements for mathematical operations has operated.

Similarities and differences between the question pools at the three ages have been briefly outlined above. More important, perhaps, are considerations of the value and purpose of the skills which are assessed within this category for different age groups of children. In relation to older children the skills of data communication and interpretation have often been referred to as 'hurdles', in the manner of sub-routines in which competence must be gained before higher level skills can be established. In primary education, the lesson of recent years has been to avoid dissociating the 'basics' from the subject as a whole. A parallel might be cited in the acquisition of reading and writing skills as integral parts of a wider enterprise of language development. Only for assessment purposes (and only then for reasons of economy) can graph construction skills justifiably be separated from the investigations to which they refer.

When the particular sub-skills are examined, continuities between the two age groups become apparent. In the use of coordinate forms, labelling conventions continue to be neglected, but to a lesser degree at age 13. The interesting question is why this should be the case. The suggestion is that coordinate forms are more profitably viewed as formal representations of associations between quantified variables, rather than a more restricted set of discrete rules and conventions. This view is supported both at age 11 and age 13, in the sense that parallels can be seen between the difficulties experienced in graph construction and in designing and implementing practical investigations.

older pupils is particularly in evidence in the category concerned with the **Use of apparatus and measuring instruments**. The younger pupils have been presented with a small range of estimating and measuring tasks mostly incorporated within practical investigations. Most of the measurement instruments used will have been encountered in other contexts than science, for measuring physical quantities such as length, area, volume, mass, etc. As well as presenting a greater range of apparatus and physical quantities within a 'circus' administration at age 13, an additional set of questions, **Following instructions for practical work**, is presented. Such science-specific activities will not have been encountered by the younger age group, and is not assessed at age 11.

A more detailed variety of *scale reading errors* is reported at age 13, but the variability in performance by reference to instrument, the particular scale used and the physical quantity under consideration are outcomes familiar at 11 and 15 also. In assessing children's proficiency in using standard measures, it is ironic to find that the particular value to be measured can markedly affect performance at all ages.

The point made above in the discussion of data communication skills, that to remove a skill from its context of use and purpose within an investigation is hardly justifiable, applies equally here. The constraints of a broadly based assessment make such a course a necessity. It is encouraging to find that, despite the decontextualisation of the measurement tasks, some light may be thrown on the difficulties which pupils encounter in evolving measurement strategies within the practical investigations. At age eleven, many pupils lack a repertoire of basic measurement skills for the commonly encountered physical quantities. This deficit must hinder their measurement strategies in exploring associations during practical investigations. A similar lament is voiced in the Age 13 Review (DES, 1988a). For example, in their attempts to estimate volumes of water, area, mass, temperature and force *most* pupils at age 13 were not within 50 per cent of the actual given value. The conclusion is drawn that '. . . competence in reading scales and use of instruments is lower than would seem necessary for the undertaking of science courses as currently organised.' The same is true in terms of the kinds of investigations involving quantification in which it is generally agreed that the younger pupils could profitably engage. It seems likely that these skills might be enhanced by more exposure to investigations during which pupils are sensitised by teaching intervention to the possibilities of measurement strategies which might meet their own requirements.

## 13.4   Use of apparatus and measuring instruments

The shift from the broader 'across-the-curriculum' view of science adopted for the age 11 assessment and the more specialist skills with which it is possible to confront

## 13.5   Observation

What assessment of this category at age 11 has in common with assessment of observation at 13 and 15 is the experience of a struggle to elucidate definitions and put those definitions into practice in the form of valid questions.

Within an assessment framework which attempts to distinguish between the conceptual and process burdens of science tasks, observation was originally viewed as posing-pupils primarily a 'process' burden of demand. For pupils at age 11, the dilemma has been to avoid the necessity for the recall of taught science, and yet maintain face validity as part of a science assessment exercise. The solution, not without contortions and difficulties, was whenever possible to use materials and phenomena possessing science face validity, yet being within the everyday experiences of children. By contrast, assessment for pupils at age 15 has always acknowledged the value of observations based on the learned constructs acquired in science lessons–theory-laden observation. The position at age 13 was initially to regard observation as an 'across-the-curriculum' skill, and a content embracing both 'everyday' and 'scientific' material was acceptable. It is now the case that only question material which raises the potential for 'scientifically relevant' observations to be made is admitted.

It seems likely that further refinements within this category will need to be made explicit both within and between the age-specific question pools. Observation is highly rated by primary and secondary teachers as a 'scientific' activity, and yet a closer examination suggests that the term lacks definition and easily slips into use as a generic term for motley classroom activities. Similarly, the fact that assessment items in this category are exceptionally well received by teachers and pupils is insufficient reason for their existence; the items are only justified when we can specify (a) precisely what skills they are demanding of pupils, and (b) how these skills relate to the assessment framework as a whole. Teaching implications may then be addressed.

It may be that the place of 'information-processing' types of items may have greater significance with the youngest age group, while those questions requiring learned science applications come to predominate in the assessment of the older age groups. While it has been possible to move to a common bank of items for use with pupils at 13 and 15, the age 11 question pool for **Observation** remains quite separate. This is not just a result of the 'appropriate content' problem discussed above. There are also practical considerations. While laboratory facilities can safely be assumed to be available to support the assessment of the older age groups, access even to water can be problematic in some primary classrooms.

These difficulties do not preclude comparisons between ages at the domain level. The same issues have been of concern at all ages, and there are clearly recognisable similarities between many items.

## 13.6   Interpreting presented information

A considerable degree of overlap exists between the question pools at ages 11 and 13. Many of the comments made in the earlier section under **Using graphs, tables and charts** apply here also, since question content is an important consideration in judging the age-appropriateness of a question. At the younger age it is possible to ask children to infer associations from data exemplifying a relationship which may be taught science at age 13. Indeed, there is an impression of a greater pupil expectation of the requirement for learned science recall by the older pupils, even though this is not the expectation of question writers.

Given the large degree of question overlap and the dialogue that has taken place encompassing all three ages, similar analyses have been conducted on the data obtained at 11 and 13. It has been found that the problems encountered in the lack of precise language usage in describing a relationship span the two age groups. For example, important aspects of an association such as the direction of a trend may be omitted, or specific instances may be offered instead of a complete pattern.

Common sets of questions concerned with data communication and interpretation have been used with all three age groups. Results are briefly summarised in Figure 13.1 of the Age 13 Review (DES, 1988a).

## 13.7   Application of learned science concepts

At all three ages, the assessment of concept application is represented by two separate groups of questions. The subcategory **Applying science concepts** comprises a domain-referenced question pool at each age, while **Generating alternative hypotheses** is represented by hand-picked questions at each of the three ages. Eight of the ten question types used at age 11 are common to all ages; one of the others overlaps with age 13, and one is unique to age 11. This unique type concerns 'life cycle' questions, which were separated because of the high element of recall rather than application.

The concept list, with its divisions into concept regions, etc. (see Appendix 9) is common to all ages. However, the specific range of concepts and the level of detail at which they are expected to be applied is tailored to age-appropriateness. Some concept areas are not translated into questions for the youngest group simply because the concept would not be expected to be available to this group. The assessment of concept application, as might be expected, is far more extensive for the older age groups. Whereas at eleven, just one overall domain of concept application is used, as indicated in Table 13.1, separate scores are derived for the areas of Physics, Chemistry and Biology at 13, and at 15 also. This restricts the possibility of overlap between the age 11 and age 13 question pools. Few questions are common to both.

Between the age 13 and 15 banks there is a far greater overlap of the question statements, to which questions are written, but not an extensive overlap of individual questions. In some cases, questions which are held in common are scored to different criteria.

As was stated in Chapter 9, the absence of any systematic exploration in depth of particular concepts as understood by any set of individuals, was neither an intention nor a possibility with random sampling from a domain of questions. Consequently, the tracking of any particular concept development is difficult within an age group, and not viable for many concepts between ages. Some work has been done in this area by the 'Children's Learning in Science Project' (Bell and Driver, 1984).

## 13.8   Planning

The Age 13 review (DES, 1988a, Chapter 10), describes the evolution of thinking which took place in the design of the assessment of **Planning investigations** at that age. The early view was influenced by considerations of the practice of typical laboratory experiments. These experiments would have been designed to demonstrate phenomena exemplifying certain theoretical constructs of science. Refinements in the **Planning** category reflect a move away from considerations of standard techniques towards more open-ended problems requiring pupils to offer dynamic and inventive descriptions of their procedures. The role of an individual's knowledge and choice in formulating a plan is accepted and accommodated, while nevertheless being appraised in terms of objective criteria based on scientific acceptability.

The assessment of **Planning** at the younger age had no equivalent laboratory based precedent to that described above. There was, of course, a tradition of 'fair testing' in primary science to call upon, but the attempt to assess by pencil and paper testing was an innovation. What is interesting to see with hindsight is the degree of convergence between the assessment structures which were developed to meet the needs of assessing primary and secondary pupils. This surely would not have been predicted at the outset, and reflects the value of the dialogue which has taken place between the primary and secondary specialists. Assessment at each age manages to combine a pupil-centred orientation with a set of assessment criteria which can identify the details of rigorous scientific plans across a range of age-appropriate content.

Work on the assessment of **Planning** was reviewed at all three ages during 1982, and resulted in the current structures being adopted for the surveys in 1983 and 1984. As a result of this review, the question pools at ages 13 and 15 were merged for **Planning parts of investigations**, and identical survey packages used for the two ages. While having some questions in common with those used for pupils at age 13, the age 11 bank consists mostly of questions unique to the younger age group, but written to the same set of question descriptors. Nevertheless, there are some broad similarities which can be identified in

pupil performance at 11 and 13. For example, the generally lower levels of performance associated with the dependent variable, measurement strategies, and use of results, are common to both ages. The independent variable is more successfully handled, particularly when discrete; conceptual dependence depresses performance at both ages.

A further observation perhaps of interest is that the assessment of **Planning** at both ages benefited from the experience of assessing practical investigations. Indeed, the shortcomings inherent in pencil and paper assessment methods of **Planning**, intended to illuminate performance, are acknowledged. Assessment at both ages also incurs assessment artefacts as the result of introducing a novel set of question demands. For example, it is impossible to know how much of what remained unstated or unrefined may have been considered implicitly self-evident by pupils. Particularly at age 11, but to a lesser degree at age 13 also, pupils centred on, and treated as the central task, aspects within the presented situation which question writers regarded as peripheral. The assessment of **Planning** has also been informative in exposing a wider range of tasks than was feasible for complete practical investigations at both ages.

## 13.9   Performance of investigations

The history and logistics of the cycle of monitoring determined that the first explorations into the assessment of practical investigations were conducted with pupils at age 11, in 1980. The justification for the innovative yet costly one-to-one assessment approach was the unparalleled validity that the activity mode of assessment made possible. Activities in which pupils could become personally engaged were more consonant with primary practice than other more abstract assessment methods. Practical assessment also managed to circumvent the reading and writing difficulties which might inhibit pupil performance in other areas, despite support from test administrators. For the older age groups, practical testing was an attempt to present pupils with an opportunity to synthesise the component activities of the framework, in tasks accessible to all abilities. Work on the **Planning** category with the older age groups contributed to the development work with age 11 pupils, and vice versa.

Comments here on the specific nature of investigations at the three ages will be brief. A separate publication (DES, 1985d) provides further details. There are recognisable similarities between the tasks as presented to pupils at 11 and 13; indeed, some tasks are used at both ages, with slight modifications in procedure. For example, the 'problems' with which pupils have been confronted tend to be amenable to a variety of equally acceptable strategies, rather than being 'closed' questions requiring standard approaches. In the sense that the practical investigations incorporate many of the skills discussed under the category headings above, many of the points raised earlier apply equally here. For example, when identifying what to measure in investigations used at age 11 pupils have to interpret the meaning of such terms as 'holding water' in relation to material properties, 'preference' in relation to animal behaviour and 'how fast' in relation to swinging boards. Fewer 11 year olds than 13 year olds understand the meaning of these terms or have an understanding which conflicts with a scientifically acceptable one. Whatever their understanding their identification of the variable determines the measurement strategy adopted.

Pupils' understanding of measurement generally was very variable. For many 11 year olds and some 13 year olds, 'measurement' was only understood as a specific procedure, often a procedure recalled by a particular instrument. A larger proportion of 13 year olds than 11 year olds have a more general understanding of measurement and attempted a quantified approach in investigations. In some cases, the requirement for the use of common laboratory procedures or measuring apparatus would be expected to be totally unfamiliar to the youngest age group, and would preclude the use of an investigation with pupils at age 11.

## 13.10  Summary

The impression may have been given as the result of the annual survey reports that have been produced, that assessment of each age group has been an independent affair. This is far from what actually happened. Although it has not been part of the assessment teams' brief to consider directly age-developmental issues, the assessment of each age group has benefited from the dialogue about issues and results which has taken place throughout the monitoring phase. The reader who is particularly concerned with the primary audience will find that similar assessment structures, issues and outcomes recur, albeit with different frequencies or magnitudes, at all three ages. Since the age-related issues were not a particular subject of enquiry, much remains to be investigated. Much of the discussion in this chapter consists of hints about links, rather than systematically investigated outcomes. However, it is hoped that further studies by the monitoring team before the next round of surveys may look more closely at developmental progression in a way that has not hitherto been possible.

# 14

## Commentary

### 14.1 Introduction

This chapter will not attempt to offer readers summaries and conclusions in the usual sense. The preceding chapters are themselves the result of compression and present summarised messages. What will be attempted here is an overview of a more qualitative kind, embracing a more abstract and generalised reflection on the expectations, achievements and implications of the whole exercise. Section 14.2 reviews the intentions and expectations of the science monitoring as they prevailed initially and as they have been modified with experience and empirical feedback. The middle part of the chapter, section 14.3, sets out the products in relation to those expectations. Finally, in section 14.4 some consideration is given to the implications for the future and the important issues which remain to be addressed.

### 14.2 Origins and expectations

This review as a whole is less a timeless picture and more a piece of history. The body of results can only be fully understood in terms of the development of ideas and methods, and prospects for the future cannot be appraised without some projection of the process of development into the future. This point of view will inform several parts of this chapter. This section will discuss two particular aspects: the development of techniques and methods and the context of expectations within which the monitoring has evolved.

Techniques and methods deserve consideration because they have reacted on aims and expectations to shift them as experience has developed. The aims and expectations of the science monitoring have themselves developed from a basis which itself evolved through discussions held several years before the first survey in 1980. The enterprise was of a novel kind, and the adopted emphases – on processes and on practical testing – meant that there was no fund of directly relevant experience upon which to draw. Since then, lessons have been learnt and many problems, both surprising and foreseen, have been solved.

Many of these problems and lessons are internal to the monitoring activity itself and will not be discussed here. Apart from their relevance to monitoring, the main developments of technique and of logistics will be of interest to those concerned with new methods of assessment (see

DES, 1985d). However, the discussion here will focus on those developments directly relevant to the appraisal and interpretation of the main results. This focus should not hide the fact that much of what is presented in this report is the outcome of technical constraints and of the choices made in accepting or overcoming these. Thus it is obvious that the choice to take on monitoring of practical work on a scale that no other national or international programme has ever attempted, has had far reaching effects on the breadth, richness and relevance of the outcomes. Less obvious is the effect of the implementation of matrix light sampling in allowing production of test results covering a wide range of types of performance whilst giving very sparse data on the overall profiles of performance of individuals. More subtle still is the connection between the range of categories of performance monitored, and the reliability of the measures in any one subcategory: a narrower range would have meant greater reliability and so enhanced accuracy in identifying differential effects on performance. Critical consideration of whether the various decisions involved in the design of the monitoring were welljudged is a matter further elaboratcd in the accompanying technical report (DES, 1988c).

In attempting to describe the expectations for the monitoring, it is again necessary to consider how these have been modified with experience. Thus the expectations discussed below are not identical as a set to those which might, formally or informally, have been laid down before 1980.

A first expectation was that appropriate methods and instruments for assessment should be developed. Further, this should be done in a particular way determined by the overall model of the aims of science teaching and by the particular ways of working within the logistic and technical constraints adopted. The particular aspiration was that the balance, between the need to create a varied and open-ended set of instruments on the one hand, and the need for reliable and orderly data on the other, should be struck in such a way that neither of these conflicting needs would be left unfulfilled.

A second expectation was that the results should be made available to all those concerned. The history of attempts to live up to this does not form part of this review, but it should be noted that the considerable efforts made, through the production of the Reports for Teachers by the teams as part of a more general dissemination programme by the APU are an important and integral part of the exercise as a whole.

A third expectation was that the surveys should give a comprehensive picture of the outcomes of school science at age 11. As with the first expectation above, any viable survey could hardly fail to give its particular picture; the critical question is whether the particular framework and mode of operation chosen could yield a valid, useful and interesting product. With the liberty of hindsight, it can be said that the point of view about primary science that has informed the framework is still the one that is held up as the basis for development by most agencies active in school curriculum development. Indeed, the results of the monitoring have served to inform and lend substance to that view so that the monitoring has worked to support its own validity. This raises two further issues.

The first is that the monitoring development occurred in a particular historical context. The aims that informed it were ahead of practice and were the principles guiding many who were in a position to promote development. At the same time, these aims were sufficiently new for their precise meaning, and thus their detailed practical implications, to be vague. What the monitoring has done, by espousing these aims and composing questions to reflect them, has been to advance the thinking by making clear, and to a degree defining, the explicit meaning and implications of these aims. This may sound an extravagant claim: its basis is that in the early years those composing questions could find hardly any examples, whether within printed texts or within selected schools where enquiries were made, of instruments which made explicit those aims which those texts and those schools professed to follow in theory. Thus the monitoring has not, as it might have done, shown where schools are in relation to what they were actually doing in 1980, but where they are in relation to what the system was trying to work out for its future in the late 1970s.

The second consequence is a more sobering companion of the first. The monitoring picture as a whole is a creature of its time; it was perhaps ahead of its time, when first planned. Part of the third expectation is the hope that the picture supported by its array of data, will form a baseline against which future developments can be appraised. Whilst there are technical problems about attempts to measure trends over time, the problem of principle that arises here is that changes may occur because the match between school aims and practice and the monitoring itself may change. If this were to happen because schools worked more effectively to the aims this would be a valid result, although in so far as they did so by teaching to the test items under the influence of published results any trend could be a self-fulfilling prophecy. However, primary school science will hardly be insulated from any further developments, ideology or method, over the next few years. Aims and practices could develop, and new compromises be struck, so that the monitoring might then fail to reflect some aspects of practice. An example that is already relevant is the emphasis now being given to technology aims within those activities in school which hitherto focused more narrowly on scientific aims.

A fourth aim was to collect information which would permit as full a description as possible of the background to pupil performance. Because of the variety of curriculum experiences available to children, science assessment was measured against the generalised criteria embodied in the assessment framework, rather than as outcomes of known and specific educational experiences. For the same reason, assessment assumed that scientific modes of thought should be possible across the curriculum. The orientation of the tasks set should permit those children having had no formal science experience to engage the questions. Nevertheless, the actual science exposure of the 10/11 age group was of unknown quality and quantity and therefore of considerable interest. It was also hoped that correlational analyses of pupil performance with background variables might reveal some interpretable associations.

The fifth and final expectation has emerged more recently. This is that the surveys might provide a useful resource and stimulus for development of the curriculum and of teaching practice. This was not one of the original aims, and it is quite at variance with any notion that the surveys should be a neutral record of what is happening. The effect has followed inevitably from the historical features described above in discussing the third expectation. As it has turned out, the questions and performance data have generally been welcomed as useful aids to development of curriculum and methods. However, substantial caveats have to be entered. The assessment framework was not built on any model of learning or teaching, and it is not possible to proceed from the results to a teaching strategy except by way of assumptions about how desirable outcomes may be promoted. These assumptions have to be made explicit and carefully evaluated – the monitoring as such will have very little to contribute to such evaluation. Even the use of monitoring questions as diagnostic instruments in schools has to be approached with great care. All of the discussion in previous chapters on the ways in which pupil responses are sensitive to context and content of questions is relevant here: an insensitive borrowing of survey questions could give a teacher a quite false impression of the effectiveness of his or her particular teaching programme, particularly in the short term in relation to specific teaching innovations (for which such borrowing is most likely to be used).

## 14.3 Products

The naive expectation of the products of monitoring would be a set of objective quantitative measures. The real product is more complex, more extensive and more limited than this.

### The framework and test instruments

The first main product is the framework itself. The framework is a product in two ways. Firstly because it represents a set of decisions in principle about what is worth monitoring and reporting, which means that it represents a view of what school science ought to achieve. Many such schemes can be produced theoretically; the science framework started in such a way. Secondly it is also a product in a technical sense in that the definition of each subdivision has been refined by the need to assess and report by reference to an explicit set of valid questions appropriate for 11 year olds. The sets of questions with their mark schemes define the extent to which it is possible to give substance to an explicit set of criteria. The development of questions has been by interaction with the definitions of the framework: the Question types were clearly defined, but the activity of question development to reflect those definitions has led to modifications in the definitions themselves. Changes have been of various kinds, but always in response to feedback from pupils. In some cases, it has been possible to define boundaries more clearly, whilst in other areas, the inextricably composite nature of responses has meant that distinctions could not be sustained, or boundaries have had to be extended.

All of this adds up to one point – that the framework, the question banks and their mark schemes now form a self-consistent whole, so that each of these is thereby of far greater significance and use than a theoretical specification of assessment aims on its own. It is hard to communicate the extent or value of this product – it can only be inferred from the examples presented in the various reports.

The intention of producing a variety of instruments for the exploration of science performance to provide both qualitative and quantitative measures has also been met. For the reasons described, these instruments cannot serve the purposes for which they were designed if they are dissociated from the rationale that prompted their development. However, technical innovations resulted from the exploration of novel assessment methods which open up new possibilities for ways of approaching assessment, and new specific techniques. In considering the particularly novel assessment techniques, the practical problems set in the **Performance of investigations** and the circus practicals used in the **Observation** category must be pre-eminent. The value of these practical testing methods should not be allowed to obscure the complementary value of the written forms of assessment. A variety of question formats and response modes have been developed. The discipline of presenting children with a focused burden of demand within any given question is a formidable constraint. The written questions may be found useful as exemplars, as well as end products.

Many test items, together with performance data, have been published in the annual survey reports and in the short reports for teachers. These serve to illustrate the framework, but particularly when they include qualitative distinctions about pupil performance may have some diagnostic value to teachers. Further written and practical items have been distributed by the APU to LEAs and teacher training institutions.

*The background to pupil performance*

The information obtained from school questionnaires is summarised in Chapter 2, which describes the background of organisation, policies and resources, goals, emphases and topics encountered by children, and the availability of various curriculum materials. At various points in this review when science performance has been discussed, a distinction has been made between general approaches to science and the more science-specific aspects. Similar distinctions can be drawn in terms of different schools' orientation towards science, and their resources, both human and material. The organisation and availability of science in some cases indicated that the subject is viewed as something encountered incidentally, if at all. Elsewhere, science may be very well defined by a post of special responsibility, the availability of materials, a curriculum document and specified time allocation.

The existence of this review pre-supposes that science should have a place in the education of 10/11 year old pupils, but what would be an appropriate exposure? Ten per cent of available curriculum time has been suggested. This criterion would be met by only one-third of schools in England and Wales, and one-fifth of those surveyed in Northern Ireland. However, the picture is not static; primary science appears to be an area of growth. The time allocated to science has increased in each country between 1980 and 1984, with a parallel increase in posts of special responsibility. Though there is evidence of an improving situation, survey schools remaining with neither a special post nor voluntary responsibility account for one-third of schools in England, half of those in Wales and two-thirds of those in Northern Ireland.

Those priorities selected by schools from lists of goals and emphases in science based activities have shown notable consistency throughout the five surveys, probably reflecting the relatively well formed sense of identity and purpose within primary education. The general goals tended to be the most popular, while specifically science-based activities received the lowest ratings. This may be interpreted as the primary schools picking up the cross-curricular integrated activities, for example in the use of reference books and applied mathematics; Independent and Middle schools' ratings suggest a greater importance attached to apparatus and equipment, probably reflecting the existence and use of laboratories. Similarly, with the selection of emphases the primary schools favoured the more general: making observations, drawing conclusions, making notes and written records and following written instructions. Among the activities least emphasised were many of a more specifically scientific nature, relevant to the design of investigations. While the orientation towards investigations and fair testing is very evident, an equivalent emphasis on good design and rigour in those tests and investigations is not. It is encouraging that primary science and the criteria implicit in the assessment framework seem to be based on the same broad assumptions about how children might be expected to operate. It is in the details of science-based behaviour that the framework defines some rather more specific possibilities than do many schools.

The other major source of background information relates to children's experience, activities and interests relating to science. Even in the area of science concept application, the particular source of children's knowledge is frequently indeterminate. It is consequently important to have some information about their exposure not just at school, but at home also, so that an indication of their total relevant experience is available. This information was summarised in Chapter 3, and is of particular interest in illuminating the gender-linked differences in performance which are so clearly in evidence at the secondary stage of education. Socially contextualised gender differences clearly exist at age 11; children have fairly clear ideas of gender-appropriate behaviour. Broadly speaking, these factors are to the disadvantage of girls, vis-à-vis science, and demand carefully considered educational strategies.

The monitoring set out to explore associations between performance and 'the circumstances in which children learn'; such relationships, if clearly established, could have been important pointers to policy about resources. In general, hardly any significant relationships have been found. We could, like Sherlock Holmes, attach significance to the dog that didn't bark in the night-time. That most of the school parameters recorded have no significant correlations with performance may be seen as evidence that they don't matter. The substantial caution to be entered is that many vary over only a very narrow range for most schools so that real effects have been hidden within the range of error of the measures. It would be ironic, if because of survey results, they were allowed to vary much more widely, so that a future survey could produce evidence that they do have a significant effect. The other reaction is to note that the surveys have not been able to explore those school variables most likely to affect performance, notably the teaching as experienced in classrooms by pupils. If this is an important determinant, it is clear that none of the resource factors recorded is so strong an influence on it that it can serve as surrogate for its effect.

Some of the differential performance outcomes which did suggest significant effects reflect stratifications in society outside the normal scope of teaching intervention. The striking effect of school catchment area repeats well-known results. For example, within England, being located in an inner city school is associated with lower levels of performance; in some activities, dramatically lower. Lower performance levels on average are also found in the survey population in the North of England or the Midlands. On average, pupils attending rural schools and pupils living in the South of England (thus tending to avoid cultural and environmental disadvantage) perform at higher levels. Gender-linked differences have also been noted.

Specific findings apart, the means of monitoring changes have been established. It remains a possibility that those factors which might serve to enhance science-specific behaviours by the establishment of particular regimes have as yet had little impact. It is almost inconceivable that trained personnel, explicit policies and curriculum materials should not have an effect on pupils' performance, but there will be some inertia felt in any attempts to establish new strategies within a school. In many schools, there will not be the opportunity to innovate on a broad front. Primary science is developing and the lesson to be learned from no detectable effect in this instance is probably to remain alert to the possibility of associations in the future.

## A picture of performance in science

The individual category chapters and the exploration of links which follows them (Chapter 5–12) comprise a more extensive and elaborated description of the science performance of pupils at age 11 than any other source, domestic or international. This is a significant product at a purely descriptive level. Its potential as a reference source to which classroom practice and expectations as well as curriculum development might find it useful to refer is also considerable. Possibly because there is such a volume of data and so many issues which could be drawn out and developed for dissemination purposes, the precise value of this resource may only become apparent as certain threads are unravelled and made more explicit. This will be a matter for dissemination in the future. The annual reports of surveys were found to be too detailed by teachers unaccustomed to reading technical reports, and have been supplemented by short reports providing a more direct message. These short reports have been pitched at a non-technical, general level. Many primary teachers will be approaching science virtually from scratch, and for this group, the basic definitions and vocabulary need to be established before the more complex messages can be entertained.

The framework and the body of questions and data do represent a significant advance in working out the educational meaning of the aim of pursuing process aims for primary school science. As well as giving a validated structure for those aims, the results begin to suggest, through analysis of the levels of difficulty and of the nature of the problems that children encounter, how these skills have to be developed. Many might think that 'process' aims are both more interesting and more assessible to children than so-called 'content' aims. This optimism may be based on an uncritical pursuit in a first wave of enthusiasm. The data, in showing how performance falls rapidly when more precise and developed levels of skills are explored, and in demonstrating how inextricably linked process and content may be, do not suggest that all will be plain sailing in the process curriculum. The data suggest pointers for the way forward, but also suggest that the business of challenging and extending children within a process orientation will demand as much skill and rigour as any attempts to pursue alternative aims might have previously required.

## 14.4 The way forward

### Dissemination implications

At first sight, it would appear a straightforward matter to inform teachers and others about the framework, the questions and the results so that they can consider the implications for their own work. There are two important complications. The first is that pupils' responses require rather sophisticated interpretation in terms of the balance and combinations of the various aspects of question burden, context, content, etc discussed particularly in Chapter 12. The potential or capability of a pupil is separated from performance by several layers of inference. Related to this is the fact that the questions are often carefully constructed by reference to tacit assumptions drawn from the experience of five years of monitoring, so that an appreciation of their significance requires detailed study of the thinking that was invested in their construction.

The second complication, already mentioned above, follows from but goes beyond the first. Use of the questions in teaching requires an understanding of the 'layers of inference'. Composition of parallel or similar questions, to reflect more directly the learning experience of particular pupils, requires some insight into the subtleties of question construction. To go further and to use the questions as a guide, *a posteriori*, to teaching aims needs very careful thought about the ways in which children learn; such thought has not been a relevant consideration for the monitoring framework. It has always been dangerous to 'teach the test'. The danger does not disappear simply because the test is more valid or appears more interesting.

Seen in this light, dissemination becomes a difficult task. What is needed is a comprehensive approach, which includes discussion of question construction, of the links between question demand and pupil response and of the matching of questions to particular teaching aims. All of this should be within a context emphasising that the specific aims of surveys are not the same as the aims of (say) formative assessment meant to accompany and help a teaching/learning strategy.

### Future monitoring

Given that the Age 11 monitoring is a good reflection of the aims currently being pursued in the development of primary science, there is clear merit in operating a future monitoring on the same bases as, and with equivalent instruments to, the first phase, so that comparability is ensured. However, this does not mean that no more work needs to be done before the next survey. This is because the description and interpretation of the monitoring reviewed in this report is not as complete as it needs to be. If the lacunae can be explored, the next monitoring will stand on a more firm and clearly understood basis.

The issues to be explored arise out of some of the concerns already discussed in this chapter. A review of the framework, question banks and mark schemes ought to be made so that clearer ways of describing the framework can be found. The factors affecting pupil responses are now better understood than they were at the outset, but the insights in some areas have been based on indirect interpretation of data, supported only by informal and limited direct investigations with small samples of pupils. There is a need to extend and develop this type of study over all areas of the framework. The outcome would be a clearer understanding of the ambiguities that lie between pupil capability or potential and the recorded or observed performance. It might also lead to ideas for new types of questions which could, by supplementing the information obtained by present means, lead to a more secure interpretation.

Since the monitoring design has not allowed either for comprehensive profiles across categories to be built up for individual pupils or for development to be studied by tracking individual pupils between monitoring ages, it is at least possible that small scale studies in which the instruments are used in these ways might throw further light on the interpretation of existing and future data. This becomes a more significant issue if the monitoring results are to be used for and related to the new developments in profiling which are now being explored on a national basis.

Finally, discussion of all of the above issues, and some others not mentioned here, could be helped by a more extensive analysis of data collected over the five years. The results set out in this report do not exhaust the possibilities of analysis of the accumulated data: they only represent what could be extracted within reasonable time constraints for a summary report.

These considerations have two policy consequences for the APU Science work. The first is that the various issues set out in this section are to be explored by the science teams in the period before the next monitoring. The results of such work should mean that in a few years time the significance of the results presented will be better understood. The second consequence is that the next monitoring will not be a mere repetition of its predecessors. It will almost certainly represent a compromise between the need to repeat, for continuity and comparability, and the need to amend or add, in order to take advantage of improved possibilities for interpretation, and perhaps in order to reflect new developments in the aims of primary science education.

# References

DES (1981) *Science in Schools. Age 11: Report No 1* Harlen W., Black P., Johnson S. London: HMSO

DES (1983a) *Science in Schools. Age 11: Report No 2* Harlen W., Black P., Johnson S., Palacio D. London: DES

DES (1984a) *Science in Schools. Age 11: Report No 3* Harlen W., Black P., Johnson S., Palacio D., Russell T. London: DES

DES (1985a) *Science in Schools. Age 11: Report No 4* Harlen W., Black P., Khaligh N., Palacio D., Russell T. London: DES

DES (1982b) *Science in Schools. Age 13: Report No 1* Schofield B., Black P., Johnson S., Murphy P. London: DES

DES (1984b) *Science in Schools. Age 13: Report No 2* Schofield B., Black P., Head J., Murphy P. London: DES

DES (1986b) *Science in Schools. Age 13: Report No 4* Schofield B., Khaligh N., Johnson S., Murphy P., Orgee A. London: DES

DES (1985b) *Science in Schools. Ages 13 and 15: Report No 3* Gott R., Davey A., Gamble R., Head J., Khaligh N., Murphy P., Orgee A., Schofield B., Welford G. London: DES

DES (1982c) *Science in Schools. Age 15: Report No 1* Driver R., Gott R., Johnson S., Worsley C., Wylie F. London: HMSO

DES (1984c) *Science in Schools. Age 15: Report No 2* Driver R., Child D., Gott R., Head J., Johnson S., Worsley C., Wylie F. London: DES

DES (1986c) *Science in Schools. Age 15: Report No 4* Welford G., Bell J., Davey A., Gamble R., Gott R. London: DES

DES (1978) *Science Progress Report 1977-78.* London: DES

DES (1978a) *Primary Education in England. A survey by HM Inspectors of Schools.* London: HMSO

DES (1983c) *APU Occasional Paper 3. Standards of Performance – Expectations and Reality* Black P., Harlen W. and Orgee A. London: DES

DES (1983d) *Science in Primary Schools.* Discussion paper

DES (1984d) *APU Science Report for Teachers: 4. Science Assessment Framework. Age 11* Harlen W., Palacio D., Russell T. Hatfield: ASE

DES (1984e) *APU Science Report for Teachers: 7. Electricity at Age 15* Gott R. Hatfield: ASE

DES (1985c) *A Review of Monitoring in Mathematics 1978 to 1982* Foxman D., *et al.* London: DES

DES (1985d) *APU Science Report for Teachers: 6. Practical Testing at Ages 11, 13 and 15* Welford G., Harlen W., Schofield B. Hatfield: ASE

DES (1985e) *New Perspectives on the Mathematics Curriculum. An independent appraisal of the outcomes of APU Mathematics testing 1978–82.* London: DES

DES (1985f) *Science 5-16: A Statement of Policy.* London: HMSO

DES (1986) *APU Occasional Paper 4. Girls and Physics: a discussion of APU survey findings* Johnson S. and Murphy P. London: DES

DES (1988a) *Science in Schools. Age 13: A Review of APU Survey findings 1980-84* Schofield B., Black P., Johnson S., Murphy P., Qualter A., Russell T. London: DES

DES (1988b) *Science in Schools. Age 15: A Review of APU Survey findings 1980-84* Archenhold F., Bell J., Donnelly J., Johnson S., Welford G. London: DES

DES (1988c) *National Assessment: the APU Science Approach* Johnson S. London: HMSO

DES (1986a) *APU Science Report for Teachers: 8. Planning Scientific Investigations at Age 11* Harlen W. Hatfield: ASE

Bell B. and Driver R. (1984) *Children's Learning in Science Project: University of Leeds:* 'Education in Science', *108*, 19–20

Comber L. C. and Keeves J. P. (1973) *Science Education in Nineteen Countries.* Stockholm: Almqvist and Wiskell

Driver R. (1983) *The Pupil as Scientist?* Milton Keynes: OUP

Driver R., Head J. and Johnson S. (1984) *The differential uptake of science in schools in England, Wales and Northern Ireland.* 'The European Journal of Science Education', *6,* 19–29

Erickson G. and Erickson L. (1984) *Females and Science Achievement: evidence, explanations and implications.* Science Education Department, University of British Columbia, Vancouver

Galton, M., Simon B. and Croll P. (1980) *Inside the Primary Classroom.* London: RKP

Glass G. V. (1982) *Meta-analysis: An approach to the synthesis of research results* 'Journal of Research in Science Teaching', *19*, 93–112

Hueftle S. J., Rakow S. J. and Welch W. W. (1983) *Images of science.* University of Minnesota: Science Assessment and Research Project

Johnson S. and Bell J. (1985) *Evaluating and Predicting Survey Efficiency Using Generalisability Theory.* 'J. Educ. Measurement', *22*, 107–119

Qualter A. (1985) *APU Science Practical Investigations: A study of some problems of measuring practical scientific performance of children* (unpublished PhD thesis). University of London

Schools Council (1980) *Learning Through Science.* London: Macdonald Educational

# School questionnaire

## APU Survey of Science at age 10/11, 1984

1. What is the age range in the school?
   (a) 5–11    (c) 8–12    (e) 10–14
   (b) 7–11    (d) 9–13
   (Please enter letter in box) ☐

2. What is the number of classes on entry?
   (eg if 3 classes, enter 3) ☐

3. What is the number of pupils on the school roll? ☐

4. Please enter in the box the number of teaching staff in the school (include any who are half-time or more, as well as full-time teachers). ☐

5. Please enter the number of teaching staff who have attended *in-service courses* or meetings on aspects of teaching science within the last three years, as follows:
   (a) a course of advanced professional study leading to a certificate or award ☐
   (b) a course amounting to more than three days in total but not included in the above. ☐

6. Is responsibility for science:
   (a) held by a special post holder?
   (b) assigned on a voluntary basis to one teacher or to a specified group of teachers?
   (c) not allocated within the school?
   (Please enter letter in box) ☐

7. *The following question applies to State Schools only*
   Please give, for the period April 1983 to March 1984:
   (a) the total sum of money which the LEA made available to the school £ ☐
   (b) the amount of other money received for *science* (eg from an LEA special grant, parents' fund-raising, etc)
   *Do not include this sum in answer to (a)* £ ☐
   (c) the money spent during this time on science equipment (consumable and non-consumable, but excluding books) by the school
   *Include money from sources in both (a) and (b)* £ ☐

8. Please indicate which of the following best describes the locality of your school:
   (a) Village
   (b) Small town (market town, small industrial town, sea-side resort, fishing port, etc)
   (c) Rural/urban fringe (villages and small towns on the edge of large built-up areas or conurbations)
   (d) Large town or city (except inner city area)
   (e) Inner city area
   (Please enter letter in box) ☐

9. Is science-based work included in the learning activities of 10/11 year olds in the school?
   (Please enter Y for Yes or N for No) ☐
   *(If NO pass to question 16)*

10. Is there a school policy relating to science-based work for 10/11 year olds?
    (Please enter Y for Yes or N for No) ☐
    *(If NO pass to question 14)*

11. Is it the school policy for the 10/11 pupils' science work to take place:
    (a) as a specified part of the curriculum (as a time-tabled subject)?
    (b) as a planned part of some broader topics (integrated with other subjects)?
    (c) as it arises?
    (Please enter letter in box) ☐

12. Is there a written document relating to science-based work which is used for 10/11 year old classes?
    (Please enter Y for Yes and N for No) ☐
    *(If NO pass to question 14)*

13. Does the document take the form of:
    (a) specific activities forming a scheme of work
    (b) specific topics or areas of study
    (c) broad guidelines which do not specify content
    (Please enter letter in box) ☐

14. What percentage of the total lesson time of 10/11 year old pupils is spent on science?
    (a) 0 or less than 5 per cent    (c) about 10 per cent
    (b) about 5 per cent             (d) about 20 per cent
                                         or more
    (Please enter letter in box) ☐

15. What, on average, is the size of class or group of 10/11 year olds undertaking science activities at the same time?
    (a) over 30      (d) 12–21
    (b) 25–30        (e) under 12
    (c) 22–25        (Please enter letter in box) ☐

16. Has your school been involved in any kind of reorganisation (eg change of age range or merger with another school) which has had an effect on the school programme within the last three years?
    (Please enter Y for Yes or N for No) ☐

17. *For schools in Wales only*
    Is the language medium (spoken and written) used by pupils in science:
    (a) entirely Welsh?
    (b) entirely English?
    (c) both Welsh and English?
    (Please enter letter in box) ☐

18. *Goals of science activities*

Please assign a rating of 1→5 to indicate the importance your school attaches to each of the following goals of science-based activities for 10/11 year olds.
1 = least important; 5 = most important.

Development of:

1. Understanding of basic science concepts, such as force, energy, evolution ☐

2. Problem-solving skills ☐

3. Ability to carry out simple experiments carefully and safely ☐

4. Enjoyment of science-based activities ☐

5. Knowledge of the natural and physical world around ☐

6. Ability to observe carefully ☐

7. Ability to plan experiments ☐

8. A questioning attitude towards the surroundings ☐

9. Ability to find information from reference books ☐

10. Appreciation of the relevance of mathematics to real problems ☐

11. Familiarity with the correct use of simple science equipment ☐

12. Recognition of patterns in observations or data ☐

19. *Emphasis in science activities*

Please read the following statements about things which pupils may be encouraged to do in science-based activities.
For each one assign a rating of 1→5 to indicate the emphasis given to it in the science activities of 10/11 year olds in your school.
1 = least emphasis; 5 = most emphasis

Pupils are encouraged to:

1. Follow carefully instructions given on a card, in a book or on the blackboard ☐

2. Make notes of observations and results during the course of their work ☐

3. Repeat any measurements or readings to reduce error ☐

4. Make a satisfactory written record of their work ☐

5. Decide on the problems they wish to investigate ☐

6. Choose what kind of record to make of their work ☐

7. Estimate a measurement before taking it ☐

8. Use scientific words correctly in discussion and in written records ☐

9. Make careful observations at first hand ☐

10. Identify the variables operating in certain situations ☐

11. Design their own experiments ☐

12. Check results using reference books where possible ☐

13. Apply scientific knowledge to many different problems or situations ☐

14. Examine their work critically for flaws in experimental method ☐

15. Pay careful attention to demonstrations ☐

16. Incorporate controls in experiments ☐

17. Read about experiments which it is not possible for them to carry out ☐

18. Draw conclusions from results or make generalisations based on observations ☐

20. *Topics encountered in the fourth year*

If, during this school year, the work of your 10/11 year old pupils will have been concerned with any of the topics listed below, through written and/or practical activity, please indicate by ticking the appropriate boxes:

| | Written work | Practical activity |
|---|---|---|
| Life cycle of any animal | ☐ | ☐ |
| Life cycle of any plant | ☐ | ☐ |
| Structure (anatomy) of any animal | ☐ | ☐ |
| Structure of any plant | ☐ | ☐ |
| Life in a particular habitat (eg wood, pond, seashore) | ☐ | ☐ |
| Food chains or webs and interdependence of living things | ☐ | ☐ |
| Properties of air (composition, pressure, etc) | ☐ | ☐ |
| Properties of water (floating, sinking, dissolving, etc) | ☐ | ☐ |
| Properties of materials (eg metals, plastics) | ☐ | ☐ |
| Forces (friction, pressure, etc) | ☐ | ☐ |
| Movement (speed) | ☐ | ☐ |
| Time | ☐ | ☐ |
| Electricity | ☐ | ☐ |
| Magnetism | ☐ | ☐ |
| Light and vision (reflections, shadows, colour, etc) | ☐ | ☐ |
| Sound and hearing | ☐ | ☐ |
| The sky (sun, moon, stars, etc) | ☐ | ☐ |
| The weather (wind, rain, temperature records) | ☐ | ☐ |
| Rocks and soil | ☐ | ☐ |
| Human food (composition, supply, nutrition, etc) | ☐ | ☐ |

21. *Topics encountered in earlier years*

Since some of these topics are introduced in earlier years, please indicate by ticking the appropriate boxes the year(s) in which each one is normally included in your school.

| | YEARS | | | | |
|---|---|---|---|---|---|
| | 7-8 | 8-9 | 9-10 | 10-11 | N/A |
| Life cycle of any animal | ☐ | ☐ | ☐ | ☐ | ☐ |
| Life cycle of any plant | ☐ | ☐ | ☐ | ☐ | ☐ |
| Structure (anatomy) of any animal | ☐ | ☐ | ☐ | ☐ | ☐ |
| Structure of any plant | ☐ | ☐ | ☐ | ☐ | ☐ |
| Life in a particular habitat (eg wood, pond, seashore) | ☐ | ☐ | ☐ | ☐ | ☐ |
| Food chains or webs and interdependence of living things | ☐ | ☐ | ☐ | ☐ | ☐ |
| Properties of air (composition, pressure, etc) | ☐ | ☐ | ☐ | ☐ | ☐ |
| Properties of water (floating, sinking, dissolving, etc) | ☐ | ☐ | ☐ | ☐ | ☐ |
| Properties of materials (eg metals, plastics) | ☐ | ☐ | ☐ | ☐ | ☐ |
| Forces (friction, pressure, etc) | ☐ | ☐ | ☐ | ☐ | ☐ |
| Movement (speed) | ☐ | ☐ | ☐ | ☐ | ☐ |
| Time | ☐ | ☐ | ☐ | ☐ | ☐ |

Electricity

Magnetism

Light and vision (reflections, shadows, colour, etc)

Sound and hearing

The sky (sun, moon, stars, etc)

The weather (wind, rain, temperature records)

Rocks and soil

Human food (composition, supply, nutrition, etc)

22. *Use of TV science programmes*
Are school television programmes used as a resource for science-based work in the school?
Please tick the appropriate boxes.

| YEARS | | | | |
|---|---|---|---|---|
| 7–8 | 8–9 | 9–10 | 10–11 | N/A |
|  |  |  |  |  |

If applicable please say which programmes are used:

_____

_____

_____

_____

_____

_____

23. *Use of microcomputer by 10/11 year old pupils*
Have your 10/11 year olds used a microcomputer at school in any of the following ways?

(a) Not at all

(b) Playing games only

(c) Simple programming

(d) Software packages (not including science)

(e) Software packages (including science)

(Please enter letter in box)

24. If there is any other information about the science work in your school that you would like to have noted please mention it here:

_____

_____

_____

126

# Science topics in the curriculum of 7–11 year olds

**Table A2.1** *Frequency of encountering science topics in the four years of junior education*

(Schools indicating each topic as a percentage of all schools; 1984 survey results)

| Topic | England | | | | Wales | | | | Northern Ireland | | | |
|---|---|---|---|---|---|---|---|---|---|---|---|---|
| | 7–8 | 8–9 | 9–10 | 10–11 | 7–8 | 8–9 | 9–10 | 10–11 | 7–8 | 8–9 | 9–10 | 10–11 |
| Life cycle of any animal | 58 | 48 | 48 | 37 | 68 | 55 | 46 | 47 | 49 | 42 | 28 | 25 |
| Life cycle of any plant | 46 | 49 | 45 | 37 | 47 | 48 | 7 | 44 | 39 | 41 | 33 | 29 |
| Structure of any animal | 16 | 23 | 30 | 35 | 19 | 20 | 33 | 35 | 9 | 16 | 16 | 15 |
| Structure of any plant | 27 | 34 | 44 | 36 | 29 | 30 | 44 | 44 | 25 | 32 | 36 | 25 |
| Life in a particular habitat | 44 | 47 | 50 | 41 | 59 | 56 | 50 | 55 | 33 | 26 | 34 | 28 |
| Food chains/webs and interdependence of living things | 12 | 22 | 35 | 36 | 25 | 16 | 29 | 34 | 10 | 13 | 18 | 24 |
| Properties of air | 15 | 26 | 37 | 38 | 22 | 32 | 44 | 53 | 8 | 10 | 30 | 36 |
| Properties of water | 43 | 36 | 44 | 38 | 51 | 49 | 50 | 50 | 31 | 22 | 35 | 38 |
| Properties of materials | 14 | 21 | 38 | 37 | 18 | 8 | 36 | 42 | 5 | 11 | 17 | 22 |
| Forces | 6 | 12 | 35 | 39 | 10 | 19 | 38 | 51 | 3 | 4 | 12 | 33 |
| Movement | 15 | 21 | 31 | 36 | 12 | 27 | 34 | 46 | 9 | 16 | 30 | 35 |
| Time | 43 | 46 | 45 | 39 | 44 | 42 | 48 | 51 | 37 | 34 | 38 | 42 |
| Electricity | 10 | 16 | 37 | 39 | 9 | 14 | 38 | 51 | 5 | 8 | 19 | 38 |
| Magnetism | 18 | 25 | 38 | 37 | 19 | 32 | 39 | 45 | 5 | 9 | 26 | 33 |
| Light and vision | 30 | 32 | 41 | 33 | 24 | 37 | 32 | 41 | 14 | 18 | 27 | 20 |
| Sound and hearing | 30 | 29 | 33 | 29 | 33 | 34 | 42 | 38 | 26 | 31 | 31 | 26 |
| The sky (sun, moon, stars etc) | 34 | 42 | 42 | 32 | 41 | 44 | 40 | 47 | 30 | 39 | 38 | 38 |
| The weather | 48 | 44 | 48 | 38 | 56 | 58 | 54 | 50 | 48 | 40 | 47 | 44 |
| Rocks and soil | 12 | 18 | 31 | 32 | 12 | 12 | 29 | 37 | 10 | 9 | 15 | 25 |
| Human food | 25 | 30 | 37 | 40 | 21 | 23 | 31 | 38 | 16 | 19 | 30 | 39 |
| Number of schools | | 410 | | | | 133 | | | | 133 | | |

**Table A2.2**  *Frequency of encountering science topics for the first time in the four years of junior education*

(Schools indicating each topic as a percentage of all schools; 1984 survey results)

| Topic | England | | | | | Wales | | | | | Northern Ireland | | | | |
|---|---|---|---|---|---|---|---|---|---|---|---|---|---|---|---|
| | 7–8 | 8–9 | 9–10 | 10–11 | Never | 7–8 | 8–9 | 9–10 | 10–11 | Never | 7–8 | 8–9 | 9–10 | 10–11 | Never |
| Life cycle of any animal | 58 | 16 | 13 | 4 | 9 | 68 | 8 | 8 | 4 | 11 | 49 | 17 | 7 | 3 | 25 |
| Life cycle of any plant | 46 | 21 | 14 | 5 | 14 | 47 | 17 | 15 | 6 | 15 | 39 | 21 | 13 | 4 | 22 |
| Structure of any animal | 16 | 14 | 19 | 14 | 37 | 19 | 8 | 19 | 14 | 40 | 9 | 11 | 10 | 8 | 62 |
| Structure of any plant | 27 | 16 | 23 | 8 | 26 | 29 | 11 | 25 | 11 | 24 | 25 | 15 | 20 | 9 | 31 |
| Life in a particular habitat | 44 | 15 | 15 | 8 | 18 | 59 | 15 | 7 | 7 | 12 | 33 | 12 | 20 | 7 | 27 |
| Food chains/webs and interdependence of living things | 12 | 14 | 21 | 17 | 36 | 25 | 7 | 18 | 11 | 39 | 10 | 8 | 11 | 14 | 57 |
| Properties of air | 15 | 17 | 21 | 16 | 31 | 22 | 17 | 23 | 18 | 20 | 8 | 5 | 25 | 21 | 41 |
| Properties of water | 43 | 14 | 17 | 9 | 16 | 51 | 14 | 14 | 7 | 14 | 31 | 12 | 22 | 12 | 23 |
| Properties of materials | 14 | 11 | 23 | 14 | 38 | 18 | 8 | 24 | 14 | 36 | 5 | 9 | 13 | 14 | 58 |
| Forces | 6 | 9 | 26 | 19 | 40 | 10 | 13 | 26 | 23 | 28 | 3 | 3 | 12 | 28 | 55 |
| Movement | 15 | 12 | 18 | 13 | 42 | 12 | 16 | 19 | 19 | 34 | 9 | 11 | 21 | 19 | 41 |
| Time | 43 | 15 | 11 | 8 | 23 | 44 | 11 | 15 | 10 | 20 | 37 | 12 | 11 | 12 | 27 |
| Electricity | 10 | 10 | 26 | 20 | 34 | 9 | 10 | 28 | 26 | 27 | 5 | 5 | 17 | 26 | 46 |
| Magnetism | 18 | 14 | 23 | 16 | 30 | 19 | 20 | 22 | 15 | 24 | 5 | 7 | 25 | 19 | 44 |
| Light and vision | 30 | 16 | 19 | 9 | 26 | 24 | 18 | 14 | 16 | 28 | 14 | 12 | 17 | 6 | 50 |
| Sound and hearing | 30 | 15 | 16 | 9 | 31 | 33 | 14 | 18 | 10 | 26 | 26 | 16 | 14 | 8 | 36 |
| The sky (sun, moon stars etc) | 34 | 19 | 16 | 7 | 24 | 41 | 17 | 12 | 10 | 19 | 30 | 20 | 14 | 11 | 25 |
| The weather | 48 | 13 | 14 | 6 | 19 | 56 | 14 | 11 | 7 | 12 | 48 | 14 | 17 | 9 | 12 |
| Rocks and soil | 12 | 11 | 21 | 15 | 41 | 12 | 7 | 20 | 17 | 44 | 10 | 6 | 12 | 17 | 56 |
| Human food | 25 | 14 | 16 | 15 | 30 | 21 | 11 | 16 | 16 | 36 | 16 | 11 | 19 | 16 | 38 |
| Number of schools | | | 410 | | | | | 133 | | | | | 113 | | |

# Experience of science topics

Have you ever done some work on these topics?

If you have, put a tick in the first box. If you would like to know more about a topic, tick the second box.

|  | Done some work | Like to know more |
|---|---|---|

### 1. Air and burning

For example:

A flame won't burn without air.

☐ ☐

### 2. Speed

For example:

Who is going faster?

☐ ☐

### 3. Dissolving things

For example:

SUGAR

Putting sugar, salt and other things in water

☐ ☐

### 4. Electric circuits

For example:

Switch

Battery

Lamp

Making the bulb light

☐ ☐

### 5. Making sounds

For example:

Notes from rubber bands

☐ ☐

**6. Growing seeds**

For example:

Beans, grass, wheat, cress.

**7. Reflection in a mirror**

For example:

LIPSTICK

**8. Shadows**

For example:

How the shadow changes

**9. Time**

For example:

Different ways of measuring time.

**10. The sky**

For example:

Star patterns.

**11. Forces**

For example:

Seeing how much force will make it slip

**12. Parts of plants**

For example:

Bract

Terminal buds

Fruit

seed

Ovary contains a seed

Leaf scar

A fruit with one seed

Stamen

Ring scar

Done some work

Like to know more

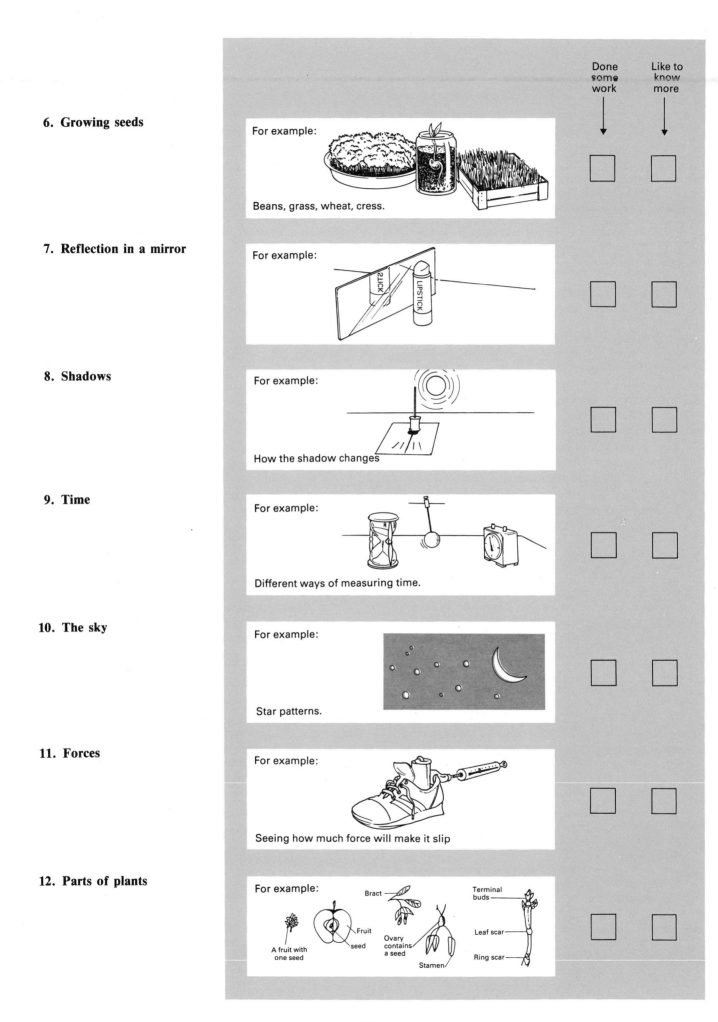

**13. Water in the air**

For example:

Drops of water on a cold can of drink.

**14. The weather**

For example:

Measuring the strength of the wind.

**15. Our food**

For example:

What food is good for you?

**16. Differences between living things**

For example:

| | Sparrow | Starling | Duck | Robin |
|---|---|---|---|---|
| Beaks | Short/Stumpy | Chisel-like | Flat | Small/delicate |
| | Hen | Moorhen | Duck | Woodpecker |
| Feet | Scratching | Running | Swimming | Climbing |

Different beaks and feet of birds that eat different kinds of food.

**17. Rocks**

For example:

Granite  Slate  Sandstone  Marble  Limestone
Some different kinds.

**18. Magnets**

For example:

Magnet

Pins

The magnet picks up steel pins.

**19. How different things live together**

For example:

Fishes, snails, plants and water fleas in an aquarium.

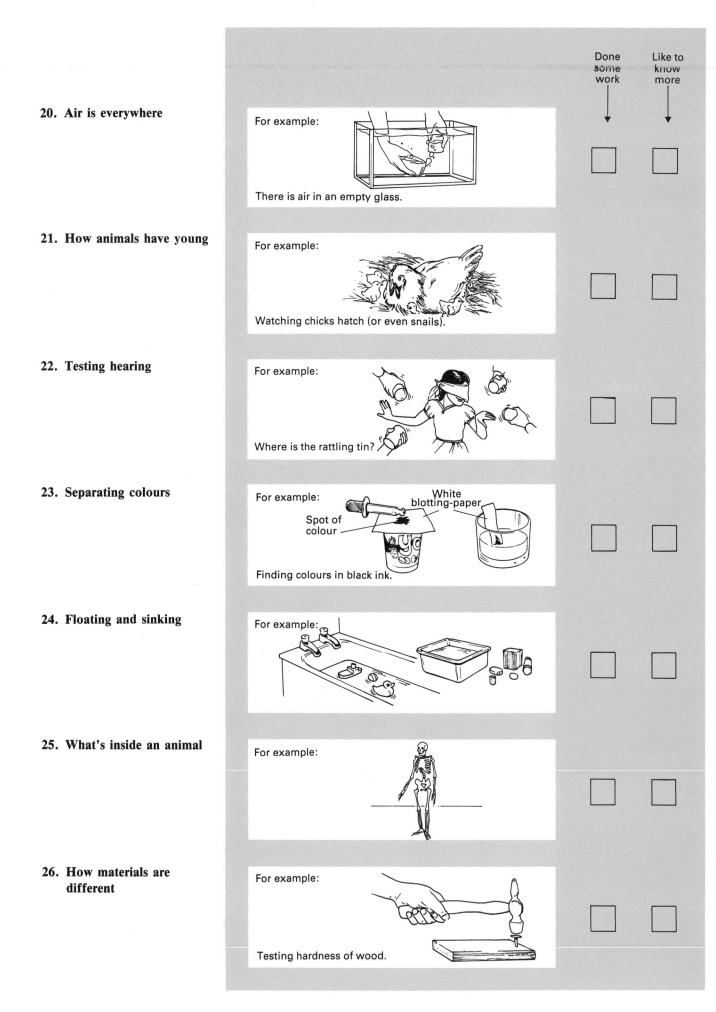

**Done some work** | **Like to know more**

**20. Air is everywhere**

For example:

There is air in an empty glass.

☐ ☐

**21. How animals have young**

For example:

Watching chicks hatch (or even snails).

☐ ☐

**22. Testing hearing**

For example:

Where is the rattling tin?

☐ ☐

**23. Separating colours**

For example:

Spot of colour — White blotting-paper

Finding colours in black ink.

☐ ☐

**24. Floating and sinking**

For example:

☐ ☐

**25. What's inside an animal**

For example:

☐ ☐

**26. How materials are different**

For example:

Testing hardness of wood.

☐ ☐

# Use of various items of equipment

| Have you ever used these things yourself? |

Put a tick by the ones you have used *at school*.
Put a tick in the second column by the ones you have used *at home or out of school*.

| | At school | At home or out of school |
|---|---|---|
| Used a hand lens (magnifying glass) _____ | ☐ | ☐ |
| Used a thermometer _____ | ☐ | ☐ |
| Used a stop watch or stop clock_____ | ☐ | ☐ |
| Used a spring balance _____ | ☐ | ☐ |
| Used a computer to play games _____ | ☐ | ☐ |
| Used a computer to do things besides playing games _____ | ☐ | ☐ |
| Used a dropper _____ | ☐ | ☐ |
| Used a compass _____ | ☐ | ☐ |
| Used a metre stick _____ | ☐ | ☐ |
| Used a measuring cylinder or jug _____ | ☐ | ☐ |
| Used a screwdriver _____ | ☐ | ☐ |
| Used weighing scales _____ | ☐ | ☐ |
| Used a microscope _____ | ☐ | ☐ |

Dropper

Measuring jug

Scales

Microscope

# Teachers helping with the development trials of the questions on pupils' experience, activities and interests relating to science

| | | | |
|---|---|---|---|
| Mr Patrick J. Acock | The Highway Primary School, The Highway, Orpington, Kent. | Mrs Carys Griffiths | Woodford Junior School, Plympton, Plymouth, Devon. |
| Mr Ian R. Bennett | Headteacher, Friarn County Primary School, Wembdon Road, Bridgwater, Somerset. | Mr Hugh Wilcox | Headteacher, Paganel Junior School, Swinford Road, Selly Oak, Birmingham. |
| Mr Alan Coode | Head teacher, Southmead Junior School, Wimbledon, London. | Mr Gwil D. Williams | Wellesbourne County Primary School, Holmbrook Road, Liverpool. |

# Experience of science-related activities

| How often do you do these things? |
|---|

For each one show whether you have *never* done it, or done it only *a few times*, or done it *often* (about once a month). Answer by putting one tick for *At school* and another for *At home/out of school*.

| | At school | | | At home/out of school | | |
|---|---|---|---|---|---|---|
| | Never | A few times | Quite often | Never | A few times | Quite often |
| 1. Watch a TV school science programme. | ☐ | ☐ | ☐ | ☐ | ☐ | ☐ |
| 2. Watch a TV programme about science (eg Tomorrow's World, Horizon). | ☐ | ☐ | ☐ | ☐ | ☐ | ☐ |
| 3. Watch science fiction on TV. | ☐ | ☐ | ☐ | ☐ | ☐ | ☐ |
| 4. Read an information book about science or scientists. | ☐ | ☐ | ☐ | ☐ | ☐ | ☐ |
| 5. Read a science fiction book. | ☐ | ☐ | ☐ | ☐ | ☐ | ☐ |
| 6. Read news about science in a paper or magazine. | ☐ | ☐ | ☐ | ☐ | ☐ | ☐ |
| 7. Watch a teacher or a scientist do an experiment. | ☐ | ☐ | ☐ | ☐ | ☐ | ☐ |
| 8. Decide for yourself how to solve a problem. | ☐ | ☐ | ☐ | ☐ | ☐ | ☐ |
| 9. Look after small animals or pets (eg mice, rabbits, fish, insects). | ☐ | ☐ | ☐ | ☐ | ☐ | ☐ |
| 10. Sow seeds or grow plants. | ☐ | ☐ | ☐ | ☐ | ☐ | ☐ |
| 11. Take things apart to see inside them. | ☐ | ☐ | ☐ | ☐ | ☐ | ☐ |
| 12. Weight out ingredients for cooking. | ☐ | ☐ | ☐ | ☐ | ☐ | ☐ |
| 13. Watch birds. | ☐ | ☐ | ☐ | ☐ | ☐ | ☐ |
| 14. Use parts from a kit to make models (eg Lego, Meccano, straws). | ☐ | ☐ | ☐ | ☐ | ☐ | ☐ |
| 15. Make up models from a kit (eg Airfix). | ☐ | ☐ | ☐ | ☐ | ☐ | ☐ |
| 16. Play with electric toy sets (cars, or trains on tracks). | ☐ | ☐ | ☐ | ☐ | ☐ | ☐ |
| 17. Play pool, billiards or snooker. | ☐ | ☐ | ☐ | ☐ | ☐ | ☐ |
| 18. Knit or sew. | ☐ | ☐ | ☐ | ☐ | ☐ | ☐ |
| 19. Collect, or just look at, wild flowers. | ☐ | ☐ | ☐ | ☐ | ☐ | ☐ |
| 20. Visit a museum or a zoo. | ☐ | ☐ | ☐ | ☐ | ☐ | ☐ |
| 21. Go fishing or pond dipping. | ☐ | ☐ | ☐ | ☐ | ☐ | ☐ |
| 22. Play draughts or chess. | ☐ | ☐ | ☐ | ☐ | ☐ | ☐ |

# Liking for science-related activities

| Would you like to try these things or do more of them? |
|---|

For each one tick *Yes, No* or *Not sure*.

|  | Yes | No | Not sure |
|---|---|---|---|
| 1. Watch a TV school science programme. | ☐ | ☐ | ☐ |
| 2. Watch a TV programme about science (eg Tomorrow's World, Horizon). | ☐ | ☐ | ☐ |
| 3. Watch science fiction on TV. | ☐ | ☐ | ☐ |
| 4. Read an information book about science or scientists | ☐ | ☐ | ☐ |
| 5. Read a science fiction book. | ☐ | ☐ | ☐ |
| 6. Read news about science in a paper or magazine. | ☐ | ☐ | ☐ |
| 7. Watch a teacher or a scientist do an experiment. | ☐ | ☐ | ☐ |
| 8. Decide for yourself how to solve a problem. | ☐ | ☐ | ☐ |
| 9. Look after small animals or pets (eg mice, rabbits, fish, insects). | ☐ | ☐ | ☐ |
| 10. Sow seeds or grow plants. | ☐ | ☐ | ☐ |
| 11. Take things apart to see inside them. | ☐ | ☐ | ☐ |
| 12. Weigh out ingredients for cooking. | ☐ | ☐ | ☐ |
| 13. Watch birds. | ☐ | ☐ | ☐ |
| 14. Use parts from a kit to make models (eg Lego, Meccano, straws). | ☐ | ☐ | ☐ |
| 15. Make up models from a kit (eg Airfix). | ☐ | ☐ | ☐ |
| 16. Play with electric toy sets (cars, or trains on tracks). | ☐ | ☐ | ☐ |
| 17. Play pool, billiards or snooker. | ☐ | ☐ | ☐ |
| 18. Knit or sew. | ☐ | ☐ | ☐ |
| 19. Collect, or just look at, wild flowers. | ☐ | ☐ | ☐ |
| 20. Visit a museum or a zoo. | ☐ | ☐ | ☐ |
| 21. Go fishing or pond dipping. | ☐ | ☐ | ☐ |
| 22. Play draughts or chess. | ☐ | ☐ | ☐ |

# Survey sampling, test distributions and marking

The pupils who took part in this survey were selected according to a two-stage stratified cluster sampling scheme. In the first stage a random sample of schools was selected, and this was followed in the second stage by the random selection of pupils of the appropriate age from within each of the participating schools.

## Selection of schools

Before selection began, the school population was stratified with respect to the variables *region, school type* and *size*. The relevant regional classification within England is shown in Table A7.1.

**Table A7.1**  *The three regions*

| North | Midlands | South |
|---|---|---|
| Merseyside* | West Midlands* | Greater London* |
| Greater Manchester* | Hereford and | Bedfordshire |
| South Yorkshire* | Worcester | Berkshire |
| West Yorkshire* | Shropshire | Buckinghamshire |
| Tyne and Wear* | Staffordshire | East Sussex |
| Cleveland | Warwickshire | Essex |
| Cumbria | Derbyshire | Hampshire |
| Durham | Leicestershire | Hertfordshire |
| Humberside | Lincolnshire | Isle of Wight |
| Lancashire | Northamptonshire | Kent |
| North Yorkshire | Nottinghamshire | Oxfordshire |
| Northumberland | Cambridgeshire | Surrey |
| Cheshire | Norfolk | West Sussex |
| | Suffolk | Isles of Scilly |
| | | Avon |
| | | Cornwall |
| | | Devon |
| | | Dorset |
| | | Goucestershire |
| | | Somerset |
| | | Wiltshire |

* Metropolitan counties in 1984.

Three types of school categories applied in England *and* Wales. **Junior-with-Infant, Junior** and **Independent**. In England a fourth group contained **Middle** schools. In Northern Ireland, schools were categorised according to their management system: *Voluntary, Controlled, Maintained*.

Four *size of age group* classifications were imposed: *up to 30 pupils, 31–60 pupils, 61–90* and *more than 90 pupils*.

Within England schools were selected from within each region-by-type-by-size classification in numbers which reflected their presence in the school population as a whole (ie schools were selected by proportional random

sampling): in other words, if x per cent of the schools in England containing 11 year old pupils were middle schools of size 61–90 pupils in the Midlands, then x per cent of the schools in the English sample were intended to be of this kind. Within Wales and Northern Ireland schools were also selected by proportional random sampling from the type-by-size or management-by-size classifications, respectively, but these countries were deliberately over-represented relative to England in the final sample so that pupil performance estimates of reasonable accuracy could be produced.

**Table A7.2**  *The sample of schools*

| | Eng | Wales | NI |
|---|---|---|---|
| Invited to take part | 509 | 173 | 174 |
| Unable to take part | 36 | 22 | 39 |
| Initial acceptance, later decline | 6 | 1 | 2 |
| Tests incomplete or not returned | 7 | 3 | 5 |

Table A7.2 provides details of the numbers of schools invited to take part in the survey and of those which finally participated. It will be clear from this table that the voluntary participation rates varied from country to country, with the Northern Ireland rate once again being relatively low (74 per cent) compared with those for England (90 per cent) and Wales (85 per cent).

## Selection of pupils

The pupils chosen to take part in the survey were selected from all of those in the participating schools. The criterion for selection depended on the pupil's birthdate; pupils whose birthdate fell within a prescribed range within any month were selected. The ranges of dates of birth used were intended to produce pupil sample sizes of approximately 17 in each school in England and 8 in each school in Wales and Northern Ireland (these countries containing high numbers of primary schools of very small size).

The group practical tests, for economic reasons, were given to just 12 pupils in each participating school in England and 6 in each participating school in Wales and Northern Ireland. Whenever the specified birthdate procedure failed to produce these ideal numbers in schools which were to undertake practical testing, the range of birthdates was extended until sufficient pupils had been drawn where these were available.

The only pupils explicitly excluded from the survey were those in special schools or in units designated as 'special' within normal schools. However, the Headteacher of each selected school was told that discretion could be used in withdrawing particular pupils from the testing sessions if it was felt that participation would cause undue distress. 12,182 pupils were chosen to take part in the survey; 149 pupils were absent from school throughout the testing period and just 44 pupils were withdrawn from testing by their Headteachers. Almost 1,600 pupils took one of the two groups practical tests.

## Test administration

The questions which were used in this survey to represent each subcategory were chosen at random from the pool of questions for that subcategory (ie a 'domain-sampling' approach to question selection was employed). This complete set of questions was then evenly distributed across an appropriate number of test packages to be administered to different, but similarly representative, random samples of pupils. The numbers of questions and the composition of each main survey package are given in Chapter 4.

Each survey school was given a variety of the written test packages (lasting about 45 minutes each) to be distributed at random among its sample of pupils (each pupil took just one of these). In addition, in a random sub-sample of the participating schools, sub-samples of these same pupils were given group administered practical tests. About 13 per cent of the pupils took both a written *and* a practical test. Testing took place during early May in England, and early June in Wales and Northern Ireland.

Pupils who were in the sample but who were absent on the day on which the school undertook a written test session were given the relevant test if they attended school at any time within two weeks of the school's main test session. This was an attempt to avoid introducing unnecessary bias into the pupil sample which would occur

if, for example, persistent absentees happened also to be lower performance in general. Economic reasons prevented such a procedure being adopted in the case of particular test sessions, which involved visits by trained administrators. For practical tests, pupils absent on the day of a test session were replaced by other randomly selected pupils who *were* present that day.

## Training and marking

Practical testers were trained in one-day training sessions held a week before the practical survey began. The training included instruction in the use of a separate detailed check-list for each investigation which was used to assess a child's performance whilst he or she was carrying it out. The testers were all practising teachers released from their schools to help with the survey (see Appendix 14).

The marking of written tests was also carried out by teachers. Each marker was trained to mark two packages and each package was shared between two members (one taking the 'a' version scripts and one the 'b' version scripts).

## Analysis samples

To most intents and purposes this survey actually comprises a series of parallel surveys, one per subcategory for which performance estimates are presented in Chapter 4.

Each written test package was distributed to approximately 500 pupils throughout England, Wales and Northern Ireland, so that in total each sub-category involved the testing of between approximately 2,000 and 3,000 pupils depending on whether the subcategory appeared in 4 or 6 test packages. Clerical errors of one kind or another resulted in the overall loss of test results for about 1 per cent of pupils at the final analysis stage.

# Question descriptors

The lists of question descriptors which follow have been used by members of the APU Science monitoring teams in writing questions to assess some of the processes and skills related to the assessment framework below. Sub-categories shown in bold correspond to those listed in recent publications.

*The assessment framework\**

| Category | Subcategories | Mode of testing |
|---|---|---|
| 1 Use of graphical and symbolic representation | **Reading information from graphs, tables and charts** **Representing information as graphs, tables and charts** Using scientific symbols and conventions | Written |
| 2 Use of apparatus and measuring instruments | **Using measuring instruments** **Estimating physical quantities** **Following instructions for practical work** | Group practical |
| 3 Observation | **Making and interpreting observations** | Group practical |
| 4 Interpretation and application | i **Interpreting presented information** Judging the applicability of statements to data Distinguishing degrees of inference | Written |
| | ii **Applying: biology concepts** **physics concepts** **chemistry concepts** Generating alternative hypotheses | |
| 5 Planning of investigations | **Planning parts of investigations** **Planning entire investigations** Identifying or proposing testable statements | Written |
| 6 Performance of investigations | **Performing entire investigations** | Individual practical |

\* One or two question descriptors have been used only at age 11, and one or two only at ages 13 and 15.

**Category 1:** *Use of graphical and symbolic representation*

| Subcategory | QD | Given | Outcome | Mode of response |
|---|---|---|---|---|
| α<br>Reading information from graphs, tables and charts | 101 | A table of (a) figures<br>(b) representative symbols<br>(c) non-representative symbols | Read off information as directed | LR and CA |
| | 102 | A schematic representation of a process or series of linked events or relationships | Read off information as directed | LR and CA |
| | 103 | Vertical or horizontal bar chart | Read off information as directed | LR |
| | 104 | Pie chart | Read off information as directed | LR |
| | 105 | Graph | Read off information as directed | LR |
| | 106 | Graph and statement of what it represents | Name the variables on the axes | LR |
| | 107 | (a) line graph<br>(b) points located by coordinates | Read coordinates of a designated point | LR |
| β<br>Representing information as graphs, tables and charts | 111 | Data and a partially completed table | Add further data to complete table | CA |
| | 112 | A partially complete schematic representation of a process, series of linked events or relationships and data to add | Add given data to complete schematic representation | Drawing |
| | 113 | Data and a partially completed bar chart | Add further data to complete chart | Drawing LR |
| | 114 | Data and a partially completed pie chart | Add further data to complete chart | Drawing LR |
| | 115 | Data and a partially completed line graph | Add further data to complete graph | Drawing LR |
| | 116 | Data in the form of pairs of related quantities | Draw axes, select scale and construct a bar chart | Drawing LR |
| | 117 | Data in the form of continuously varying quantities of pairs of related quantities | Draw axes, select scale and plot points and draw line graph | Drawing LR |
| | 118 | A pair of labelled axes, and (a) and (b) points to plot (c) data | Construct (a) bar chart representing data (b) points (c) line graph—as directed | Drawing LR |
| γ<br>Using scientific symbols and conventions | 121 | Section diagram of assorted objects, and a list of names with some redundancy | Identify the objects by matching names to objects | LR |
| | 122 | A 3-D drawing of an experimental set-up using general lab. apparatus | Make a conventional section drawing | Drawing |
| | 123 | A conventional section drawing of a set-up using general lab. apparatus | Propose names for the components of the set-up | LR |
| | 124 | A 3-D drawing of a circuit | Draw a conventional circuit diagram | Drawing |
| | 125 | A conventional circuit diagram | Propose names for the components of the circuit | LR |

*Mode of response*

CA—Coded answer
LR—Limited written response

**Category 2:** *Use of apparatus and measuring instruments*

| Subcategory | QD | Given | Outcome | Mode of response | Mode of marking |
|---|---|---|---|---|---|
| α<br>Using measuring instruments | 201 | Choice of units or description of physical quantities | Select from four or five alternatives | CA | 1 |
| | 202 | Physical quantity measured by a set up instrument | Give a value with units | LR | 1 |
| | 203 | Physical quantity, object or event, and instrument(s) for measuring or observing it | Employ appropriate instrument(s) to: give an answer or give a value with units or leave a measured quantity | LR<br>LR<br>A | 1<br>1<br>2 |
| β<br>Estimating physical quantities | 211 | Objects or events and units of physical quantities | Give a value | LR | 1 |
| | 212 | Supply of material and an amount specified | Leave or indicate the right amount of material | A | 2 |
| γ<br>Following instructions for practical work | 221 | Instructions, in the form of a conventional diagram, for setting up apparatus for a stated purpose | Set up apparatus | A | 3 |
| | 222 | Detailed instructions for completing an unfamiliar task | Comply exactly with instructions to complete the task | A<br>LR | 2<br>1 |
| | 223 | Detailed instructions for completing an unfamiliar task | Comply exactly with instructions to leave a product | A | 2 |
| | 224 | Instructions for task that explicitly refer to standard techniques used in laboratories | Follow instructions, using the correct procedures, in order to complete the task | A | 4 |
| | 225 | Instructions for task that require standard techniques used in laboratories | Follow instructions, recalling and using the correct procedures, in order to complete the task | A | 4 |

*Mode of response*
CA—Coded answer
LR—Limited written response
A —Action

*Mode of marking*
1 Assess written response
2 Inspect/check quantities at end of test period
3 Inspect each pupil's product during test period
4 Observe pupil and fill in prepared schedule

**Category 3:** *Observation*

Making and interpreting observations

| QD | Given | Outcome | Mode of response |
|---|---|---|---|
| 301 | Objects, photographs | Identify each object using a branching key | CA/LR |
| 311 | Objects, photographs or diagrams | (a) Group objects into self-defined classes | Action |
| | | (b) Identify rules used to classify the objects and add further objects to classes | LR |
| 312 | At least two objects, events, photographs or diagrams | Give a specified number (3) of similarities and differences or as many differences as possible | ER |
| 314 | Event | Make a record of change | ER |
| 315 | Objects and drawings, or photographs and drawings | Select the matching drawing | CA |
| 316 | Objects or photographs | Make a scientific dawing | Drawing |
| 319 | Set of photographs or drawings or a sequence some of which may not belong to that sequence | Discard those which do not belong to the sequence and arrange the remainder in sequence | CA |
| 321 | Events | Make a record of observations and give an explanation | ER |
| 323 | Events | Make a record of changes and make a prediction consistent with the data | LR |
| 324 | At least two events or photographs or diagrams and a list of predictions | Note the differences and select a prediction consistent with the data | LR and CA |
| 325 | Events | Make a record of changes and identify a pattern in the observed changes | ER |

*Mode of response*
LR—Limited written response
ER—Extended response
CA—Coded answer

# Category 4: *Interpretation and application*

## 4 i: Interpretation

| Subcategory | QD | Given | Outcome | Mode of response |
|---|---|---|---|---|
| | 401 | Data embodying a pattern, regularity or relationship | Generate a description of the regularity | ER |
| | 402 | Data as in 401 | Generate a description, and use to generate a prediction | ER +LR |
| | 403 | Data as in 401, and a minimum of four predictions | Generate a description and use to select a prediction | ER +CA |
| α Interpreting presented information | 404 | Data as in 401 | Generate a prediction based on a regularity in data | LR |
| | 405 | Data as in 401 and a minimum of four predictions | Select a prediction using regularity in data | CA |
| | 406 | Data as in 401, and a minimum of four 'descriptions' | Select a description of the regularity in data | CA |
| | 407 | Data as in 401 | Generate a prediction and justify it | LR +ER |
| | 408 | Data as in 401, and a minimum of four predictions | Select a prediction and justify the choice | CA +ER |
| β Judging the applicability of statements to data | 411 | Equivocal data and a statement (or pair of contradictory statements) | Assess and discuss validity of presented statement in relation to data | ER |
| | 412 | Data and a minimum of four statements | Assess the validity of the statements in relation to data and identify those consistent with it | CA |
| γ Distinguishing degrees of inference | 421 | A 'snapshot' of an event (in words or line drawing) and five possible accounts of it | Select the account which makes the fewest additional assumptions | CA |

*Mode of response:*
ER—Extended response
LR—Limited written response
CA—Coded answer

**Category 4:** *Interpretation and application*—continued

## 4 ii: Application

| Subcategory | QD | Given | Outcome | Mode of response |
|---|---|---|---|---|
| | 430 | Diagrams of stages in a sequence | Re-order according to accepted concepts | LR |
| | 431 | Data | (a) Describe a relationship based on data *and* accepted concepts and use it to generate predictions *or* (b) Generate predictions giving reasons based on data *and* accepted concepts | ER |
| | 432 | Data | Generate predictions based on data and accepted concepts | LR |
| | 433 | Data and a minimum of four predictions | Select a prediction giving reason based on data and accepted concepts | CA +ER |
| | 434 | Data and a minimum of four predictions | Select a prediction based on data and accepted concepts | CA |
| ʕ Applying science concepts | 435 | Data, description of an event or situation | Give an explanation consistent with the data and accepted concepts | ER |
| | 436 | Data, description of event or situation, and one or more hypothesis/explanation | Assess validity of each hypothesis/ explanation in relation to data and accepted concepts | ER |
| | 437 | Data, description of event or situation, and a minimum of four predictions or hypotheses/explanations | Select the best hypothesis/explanation in relation to data *and* accepted concepts | CA |
| | 438 | Data, description of event or situation, and a minimum of four hypotheses/explanations | Select all the hypotheses/explanations which are consistent with the data *and* accepted concepts | CA |
| | 439 | Data and minimum of two predictions | Select one prediction and give reason based on data and accepted concepts | LR +ER |
| ε Generating alternative hypotheses | 441 | Data, description of event or situation where there is no single obvious explanation | Generate alternative hypotheses/ explanations consistent with data *and* accepted concepts | ER |

*Mode of response:*
ER—Extended response
LR—Limited written response
CA—Coded answer

**Category 5:** *Planning of investigations*

| Subcategory | QD | Given | Focus | Outcome |
|---|---|---|---|---|
| α Identifying or proposing testable statements | 501 | Four or five statements, one of which: (a) can be tested scientifically (b) cannot be tested scientifically | — | Select the statement which can be tested scientifically / Select the one which cannot be tested scientifically |
| | 503 | A general statement or opinion | — | Re-write as a (number of) statement(s), each of which can be tested. |
| γ Planning entire investigations | 521 | A proposition in a testable form | — | *Plan* a procedure to test, resolve or determine the point at issue (taking into account control of variables and selection of equipment). |
| β Planning parts of investigations | 515 | A statement of an investigation which may or may not include operational details of how the investigation is to be performed | Variables to be controlled | To select or generate variables in an investigation which should be kept constant, or to criticise the control of a particular variable |
| | 512 | A statement of an investigation | Variables to be changed (the independent variable) and controlled | To select or generate variables in an investigation which should be kept constant (controlled variables) and which should be systematically varied (independent variable) |
| | 516 | A statement of an investigation which contains operational details of how the investigation is to be performed | Operational details concerning the variables to be changed (the dependent variable) and controlled | To give or select or criticise operational details of the variables in an investigation which should be kept constant (controlled variables) and which should be systematically varied (independent variable) |
| | 514 | A description of a procedure specifying the variables changed (independent variable) and measured (dependent variable) | The problem being investigated | To select a statement of the relationship between dependent and independent variables |
| | 517 | A statement of an investigation with operational details of conditions which should be systematically varied (the independent variable) and, where appropriate, those which should be kept constant (controlled variables) | Operational details concerning the variable to be measured (the dependent variable) | To generate, select or criticize a procedure for measuring the dependent variable |
| | 518 | Describes an investigation, including details of operationalisation of dependent, independent and controlled variables | Procedures which ensure valid measurements of either the dependent or the independent variable | To explain how a given procedure ensures valid measurement procedure or say why it would not ensure validity of measurement |
| | 519 | Describes an investigation with experimental details, including the kind of measurement taken | The use of judgements/measurements in solving a problem | To describe how the measurements taken during the investigation could be used to solve the problem at issue |

# Science concepts and knowledge used in subcategory 4ii, 'Applying' questions at age 11

## Living things

### A   Interaction of living things with their environment

#### i   *Interdependence of living things:*

Living things depend on each other in various ways.

Some animals eat plants and some eat other animals, but all animals ultimately depend on green plants.

Living things are usually well suited in form and function to their natural environment.

#### ii   *The physical and chemical environment:*

There is air around the Earth.

Water is essential to life.

Soil, a mixture of things, comes from rocks and living things.

Plants take substances from both the air and the soil.

Substances taken from the soil must be replaced to maintain fertility.

Changes in the physical environment due to seasonal cycles are often matched by changes or events in the living world.

Air contains water vapour.

### B   Living things and their life processes

#### i   *Nutrition:*

All living things need food for growth.

Green plants can make food, animals cannot.

#### ii   *Reproduction:*

Living things produce offspring of the same 'species' as themselves.

The life cycle of any living thing is repeated in each generation.

#### iii   *Sensitivity and movement:*

All living organisms have means of receiving information from their environment.

Different senses can detect different kinds of information.

In humans the senses include sight, touch, hearing, taste and smell.

## Force and energy

### C   Force

#### i   *Movement and deformation:*

The speed of an object means how far it moves in a given period of time.

The average speed of an object is found by dividing the distance moved by the time taken.

To make anything move (or change the way it moves) there has to be a force (push, pull or twist) acting on it.

To change the shape of an object there has to be a force acting on it. The force which an object can stand before breaking depends on its shape as well as on the material from which it is made.

#### ii   *Properties of matter:*

The larger the area over which a force is spread the smaller the force on each part.

Water tends to flow until its surface reaches a common level.

Objects completely immersed in a liquid displace a volume of liquid equal to their own volume.

Whether an object floats or sinks depends both on the material from which it is made and on its shape.

#### iii   *Forces at a distance:*

Magnets attract and repel other magnets and attract magnetic substances.

#### iv   *The Earth in space:*

All things are pulled towards the centre of the Earth; it is this force which makes them feel heavy.

The apparent movements of the sun, moon and stars follow a regular pattern.

## D Energy

### i Work and energy:

There is a variety of sources of energy such as food, fuel and stretched springs.

Moving objects have energy which they lose when they are stopped.

### ii Electricity:

A complete circuit of conducting material is needed for a steady current to flow between the terminals of a battery.

### iii Waves:

Objects can be seen because of the light which they give out or reflect.

Light travels (in a uniform medium) in straight paths or rays.

Sound comes from vibrating objects.

## Materials and their characteristics

### E The classification and structure of matter

#### i States of matter:

In general a substance can be classified either as a solid or a liquid or a gas.

The processes of melting, freezing, evaporating and condensing do not change what a substance is made of.

Energy (often in the form of heat) is required for melting and for evaporation to take place.

#### ii Metals and non-metals:

Materials can be classified in many different ways into groups, such as metals, plastics and wood, according to their properties.

### F Chemical interactions

#### i Solutions:

Some substances dissolve in water; others do not, but may dissolve in other liquids.

# Examples of pupils' investigations

**Example of pupil's investigation (boy)**

*Question selected:* How hard can it pull?

*Description of investigation:*
Picks up balance pan, studies rest of equipment for 3 min. Picks up knife and string—leaves down knife—ties knife to end of string, cuts off approx. 15 cm of string—forms loop at other end of string—puts loop over snail's shell. Snail retreats into shell—takes loop from shell. Now gently places loop over shell—snail comes out of shell. Looks at snail through lens—pushes out knife to 'stretch' out string—snail near edge of glass. Moves snail towards centre—observes occasionally using lens. Watches knife—knife moves with jerks. Notes on his sheet. Snail tries to 'eat' string. Takes ruler, measures how far he thinks the knife has moved. Snail climbing over string and out of loop. After finishing writing notes, looks at snail using lens. Picks up dropper, returns snail to centre of glass. Unties knife, ties on dropper. Gently puts loop over snail's shell. Observes through lens. Snail pulls dropper along glass. Uses ruler to measure distance (no timing). Moves snail to centre of glass, picks up balance, zeroes it, weighs knife, records weight. Snail crawls out of loop. Unties dropper. Picks up bran bottle, puts it down again. Moves snail towards middle of glass, places ruler along glass, times how long snail takes to travel in 1 min. Takes torch, shines it at front of snail. Snail moves away from light. Notes on his sheet. Takes scales, checks zero, checks weight of dropper and knife.

*Aspects clarified in discussion:*
Shone light at snail to see how quickly it moved away from it. Would not use any heavier weights in case he would hurt snail.

**Example of pupil's investigation (boy)**

*Question selected:* What food does it like best—

*Description of investigation:*
Cuts piece from apple (1 cm) place (1 cm) from snail. Snail moved past. Boy moves apple in front again. 1 min. 20 secs. wait—'Snail seems to drink from over the water?' Writes notes. Tries mixing some bran with the water using the end of the dropper—puts 2 cm away—'Snail has drunk all first water'. Snail advances to eat some of the water and bran mixture. 'It is eating

it' 'It's eating the bran' 'I think it is anyway'. Picks up magnifying glass to look closer. Writes notes. Chops apple to tiny one mm pieces—decides to see if it likes the juice—crushes apple with the knife. Snail eats. 'Took shorter time than with the bran'. (Checks to see if bran smells?) Observes that snail has eaten all of 1 cm crushed apple—tries 1 cm piece of apple skin. Snail leaves skin and goes past to a patch of apple juice—drinks that. Writes. Cuts small 1 cm rings from white end of spring onion. Observes snail with magnifier. Observes snail antennae keeping retracting from onion. Chops off end of spring onion (green—'Which does not smell so much'). (In each case the boy put food about 1 cm from snail. The snail advanced each time and ate or drank.) Watches snail investigating—1 min. Decides it doesn't like the top. Writes notes. Cuts carrot into 3 mm cubes—puts in front of snail—snail advances and climbs straight over the carrot eating none. Boy moves snail to centre, cuts more carrot, puts it in front of snail in new position. Drops water on carrot. Crushes mixture (poorly!) in water. Snail advances, but leaves the carrot and drinks the water surrounding the crushed carrot.

*Aspects clarified in discussion:*
None recorded

**Example of pupil's investigation (boy)**

*Question selected:* How fast can it move?

*Description of investigation:*
Cuts piece of bread (about 2 cm long) and places directly in front of snail. Removes after 1 min. and records. Takes torch and shines it a) left eye—1 cm away b) above 1 cm away. Stops after 45 secs. and records. Takes piece of carrot (2 cm²) holds it above snail (10 secs. at 10 cm) then puts it directly into snail's path. Stops this activity after 2 mins. and substitutes lettuce (small piece). Records. Removes lettuce and substitutes a small (two-thirds cm) piece of apple (this after approx. 4 mins.). Takes apple away (1 min.), places black paper on glass, transfers the snail to this then, after 1½ mins. transfers to polystyrene tile—waits for another minute and places the small piece of apple in front of snail. Removes snail to carpet tile after 3 mins. and carefully observes. After 3 mins. transfers to scales pan and weighs snail and records this. Puts snail back on carpet tile (2 mins.) then on to glass and

sprinkles bran directly in front of snail. Writes. Places tape measure along glass with snail's 'tail' on zero cm. Tempts snail with lettuce and starts clock. Places bits ($\frac{1}{2}$ cm) lettuce at intervals along the tape measure.

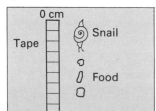

Tries keeping snail on 'track' and stops clock at 2 m 51 sec.

Removes measuring tape and writes.

Cuts small piece of potato and offers it to snail by hand (c. $1\frac{1}{2}$ cm). Shines torch close to snail's head (2 mins.). tries piece of carrot again, writes.

*Aspects clarified in discussion:*
Torch? 'To see if the light attracts him'.
'He doesn't like light because he is familiar with the dark'.

**Example of pupil's investigation (boy)**

*Question selected:* What food does it like best?

*Description of investigation:*
Took small piece of bread, placed it adjacent to snail's head and observed using eye for 10 secs. then hand lens for 30 secs. Snail has been eating bread. He made notes. Took 5 cm length of carrot, asked if he could cut it and then put it away. Snail eaten all bread. Picked up glass to observe by eye from beneath. Offered snail whole apple at its head. Snail began to crawl up side of apple. Observed by eye for 5 secs. then hand lens for $1\frac{1}{2}$ mins. Made notes. Observed with hand lens for 5 secs. Made notes. Apple and snail toppled, he placed them at centre of glass. Took a pinch of bran, put 10 cm away from apple, took 12 cm$^2$ lettuce and put it near bran, $\frac{1}{2}$ onion other side of bran, 5 cm carrot, near onion—all about 20 cm from snail on apple (see diagram):

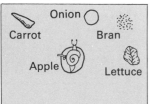

Took snail off apple and placed it in centre of arc of food, put apple away. Put lump of carrot in front of snail's head. Made notes and added notes to earlier notes. Snail crawled onto carrot. After 10 secs. he observed, using eye. Took snail off carrot, placed it in centre and made notes. Put bran in front of its head. Observed with hand lens for 10 secs. Made notes. Snail appeared to ignore bran. Put onion at snail's head, observed with eye for 20 secs. Started to make notes but stopped. Adjusted position of onion so that cut side was offered to snail, observed with hand lens for 2 secs., took onion away. Put lettuce at snail's head, observed with hand lens for 20 secs. Picked up snail and placed it 10 cm away from lettuce. Made notes. I asked if he had finished.

*Aspects clarified in discussion:*
'He ate the bread, did not touch others, just went over them. He ate all the bread. I looked closely at others and he did not eat them, there were no marks at all'. I asked if he wanted to say something about the onion because it was crossed out but he said no.

**Example of pupil's investigation (girl)**

*Question selected:* How fast can it move?

*Description of investigation:*
Gets slice of apple, places 12 cm in front, times for 10 secs. Removes apple, times for 10 secs. Lays onion 10 cm in front, having measured distance, timed for 10 secs. Replaces onion. I put snail on corner of glass. Offers lettuce opposite corner, measuring distance, sets timer for 10 secs. Removes lettuce. Shines torch, approx. 5 cm above head, for 5 secs., removes torch. Picks up carrot then moves snail to edge of glass, offers carrot 12 cm in front, times for 10 secs. Removes carrot, breaks off 3 cm$^3$ bread, places 10 cm in front, for approx. 5 secs (*sic*), removes. One crumb left behind–offers close to snail (it is not eaten). Offers apple, 6 cm in front, removes after several seconds. Offers bran, 4 cm to sides of head, snail approaches left-hand flakes.

*Aspects clarified in discussion:*
Food was given as a bait. Timer set to give a guide of distance covered in time.

**Example of pupil's investigation (girl)**

*Question selected:* Does it move faster on some surfaces?

*Description of investigation:*
Transfers snail to black paper. Tempts with half a carrot (7 cm away) (2 mins.). Moves carrot back–waits and observes (5 mins.). Takes snail off black paper and transfers to carpet tile. Uses same pattern again (carrot, 7 cm away). Waits and observes (3 mins.). Transfers to glass ('I don't think it likes carrots'). (1 min.). Tries polystyrene tile with carrot 'It seems to move quicker on light colours and slower on dark colours (tile, black paper).' 'It also sucks harder on the polystyrene tile than the other. It seems to use more of its body.' 'A dark colour could mean a cold surface.' Transfers the snail back on to glass (temporary) then back on to black paper. 'Seems to be moving faster now–and he's going the right way!' (towards the carrot). 'Because of the smoother surface he uses his pad to grip more.' Transfers (after 2–3 mins.) back to carpet tile. Places under plastic beaker on edge of polystyrene tile. Waits to see if snail goes in. 'He doesn't like this.' 'He's turning away–perhaps he knows from the vibrations of the air.'

*Aspects clarified in discussion:*
Beaker used to see if snail would crawl inside.

**Example of pupil's investigation (boy)**

*Question selected*: Does it move faster on some surfaces?

*Description of investigation*:

Gets carpet tile and transfers GALS from glass sheet to carpet tile (edge). Pauses for ~10 secs. and starts stop-clock. Puts pencil about 5 cm away from snail and then removes pencil almost immediately. Stops clock after 1 minute. Uses ruler to measure distance travelled. Writes notes. Transfers GALS to polystyrene tile–same position relative to carpet tile–at edge but snail facing inwards. Slight pause, starts stop-clock. Times for 1 minute and measures distance snail travelled from edge of tile with ruler. Writes notes. Transfers snail to edge of glass sheet (back tip of snail just touching edge of glass not on the taped edge); same position relative to carpet and polystyrene tiles. Times for 1 min. and writes notes. Places paper towel at edge of glass sheet–snail put on to paper towel–back tip of snail lined up with edge of towel. Pauses for 2 minutes looking intently at GALS–starts stop-clock–times for 1 min. Measures distance from edge of paper towel to *front* of snail (*as before*). Writes notes at b) and then at c) on sheet. Reads over notes and results.

*Aspects clarified in discussion*:

Thought of using pencil originally to see how long it would take for snail to travel between material edges and pencil. Thought this would take too long. Reason for pauses–'I waited till the head was opened up'. No explanation offered as to why GALS wasn't put right at the edge of the taped glass sheet.

**Example of pupil's investigation (boy)**

*Question selected*: Can it hear?

*Description of investigation*:

Surveys equipment briefly. Breaks off piece of onion with finger (~4 cm²). Holds onion piece ~4 cm away from front of snail. Watches 20 secs. Discards onion. Snaps fingers near (~5cm) snail's head. Writes note. Takes piece of lettuce ~6 cm², holds in front of snail for ~10 secs., puts lettuce down in front of snail, gets piece of carrot (~4 cm³) and places beside lettuce in front of snail. Watches for ~5 secs. Uses fingers to break off tiny piece of carrot and lettuce (each ~one-quarter cm³), puts in front of snail–discards rest of carrot and lettuce and watches snail for about 10 secs. Writes note. Uses dropper–drops 3 drops of water in front of snail near lettuce and carrot–watches for ~5 secs. Writes note. Takes bran–sprinkles small amount near snail's mouth (no longer near carrot and lettuce and water). Immediately uses dropper and drops ~5 drops of water onto bran flakes on glass. Uses ruler to measure antennae. Writes note. Uses torch–shines in front of snail for about 4 secs. Puts torch aside. Writes note.

*Aspects clarified in discussion*:

'When I clicked my fingers he turned around as if he had heard it.'

# Difficulties reported by schools concerning written-test administration

**A11.1** The science assessment depended on more than just the goodwill of the teaching profession. Administrative experience and professional support and judgement in guiding children through the written tests were also prerequisites. During each survey, science test booklets were administered to pupils in between 800 and 1,000 participating primary or middle schools. The assessment teams and the Monitoring Services Unit of the NFER made every effort to ensure that the exercise proceeded as smoothly as possible with minimal disruption to schools and pupils. However, in case of difficulties occurring, schools were invited to comment on the end of the sheet outlining administration procedures, and to return their comments to the Monitoring Services Unit. These comments were then forwarded to the team at Chelsea (King's), and afforded an insight into reactions at the classroom level. In fact, given the well protected anonymity of participants, feedback directly from schools in this form was invaluable.

The sentence inviting comments read:

'Please comment on any difficulties you encountered in administering this test. Thank you.'

About half of one page of A4 was free for written comment.

The first point to make about responses is that 'difficulties' may vary in both objective and subjective magnitude. (The MSU team could have been contacted by telephone to offer advice or clarification, should an urgent response have been required.) Between 1981 and 1984 (the 1980 pilot survey is not included in this discussion) written response rates ranged from 6 per cent to 11 per cent. Of these, about a quarter of respondents used the space not to express difficulties, but to state explicitly that there were *no* difficulties or that teachers and/or children had enjoyed the experience.

In the summary which follows, responses have been allocated to one of four broad categories: pupils' reading or language, administration, question/test package queries, and comments not expressing difficulty. Where comments relating to more than one category have been offered, all have been collated. Thus the number of responses is greater than the number of respondents. Table A11.1 (p. 152) summarises this information.

## A11.2 Pupils' reading and language difficulties

Consistently, the most frequently mentioned difficulty concerned reading, language or written expression problems. This area was mentioned by between 2.6 per cent and 6 per cent of the whole sample, the highest figure occurring in 1983 when the science assessment was accompanied by a reading comprehension test. It is possible that this reading test had focused teachers' attention on reading and language; the mean for the other three years was 2.9 per cent. Problems in this area essentially concern discrepancies between the language demands of questions and the language competence of pupils. It was not always possible to distinguish implicit criticisms of questions from expression of concern about pupils' reading/language ability. Exceptions to this comment are seen where reference is made explicitly to low ability or second language/ethnic minority factors; these two groups account for an average 30 per cent of responses in the reading/language difficulty category. Also averaging 30 per cent of reading/language difficulties over the four years were those comments grouped under, 'pupils required support with reading'. In fact, the administration instructions specifically asked that childrens' reading should be supported:

'Since the test is assessing pupils' thinking about problems, we are keen that their responses should not be unduly affected by poor reading ability. Thus, for any pupil who cannot read well or asks for help, please read a question to him or her privately, once slowly whilst pointing out words, and a second time at normal speed. For pupils who ask for individual words, these can be read without giving the whole question.'

Those responses which refer to the need for reading support are not always easily interpretable in this light, though amongst them were those which simply registered agreement:

'The children enjoyed this test. It was especially popular with the less able readers who nevertheless are interested in science. They were able to get help with words they couldn't read and there was no undue pressure of time on them.'

It could have been the case that where several children with reading difficulties were congregated in one of the larger testing groups, each child having a different test

**Table A11.1** *Categorisation of responses from schools reporting difficulties with written-test administration, 1981-4, as percentage of responding and participating*

| | 1981 | | 1982 | | 1983* | | 1984† | |
|---|---|---|---|---|---|---|---|---|
| Difficulties encountered | Resp. n = 65 | Part. n = 1031 | Resp. n = 84 | Part. n = 993 | Resp. n = 93 | Part. n = 874 | Resp. n = 76 | Part. n = 85 |
| **Pupils' reading or language difficulties** | | | | | | | | |
| Pupils required support with reading | 12 | | 14 | | 16 | | 9 | |
| Specified lower ability range | 5 | | 5 | | 17 | | 7 | |
| Ethnic minority | 3 | | 4 | | 5 | | 7 | |
| Other language/vocabulary difficulties | 17 | | 10 | | 16 | | 15 | |
| Written expression difficulties | 1 | | 1 | | 3 | | 3 | |
| | 40 | 2.5 | 34 | 2.8 | 58 | 6 | 39 | 3.4 |
| **Administration difficulties** | | | | | | | | |
| Test duration >45 minutes | 11 | | 17 | | 22 | | 12 | |
| Different test for each child | 1 | | 5 | | 2 | | 4 | |
| Smaller testing groups required | — | | — | | 1 | | — | |
| Local administration problems | 11 | | 6 | | 1 | | 8 | |
| | 23 | 1.4 | 28 | 2.3 | 26 | 2.8 | 24 | 2.1 |
| **Question/test package queries** | | | | | | | | |
| Question content queried | 10 | | 11 | | 2 | | 3 | |
| Question layout queried | 3 | | 4 | | 3 | | 4 | |
| Diagrams or drawings queried | 5 | | 2 | | 7 | | 1 | |
| Printing/binding problem | 15 | | 6 | | 2 | | 13 | |
| | 33 | 1.9 | 23 | 1.9 | 14 | 1.5 | 25 | 2.2 |
| **Comments not expressing difficulties** | | | | | | | | |
| No difficulties | 14 | | 18 | | 11 | | 16 | |
| Positive reaction of pupils/teachers | 11 | | 11 | | 3 | | 1 | |
| | 26 | 1.5 | 29 | 2.4 | 14 | 1.5 | 17 | 1.5 |

* Reading comprehension test included in test booklets.
† Pupil questionnaire included in test booklets.

booklet, the demands on teacher support became problematic. Teachers administered the tests in their own schools to pupils with whom they were presumably familiar. The overall impression is that the teachers coped extremely well with the demands made on them, and made strenuous efforts at overcoming reading difficulties. Not surprisingly, respondents commenting on the demand for reading support often mentioned administrative problems of time, or the problem of having a variety of test packages. These issues are discussed in the next section. Apart from the very small number of comments concerned with written language, the remaining bulk of comments conveyed by an average 34 per cent of respondents (just over 1 per cent of the total samples on average) specified language or vocabulary as being sources of problems. In view of the difficulties involved in presenting novel and complex questions in a straightforward manner (especially in **Planning** and **Interpreting**) some expression of language difficulties is not surprising. While these are no grounds for complacency, the relatively small numbers drawing attention to difficulties in this area indicates that language demands are not insurmountable. Considerable effort was expended by the assessment team, in consultation with teachers and other experts, in tailoring print, vocabulary and sentence construction to the age group. The great majority of children seemed, with teacher support, to have managed the reading, language and writing demands. As one respondent remarked:

'Even the child the teacher felt would be distressed by the test was not disturbed at all.'

On the other hand, coping with the words did not necessarily imply that the question was within range:

'Script too difficult. Could read the words but failed to appreciate the implications involved.'

As the performance estimates for **Interpreting, Applying** and **Planning** clearly reveal, the 'implications' were indeed difficult for the majority of the age group.

## A11.3 Administration difficulties

It was intended that reported difficulties would be related to administration; this section refers to the procedural 'nuts and bolts'. Difficulties in this area were mentioned by just over 2 per cent of the total sample.

Most respondents in this category commented that the estimate of average test duration of 'about 45 minutes' was an under-estimate. Children had been encouraged to 'try all the questions' and it was clear from some teacher's comments that there had been problems in some cases of prising children away from the booklets, such had been their persistence. For example:

'. . . pleasantly surprised at the way even the poorest (and the sample included at least two remedial children whom I seriously thought might become upset) managed to plod to the end . . .'

Once again it is apparent that although schools were specifically asked to comment on difficulties, responses tended to be framed in positive terms with a constructive intent:

'Our less able pupils required well over one hour to complete. Just a comment, not a difficulty!'

(This comment is from the 1983 survey when possible extra administration time was allowed for the reading comprehension test.)

The random distribution of test packages to schools was a source of difficulty for some administrators. There were good reasons for such a procedure, ensuring as it did that pupils in each school would be assessed on as wide a range of skills as possible (and incidentally reducing opportunities for collusion between pupils). However, there were reading difficulties, the teacher's role was complicated. As one teacher put it:

'Difficulties arose in the context of eleven children of widely varying ability simultaneously attempting eleven different test papers. In retrospect it would have been better if they had been split into two or perhaps three groups to be tested at different times.'

The final grouping within this category includes comments on factors which were totally beyond the control of the monitoring teams or the MSU. This example embraces two separate points:

'Unfortunately all the rest of the class have to be kept quietly occupied whilst the fourth year children do the test. Local airfield had a "war" today so lots of jets overhead.'

## A11.4   Question/test package queries

The average rate of comment for the whole sample over four years was 1.9 per cent, and as much as half of this amount was accounted for by printing or collating difficulties. For example, in 1981, comments on a page which was duplicated in some test packages inflated responses in this area. In 1984, there were acknowledged problems with the staples which provided a temporary attachment of the questionnaires to the test packages.

Perhaps of more interest are those comments which refer to the content or organisation of individual questions or test packages. The following comment clearly indicates that the phenomenon of children importing personal knowledge in order to address questions, reported in the **Interpreting** subcategory, was noticed in the classroom. Information, derived from a consumer magazine, about the price of a range of fruits at different times of the year was presented and children were required to read from it as directed:

'The child said that fruit is cheap at Harvest time and dearer in December because of Christmas. She was very reluctant to use the graph as it conflicted with her experience.'

Schools represented by only a small number of pupils saw only a restricted range of questions. In these circumstances, comments about the imbalance of the science assessment based on an incomplete picture arise from a misapprehension. The following comment was almost unique in condemning the assessment exercise on grounds of children being unaccustomed to the demands made on them:

'For children who are not accustomed to such testing, these tests were unnecessarily disturbing. Hence their value as a guide to science in primary schools is totally unreliable.'

Most comments in this area tended to be far more specifically related to question layout, etc., for example:

'Printing of some graphs not as clear as might be . . . the drawings of the pea plants . . . were not consistent . . . the children enjoyed (on the whole) doing the questions . . .'

It is encouraging to see that there is a steady decrease in the number of such comments between 1981 and 1984, as the monitoring teams have managed largely to iron out this type of problem.

## A11.5   Comments not expressing difficulties

Unsolicited expressions of approbation are most welcome. In the context of the science assessment of pupils at age eleven (many of whom will have had little exposure to science) such comments provide an encouraging endorsement of the techniques developed, and a fitting note on which to draw this section to a close:

'No difficulties were encountered. The children thoroughly enjoyed taking part in this test.'

## A11.6   Summary

Participating schools were invited to comment on any difficulties experienced in the test administration. Response rates between 1981 and 1984 ranged from 6.3

per cent to 10.6 per cent, with up to one quarter of these consisting of unsolicited comments expressing satisfaction.

Difficulties were encountered in approximately equal measure in:

—language and reading;

—the practicalities of administration; and

—the question or test package content or organisation.

Detailed examination reveals that the comments offered tended to be constructive, and compatible with a positive regard for the science assessment exercise as a whole.

The booklet entitled 'Science Age 11 Sample Questions' included some **Observation** questions (Category 3) not previously reported. In order that more use may be made of the results of APU Science surveys, mark distributions for these questions, together with a page number reference in the above booklet, are given in this appendix.

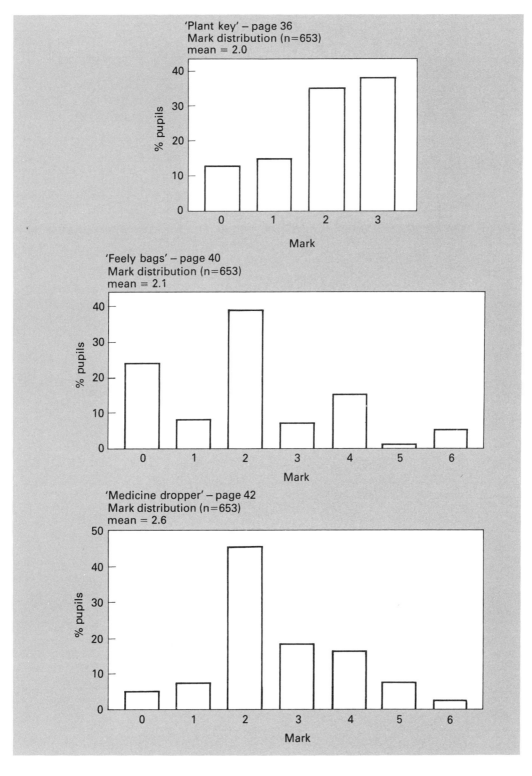

'Plant key' – page 36
Mark distribution (n=653)
mean = 2.0

'Feely bags' – page 40
Mark distribution (n=653)
mean = 2.1

'Medicine dropper' – page 42
Mark distribution (n=653)
mean = 2.6

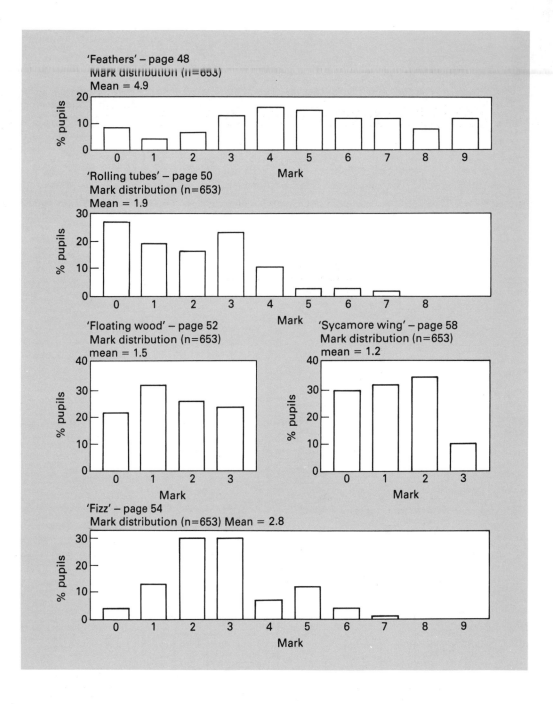

'Feathers' – page 48
Mark distribution (n=653)
Mean = 4.9

'Rolling tubes' – page 50
Mark distribution (n=653)
Mean = 1.9

'Floating wood' – page 52
Mark distribution (n=653)
mean = 1.5

'Sycamore wing' – page 58
Mark distribution (n=653)
mean = 1.2

'Fizz' – page 54
Mark distribution (n=653) Mean = 2.8

156

# Membership of groups and committees*

## 13.1  The Monitoring teams

*Kings's:*
Director — Paul Black

Research and Development (ages 11 and 13) — Patricia Murphy (Deputy Director)
Anne Qualter
Peter Swatton
Robert Taylor

Secretary — Julie Jones

*Leeds:*
Director — Fred Archenhold
Technical Director — Roger Hartley

Research and Development (age 15) — Geoff Welford (Project coordinator)
James Donnelly

Data Analysis — Sandra Johnson (Deputy Director)
John Bell

Secretary — Jan Akkermans

## 13.2  APU Steering Group on Science

| | |
|---|---|
| Mr A. G. Clegg, HMI Chairman | Professional Head of the APU |
| Mr W. F. Archenhold | Director, Science Monitoring Team, University of Leeds |
| Professor P. J. Black | Director, Science Monitoring Team, King's College London |
| Mrs S. Dean | St Martin's College, Lancaster |
| Mr N. B. Evans, HMI | HM Inspectorate (Wales) |
| Mr A. Giles | British School Technology, Trent Polytechnic |
| Mr E. O. James | Deputy Head, Southlands Schol |
| Miss R. Jarman | Department of Education for Northern Ireland |
| Professor R. Kempa | Department of Education, University of Keele |
| Dr W. J. Kirkham | Director, Secondary Science Curriculum Review |
| Mr E. R. Little, HMI | HM Inspectorate |
| Mr H. Wilcox | Headteacher, Paganel Junior School, Birmingham |

## 13.3  Monitoring Services Unit (NFER)

Mrs B. Bloomfield–Head of Unit

Mrs A. Baker–Deputy

Mrs E. Elliott

Mrs M. Hall

Mrs B. Woodley

Mrs J. Cowan–Secretary

## 13.4  APU Consultative Committee

| | |
|---|---|
| Professor J. Dancy (Chair) | School of Education, University of Exeter |
| Miss J. E. L. Baird | Joint General Secretary AMMA |
| Dr P. Biggs | Senior Adviser, Wiltshire LEA |
| Mrs M. J. Bloom | Project Leader for Building and Civil Engineering, National Economic Development Office |
| Mr P. Boulter | Director of Education, Cumbria (ACC) |
| Dr C. Burstall | Director, National Foundation for Educational Research |
| Professor C. B. Cox | Department of English Language and Literature, University of Manchester |
| Mrs J. Davies | Howbury Grange School, Bexley |
| Mr G. Donaldson | Flint High Comprehensive School (NUT) |
| Mr I. Donaldson | NAS/UWT |
| Mr H. Dowson | Deputy Headmaster, Earl Marshall School, Sheffield (NUT) |
| Councillor G. Driver | Councillor, Leeds City Council (AMA) |
| Professor S. J. Eggleston | Department of Education, University of Keele |
| Mr A. Evans | Education Department, NUT |
| Mr D. Fox | Accountant, Chairman of National Education Association |
| Mr C. Gittins | Longsands School, St. Neots (SHA) |
| Dr A. Grady | Middlesex Polytechnic |
| Mr P. L. Griffin | Windsor Clive Junior School (NUT) |
| Mr K. S. Hopkins | Director of Education, Mid-Glamorgan (WJEC) |
| Mr C. Humphrey | Director of Education, Solihull (AMA) |
| Mr S. A. Josephs | MacMillan Education Ltd. |
| Mr J. A. Lawton | Kent County Council (ACC) |
| Mr G. M. Lee | Doncaster Metropolitan Institute of Higher Education (NATFHE) |
| Mr J. M. Leonard | General Inspector, Walsall LEA (AMA) |
| Mr M. J. Pipes | Headmaster, City of Portsmouth School for Boys (NAHT) |
| Mr G. R. Potter | Director of Education, West Sussex LEA (ACC) |
| Miss C. L. Richards | (CBI) Understanding British Industry Project, Birmingham |
| Mr R. Richardson | Advisory Head, ILEA (NUT) |
| Professor M. D. Shipman | School of Education, Roehampton Institute |
| Mr P. Smith | Springfield Lower School, Bedford |
| Mr S. C. Woodley | The Kings School, Canterbury |

*At 1 January 1987.

**Assessors**

| | |
|---|---|
| Mr A. Gibson | HM Inpectorate |
| Mr K. A. Smart | Department of Education for Northern Ireland |
| Mr N. Summers | DES |
| Mr D. Timlin | Welsh Office Education Department |

**13.5 APU Advisory Group on Statistics**

| | |
|---|---|
| Mr M. D. Phipps (Chair) | Administrative Head of the APU |
| Professor V. Barnett | Department of Statistics, University of Sheffield |
| Professor D. J. Bartholomew | Department of Statistics, London School of Economics and Political Science |
| Mrs B. Bloomfield | National Foundation for Educational Research |
| Mr T. Christie | Department of Education, University of Manchester |
| Mr J. Gardner | Chief Statistician DES |
| Mr D. Hutchinson | Chief Statistician, National Foundation for Educational Research |
| Mrs S. Johnson | Centre for Studies in Science Education, University of Leeds |
| Professor T. Lewis | Faculty of Mathematics, Open University |
| Professor R. Mead | Department of Applied Statistics, University of Reading |
| Mr A. Owen | Her Majesty's Inspectorate |
| Mrs V. Scott | WOED |
| Dr A. S. Willmott | University of Oxford Delegacy of Local Examinations |

**13.6 APU Management Group**

| | |
|---|---|
| Mr M. D. Phipps | Administrative Head of the APU |
| Mr A. G. Clegg | Professional Head of the APU |
| Mr P. J. Silvester | |
| Mr M. E. Malt | |
| Mr D. Sleep | |
| Miss H. Bennett | |
| Mrs M. L. Pooley | |
| Miss N. E. Mitchell | |
| Miss T. E. Pilborough | |

# Administrators of practical tests – 1984 survey

| Group | | Individual | |
|---|---|---|---|
| *England* | | *England* | |
| Mr R. Allen | Primary Science Resource Centre, East Barnet | Mr A. Blank | (on secondment) Rugeley, Staffs. |
| | | Mr F. Bristow | Science & Technology Centre, Bridgwater |
| Mr B. Barkway | Church Lawton Gate Primary School, Stoke-on-Trent | Mr L. Edwards | Greenhill Middle School, Halesowen |
| Mr D. N. Byrne | Tottington South County Primary School, Bury | Mr C. Johnston | New College, Faculty of Education, Durham |
| Mr C. Drake | Concord Middle School, Sheffield | Mr I. MacGregor | Bunwell County Primary School, Norwich |
| Mrs B. Dunnachie | Prince's Plain Primary School, Bromley | Mr P. Middleton | Moorlands Junior School, Sale |
| Mrs C. Griffiths | Woodford Junior School, Plymouth | Mr J. Mulvany | Highcliffe County Junior School, Leicester |
| Mr A. McFarland | Avon Education Authority, Bristol | Miss H. Murray | Towers Junior School, Hornchurch |
| Mrs K. Machin | Hengrove County Middle School, Ashford, Middx. | Mr E. Parkinson | Elaine Avenue Junior School, Rochester |
| | | Mrs S. Pearson | Five Acres Primary School, Bicester |
| Mrs P. Mackenzie | (retired) Liverpool | Mrs E. B. Rhodes | Priestmead Middle School, Kenton, Middx. |
| Mr K. Rooke | Delapre Middle School, Northampton | | |
| Mr R. Shipman | Lickey First & Middle School, Birmingham | Mr J. Robinson | Gonville Primary School, Thornton Heath |
| | | Mr A. Row | Charville Junior School, Hayes, Middx. |
| Mr A. Stewart | High Oakham Middle School, Mansfield | Mr D. Soerbutts | Otley All Saints Middle School, Otley |
| Mr I. Thompson | County Primary School, Selby | *Wales* | |
| Mrs G. Woodford | Becontree Junior School, Dagenham | Mr R. Davies | Johnstown Junior CP School, Wrexham, Clwyd |
| *Wales* | | Mr D. R. Howells | Durham Road Junior School, Newport, Gwent |
| Mr P. A. Clarke | Alway Junior School, Newport, Gwent | | |
| Mr W. D. Griffiths | Ysgol Cymraeg y Santes, Merthyr Tydfil, Dyfed | Ms E. Huws | Ysgol Glan y Mor, Pwellheli, Gwynedd |
| | | Mr C. Vernon Jones | Science Adviser, Clwyd Education Authority |
| Mr I. L. Hill | Gors Junior School, Swansea, W. Glam. | Mrs N. Lucas | Knelston Primary School, Gower, W. Glam. |
| Mr D. M. Lewis | Ogwr Teachers' Centre, Bridgend, S. Glam. | | |
| Mr P. Maddocks | Ysgol y Moelwyn, Blaenau Ffestiniog, Gwynedd | Mrs A. Morris | Springwood Junior School, Cardiff |
| | | Mr N. Tuffnell | Ysgol Trefonnen, Llandrindod Wells, Powys |
| Mrs G. Thomas | Carrog C. P. School, Nr. Corwen, Clwyd | | |
| | | *Northern Ireland* | |
| *Northern Ireland* | | Miss G. Gibson | Howard Primary School, Moygashel, Dungannon |
| Mrs E. Burton | Newtownards Model Primary School, Newtownards | | |
| | | Mr W. Hoy | Ballyclare Primary School, Ballyclare |
| Mr D. Cheney | Iveagh Primary School, Rathfriland | Mr R. McClintock | Ballymena Primary School, Ballymena |
| Mr M. Gowland | Armoy Primary School, Ballymoney | Mrs M. McKeown | Aughnacloy Primary School, Aughnacloy |
| Mr W. Manning | Ebrington Primary School, Londonderry | Mr S. O'Driscoll | St Colman's Abbey Primary School, Newry |
| Mr D. Nixon | Jones Memorial Primary School, Enniskillen | | |
| | | Dr J. Sweeney | St Joseph's Training College, Belfast |
| Mr D. Owen | Cairnshill Primary School, Newtownbreda | Mr E. Young | Newtownstewart Primary School, Newtownstewart |

# 'Shadows' check-list

Pupil No.

Boy ☐
Girl ☐

| No. | Category | Description | |
|---|---|---|---|
| 1. | | Torch, ball, box each moved one at a time when results taken | |
| 2. | | Torch and ball both moved when results taken | |
| 3. | **Torch** | Effect of varying position observed | |
| 4. | | Full range of positions explored (X for restricted range/not at all) | |
| 5. | | Result judged by eye whilst size changing (no measurement) | |
| 6. | | Repeated for different positions of ball or box | |
| 7. | | Sizes of shadow measured | |
| 8. | | Positions of torch measured | |
| 9. | **Ball** | Effect of varying position observed | |
| 10. | | Full range of positions explored (X for restricted range/not at all) | |
| 11. | | Result judged by eye whilst size changing (no measurement) | |
| 12. | | Repeated for different positions of torch or box | |
| 13. | | Sizes of shadow measured | |
| 14. | | Positions of ball measured | |
| 15. | **Box** | Effect of varying position observed | |
| 16. | | Full range of positions explored (X for restricted range/not at all) | |
| 17. | | Result judged by eye whilst size changing (no measurement) | |
| 18. | | Repeated for different positions of torch or ball | |
| 19. | | Sizes of shadow measured | |
| 20. | | Positions of box measured | |
| 21. | **Repetition** | Movements repeated for checking pattern | |
| 22. | **Result** | Notes or results written during investigation | |
| 23. | | Results reported for each separate variable | |
| 24. | | Correct relationship reported for torch position variation | |
| 25. | | Correct relationship reported for ball position variation | |
| 26. | | Correct relationship reported for box position variation | |
| 27. | | Category of pattern statements | |
| 28. | **2 × shadow** | Diameter of ball measured | |
| 29. | | Circumference of ball measured (part or whole) | |
| 30. | | Distances measured | |
| 31. | | Distances made equal (with or without measurement) | |
| 32. | | Shadow measured | |
| 33. | | Shadow size within 1 cm of 2 × ball | |
| 34. | | Distance measured to nearest mm (9 for 2 mm, X for >2 mm) | |
| 35. | **Ball move** | Torch moved in correct direction | |
| 36. | | Torch moved to approx. correct position | |
| 37. | **Torch move** | Box moved in correct direction | |
| 38. | | Box moved to approx. correct position | |
| 39. | | Pattern of equal distances noticed with help | |
| 40. | | recognised only when pointed out | |
| 41. | | Willingness to be involved in the investigation (A, B, C) | |

## Administrator's notes for Shadows investigation, Interview + Category 2 (length, mass, area)

### Shadows investigation

Equipment:  3 cm diameter polystyrene ball mounted on wooden block
Duracell torch + 2 spare cells
Box approx. 27 × 31 × 23 cm with lid
Sheets of 2 mm graph paper, one stuck to side of box cm tape measure
Shadows graph and bar chart in plastic case

### Introduction of investigation

Arrange the box, torch, ball and tape as shown in the diagram.

*These are some things that are for you to use to do an investigation about shadows. You know what a shadow is, do you?*

Remove ball temporarily and put you hand in front of the box, switch on the torch and point out the shadow. Then replace ball.

*There we have a shadow of the ball. We can make it larger or smaller by moving the torch, the ball or the box.*

Move the ball and torch *together* to vary the size of the shadow. Then move the box to and fro.

*In a moment you can make the shadow change size and find out what is the effect of moving the torch, the ball and the box. Here is a paper for you to use.*

Hand child the pupil's sheet. Point to each part as it is mentioned.

*Here it says what you have to do–'Find out how the size of the shadow changes when you move the torch, the ball, the box.' This space here at (a) is for you to use to put down notes or results as you go along if you want to. Then at (b) you write down your result. Are there any questions you would like to ask before you start?*

Answer any question about what the problem is but avoid stating procedures or indicating that the three variables (position of torch, ball and box) have to be varied one at a time. Questions about *how* to tackle the problem should be answered in this way: *You think about that* or *There are several ways of doing this, you decide which is best.*

When there are no further questions:

*Now whilst you are doing the investigation I shall be putting down some notes about what you do. There aren't marks, so don't worry. It just gives us a record of how you tackled the problem.*

*Before you start, to make sure I have explained everything clearly, you tell me what you are going to try to find out.*

When you are satisfied that the child has grasped the problem, tell him/her to go ahead.

### Observations during activity

During the activity do not interrupt the pupil. If (s)he asks a question, reply briefly: *You decide how to do it* or *You can use any of the things here in any way you want.*

Watch carefully what (s)he does. Complete check-points 1–24 using the following guidelines. Put a ✓ or X for *every* check-point.

| | |
|---|---|
| 1 | Child may 'play' or investigate somewhat randomly at first. Distinguish this from movements carried out when results are taken. Put X only if variables are never changed one at a time to investigate their separate effects. |
| 2 | Tick if torch and ball are both moved and effect of each is not investigated separately. (See also check-points 6, 12, 18.) |
| 3, 9, 15 | Tick if position varied in order to observe effect. This excludes moving the object during the course of investigating the effect of another variable (see check-points 6, 12, 18). |
| 4, 10, 16 | 'Full range' means moved in both directions from starting point and more than a few cm in each direction ie not just forward and back to starting position and not just 5 cm or so in each direction. Put A if not moved at all or only over a restricted range. |
| 5, 11, 17 | Tick if no measurement of either shadow size or positions of torch, ball or box. All results judged by eye. |
| 6, 12, 18 | Refers to effect of one variable being observed, then repeated after positions of other object changed (eg effect of torch position variation observed with ball close to box, then observed again with ball further away from box). Distinguish from case where two variables are changed all the time when results are taken. |
| 7, 13, 19 | Tick if shadow size is measured, using tape or divisions on box, systematically for all results. |
| 8, 14, 20 | Tick if attempt made to measure positions of torch, ball, box from same point each time. |
| 21 | Tick if any movement is repeated in exactly the same way to check the observation of its effect. |
| 22 | Tick if note at (a) or results at (b) were put down during the course of the investigation. X for only at end with or without a reminder. |

161

**Discussion with pupil**

If pupil appears to have stopped and if nothing has been written at (b) wait to be sure (s)he is not just pausing and the ask:

*Have you finished?* If answer is 'Yes':

*Remember you have to write down what you have found, at (b) on the paper.*

When (s)he has done this, look over the paper with him/her.

*Can I see what you have found?*

If necessary ask the child to clarify what has been written so that you can complete check-points 23–26; eg if the child has written 'It gets bigger' ask him/her to say what gets bigger and when does it get bigger.

**Leave check-point 27 blank**

Put the child's sheet aside and complete the remaining check-points as follows. Start by asking the child:

*Now will you make a shadow that is twice the size of the ball, as nearly as you can?*

28  Tick if pupil attempts to measure the diameter of the ball (X if no attempt at measurement or circumference measured).

29  Tick if pupil attempts to measure the circumference of the ball either half way round or all round.

30  Tick if some attempt to measure distances between torch and ball and ball and screen (regardless of whether these are made equal).

31  Tick if pupil appears to be equalising the distances between torch and ball and between ball and screen either by eye or measurement.

32  Tick if the shadow is measured either using the tape or the grid on the box (X for judged by eye only).

33  When pupil has finished, judge the size of the shadow yourself. Tick if shadow size is within 1 cm of twice ball size (base your judgement on the grid). If the shadow is not within 1 cm of twice the ball size, move the torch so that it is, with the comment *Let's see if we can make it a bit closer to twice the size? How's that?*

34  Ask the child to measure where the line on the side of the block comes to on the tape when you hold the end at the front of the box. Read the distance yourself. (This is a Category 2 item.) Record as ✔ if child measures to nearest mm, 9 for nearest 2 mm and X for outside 2 mm).

Now move the *ball* nearer to the box so that the shadow size changes noticeably. *Now the shadow isn't twice the size any more, is it? Can you make it twice the size again by moving just the torch?* Before the child moves the torch, TURN IT OFF.

35  Tick if the child moves the torch towards the ball, X if moved away from it.

36  Tick if the distances torch to ball and ball to box are made about equal (judge by eye).
Let child turn on the torch 'to see if that is about right'.
Then move the torch away from the ball so that the shadow is no longer twice the size. *This time can you make it twice the size again by moving just the box?* TURN OFF THE TORCH.

37  Tick if box moved away from the ball. X if moved towards it.

38  Tick if distances made about equal.
Let child turn on the torch to check. Then ask *Did you notice anything about where the torch, ball and box were when the shadows were twice the size of the ball?*

39  Tick if child indicates recognition of equality of distances from torch to ball and ball to box. Put X if child does not recognise this, but point it out. *Each time this distance was about the same as this distance. Let's see if this works for another position.* Move the box closer to the ball and ask child to move the ball to make the shadow twice the size. TURN TORCH OFF.

40  Tick if ball moved to make distances about equal. Let child check by turning torch on.

41  Rate the child's general willingness to engage in the investigation using codes A, B, C as follows.

A  evidence of real interest in investigation, looking carefully and intently at what happens, actions deliberate and thoughtful

B  willing to carry out investigation, but no sign of great enthusiasm or special interest

C  carries out only the minimum necessary, may look bored, uninterested or scared.

**Interview to follow Shadows investigation**
(Record on reverse of check-list. ✔ = Yes, X = No unless otherwise stated)

42  *Have you ever done anything about shadows before, using a lamp or the sun? Either at school or at home or out of school?*

43 *You found something out about the shadow just now, didn't you? I didn't tell you how the size changed, you found it out. Have you ever done that before-used equipment to find something out (not just with shadows but with anything else)?*

44 *You had to measure a distance just now. Have you ever used a tape measure or a ruler to measure things before (not just to draw straight lines)?*

*Let me show you what a girl/boy did. She/he kept the ball and the box in the same places and moved the torch (refer to the equipment).*
*She/he measured the sizes of the shadow when the torch was at different distances from the ball. Then she/he drew this graph* (show).

45 *Have you ever drawn a graph like this?*

46 *There is a different kind of graph where you draw blocks and sometimes colour them in, like this one* (show).
*Have you ever drawn one like that?*

47 Turn back to line graph:

*Have a look at this one again. What does it tell you about the way the size of the shadow changed when the torch was moved?*
Write down the child's answer verbatim. Leave code square blank.

48 *Can you tell me from the graph how big the shadow was when the torch was 30 cm away?*

49 *Can you tell me from the graph how far the light was when the shadow was 5 cm in size?*

50 *Have you ever used a graph in this way, to tell you about what someone found out?*

51 *Have you used a bar chart to tell you about what someone found out?*

# Index

Printed in the United Kingdom for Her Majesty's Stationery Office
(45/88) Dd239898 2/89 C40 G443 10170